PHILOSOPHY THROUGH FILM

Many of the classic questions of philosophy have been raised, illuminated, and addressed in celluloid. In this Third Edition of *Philosophy through Film,* Mary M. Litch teams up with a new co-author, Amy Karofsky, to show readers how to watch films with a sharp eye for their philosophical content. Together, the authors help students become familiar with key topics in all of the major areas in Western philosophy and master the techniques of philosophical argumentation.

The perfect size and scope for a first course in philosophy, the book assumes no prior knowledge of philosophy. It is an excellent teaching resource and learning tool, introducing students to key topics and figures in philosophy through thematic chapters, each of which is linked to one or more "focus films" that illustrate a philosophical problem or topic.

Revised and expanded, the Third Edition features:

- A completely revised chapter on "Relativism," now re-titled "Truth," with coverage of the correspondence theory, the pragmatist theory, and the coherence theory.
- The addition of four new focus films: *Inception, Moon, Gone Baby Gone,* and *God on Trial.*
- Revisions to the General Introduction that include a discussion of critical reasoning.
- Revisions to the primary readings to better meet the needs of instructors and students, including the addition of three new primary readings: excerpts from Bertrand Russell's *The Problems of Philosophy,* from William James's *Pragmatism: A New Way for Some Old Ways of Thinking,* and from J. L. Mackie's "Evil and Omnipotence."
- Updates and expansion to the companion website.

Films examined in depth include:

Hilary and Jackie	*Crimes and Misdemeanors*
The Matrix	*Gone Baby Gone*
Inception	*Antz*
Memento	*Equilibrium*
Moon	*The Seventh Seal*
I, Robot	*God on Trial*
Minority Report	*Leaving Las Vegas*

Mary M. Litch has taught Philosophy at Yale University, the University of Alabama at Birmingham, and the University of Massachusetts at Amherst. She is currently Director of Academic Technology and Digital Media at Chapman University, where she also teaches Philosophy.

Amy Karofsky teaches Philosophy at Hofstra University.

"This *Third Edition* of *Philosophy through Film* is a valuable book for introducing students to the wonder of philosophical exploration and the power of philosophical reasoning to force us to reevaluate our reflexive responses to fundamental questions, such as the nature of truth or the self. Litch and Karofsky have added more recently released films familiar to undergraduates, such as *Inception* and *Gone Baby Gone,* and refocused chapters to better clarify the variety of philosophical positions taken on enduring philosophical questions. What I find valuable about *Philosophy through Film* is that it argues that films can make philosophical arguments by drawing us wholly into fictional worlds that enable us to entertain new ideas about truth, reality, or free will in ways that mere argument sometimes cannot."

–Jennifer Hansen, St. Lawrence University

"With clarity that doesn't compromise rigor, Mary Litch and Amy Karofsky introduce readers new to philosophy to some of its most enduring concerns and seminal questions, including skepticism, personal identity, artificial intelligence, and political philosophy. Coupling penetrating analyses in thematic chapters with excerpts from classical works by Plato, Descartes, Hume, Kant, Mill, Sartre, and others in the philosophical canon, *Philosophy through Film* connects central philosophical questions to focus films from popular culture that students will recognize and understand. In so doing the book reveals the presence of philosophical issues in the context of everyday life, enabling instructors to capture a wider audience than one might otherwise hope to reach in an introductory philosophy course."

–Mark Uffelman, Millersville University

"Building upon the strengths of previous editions while expanding its coverage of topics and bringing new films into focus, *Philosophy through Film* offers a readable and engaging introduction to a wide range of philosophical questions: about what is real, what we can know, how we should act, and what it all means. Popular films such as *Inception* and *The Matrix* provide a rich repository of situations and examples, that not only help to bring these questions to life but offer surprising insights into their solutions. Highly recommended for the introductory philosophy classroom, as well as for anyone who likes movies that make you think."

–Nathan Andersen, Collegium of Letters, Saint Petersburg, FL

"This book is fabulous! Since its first edition, *Philosophy through Film* has served as an outstanding text for both topical introduction to philosophy courses and philosophy and film courses. The writing is very clear, organized, well-researched, and, most importantly, thought provoking. It tackles core philosophical issues in a serious way, yet at the same time remains accessible and exciting to even beginning philosophy students. A unique feature of this book is that it confines itself to a manageable set of films, which can easily be viewed within the timeframe of a single semester. This third edition builds on all the strengths of the previous ones, while including just the right amount of new material to keep it current."

–James Fieser, University of Tennessee at Martin

PHILOSOPHY THROUGH FILM

Third Edition

Mary M. Litch
Amy Karofsky

Routledge
Taylor & Francis Group

NEW YORK AND LONDON

Please visit this book's companion website for links, organized by chapter, to online resources on some of the philosophers and topics discussed in the book: www.routledge.com/9780415838627

Third edition published 2015
By Routledge
711 Third Avenue, New York, NY 10017

and by Routledge
2 Park Square, Milton Park, Abingdon, Oxon, OX14 4RN

Routledge is an imprint of the Taylor & Francis Group, an informa business

First edition published 2002 by Routledge

Library of Congress Control Number: 2014943152

ISBN: 978-0-415-83862-7 (hbk)
ISBN: 978-0-415-83932-7 (pbk)
ISBN: 978-0-203-77229-4 (ebk)

Typeset in Baskerville
by Cenveo Publisher Services

CONTENTS

PREFACE

Philosophy through Film is geared for use as the primary textbook in a first course in philosophy and covers the same topics as a standard introductory text. However, the novel avenues for philosophic exploration opened up by the use of film make *Philosophy through Film* appropriate for an upper-level course in some contexts. The movie enthusiast interested in a deeper understanding and appreciation of films may also find the book engaging and informative.

Some feature films may be interpreted as attempts to provide answers to classic questions within philosophy. This is an underlying assumption of *Philosophy through Film.* Each chapter examines one such question in an approachable yet philosophically rigorous manner, using one or two focus films as a source for the standard positions and arguments associated with that question. The discussion of the films in question is fully integrated into the discussion of the philosophical issue within the authored portion of the book: the films are not mere "add-ons" to an otherwise straightforward introductory philosophy text. One consequence is that the bulk of each chapter is most fruitfully read after viewing the relevant films. Each chapter begins with a brief introduction (to the topic and to the films) to be read first; however, the remainder of each chapter assumes that the reader has already seen the one or two films associated with that chapter and has them freshly in mind. Associated with each chapter is one, two or three readings from primary sources that are collected together at the end of the book. For those instructors who wish to assign readings from the most historically significant texts mentioned in each chapter, those readings are available. For those instructors who prefer to use *Philosophy through Film* as an authored text, that is also an option: while occasional reference is made to a relevant reading, any passages from these texts discussed in detail in a chapter will be quoted in that chapter.

The focus films associated with each chapter run the gamut in styles and genres. The main requirement for inclusion was philosophical relevance: Does the movie "cover the topic" in a way that will be familiar to philosophers? A second requirement for inclusion is that the film is engaging for the typical American undergraduate. This means that many of the focus films are high-budget, high-production value films that initially saw wide theatrical release. (We have included a few titles that don't fit this model, but they are the exception rather than the rule.) Thus, even though Netflix and other commercial web-based video rental companies have made it very easy to find and screen low-budget films that did poorly during their theatrical run, we have opted to stick to a modified version of the blockbuster test applied in choosing titles for the first edition.

For the third edition, the chapter on relativism has been significantly revised to include a consideration of several other theories of truth, including: the correspondence theory, the pragmatist theory, and the coherence theory. The chapter, renamed, "Truth," now appears as the first chapter in the third edition, followed by "Skepticism." Some older titles have been swapped out in favor of the following recent releases: *Inception* (2010), *Moon* (2009), and *God on Trial* (2008). And *Gone Baby Gone* (2007) has been added to the discussion of Ethics. In addition, three new readings have been added to the Readings from Primary Sources.

We would like to thank the many students at Hofstra University who offered suggestions for movies to consider for inclusion in this edition and to the members of the Chapman University Philosophy Club for providing useful comments on some of those films. Also, deepest gratitude to Judy Karofsky for reading and providing helpful comments and suggestions on the drafts of each revised chapter for the third edition. As always, responsibility for any leftover errors remains our own.

ACKNOWLEDGMENTS

The authors and publisher would like to thank the following for permission to use copyrighted material:

Arete Press for René Descartes, "Meditation One" in *Meditations on First Philosophy*, trans. Ronald Rubin, © 1985 Arete Press, Claremont, CA.

Cambridge University Press for excerpts from John Searle, "Minds, Brains, and Programs" in *The Behavioral and Brain Sciences*, Vol. 3 (1980), pp. 417–457.

Oxford University Press for excerpts from A.M. Turing, "Computing Machinery and Intelligence" in *Mind* (1950).

Oxford University Press for J. L. Mackie, "Evil and Omnipotence," *Mind* Vol. 64 (April 1995), pp. 200–212.

Pearson Education for excerpts from St. Augustine, *On Free Choice of the Will*, 1st edn, trans. Anna Benjamin and L.H. Hackstaff, pp. 3, 6, 8, 34, 88, 90, 94–96, 139, 140–141. © 1964 Pearson Education, Upper Saddle River, NJ.

Penguin Group (UK) for excerpt from Albert Camus, "The Myth of Sisyphus," trans. Justin O'Brien (1955), pp. 119–124. Translation copyright © Justin O'Brien, 1955.

Philosophical Library for excerpts from Jean-Paul Sartre, "Existentialism is a Humanism" in *Existentialism and Human Emotions*, trans. Bernard Frechtman, © 1947 Philosophical Library, New York, NY.

Random House for excerpt from Albert Camus, The Myth of Sisyphus, trans. Justin O'Brien (1955). Translation copyright © 1955. Copyright renewed 1983 by Alfred A. Knopf, a division of Random House, Inc. Used by permission of Alfred A. Knopf, a division of Random House, Inc.

Every effort has been made to contact copyright holders for their permission to reprint material in this book. The publishers would be grateful to hear from any copyright holder who is not here acknowledged and will undertake to rectify any omissions or errors in future editions of this book.

INTRODUCTION

0.1 What Is Philosophy?

While it is hard to give a one-sentence definition of the term *philosophy*, it is relatively easy to describe the field by reviewing some of the classic questions philosophers study. Here are some examples. What is truth? Is it objective or subjective? What are the limits of human knowledge (for example, can I *know* that an external world exists?) Does it even make sense to talk about the way that the world is apart from our conceptualization of it? What is the nature of reality? What makes me *me*? What does it mean to have a mind? What distinguishes morally right from morally wrong action? Under what circumstances can I be held morally responsible for my actions? Do I have an obligation to obey the laws of the state? Does God exist? If so, is that God worthy of praise and adoration? Does life have meaning? If so, is God a necessary prerequisite to making sense of life's meaning? At first glance, nothing seems to tie these diverse questions together, leaving the impression that they are all considered "philosophical" questions only because of some historical accident in the development of the Western intellectual tradition. On closer examination, however, the questions are seen to share at least one attribute in common— they are all basic questions. By basic, we mean that each of these questions must be among the first questions asked when building a framework for thinking about and acting in the world.

The usual method employed by philosophers in examining one of these questions is to describe and then argue for a particular answer to it. An **argument** is nothing but a set of reasons that are given to back up or justify some statement. For example, the skeptic argues for the view that we cannot know that an external world exists by giving us reasons to believe that we cannot have such knowledge.

1

0.2 Can a Film Carry Philosophical Content?

The usual form in which philosophical discussions are carried out is the written or spoken word. But is the written or spoken word the *only* medium in which philosophical positions and arguments can be expressed? An assumption of this book is that a film, with the assistance of some supplementary written material to guide the viewer in the right direction, can be used to present philosophical positions and arguments in a way that is both rigorous and entertaining.

Over the past decade, academic philosophy has seen significant growth in interest in the question: Can a film carry philosophical content? In a way, though, this question is not new. The ancient Greek philosopher Plato, in his Allegory of the Cave, described a rudimentary movie house 2300 years before the invention of moving pictures. According to Plato, nothing of philosophical interest could go on in that rudimentary movie house. To see why Plato held this view, and, more importantly, to see if his reasoning is relevant to us, it is useful to consider the role that the Allegory played in the larger work, *The Republic*, of which it is a small portion. The Allegory of the Cave is included in Readings from Primary Sources.

In the Allegory of the Cave, Plato asks us to imagine prisoners chained from birth in an underground cave. They are each chained in a way that severely restricts movement. As a result, they can only see one of the cave walls. The cave is poorly illuminated by a single torch a considerable distance behind the chained row of prisoners. Occasionally, a guard will walk between the torch and row of prisoners, and his shadow or the shadow of some object he is carrying will be cast on the wall in front of the prisoners. Since the prisoners cannot turn their heads to see the torch or the guard (or their fellow prisoners), they naturally mistake the shadows they are seeing for "reality." If the guard speaks while walking past, the prisoners are likely to assume that it is the shadow that is speaking. There are several points of similarity between the prisoners in Plato's cave and people in a movie house. One point of similarity is that both sets of people have their attention focused on what is being projected on the wall in front of them. Also, both sets of people can become so drawn in to what is happening in the fictional shadow world that they mistake it for reality. (It is part of the folklore of early cinema that movie-goers occasionally mistook movies for reality; thus, the screening of a short film showing a locomotive speeding towards the camera would cause everyone to run out of the theater in panic. Even today, one regularly sees viewers so drawn in to the fictional world presented in a film that they cry when a sympathetic character suffers or become embarrassed when a character does something silly.) There are some important differences between the prisoners in the Allegory of the Cave and modern movie-goers. The most obvious of these is that modern movie-goers know about the outside world and its relationship to the movie they are watching; whereas, Plato's prisoners only know the shadow world.

After describing the cave interior and the situation of the prisoners, the Allegory of the Cave continues as follows. Plato asks us to imagine that one of the prisoners is freed and struggles out of the cave. His initial response would be confusion: What is this I am seeing now? He may desire to return to the safety and familiarity of the cave environment. If he perseveres in the outside world, he will come to understand that everything he experienced in the cave was unreal and he will begin to pity the prisoners who are still chained there. If one examines the Allegory of the Cave in the context of the surrounding text in *The Republic*, one sees that the story is much more than a premonition of cinema. For Plato, the prisoners chained in the cave are the masses of humankind who walk around in the visible world, mistaking it for reality. These masses fail to understand that the world they experience through the senses is a poor reflection of true reality–a reality that is accessible only through philosophical inquiry. To the extent that we have our attention drawn away from the world of the intellect and toward the world of the senses, to that extent we move away from philosophy. So, for Plato, the cave symbolizes a mistake about what is real and about where knowledge of true reality is to be found.

Does this mean that Plato would have a similarly dim view of the ability of cinema to offer us philosophical insight? It seems not. First, in rejecting the cave as a possible venue for philosophical inquiry, Plato was thinking of the cave as a place of sense-based experience only, not a place in which abstract ideas could be communicated. His rejection of the cave as a possible locale for philosophical inquiry was a rejection of an empirically based method for doing philosophy, not a rejection of "shadows" as a possible medium for reproducing philosophical arguments. Second, Plato wrote most of his works (including *The Republic*) in dialogue form. Many scholars believe that this choice of the dialogue form was based on his view that discussion–dialectical give and take–was the best, perhaps the only means for gaining philosophical insight. *The Republic* is a work of philosophy because it reproduces a discussion on an appropriate set of topics. Is there any difference between a written copy of *The Republic* and a dramatic reading of it that bears on its status as a work of philosophy? Is there any difference between a dramatic reading of *The Republic* and a screening of a filmed dramatic reading of it that bears on its status as a work of philosophy? We believe that the answer to both of these questions is no.

Some contemporary philosophers would disallow a filmed dramatic reading of *The Republic* as positive evidence that a film can carry philosophical content. They would object that the question: Can a film carry philosophical content? presupposes that we consider only the specifically cinematic attributes of film (that is, a film's visual and the narrative elements) in answering the question.[1] Thus, philosophy that takes place in dialogue[2] or is embedded in structural elements of a film[3] is off-limits. Given our present interest in using film in the instruction in philosophy, we have no qualms about taking philosophical content wherever we can find it.

Thus, film offers the philosopher the full expressive power of language, plus the visual and narrative elements that makes film such a good vehicle for introducing students to philosophy. Film, like other forms of fiction, can even make the transition to philosophical thinking easier. We mentioned above that one of the classic questions within philosophy is: Can I know that an external (mind-independent) world exists? At first glance, this may strike you as an absolutely preposterous question. "Of course, I can!" you answer. Indeed, the original question may strike you as so preposterous that it doesn't deserve serious thought. A movie can be an effective tool for introducing a philosophical topic, because it allows the viewer to drop many preconceived notions. We are all used to suspending our commonsense views about how the world works in the context of fiction. This suspension can be used to the philosopher's advantage. Consider the film *Inception*. It first draws the viewer into the fictional world created by the film, pointing out that the protagonist cannot know that *his* experiences represent an external world or that *his* memories correspond to experiences he had in the past. It is only once the viewer has accepted this that the film's subtext becomes clear: *the viewer* is in exactly the same position as the character. This realization can produce an "Aha!" experience–a sense of sudden understanding–that skepticism (the thesis that we cannot know that an external world exists) is not so preposterous after all!

Other films can have the same force. Indeed, our main criterion for using films in this book is that they do just that–that they present and defend an answer to one of philosophy's classic questions. Whether the writer or director responsible for a film had the intention of doing philosophy is beside the point. Each film we will be discussing deals with one or more of the questions posed in the first paragraph of this chapter. *Hilary and Jackie* may be interpreted as presenting arguments for relativism–the view that the truth of all statements can only be judged relative to a conceptual scheme and other background assumptions. As already noted, *Inception* offers us a defense of skepticism, as does *The Matrix*. *Moon* and *Memento* consider what makes a person who she is: Is it my body, my mind, or my immaterial soul that identifies me at birth as the same person I am now? *I, Robot* poses questions at the intersection of philosophy and artificial intelligence: What does it mean to have a mind? What does it mean to be a person (in the sense of someone who has moral rights)? *Memento* (again), along with *Minority Report*, considers the question of whether human beings are free: Do I have free will, or are all of my actions determined by the laws of nature governing the universe? *Gone Baby Gone* and *Crimes and Misdemeanors* examine the nature of morality: When faced with a decision, how do I know which choice is *right*? And which ethical theory is the correct one to use to figure that out? *Antz* and *Equilibrium* address problems within political philosophy: Do I have an obligation to obey laws? What is a *just* state? The next two films, *The Seventh Seal* and *God on Trial*, consider the problem of evil: it seems that God can't exist, because if God did exist, there wouldn't be so much suffering in the world. Even if we assume that God exists, is a God that allows so much suffering worthy of our praise and adoration? *The Seventh Seal* is also a useful source for discussion of the role God plays in making human existence meaningful. *Crimes and Misdemeanors* also raises this topic at several points. Finally, *Leaving Las Vegas* addresses the existentialist question outside of a religious framework: Does life have meaning?

0.3 Tips on How to Watch a Film Philosophically

Films can offer philosophical content in several different ways. As we have noted, a film can simply reproduce a position or an argument in its entirety via dialogue, thereby offering up philosophy in its usual linguistic form. While this does occasionally occur, it is quite rare. Much more common is the case in which a film offers us a fictional world with the key elements of a thought experiment and sufficient context within the film to interpret those elements *as* a thought experiment.

When presenting a thought experiment within the more traditional vehicle for philosophy–the essay–a philosopher describes a hypothetical situation and asks the reader how she interprets what is going on: for example, would she assent to statement X's being an accurate description of the situation? To take a particular example, suppose a philosopher were investigating what criteria determine whether a person at one time is the same person as a person at another time. The philosopher might describe the case of someone who has a form of amnesia that causes him to forget everything that happened prior to a few minutes ago.[4] The philosopher might then pose the following question: Is the person who goes to bed at the end of the day the same person as the person who wakes up that next morning? The reader would then be left to determine what her intuitions tell her about such a case. The role that this particular thought experiment plays would depend on the context in which the philosopher is using the thought experiment; perhaps, the philosopher assumes the reader will say that the person who wakes is a different person from the person who went to bed. This response would then be used by the philosopher as evidence against a theory that tied personal identity to physical continuity of the body. The pattern exemplified in this thought experiment is typical: a philosopher

(i) presents theory T, (ii) presents a hypothetical situation, S, (iii) notes that T makes some prediction, P, related to S, (iv) asks the reader whether they agree with P, (v) explicitly notes that a discrepancy between P and the reader's intuitive response implies that T is false. How would this pattern of thought experiment be realized in film? Step (ii) is easy, since it is the job of a fiction film to present a series of hypothetical situations. Steps (i), (iii) and (v) are a bit trickier, but not impossible: they might be stated or at least alluded to in dialogue. Step (iv) is something the viewer does on his own. The film can encourage the viewer to take this step in various ways; the most common method is to depict a conversation among several characters in which one character insists that P is true and the other insists that P is false. Once steps (i) through (v) have been recognized by the viewer, the argument is complete. Films differ in how explicit the various steps are: in some cases, one or more of the steps are a bit of a stretch. In that case, some prior knowledge of the relevant philosophic topic can help fill in the gaps. That is one of the functions performed by this book.

It should be noted that the legitimacy of thought experiments within philosophical argumentation has been a controversial topic within academic philosophy. Given that a significant number of the film-based arguments we will consider in the following chapters involves the use of thought experiments, this debate affects the legitimacy of using film to explore philosophical topics. Unfortunately, examining this debate further would take us too far afield. Therefore, throughout this book, we will assume that the use of thought experiments in argumentation is legitimate.

Obviously, for Hollywood blockbusters, the purpose of the film is to entertain audiences and, ultimately, to make money; the purpose is not to engage in philosophy. However, in watching even some very mainstream commercial films, one sees in the construction of the story, the dialogue and the visual elements that the screenwriter and director are running into philosophical topics and discovering independently how to reason through them. This should not be surprising. Philosophy is, after all, supposed to make sense, even to people who are not academic philosophers.

There is one other role that film can play in the context of philosophy. A movie can help the viewer to *think critically* by presenting her with views to which she has not (yet) been exposed. Think back, again, to Plato's Allegory of the Cave. The prisoners believe that the shadows on the wall are *real* people and *real* objects and not merely shadows of them. They believe this because this is all they have ever known and because everyone else in the cave believes the same. When the prisoner who has been freed leaves the cave, the brightness of the sun is painful to his eyes (remember, he has been in a dark cave all of his life). But slowly he becomes acclimated to the light and is able to look around at the world outside of the cave. He sees real trees and real animals and, as a result, comes to realize that much of what he took to be true about the world when he was in the cave is in fact false.

A **critical thinker** will be open to examining her own beliefs and the reasons that she has for holding them. She will try to recognize when a belief is the product of her upbringing or the culture in which she lives and to be aware of any biases that she might have as a result. For example, if I was raised by my parents and community to believe that *guns are bad*, I may tend to reject any reasons in support of gun ownership, even if they are strong. To think critically, I must try to avoid being too emotionally or psychologically attached to my anti-gun position that I will not allow anything to count against it. Instead, I will work to be open-minded about views that differ from my own and to take opposing views seriously, without immediately rejecting them. I will also accept the genuine possibility that my own beliefs may turn out to be false. Like the prisoner coming into the bright sun for the first time, it can be disconcerting to come face-to-face with a new and different perspective. It can also be quite troubling to discover that a long-held belief may not be true, especially when it is a core belief upon which many life-decisions are based. But a critical thinker will recognize that it is better to hold a belief for good reasons, than to hold it only because it is the view that she has always held or because her family and friends believe it to be true.

Most likely, you already hold some views with respect to many of the issues that will be explored in the movies and covered in the following chapters. You may find that some views match up with your own and that some don't. There may be some explanations that you have never encountered before and some accounts that differ from the one that you take to be correct. As you explore various solutions to the problems, try to evaluate them as a critical thinker. As much as possible, attempt to maintain some distance from your own views, consider different notions in a fair-minded way, and assess whether there are good reasons supporting a position before accepting or rejecting it.

0.4 The Layout of the Book

Even though philosophy through film is an unorthodox approach to teaching philosophy, the topics have been chosen to cover roughly the same material as a standard introductory textbook. Each chapter corresponds to one of the classic questions within philosophy. The structure within all of the chapters follows the same pattern. The first two or three sections serve as a general introduction to the topic and are intended to be read *before* that chapter's focus film or films are screened. Sections thereafter will make repeated reference to the film(s), so they are best read only *afterward*. Corresponding to each chapter is one or more readings from primary sources. These readings have been selected based on their significance within the history of philosophy and their offering of complete arguments on central issues within the space of just a few pages. The appendix contains plot summaries by elapsed time (through minute marks) for all fourteen focus films. It may be useful to refer to these at various points, either while watching the film or while reading the latter sections in each chapter.

Notes

1. See, for example, Thomas Wartenberg, *Thinking on Screen: Film as Philosophy* (New York: Routledge, 2007).
2. There are many examples of the use of dialogue in a film as a vehicle for philosophy. One example in particular is Professor Levy's soliloquies in *Crimes and Misdemeanors*. Another example is the dialogue in *God on Trial.*
3. An example of a structural element in a film as a vehicle for philosophy is our use of the structuring of the presentation of the multiple perspectives in *Hilary and Jackie.*
4. What we have described is the story line for the film *Memento*, one of the focus films for Chapter 3 on personal identity.

1

TRUTH

Hilary and Jackie (1998)

[T]he truth is that you're not special.
–from *Hilary and Jackie*

A philosopher searches for the *truth* about the world. But what is the nature of *truth*? What does it mean for a statement to be *true*? In this chapter, we will consider various responses to these questions. In the first two sections, we will examine two different theories of truth: the correspondence theory of truth and the pragmatist theory of truth. We will then discuss the movie *Hilary and Jackie*, a "multiple-perspective film" that retells the "same" story from different perspectives. The viewer must wonder whether there is a *true* interpretation of the events or whether *all interpretations of the events are true*. Section 1.3 offers a brief introduction to the film that will draw your attention to things to watch for during your viewing. The material beginning with Section 1.4 makes heavy reference to the movie, so it is most profitably read *after* you have finished watching the movie. In the remaining sections of the chapter, we will explore some theories of relativism with respect to the truth.

1.1 The Correspondence Theory of Truth

The Greek philosopher, **Aristotle** (384 B.C.E.–322 B.C.E.), one of the earliest and most influential philosophers in the history of Western thought, explains truth and falsity like this: "To say of what is that it is not, or of what is not that it is, is false, while to say of what is that it is, and of what is not that it is not, is true."[1] Notice that Aristotle defines truth and falsity in terms of what we *say*. When we think and talk about the world around us, we do so by using combinations of words that form statements. The Greek word *logos*, from which *logic* is derived, can be translated as *argument from reason*, the method by which philosophers justify true statements. But *logos* can also mean *word* and *sentence*. So, for Aristotle, it is not the facts about the world that are true or false; it is what we *say* about the world that is true

9

or false. Truth, then, is a property of a *statement*. According to Aristotle, a statement is true when it conveys what is in fact the case, and a statement is false when it expresses what is not in fact the case. For example, if I say, "A dog is an animal," I am saying of a dog that *is* in fact an animal that it *is* an animal, and so my statement is true. If I assert, "A dog is not an animal," I am saying of a dog that *is* in fact an animal that it *is not* an animal, and so my statement is false.

Bertrand Russell (1872–1970) offers a theory of truth that is similar to Aristotle's. Russell provides an explanation of his theory of truth in his book, *The Problems of Philosophy* (1912). Selections from the chapter, "Truth and Falsehood," are provided in Readings from Primary Sources. In that chapter, Russell explains *truth* and *falsity* in terms of the way that a person's statement or belief matches up with reality: "… a belief is true when there is a corresponding fact, and is false when there is no corresponding fact."[2] In other words, a true belief matches up with what is in fact the case, and a false belief does not. So, according to both Aristotle and Russell, there are two things involved in truth: (1) a statement (or belief) and (2) reality or facts. When (1) *corresponds* with (2), we have a true statement (or belief). This is the **correspondence theory of truth**.

According to Russell, facts about the world are independent of thought. In other words, there is a mind-independent reality—a world made up of objects that exist independently of what anyone or any group of people happens to think. **Cognitive objectivism** is the position that combines the thesis that the world is mind-independent and the correspondence theory of truth. So, the cognitive objectivist holds that what makes a statement or a belief true is its relationship to a fact about the world. And since the world is mind-independent, minds do not decide what is true and what is false. Truth is *objective*.

Initially, the correspondence theory of truth might sound like a very plausible account of truth; it seems to make sense to say that a proposition is true if it matches up with a fact out there in the world. However, the skeptic (whom we will discuss in detail in the next chapter) argues that it is impossible to ever *know* that a belief corresponds to reality. The skeptic will maintain that a person can only have direct access to her own *sense data*. You might have the *sensation* that a ball is red because that is how it looks to you. But, the skeptic argues, how do you know that the ball is *really* red? How can you ever be sure that the way that the ball *appears* to you inside your head is the way that the ball *really* is in the external world? You would have to "get outside your own head" to compare your *perception* of the red ball with the ball as it is in reality in order to determine whether what you are seeing matches up with a ball that is really red. But, *you can't get outside of your own head*! You can never have *direct* access to the external world of mind-independent objects; you only have direct access to your own internal world of sensations and perceptions. Because you can never compare your sense data with some fact out there in the world, it seems that you can never *know* whether how things *appear* to you corresponds to how things *really* are. And, if you can never know whether your beliefs match up with a mind-independent fact, then you will never be able to use the correspondence theory of truth to show that any of your beliefs is true. The skeptic concludes that the correspondence theory fails as a theory of truth because it cannot work to give a definite answer about whether any statement is true.

1.2 The Pragmatist Theory of Truth

William James (1842–1910), an American philosopher and psychologist, raises a different objection against the correspondence theory of truth. Excerpts from James's book, *Pragmatism*, are provided in Readings from Primary Sources. In the first passage, James explains that the correspondence theorist (whom James calls the "intellectualist") is right to characterize a true idea as one that is in "agreement" with reality. However, James argues that the definition of *agreement* that the correspondence theorist uses is in some sense too strict because many of our ideas are not exact copies of reality. James asks the reader to think of a clock and the way that it works. If you are like James, your idea of the *time keeping function* of the clock fails to accurately capture the *real* workings of the clock (unless, of course, you are a clockmaker). And, when you consider the *elasticity* of the clock's springs, most likely your idea of elasticity doesn't *exactly* match up with what elasticity *really* is. James concludes that the correspondence theory cannot work because so many of our ideas fail to be exact copies of reality: "Where our ideas cannot copy definitely their object, what does agreement with that object mean?"3

Rather than taking *agreement* to mean "corresponding to reality," James maintains that an idea *agrees* with reality when its being true is "helpful in life's practical struggles." A true idea has "cash-value in experiential terms," in other words, it is *useful* in helping the person to function in the world:

> If I am lost in the woods and starved, and find what looks like a cow-path, it is of the utmost importance that I should think of a human habitation at the end of it, for if I do so and follow it, I save myself. The true thought is useful here because the house which is its object is useful.4

Thus according to the **pragmatist theory of truth**, an idea is *true* when it is practical. And we don't need "complete verification" that the idea matches up exactly with reality, we only need to show that the belief *works*: "Just as we here assume Japan to exist without ever having been there,

11

because it WORKS to do so."[5] In this way, the pragmatist can avoid the skeptic's objection that is raised against the correspondence theory. Whereas the correspondence theorist must prove that a belief matches up with reality, the pragmatist only needs to show that the consequences of holding the idea will have practical value:

> Any idea that helps us DEAL, whether practically or intellectu-
> ally, with either the reality or its belongings, that doesn't entangle
> our progress in frustrations, that FITS, in fact, and adapts our
> life to the reality's whole setting, will agree sufficiently to meet the
> requirement. It will hold true of that reality.[6]

So, both Russell and James believe that there is a mind-independent world and both hold that a true idea must agree with that world. However, the two philosophers differ with respect to what it means for an idea to "agree" with reality. While Russell claims that a true idea *corresponds* with reality, James maintains that a true idea is *useful* when dealing with reality.

Russell raises an objection against James's pragmatist theory of truth. Russell explains that since it *works* to believe that Santa Claus exists, then, on James's account, the belief that Santa Claus exists must be *true*–even though we know that it is false that Santa Claus exists.[7] Because this objection can work for many such beliefs, it seems to follow that pragmatism encourages the belief in false statements. This objection may seem a bit childish. However, in another work, James makes the case that religious belief is justifiable because a person is better off believing that God exists.[8] Since James makes the case that a person can choose to believe in God when it is pragmatic for her to do so, he would need to show why that same line of reasoning wouldn't work in the case of the belief in Santa Claus.

Perhaps a more pressing problem for the pragmatist account concerns the characterization of a true belief. According to James, an idea is true if it is useful and helps to lead to a better life. But what does it mean to say that an idea is *useful?* And, does a true belief need to be useful to everyone or just the person who is considering the idea? Also, the skeptic might argue that because we can't see the future, we can never know whether holding a particular belief will have good consequences and lead to a better life. Think back to the cow-path example. Say that I follow James's advice and take the path because I believe that there is a house at the end of it. But, as it turns out, I am mistaken. There is no house at the end of the path, there is just a big old grizzly bear that eats anything that comes his way. One might argue that the pragmatist theory is problematic because it may encourage us to adopt beliefs that result in very bad consequences that we cannot foresee.

Finally, one might argue that the pragmatist must concede that the same belief could be true for one person but false for another. If a belief works for one person but not for another, then it would seem that the belief could be both true (for the person for whom it works) and false (for the person for whom it doesn't work). For example, James suggests that if believing that *God exists* helps you to deal with life, then you are justified in believing that it is true that *God exists*. But, if I think that it is not useful to believe that *God exists*, then, for me, it is false that *God exists*. It may be the case, then, that the pragmatist is ultimately committed to some form of *relativism* with respect to the truth.

We will be able to better consider this objection, once we have examined various forms of relativism. But, first, let's take a look at the movie.

1.3 An Overview of the Movie (*Hilary and Jackie*)

HILARY AND JACKIE (1998). DIRECTED BY ANAND TUCKER.
STARRING EMILY WATSON, RACHEL GRIFFITHS, JAMES FRAIN,
DAVID MORRISSEY

The most important thing to know about *Hilary and Jackie* for the purposes of this chapter is that it is a multiple-perspective film: telling the same story from the perspectives of several different characters. On many points, these retellings disagree with one another. The rest of this chapter will be concerned with the philosophical import of this disagreement.

While the multiple-perspective structure of the film should be obvious, it is useful to have it in mind, since, right from the beginning, the film is dropping hints about when perspective changes and what to make of those changes. In the plot summary for the movie included in the Appendix, we have tried to make explicit when perspective changes. It may be helpful to read the Appendix entry while watching it, in order to see when the various switches in perspective occur, for, while the filmmaker has provided us with explicit labels ("Hilary and Jackie," "Hilary" and "Jackie") for the first three-quarters of the film, by the end, perspective is switching at a rather fast clip from Hilary to Jackie and back again, and, by now, no labels are provided.

Based on the book by brother and sister Hilary and Piers du Pre (originally entitled *A Genius in the Family*, later retitled *Hilary and Jackie*), the film *Hilary and Jackie* follows the lives of the two du Pre sisters from their childhood in 1950s England to sister Jackie's rise to stardom as one of the world's preeminent cellists. The two girls, both musicians (sister Hilary plays the flute), are originally very close, but Jackie's increasing success and celebrity tear them apart. The trajectories of their lives diverge even more as Hilary settles down, marrying her first love Kiffer Finzi, while

Jackie becomes ever more isolated in the role of "musical genius," eventually marrying the gifted pianist and conductor Daniel Barenboim. Jackie's increasing isolation and unhappiness with the life she has chosen (or, from her perspective, the life she had thrust upon her) is brought to a head during a fateful visit to Hilary and Kiffer's country home. When Hilary and Piers du Pre first published the book detailing their family's lives, it caused quite an uproar among the classical music community, within which Jacqueline du Pre had been almost deified. Some suggested that Hilary's picture of Jackie was the result of envy and jealousy at her sister's musical success. The film's release only reignited the controversy. Gossip column flap aside, the charge that Hilary and Pier's portrayal of Jackie is colored by subjectivity only adds to the philosophical usefulness of the film in exploring the issue of truth.

The Appendix entry for *Hilary and Jackie* gives plot summaries and corresponding minute marks (the total amount of time that has elapsed since the opening credits began) for the major scenes.

1.4 What Really Happened?

So, you've just finished watching *Hilary and Jackie*. What happened? What *really* happened?

There are a couple of significant differences between *Hilary and Jackie* and the other films that are used in this book. First, unlike most of the other films presented in this book, the philosophical import of *Hilary and Jackie* is not found in the story or in bits of dialogue, but in the structure of the film. In the film's various retellings, the viewer is made aware of the markedly different interpretations each of the characters puts on the "same" set of events. Most films (and virtually all mainstream Hollywood movies) convey a story from a single omniscient or quasi-omniscient perspective: the film's narrative is not bound by the knowledge or point of view of any single character. Rather, it is as if the narrative is being generated by some disinterested spectator who can observe events taking place without regard for distance in time or place. Within this narrative convention, questions about what to make of differing interpretations never come up. However, *Hilary and Jackie* confronts us with different pictures of the world, and thereby forces us to try to make sense of these differences. What is responsible for generating the differences? What do the differences tell us about the nature of *truth*?

Hilary and Jackie also differs from the other films in this book because it is based upon a *true* story; the events that unfold are based upon events that really happened. Most of the other movies used here are purely fictional, and the writer makes up all of the events. In the case of fictional films, it doesn't make sense to ask what *really* happened. In some cases, the writer may even intentionally leave the ending ambiguous, with no intended true interpretation. However, because most of the events that are depicted in *Hilary and Jackie* really occurred, we can meaningfully explore the question of which interpretation is the *correct* interpretation.

Let us begin our investigation of the film by looking at its narrative structure. The first label identifying whose perspective is being offered occurs at the 3:30 minute mark, as the words "Hilary and Jackie" flash briefly on the screen. This shared perspective lasts through the two girls' childhood and teenage years, ending on the night of the Italian wedding (MM 23:20).[9] Hilary's perspective (clearly demarcated as the name "Hilary" flashes on the screen) picks up when she awakens the next morning to find that Jackie has gone. We are then presented with events as experienced by Hilary over the next decade or so of fictional time. We will come back shortly to discuss several key events in this series; first, though, we will lay out the rest of the film's structure. At MM 63:30, the word "Jackie" flashes on the screen, and we are back in Italy the morning after the wedding as Jackie is awakened early to catch a train for her next performance. For the next twenty-seven minutes of the film, we review roughly the same time span, now from Jackie's perspective. Beginning at MM 90:00, perspective shifts back and forth from that of Jackie to that of Hilary. This time, though, we are not provided with labels to warn us of the changes in perspective. Other clues (for example, scenes in which only one sister is present) are needed. The film ends as Hilary and Piers are driving back after Jackie's death.

Events recounted from Hilary's and Jackie's perspectives have much in common. A careful viewer should have little problem recognizing that many events described from Jackie's perspective match up with those from Hilary's. However, there are three events recognizable in both Hilary's and Jackie's perspectives where there is major disagreement about what really happened. These three events are: Kiffer's first "visit" to the du Pre home; the nighttime conversation between Hilary and Jackie, when Hilary announces her engagement to Kiffer; and circumstances surrounding Kiffer and Jackie having sex. Let's start with the last event and work our way back in time. (In the part of the film relating events from Jackie's perspective, the sex act is implied at MM 85:00. The corresponding event from Hilary's point of view occurs at MM 55:20; however, Jackie's initial request to sleep with Kiffer occurs earlier, at MM 47:00.) This event from Jackie's point of view is barely recognizable as the same as what we had seen from Hilary's point of view. Hilary viewed the act as the effect of Jackie's uncaring manipulations—her desire to get what she (Jackie) wanted, irrespective of the cost to those around her. From Jackie's perspective, there is no trace of the manipulations that loom so large from Hilary's point of view. Rather, the sequence of events leading up to sex is: Kiffer comes into Jackie's room, notices that she is very upset, and comforts her. Sex between the two of them isn't shown, but we can easily imagine it as the continuation of this scene. There is no hint that it is anything other than a spontaneous act on both their parts.

The second event that differs sharply in interpretation is the nighttime conversation between the two sisters, as Hilary wakes Jackie up to announce her engagement to Kiffer. (This begins at MM 35:20 from Hilary's point of view and MM 73:00 from Jackie's point of view.) From Hilary's point of view, Jackie is very cruel. When asked why she is marrying Kiffer, Hilary responds, "Because he makes me feel special." Jackie replies, "[T]he truth is, you're not special." Compare this with the conversation as related from Jackie's point of view. That same line ("the truth is, you're not special") is still there, but its meaning has changed significantly. Here it is Hilary who is the cruel one.

The final event we would like to consider occurs shortly after Kiffer barges into the du Pre home. (Hilary's take on this begins at MM 30:55, Jackie's at MM 72:50.) Even at this early juncture (not very much fictional time has elapsed since the wedding in Italy when the two perspectives started to diverge), clear differences are noticeable. Missing from Hilary's version of events is any sense that Jackie is disappointed by Hilary's choice to spend time with Kiffer, even though Jackie has come back home to see her.

Perhaps your initial reaction is to try to reconcile the diverging stories, discovering the hidden truth that both versions of events were based upon. This reaction discloses an objectivist leaning: one assumes there are facts about what happened and one tries to use the conflicting stories as clues to discovering the facts. However, it is not at all obvious what this "hidden truth" would be. One might even argue that there is no such "hidden truth," and that there are, instead, just different interpretations that result from the different ways that the events were perceived.

In general, there are four alternatives we can take in order to reconcile the differences:

1. We can reject one of the interpretations as untrue and based on misinformation.
2. We can reject one of the interpretations as untrue and the result of lying.
3. We can reject one of the interpretations as untrue and the result of self-deception.
4. We can accept both of the conflicting interpretations as true by adopting a relativistic stance.

The first three are objectivistic options. In each of these cases, there is some objective truth about what happened in the mind-independent world, and the different interpretations result from an error of some sort: one (or both) of the characters simply failed to represent the actual facts accurately. The fourth option is relativistic. In this case, each of the different interpretations is true *relative to the person who provides it.* *Hilary and Jackie* does not *force* us to adopt the relativistic option, but the multiple-perspective structure of the film offers relativism as an avenue that deserves exploring. So, let's consider some forms of relativism.

1.5 The Coherence Theory of Truth

In Section 1.1, we saw that the skeptic raises an objection against the correspondence theory of truth: because we can't get outside our own heads to see whether a belief matches up with the external world, we can never use the correspondence theory to determine whether any given belief is true. The skeptic's objection concerns the fact that we do not have direct access to the external world; we only have direct access to our own internal world of perceptions and beliefs. So, why not just define truth in terms of what we can have access to, namely, our beliefs? Rather than characterizing truth as a relation between beliefs and facts in the mind-independent world, the *coherentist* maintains that a belief is true when it *coheres* with the system of beliefs that a person holds. On the **coherence theory of truth**, I know that a certain belief is true by holding it up against all of my other beliefs. If that belief is consistent with my other beliefs, then it is true; if it contradicts my other beliefs, then it is false. For example, let's suppose that in 1960 Hilary believes the following: *my sister was born in 1945; it is now 1960; I am now 18 years old,* and say that she also holds the belief: *I am younger than my sister.* When Hilary compares all of these beliefs together, she can see that the last belief does not cohere with the first three, so she would know that the belief, *I am younger than my sister,* must be false.

It is important to see that the proponent of the coherence theory does not necessarily deny that there is a mind-independent world. The coherentist merely thinks that *we can never have direct access to it.* Like the skeptic, the coherentist rejects the correspondence theory of truth because there is no way to verify whether the information that a person has about the world is true. Since the correspondence theory of truth is one of two theses that make up *cognitive objectivism,* the coherentist's denial of the correspondence theory amounts to a rejection of cognitive objectivism. Instead, the coherentist defends **truth relativism**, the view that truth is *relative* to a person's *conceptual scheme.*

A **conceptual scheme** is the set of concepts and rules that a person uses to shape and organize her thoughts and to process sensory information to form her system of beliefs. When a person receives sense data, the cognitive machinery of the mind works on the sensory stream to produce a coherent account of the world. So, as I look around right now, I am receiving visual sense data—I see colors and shapes in various positions. My mind interprets that sensory information in terms of interrelated objects. The colors and shapes that I see are immediately interpreted as *a white and yellow coffee cup on a desk next to a stack of books.* Without *concepts* like "white," "yellow," "coffee cup," "on," "desk," "next to," "stack," and "books," my sensory stream would not reveal a coherent world. Rather, it would be, to use William James's words, a "buzzing, blooming confusion"–there would be no regularity from one moment to the next and no objects persisting through time. For that matter, there would be no objects at all; there would just be uninterpreted patches of color of various shades. If I lacked the concept "coffee cup," I might interpret the set of white and yellow patches that I experience as part of the desk, or I might interpret the patches of color as distinct objects that do not go together to form a larger object. My *conceptual scheme* is the set of concepts that I use to interpret the sense data into diverse objects related in various ways, and it is what allows me to divide up the world in a way that makes sense to me and helps me to interact with it. When I drink from the coffee cup, I manipulate it in a particular way, with the result that there is less liquid in the cup than when I started the action. All this is as it should be–as common sense and my conceptual scheme tells me that the world is.

It may be the case that different individuals have different conceptual schemes. Cultural anthropologists return from the field with reports of individuals who seem to use quite different conceptual schemes to interpret their experiences. What initially appear to be irrational beliefs are shown to "make sense" in the context of the culture-specific conceptual schemes. And, it may even be the case that individuals within a culture have varying conceptual schemes. For example, consider, again, the various scenes in *Hilary and Jackie* that depict two very different versions of the same event. The coherentist might maintain that the different interpretations that the two sisters have of the events in their lives are due to their different conceptual schemes. Thus, the coherentist might explain that if Hilary believes that one interpretation is true, and it coheres with her conceptual scheme, then it is true. While, at the same time, Jackie might believe that that same interpretation is false, and if the interpretation is inconsistent with *her* conceptual scheme, then it is false.

It is important to see that the coherentist and truth relativists, in general, do not rule out the possibility that some conceptual schemes can be rejected outright as irrational. The coherentist will maintain that a conceptual scheme is irrational if it allows the person to hold two incoherent beliefs. If Hilary's conceptual scheme results in the belief that Jackie was born in 1945 and the belief that Jackie was not born in 1945, then, according to the coherentist, there is something wrong with Hilary's conceptual scheme.

Russell raises an objection against this particular aspect of the coherence theory of truth. (The passage containing the objection is included in

Readings from Primary Sources.) In that passage, Russell argues that, even though the coherentist wants to maintain that we cannot get at objective truths, the coherentist must actually make use of some objective truths in the defense of the coherence theory. As we just explained, the coherentist maintains that a conceptual scheme is irrational if it allows a person to hold two contradictory beliefs. So, in order for the coherence theory to work, it must be *true* that *two incoherent beliefs cannot both be true*. But, then there is (at least) one true statement—*that two incoherent beliefs cannot both be true*—that we can know and that is true independent of any person's beliefs. The claim that *two contradictory statements cannot both be true* is called the **principle of noncontradiction** (what Russell called the principle of *contradiction*). Russell concludes that the coherence theory of truth fails because, while it claims that objective truth is beyond our grasp, the coherence theory must actually presuppose the objective truth of the principle of noncontradiction.

1.6 Cognitive Relativism

In the previous section, we examined a less radical form of cognitive relativism: truth relativism (of which the coherence theory is one example). In this section, we will take a look at cognitive relativism, in general.

The name most closely related with relativism in the ancient world is that of **Protagoras** (ca. 480–421 B.C.E.), a slightly older contemporary of Socrates. Although the bulk of Protagoras's writings is no longer extant, a few tantalizing fragments have managed to survive (mostly in the context of criticisms of relativism by subsequent generations of Greek philosophers). The most famous among these is: "Man is the measure of all things: of what is, that it is; of what is not, that it is not."[10] Here we see that what is *true* is entirely up to us to decide. According to Protagoras, man is the ultimate arbiter of what is true and what is false.

Let's examine some of the main empirical arguments for cognitive relativism. The first argument begins with the pervasive differences of opinion one observes among people, coupled with the claim that there is no objective standard to use in adjudicating between the differing views— no objective standard to use in deciding which view is true and which view is false. Clearly, different opinions are offered by Hilary and Jackie. Does difference of opinion by itself constitute evidence in favor of cognitive relativism? We think not. This can be seen by considering a related argument, one that shows the structural unsoundness of inferring cognitive relativism based solely on a difference of opinion.

This related argument goes as follows.[11] Different individuals have different views on whether the earth is flat or not. In general, there is a high degree of intracultural agreement on this question. Thus, among adults within a given culture, the probability that an individual holds the flat-earth

19

hypothesis is closely correlated with whether her cultural peers hold this hypothesis. (Since conceptual schemes play a large role in cognitive relativism, and since conceptual schemes are largely culture-specific, this intracultural agreement is potentially relevant to the argument–it strengthens the relativist's case.) However, intercultural diversity and intracultural uniformity on the question of the earth's shape do not entail that there is no objective fact of the matter about whether the earth is flat or not. A consistent cognitive objectivist can say that some cultures (namely, those cultures in which the flat earth hypothesis is widespread) are just mistaken on this point. The burden of proof is on the relativist to show how difference of opinion implies relativism; so, the objectivist's response is not begging the question. In general, mere difference of opinion does not constitute evidence in favor of relativism. In order to argue for cognitive relativism, we must be offered more; we must be offered reasons to believe that there is no way of adjudicating between the differing views.

Hilary and Jackie does just that. As viewers, we are offered not only difference of opinion but also enough of Hilary's and Jackie's history to understand how and why their later conceptual schemes diverged. Consequently, the film does offer us reasons to believe that *both* sisters' accounts of events are true.

So far, all we have done is catalog a list of differences between Hilary's and Jackie's takes on events. As stated above, this sort of difference does not, in itself, argue for cognitive relativism. For that, we must be presented not only with a difference of opinion but also with some reason to think the difference is the result of incompatible but equally valid conceptual schemes. Otherwise, the cognitive objectivist can dismiss the differences as being the result of misinformation or deception of some sort. *Hilary and Jackie* provides us with evidence of differing conceptual schemes. We see that differences in interpretation of later events can be traced back to differing experiences during the time period when the two sisters are separated. Given these previous experiences, Hilary's take "makes sense," as does Jackie's, even though the two are at odds with one another.

There are three events that provide us as viewers with information about how and why the two sisters' interpretations of later events diverge. In each case, one of the sisters lacks relevant information about what is happening with the other. The three events all occur fairly early in fictional time after the Italian wedding. Indeed, the first event to be discussed happens that very next morning after the wedding, as first Jackie wakes up, then Hilary. In some ways, Hilary's take on these events stretches credulity, but we will disregard that as within the bounds of artistic license. (For this event from Hilary's perspective, see MM 23:40, for Jackie's, see MM 64:10.) Hilary wakes to find Jackie already gone. Hilary's reaction shows that this was not something she had expected. (This is the aspect that appears to stretch believability–that Hilary would not have been informed of Jackie's upcoming concert in Berlin and the need for an early departure.) From Hilary's perspective, Jackie had abandoned her there, without bothering to wake her or even write a "goodbye" note. When we finally get around to seeing Jackie's take on things, we start with exactly this event. Jackie is awakened by a man telling her she is running very late. She wants to wake Hilary and say good-bye but is told that there is no time for that. She receives assurance that Hilary's transportation back to England has already been taken care of.

The second event that helps us understand why the two sisters' conceptual schemes diverged involves the package of laundry. (See MM 27:00 and 71:00 for Hilary's and Jackie's takes, respectively.) In some ways, this event is emblematic of the whole film. Jackie, desperately homesick, is overjoyed to receive a reminder of home in the form of the familiar smell of her cleaned clothes. For her, the washed laundry has much more import than merely having clean clothes to wear again. Hilary, unaware of Jackie's current mental state, interprets the dirty laundry as evidence that Jackie doesn't care about the family she has left behind. To the extent that Jackie thinks about them at all, it is as someone to do her laundry. This is emblematic of the film because it shows not only how different prior experiences can lead to different interpretations of shared events, but also how those differences in interpretations tend to reinforce the differences.

The final event that helps to explain how the two sisters' conceptual schemes diverged is Jackie's first noticing that something is wrong with her. Recall the chronology leading up to Jackie's unannounced arrival at Hilary and Kiffer's country home. Jackie has altered perception (MM 81:50). Jackie breaks the glass backstage and notices that her hand is shaking badly (MM 82:40). Jackie appears to know that something is seriously wrong with her—something that may make it impossible for her to continue playing the cello. She tries to talk about it with Danny, asking him how he would react if she were to give up the life of a concert cellist and become an "ordinary" person. Danny's response is very discouraging (MM 83:20). Hilary is not aware of any of this.

Do these differences in take amount to a difference in conceptual scheme? When we introduced the notion of a conceptual scheme in Section 1.5, we used a somewhat simplistic example as illustration. The way we described it there, two people have differing conceptual schemes if they segment their respective perceptual streams differently. For example, I interpret a set of yellow and white color patches as a coffee cup (a distinct object). Someone else (someone who lacks the concept "coffee cup") interprets a similar set of yellow and white color patches as part of the desk. The examples of differing interpretations we have drawn from *Hilary and Jackie* are not so straightforward as the coffee cup example. The most important respect in which the two sisters' interpretations differ regards the motives each imputes to the other sister in making sense of that sister's behavior. There seem also to be differences in what each sister pays attention to. Thus, in certain shared scenes (for example, the nighttime conversation in which Hilary announces her engagement), elements from one version of events are missing in the other and vice versa. These differences *do* amount to a difference in conceptual schemes, because the mutually incompatible world that each sister constructs is internally coherent and differs from the world constructed by the other sister in predictable ways. In Hilary's world, some of the bad things that befall her are the direct result of the actions of her self-absorbed sister. In Jackie's world, the loneliness and fear she feels are not assuaged when she seeks comfort from Hilary. If anything, Hilary's rejection of her only heightens those feelings.

So, consider the view that *Jackie was cruel.* Hilary believed that Jackie was cruel, while Jackie did not think that of herself. Whose take on events was superior: Hilary's or Jackie's? Which sister is *correct?* Does this question even make sense? It seems that the correspondence theorist would claim that since Hilary believes that it is true that *Jackie was cruel* and Jackie believes that it is false, only one of the two sisters can be correct. The coherentist may suggest that because the belief that *Jackie was cruel* is coherent with Hilary's system of beliefs, it is true with respect to Hilary. Yet, since the belief that *Jackie was cruel* is *in*consistent with Jackie's belief system, it is false relative to Jackie's conceptual scheme. However, keep in mind that the coherentist, as a truth relativist, holds that rationality is universal and that it is universally true that it is *ir*rational to hold two contradictory beliefs. The coherentist would thus allow for the possibility of judging the adequacy of the two competing conceptual schemes. In this case, the coherentist might explain that Jackie's conceptual scheme has been impaired by her deteriorating mental condition due to the MS, preventing her from adequately assessing the coherence of her own beliefs.

The cognitive relativist would maintain that the belief that *Jackie was cruel* is true relative to Hilary's conceptual scheme and false relative to Jackie's. But, unlike the coherentist, the cognitive relativist does not think that rationality is universal. According to **relativism of rationality**, there is no way to adjudicate between the two competing conceptual schemes. Some relativists with respect to rationality might argue that the only criterion other than objective truth that could be used in rating the two sister's conceptual schemes is the overall rationality of each scheme; however, since there is no rational foundation, there is no available criterion to use to judge between the two schemes. Other rationality relativists might argue that rationality itself is internal to a conceptual scheme. And so there is no such thing as a conceptually neutral version of rationality that could be used to compare the two different conceptual schemes with one another. Hilary would grade her own conceptual scheme based on the notion of rationality that goes along with *her* scheme, and she would judge her conceptual scheme to be quite rational. Jackie would grade her own conceptual scheme on *her* notion of rationality and, again, she would find her own conceptual scheme to be quite rational.

What about the viewer's take on the two sister's competing conceptual schemes? It seems that most people think that Hilary's way of interpreting the events is correct. Hilary is the "good" sister, the long-suffering victim, and Jackie is the "bad" sister, the one who manipulates and uses others to get her way. While the typical viewer reports that her picture of Jackie softened somewhat after seeing things from Jackie's point of view, the bias in favor of Hilary and her perspective remains. (It would be interesting to see whether reversing the order of presentation of perspectives had any effect on this trend.) When asked *why* they voted in favor of Hilary's perspective as most accurate and/or trustworthy, the answer varies. Most people say something like, "Hilary's interpretation of events strikes me as most plausible." However, when asked to elaborate, or to cite a particular event and explain why Hilary's interpretation is more plausible than Jackie's, no answer is forthcoming.

1.7 Nietzschean Perspectivism and Postmodernism

According to the relativity of rationality, "what warrants belief depends on canons of reasoning ... that should properly be seen as social norms, relative to culture and period."[12] In its most extreme form, relativism of rationality even questions whether the laws of logic have any sort of objective status. According to **relativism of logic**, laws of logic (for example, the law of noncontradiction) are merely social norms; they do not reflect laws governing the mind-independent world. The most radical relativists do not even require that I be minimally consistent in my beliefs, assuming that my conceptual scheme does not recognize the law of noncontradiction. In the words of Walt Whitman, "Do I contradict myself?/very well then I contradict myself,/(I am large, I contain multitudes.)"[13] In this section, we look at the two most radical members of the cognitive relativism family: Nietzschean perspectivism and postmodernist relativism.

Friedrich Nietzsche (1844–1900) lived in the nineteenth century, thus he predates the birth of postmodernism. However, he is the first major philosopher to espouse relativism of rationality, the point of departure for postmodernism. Indeed, he was also prescient of postmodernism in emphasizing the role language plays both in fixing our conceptual schemes and in creating the very idea of objective truth.

Nietzsche had a rather strange writing style, preferring to express his ideas with highly elliptical prose and copious self-contradictions. Some have argued that this writing style was exactly what was called for, given the message: Nietzsche wanted to jar his readers into seeing that many of the things they currently believed were not objectively true, without thereby putting something equally untrue in their place.[14] The use of multiple perspectives, in both film and literature, serves a similar purpose. We, as viewers, are shown several incompatible descriptions of the world and asked not to pick which one is the objectively correct one (or even which is closest to objective truth) but to conclude that they are all true relative to the perspective of their respective narrators. As Nietzsche tells us,

> There are no facts, only interpretations.
> As though there would be a world left over once we subtracted the perspectival![15]

Contrary to the implication of the second quotation above, he was no idealist: there was a world left over after the subtraction of the perspectival. As Arthur Danto notes in writing about Nietzsche, "[T]here was a world which remained over, tossing blackly like the sea, chaotic relative to our distinctions and perhaps to all distinctions, but there nevertheless. ... A blind, empty, structureless thereness."[16] So, Nietzsche's conceptual relativism was the result of what he saw as a qualitative mismatch between our distinctions (that is, the concepts we use in structuring the world of experience) and the mind-independent world.

Because of his repeated emphasis on the ineluctably perspectival nature of all observation and knowledge, Nietzsche's version of cognitive relativism has come to be called "perspectivism." But Nietzsche didn't stop there, with merely a negative description of what the world wasn't. His perspectivism had a positive aspect as well. To the extent that you can say what it is, the world is "made up of points of origin for perspectives, ... occupied by active powers, wills, each seeking to organize the world from its perspective, each locked in combat with the rest."[17]

Does this mean that every conceptual scheme is as good as every other one? Nietzsche would answer: No. The wills are in combat. The victor shall be the will whose perspective incorporates the conceptual scheme that most facilitates life. For Nietzsche, "Truth is that sort of error without which a particular class of living creatures could not live."[18] So, Nietzsche does not use some objective standard of rationality in judging the adequacy of a conceptual scheme, but rather a pragmatic standard: a conceptual scheme is adequate if it allows one to thrive.

Postmodernism's history as a distinct school of thought begins in the mid-twentieth century within the philosophy and literary criticism in France and Germany, as a reaction to the devastation of the Second World War. For the postmodernists, Hiroshima and the Holocaust showed without a doubt that humanity is not progressing toward some objective goal, as the modernists' inherent faith in the universality of rationality had led many to believe.

Postmodernism's starting point is the claim that there are no objective standards either for determining the truth or falsity of individual judgments or for judging the adequacy of conceptual schemes. Members of the mainstream Western tradition mistakenly believe in objective standards because our language has created the myth of a mind-independent world against which judgments can be compared. According to Gene Blocker, one of the goals of postmodernism is to expose this myth of the mind-independent world as a myth

> by "deconstructing" language, that is, by showing first the gap between word and object, language and reality, and then by showing that the so-called reality is simply created by the language itself. Deconstruction shows how language has constructed what we call "reality"; it then deconstructs these linguistic constructions. What this basically accomplishes, where successful, is to expose as myths linguistic descriptions which masquerade as reality–the myth of [the correspondence theory of truth], the myth of universal cross-cultural objectivity and rationality, the myth of neutral, value-free scientific investigation, and so on. ... The things we refer to are not real, objective parts of reality; they are just ways of speaking which have caught on, become popular and then "internalized" so that we wrongly assume they accurately describe and reveal an independent reality.[19]

Even the distinction between what is or is not a value judgment is overthrown. According to postmodernism, all judgments are colored by human values and emotions. Even if the notion of a "disinterested observer" made sense, there is no neutral, value-free vocabulary in which to express judgments. As noted in the quote above, even science, presumed by many to be the epitome of rationality and the search for objective truth, is value-laden. As such, Alison Jaggar notes, "the conclusions of western science thus are presumed ... [to be] uncontaminated by the supposedly 'subjective' values and emotions that might bias individual investigators. ... [However,] it has been argued that it does not, indeed cannot, eliminate generally accepted social values."[20]

The upshot of **postmodernist relativism** is the legitimization of *all* points of view. There is no such thing as objective truth. There is no such thing as universal rationality. The canons of logic are merely one set of social norms among others with no special claim to universal acceptance. Many postmodernists even reject the possibility of employing pragmatic criteria for adjudicating between conceptual schemes.[21] Taken to its extreme in postmodernism

> [t]here are no external standards nor even internal standards of personal or cultural consistency and coherence to restrict us. We are therefore free to go with what seems at the moment compelling to us and we are guided in our articulations only by the desire to persuade, to gain a receptive following.[22]

To many objectivists, and even modernist (truth) relativists, this sounds like intellectual anarchy. It should therefore come as no surprise that the postmodernist challenge to modernism's assumption of the universality of reason has been greeted with great apprehension within mainstream Anglo-American philosophy.

Is *Hilary and Jackie* a film that can be used to support the postmodernist cause? Yes and no. On the affirmative side, it presents not one complete and consistent picture of the world but a pair of perspectives; this much is in agreement with postmodernism. On the negative side, whether this was intentional or not, *Hilary and Jackie* seems to prefer one interpretation at the expense of the other–Hilary's perspective is judged as objectively better. (Although, as we noted earlier, viewers were unable to explain what about the film led them to that conclusion.)

Just as postmodernist philosophers hold that there are no objective facts, postmodernists within literary and film criticism hold that there is no such thing as the meaning of a work of art (for example, a film). Thus, if some viewers interpret *Hilary and Jackie* as a postmodernist film, then it is for them. "Meaning" arises only in the confluence of a work of art and a point of view.

1.8 An Assessment of Relativism

In a pluralistic society like the United States, tolerance is an absolute necessity. Some argue that one way to foster tolerance is to convince everyone that cognitive relativism is correct. If there is no such thing as absolute truth, but only truth relative to a conceptual scheme, then two individuals can both be right on some issue, even if those two individuals disagree with one another. I am less likely to act intolerantly toward someone with whom I disagree if I think that that person's views may be true (relative to their own conceptual scheme, of course). While the above line of reasoning looks good on the surface, we believe it has one serious flaw–that is the form of tolerance that emerges from relativism is not very attractive. It should not be confused with the form of tolerance that emerges from traditional liberalism.

Let us take a closer look at tolerance *à la* relativism. Suppose that I am someone who categorizes members of certain races as fully rational and members of other races as less than fully rational. Suppose further that I am someone who holds that I have serious moral obligations only to creatures that are fully rational. Thus, I believe that I don't have serious moral obligations to members of some racial groups. As a result, when I make decisions, I may not take their well-being into account to the extent I take into account the well-being of those I judge to be fully rational humans. A consistent cognitive relativist would have to admit that a racist conceptual scheme is not objectively better or worse than any other. Thus, a consistent cognitive relativist cannot reject my conceptual scheme on the grounds that it is mistaken. Similarly, a consistent cognitive relativist cannot object that those actions of mine based on my racist categorization of humans are done in error, so long as my actions are consistent with my racist conceptual scheme. Even more importantly, moral condemnation of my racist actions is beyond the reach of the cognitive relativist.

This is the version of tolerance that arises out of cognitive relativism: so long as someone is acting in a way that "makes sense" given her (or her culture's) conceptual scheme, that person is not acting in an incorrect or immoral manner. But this is not a version of tolerance that is very appealing, for it requires that I tolerate individuals and societies, no matter what they do. Genocide, human slavery, the subjection of women–all of these things have been practiced by some societies. (Alas, some societies continue to practice them even now.) The consistent cognitive relativist must tolerate these sorts of practices, along with the less objectionable ones. Contrast the version of tolerance emerging out of relativism with that emerging out of traditional liberalism, according to which individuals may act as they like as long as they do not infringe on the rights of others. It is this latter version of tolerance that is required to prevent a society from succumbing to either tyranny by the dominant group or Balkanization as the society rips apart into its separate subcultures. If a stable pluralism is a benefit for society (as we believe it is), then it is not relativism but objectivism that is most likely to achieve it.

So, the argument for cognitive relativism based on its relationship with tolerance is actually an argument *against* cognitive relativism. Are there other such arguments? One problem the cognitive relativist faces is explaining just what intellectual investigation (within both the sciences and the humanities) is striving for, if not knowledge of the objective truth. It seems as though we already have knowledge in the relativist sense, so what's the point of continuing the search?

A second difficulty for cognitive relativism is explaining why science and technology have been so successful. This difficulty is especially acute for postmodernism, which classifies science as "just one among many equally good approaches to improving our understanding of the world." The postmodernist responds by noting that science and technology are successful relative to their own criterion for success (namely, controlling the environment); but not necessarily successful relative to some other criterion (for example, living in harmony with the environment). One person's idea of success is another person's idea of failure. We will leave it for you, the reader, to decide whether this response is adequate.

Yet another difficulty arises because, while the relativist wants to maintain that there are no objective truths, it seems that the relativist is ultimately committed to the claim that there are at least some objective truths. Think back to *Hilary and Jackie*. The film provides two different interpretations of *events that happened*. So, at the very least, it must be the case that *something happened*, even if there are differences of opinion with respect to what *in fact* happened. Thus, one could argue that since any interpretation must be an interpretation *of* something, at the very least, whenever there is an interpretation, there must be *something* that is being interpreted, even if there are different accounts of what that something is. So, it may be the case that even the most radical relativist would have to concede that it is an objective fact that *there is something*.

By far the most oft-cited criticism of cognitive relativism is that it is self-refuting.[23] If the truth of all judgments is relative, then the truth of the judgment "cognitive relativism is correct" is itself relative: it is true according to some conceptual schemes and false according to others. If one goes the extra step to relativism of rationality, those conceptual schemes in which conceptual relativism is true have no better claim to our allegiance than those conceptual schemes in which it is false. Thus, for the relativist about rationality, anyone like us (with a conceptual scheme that makes cognitive relativism false) can truly say that cognitive relativism is false.

Discussion Questions

1. Look, again, at James's example involving the *cow-path*. How would the correspondence theorist assess the truth-value of the belief *that there is a house at the end of the path*? How would the coherentist assess it? The perspectivist?
2. What are similarities between Nietzsche's perspectivism and James's pragmatism? What are some differences? How might James argue that pragmatism is not a form of relativism?
3. Can you think of one event or one fact from the movie *Hilary and Jackie* that the objectivist would argue *must* be objectively true? How might the cognitive relativist argue that that fact is not objectively true?

4. Did you start out the chapter as a cognitive relativist? Or now, after having finished the chapter, are you a cognitive relativist? If your view changed, why did it change?

5. Russell objects to cognitive relativism because it entails that *no belief can be false*. First explain Russell's objection against cognitive relativism. Then, try to come up with a statement that *must be false*.

6. Does the universality of rationality necessarily mean that humanity must progress towards a common goal? Can you provide an example of two different cultures that each has a different idea about what the ultimate goal really is? Now take a look at those goals again and explain the underlying basis for each. Is the basis the same? Does this affect the way that you initially responded to the first question of this discussion question?

7. As you were watching *Hilary and Jackie*, did you find yourself assuming that Hilary's account of events was the more trustworthy of the two? If so, can you isolate what led you to this position?

Annotated List of Film Titles Relevant to Truth

Rashomon (1950). Directed by Akira Kurosawa. Starring Toshiro Mifune, Masayuki Mori, Machiko Kyo, Takashi Shimura, Minoru Chiaki.
Rashomon, like *Hilary and Jackie*, is a multiple-perspective film: it tells the same story several times over from the point of view of different characters.

Citizen Kane (1941). Directed by Orson Welles. Starring Orson Welles, Joseph Cotten, Ray Collins, Dorothy Comingore.
Citizen Kane is the reconstruction of one man's life, as told from the points of view of several people who knew him. "Rosebud," the enigmatic dying last word of the title character, sets a newspaper reporter off on a quest to understand what the word signifies by interviewing several of Kane's associates. In the process, he discovers that each interview subject presents a very different version of the man. Whose portrayal is most accurate? Does that question even make sense?

Go (1999). Directed by Doug Liman. Starring Sarah Polley, Desmond Askew, Katie Holmes.
Drug deals, sex, violence, pyramid schemes, a road trip to Las Vegas, supermarket check-out cashiers: these elements are thrown into the hopper, shaken, and strewn out to form the backbone of a multiple-perspective film. *Go* has the fast-paced, almost frenetic feel typical of young directors weaned on music videos. It's a fun, darkly comic ride.

Courage Under Fire (1996). Directed by Edward Zwick. Starring Denzel Washington, Meg Ryan, Matt Damon.
A classic example of the multiple-perspective film.

He Said. She Said (1991). Directed by Ken Kwapis, Marisa Silver. Starring Kevin Bacon, Elizabeth Perkins, Sharon Stone.

This lightweight comedy attempts to answer the question: Do men and women live in different worlds? It offers the male and the female perspective on a love affair that develops between two polar-opposite newspaper editorial writers.

Melinda and Melinda (2004). Directed by Woody Allen. Starring Radha Mitchell, Chloë Sevigny, Johnny Lee Miller, Amanda Peet, Will Ferrell.

Several old friends meet at a restaurant for dinner and end up in a heated debate over whether life is essentially comic or tragic. They decide to settle matters by considering and then retelling the "same" story first as a tragedy, then as a comedy.

Annotated List of Book Titles Relevant to Truth

"Classics" in the History of Truth

ARISTOTLE

Metaphysics. Aristotle presents an early version of the correspondence theory of truth.

WILLIAM, JAMES

Pragmatism: A New Name for Some Old Ways of Thinking. James presents and defends the pragmatist theory of truth. An excerpt from *Pragmatism* can be found in Readings from Primary Sources.

IMMANUEL KANT

Critique of Pure Reason, first published in German; first edition 1781, second edition 1787. This is where cognitive relativism in the modern era comes from (even though Kant would deny it).

Prolegomena to Any Future Metaphysics, first published in German, 1783. Kant attempts to boil down the theory laid out in his *Critique of Pure Reason* in a form that will be more accessible than the larger work. A brief excerpt from the *Prolegomena* is reproduced in Readings from Primary Sources.

FRIEDRICH NIETZSCHE

Unpublished Notes, published posthumously in the German multi-volume collection *The Works of Nietzsche*, 1958. Citations of the *Unpublished Notes* here are from the third volume, as translated by Arthur Danto. Nietzsche is one of the most widely read (and widely misunderstood) Western philosophers. To precipitate out the philosophical substance from the surrounding literary fireworks, Danto's *Nietzsche as Philosopher* (New York: Columbia University Press, 1965) is an excellent source. The reader doesn't miss the flavor of Nietzsche's writings, while making Nietzsche's philosophy as clear as possible.

THOMAS KUHN

The Structure of Scientific Revolutions (Chicago, IL: University of Chicago Press, 1996; first published 1962). While Thomas Kuhn's seminal work is generally considered as a work in the philosophy of science, it has been widely influential throughout philosophy. It is moderately easy reading; hence it is accessible to the determined lay reader. In the book, Kuhn explores the relationship between conceptual schemes, theories, and observation and the nature of theory choice.

Collections of Essays and Single-Author Books on Truth

Simon Blackburn, *Truth: A Guide* (New York: Oxford University Press, 2005). An examination of various arguments and positions on truth from the leading theories of the twentieth century. Blackburn attempts to pave the way for a position set somewhere in between objectivism and relativism.

Paul Feyerabend, *Against Method* (New York: Routledge, 1988). Feyerabend starts with Thomas Kuhn and goes one better. In this work, Feyerabend argues that Western science is not a homogeneous set of methods; there is no universally applicable set of standards that may be used to adjudicate between conflicting theories (as Kuhn has argued).

Nelson Goodman, *Ways of Worldmaking* (Indianapolis, IN: Hackett, 1978). Goodman argues that it is possible for several irreconcilable versions of the world to be right, and considers how taking relativism seriously would alter our standard understanding of "truth."

Martin Hollis and Steven Lukes, eds., *Rationality and Relativism* (Cambridge, MA: MIT Press, 1982). Another very good collection of essays, with several contributions focusing on relativism within sociology and cultural anthropology.

Richard L. Kirkham, *Theories of Truth: A Critical Introduction* (Cambridge, MA: MIT Press, 1992). An examination and comparison of various theories of truth from the history of Philosophy.

Jack Meiland and Michael Krausz, eds., *Relativism: Cognitive and Moral* (Notre Dame, IN: Notre Dame University Press, 1982). An excellent collection of essays by the most important philosophers writing in the area of relativism.

Bertrand Russell, *Problems in Philosophy* (Oxford: Oxford University Press, 1912. Released as Ebook: The Project Gutenberg, 2009). This small book is amazingly accessible for the beginning philosopher. In the chapter, "Truth and Falsehood," Russell defends the correspondence theory of truth. An excerpt from that chapter is available in Readings from Primary Sources.

Related Works

Alburey Castell, Donald Borchert, and Arthur Zucker, eds., *Introduction to Modern Philosophy* (Upper Saddle River, NJ: Prentice Hall, 2001). A collection of essay-length works in modern philosophy, arranged by topic; chapter 9 is particularly useful.

Hilary and Piers du Pré, *Hilary and Jackie* (originally entitled *A Genius in the Family*) (New York: Ballantine, 1997). This is the book on which the film is based.

Plato, *Theaetetus* and *Protagoras*, originally published in Greek. These two dialogues by Plato (427–347 B.C.E.) discuss the ramifications of Protagoras's famous one-liner "Man is the measure of all things."

Notes

1. Aristotle, *Metaphysics* Bk. IV, part 7.
2. Bertrand Russell, *The Problems of Philosophy* (1912), (The Project Gutenberg, 2009), chapter XII, "Truth and Falsehood."
3. William James, *Pragmatism: A New Name for Some Old Ways of Thinking* (1907), (The Project Gutenberg, 2004), Lecture VI, "Pragmatism's Conception of Truth."
4. Ibid.
5. Ibid.
6. Ibid.
7. Bertrand Russell, *History of Western Philosophy* (London: George Allen and Unwin Ltd., 1946), "William James," chapter 29, 845–46.
8. William James, *Will to Believe and Other Essays in Popular Philosophy* (New York: Longmans, Green, and Co., 1912), chapter 1, "The Will to Believe."
9. Henceforth, we shall cite a minute mark–the number of minutes that have elapsed in the movie since the opening credits began–as "MM." A plot summary for each of the focus films, along with the minute marks for the important scenes, is given in the Appendix.
10. This is the opening sentence from Protagoras's book *On Truth*. It is the only surviving fragment from that work.
11. The following is a reworking of the argument against relativism in James Rachels, *The Elements of Moral Philosophy*, 3d edn (New York: McGraw-Hill, 1999).
12. Martin Hollis and Steven Lukes, *Rationality and Relativism* (Cambridge, MA: MIT Press, 1982), 10.
13. Walt Whitman, "Song of Myself," in *Leaves of Grass* (Philadelphia, PA: David McKay, 1891–92), 51.

14. See, for example, Arthur Danto's *Nietzsche as Philosopher* (New York: Columbia University Press, 1965), 97.
15. Friedrich Nietzsche, *Aus dem Nachlass der Achtzigerjahre*, vol. 3 of *Nietzsches Werke in Drei Bände*, ed. Karl Schlechta (Munich: Carl Hanser Verlag, 1958), 903 and 705, respectively. These passages are as translated by Danto in *Nietzsche as Philosopher*.
16. Danto, *Nietzsche as Philosopher* (New York: Columbia University Press, 1965), 96.
17. Ibid., 80.
18. Friedrich Nietzsche, *Aus dem Nachlass*, 814.
19. Gene Blocker, "The Challenge of Post-Modernism" in *Introduction to Modern Philosophy*, 7th edn, ed. Alburey Castell, Donald Borchert, and Arthur Zucker (Englewood Cliffs, NJ: Prentice Hall, 2001), 554–55.
20. Alison Jaggar, "Love and Knowledge: Emotion in Feminist Epistemology" in *Introduction to Modern Philosophy*, ed. Castell, Borchert, and Zucker, 535.
21. Nietzsche, a postmodernist in all but name, held that a pragmatic criterion for judging adequacy was universally valid.
22. Blocker, "The Challenge of Post-Modernism," 558–59.
23. The criticism originates with Plato, in his discussion of Protagoras's views in the *Theaetetus*.

2

SKEPTICISM

The Matrix (1999) and *Inception* (2010)

Morpheus: You have the look of a man who accepts what
he sees, because he is expecting to wake up. Ironically,
this is not far from the truth.

–from *The Matrix*

Cobb: If this is my dream why can't I control this?
Mal: Because you don't know you're dreaming!

–from *Inception*

We are all used to thinking that our senses reveal a world that exists
independently of our minds. But is this belief justified? What can I
know about this external world? Can I be sure that what my senses
report to me is accurate? Maybe my senses are giving me radically
misleading information about what is going on in the world outside of
my mind. Can I even know that an external world exists? Philosophers
have been examining these questions for centuries. As we saw in the
Introduction and in Chapter 1, some philosophers hold a position
called **skepticism**, according to which genuine knowledge in such
matters is unattainable. The science-fiction virtual-reality genre is ideal
for introducing this topic. The movies *The Matrix* and *Inception* are both
excellent sources for the standard arguments supporting skepticism
and for hints at how modern philosophers have reacted to these arguments. Our advice is to read up to and including Section 2.3, then to
watch the movies before resuming reading the rest of the chapter. The
first two sections introduce the topic of skepticism in very general
terms; having it under your belt *before* viewing *The Matrix* and *Inception*
will help you extract more of the philosophical content out of the
movies. The material beginning in Section 2.4 makes constant reference to the movies, so it would be most profitably read after viewing
the movies.

2.1 What is Skepticism?

In everyday discourse, to call someone *skeptical* is to say that that person is prone to disbelieve what others say. It is commonplace to show distrust or disbelief in what a politician is promising by stating, "I'm skeptical." The term *skepticism* as it is used within philosophy has a slightly different, albeit related meaning. Someone who is skeptical about X in the *philosophical* sense is someone who claims that it is impossible to know whether X is true or false. To see this more clearly, consider the following statements:

S1: George Washington was the twenty-first president of the United States.
S2: 2,356,717 is a prime number.
S3: I am not dreaming right now.

Suppose you were asked, for each of *S1*, *S2*, *S3*, whether you *know* with absolute certainty that that statement is true. What would your response be? Here is how your answers might go:

S1': I know that *S1* is definitely false.
S2': I don't know about *S2*, maybe it's true, maybe it's false. If I were a math whiz or someone with some time to kill, I could probably figure out, though, whether *S2* is true or false.
S3': I'm not quite sure what to make of *S3*. I tend to *believe* that I'm not dreaming right now, but I can remember times in the past when I thought I wasn't dreaming, only to wake up a few minutes later when my alarm went off. The more I think about *S3*, the weirder *S3* seems. At least if asked whether *S2* was true or false, I could think of a way to figure it out. But *S3* is qualitatively different. I can't think of a calculation I can carry out or a test I can perform that would give me conclusive evidence either way. I guess the correct thing to say in this case is that *I can't know with absolute certainty whether S3 is true or false.*

The response given in *S3'* above captures exactly what philosophers mean by skepticism: skepticism is the view that knowledge is not attainable. Note the difference between skepticism in its everyday usage and its philosophical usage. According to the former, skeptics are deniers. According to the latter, skeptics are doubters.

It is possible for someone to be skeptical about some domains but not about others. Thus, a *moral* skeptic claims it is not possible to know whether moral statements are true or false; however, this moral skeptic may think knowledge is attainable in other areas. Such circumscribed versions of skepticism will not be discussed further. The version of skepticism that this chapter deals with is all-encompassing. Sometimes the term *epistemological skepticism* is used to distinguish this all-encompassing version of skepticism from versions that involve more limited claims. (*Epistemology* is the name of the subarea of philosophy that studies what knowledge is and how knowledge claims are justified.)

Skepticism has a long history, which predates the advent of virtual reality movies by some 2300 years. The first skeptics lived in ancient Greece in the third and fourth centuries B.C.E. in the generation after Aristotle. While none of the writings from these very early skeptics survived, we are familiar with their views based on the writings of later skeptics who had had access to those original documents. Among the latter group, Sextus Empiricus (175–225 C.E.) has been the most influential in defining ancient skepticism. According to the ancient skeptics, all one's claims to knowledge are to be rejected, except for the knowledge of one's current perceptual state. Thus, I can know that I am having a visual impression of redness right now (a current perceptual state), but I cannot know that that impression of redness is caused by, or represents, or has anything whatsoever to do with goings-on outside of my own mind. Notice that these ancient skeptics are not claiming that my current impression of redness is not caused by something outside of my mind (remember, skeptics are *doubters*, not deniers). They are "merely" claiming that I have insufficient evidence to know whether my current impression of redness is thus caused by an *external* object (that is, an object that is mind-independent, that exists external to the mind). The ancient skeptic, just like his modern counterpart, would say that active *dis*belief in the existence of an external world is just as unfounded as active belief in such a world. Strange as it may sound, the ancient skeptics held that the natural psychological response to adopting skepticism would be a blissful detachment from the world. Whether the ancient skeptics were blissfully detached is anyone's guess; the modern response to skepticism has been repugnance. (Watch for the responses offered by characters in *The Matrix* and *Inception* when the skeptical hypothesis enters the picture–do they become blissfully detached?) Philosophers are like other people in finding something profoundly unsettling about skepticism. Indeed, much of the epistemology done in the modern era can be interpreted as an attempt to refute skepticism. So deep is the disdain for skepticism among some philosophers (e.g., George Berkeley, whom we shall meet in Section 2.6) that they will reject any assumption, solely on the grounds that it will lead to skepticism.

The strain of skepticism that began in ancient Greece died out during the Early Middle Ages and had no or only very few adherents in Europe for over a thousand years. It wasn't until the religious and scientific revolutions of the fifteenth and sixteenth centuries that interest in skepticism reemerged. This reemergence was further spurred by the republication of the writings of Sextus Empiricus in the middle of the sixteenth century. The time was ripe for philosophers to grapple once again with doubt. By far the most influential writer on the topic of skepticism during this time was the French philosopher René Descartes (1596–1650). In retrospect, historians of philosophy have marked his emergence as the beginning of philosophy in the modern period.[1] Descartes laid out skepticism in the form that it has retained to this day. Because of his influence, we have allocated all of Section 2.2 to a discussion of his views. The work by Descartes discussed in Section 2.2 is reproduced in Readings from Primary Sources towards the end of this book. Skepticism remained on philosophy's front burner for the rest of the seventeenth and most of the eighteenth centuries. Another highly influential philosopher of this period, David Hume (1711–1776), refined the arguments for skepticism still further, showing just what would be required to justify a claim to know that an external world exists, and showing how this requirement could not be satisfied—not even in theory. We shall discuss some of these arguments in Sections 2.4 and 2.5.

2.2 Descartes's Formulation

The most influential work ever written on skepticism is the first essay in *Meditations on First Philosophy*, originally published by **René Descartes** in 1641.[2] In this essay, Descartes lays the framework for modern skepticism and sets the standard according to which any presumed refutation of skepticism must pass muster. In the remaining five essays that make up the *Meditations*, Descartes sets forth what he believes to be a refutation of skepticism. While philosophers greatly admire the thoroughness and ingenuity of the arguments Descartes offers in favor of skepticism, most philosophers believe Descartes's "solution" to the problem of skepticism presented in the second through sixth essays doesn't work. Thus, Descartes's *Meditations* have become the classic source for skepticism, rather than the refutation of skepticism that Descartes had intended the work to be.

The complete first essay from Descartes's *Meditations on First Philosophy* is reproduced in Readings from Primary Sources towards the end of this book. In this essay, Descartes sets about trying to find a belief whose truth he cannot possibly doubt. He notes that his senses have deceived him in the past; so, any belief based on the report of his senses can be doubted. (Recall the distinction emphasized above between doubting the truth of a statement and believing it to be false.) Furthermore, he recalls having experiences while dreaming that were indistinguishable at the time from experiences while awake. Thus, while close and careful examination of an object in good light is normally sufficient to dispel concerns that his senses are deceiving him, close and careful examination in good light is wholly insufficient for distinguishing "real" reality from the "virtual" reality created within a dream. He decides that he is looking for indubitability in the wrong place. If he has any indubitable beliefs, they are more likely to be found within the domain of pure mathematics (for example, arithmetic statements such as "2 + 3 = 5"). On further consideration, however, he decides that, even here, doubt is possible. Descartes believes that an all-powerful God exists–a God who created him and would not allow him to be massively deceived. He admits, though, that his belief in the existence of God can be doubted. Perhaps the truth is that, instead of God, an all-powerful and evil demon exists; this demon has created Descartes so that he constantly falls into error, even when he performs simple calculations such as adding 2 and 3. He cannot know for sure that this is not the case. If such an evil demon exists, then even beliefs based solely on his powers of reason are called into doubt. Descartes decides to adopt the hypothesis that just such an evil demon exists, not because this hypothesis is well founded (quite the contrary, Descartes would say), but because such a hypothesis will steel Descartes in his resolve not to allow in any belief as indubitable if that belief has the slightest shred of grounds for doubt. It is on this note of abject skepticism that his first meditation ends.

As mentioned above, Descartes believed he had refuted skepticism in the later essays. While most of the remainder of the *Meditations on First Philosophy* lie outside the scope of this chapter, there is one item from the beginning of the second meditation that bears remarking upon. In his search for a belief whose truth he could not possibly doubt, Descartes settles upon the statement "I exist." He bases the indubitability of this statement on the reasoning that even if the evil demon exists and is constantly causing him to fall into error, Descartes could not possibly be mistaken in believing he exists as a thing that thinks–as a thing that doubts. This is because he would at least have to exist as a thing that was being deceived. Thus, Descartes formulates the argument "I think; therefore, I exist" (in its original Latin, *cogito, ergo sum*) as showing beyond a shadow of a doubt that he exists.

2.3 An Overview of the Movies

THE MATRIX (1999). DIRECTED BY ANDY AND LARRY WACHOWSKI. STARRING KEANU REEVES, LAURENCE FISHBURNE, CARRIE-ANNE MOSS

The Matrix is the first film released in what eventually became a movie trilogy exploring a futuristic world in which computers have enslaved humankind. The humans are farmed as an energy source and their nervous systems are hooked into computers that create a perfect virtual world for each of them. While fancy computers are not, strictly speaking, necessary for a discussion of skepticism (after all, Descartes managed to do just fine back in the seventeenth century making reference only to the virtual world created in normal, human dreams), bringing technology into the picture makes skepticism an easier sell. Neo, the main character in *The Matrix*, is asked the question "How would you know the difference between [a] dream world and a real one?"[3] He (and we, the viewers) realizes that there is no way to tell the difference.

Inception (2010). Written and directed by Christopher Nolan. Starring Leonardo DiCaprio, Joseph Gordon-Levitt, Ellen Page

Inception allows us to explore the question whether we can ever be certain that we are not dreaming. The main character, Dominic Cobb, is a thief-for-hire. He and his team of specialists have figured out how to enter a person's dream and extract valuable secrets from that person's subconscious. This time, however, rather than stealing an idea, Cobb and his team must figure out how to plant an idea in the victim's mind, a process called *inception*. They devise a plan according to which they will go three levels deep—a dream within a dream within a dream.

For the viewers, the film can be quite confusing to watch (especially the first time through). We have to keep track of different dream levels and different dreamers. The confusion starts with the opening scene (a scene that is repeated later in the movie) and continues to the end of the movie when we're left wondering whether Cobb successfully returns to reality. In the story line for this movie that is provided in the Appendix, the different dream levels have been indicated to make it easier to follow a straightforward interpretation of the film. (Whether that is the *correct* interpretation will be discussed later in this chapter).

If you are following our advice given at the beginning of the chapter, now is the time to watch *The Matrix* and *Inception*.

2.4 Cobb and Neo as Embodiments of Descartes's Problem

So, you have just finished watching *Inception*. What happened in the movie? Did you wonder whether Cobb is stuck in limbo at the end or whether he was really awake and seeing his real kids? Is this all a dream? It's difficult to know. In the first scene, Cobb wakes up on a beach with waves washing over him. He is then taken to a room to meet with a very old Saito. Saito tells Cobb that he reminds him of someone, "a man I met in a half-remembered dream." The scene shifts to what feels like a flashback of another conversation between Cobb, Arthur, and a younger Saito in a room very much like the one we just saw. Then, Cobb "wakes up" after having been dunked in a bathtub (MM 11:29). And, at MM 14:35, Cobb wakes up on the train. So, in the first fifteen minutes of the movie, the viewer sees Cobb in limbo, then waking up in a dream, and then waking up in (what might be) reality. Since we've already seen a couple of scenes in which Cobb wakes up, only to wake up again, how do we know–and how does *Cobb* know–that he isn't in yet another dream? Is there any way to prove that Cobb is not dreaming?

Descartes explains that "there are no reliable signs by which [a person] can distinguish sleeping from waking."[4] The problem is that any test that one might use to prove that he is not dreaming can be replicated in a dream, because any such test will involve a sensory experience. For example, say that I ask someone to pinch me right now to prove that I am not dreaming. Quite clearly, the experience of feeling the pinch won't work to prove to me that I am not dreaming since I could merely be dreaming that I have been pinched. As we will see, even the pain that I might feel may not be genuine because it may be possible to have the sensation of pain in the absence of any actual physical injury. As Descartes recognizes, it is impossible to know that a perception is genuine *in a given moment*–one may wake up afterwards and retroactively discount a perception one experiences while asleep as unreal, but while it is happening, there is nothing to distinguish it from a waking perception.

Inception adds a couple of other features that work to further enhance the skeptic's argument. The first is *lucid dreaming*. In a typical dream, the dreamer is passive. The dream happens and the dreamer has no control over his own actions. In a lucid dream, the dreamer is consciously aware that he is dreaming and can actively direct his own movements. In *Inception*, the lucid dreams that some of the characters have are so like reality that it is difficult for the victim to know that the events are occurring in a dream. For example, at MM 85:23, Cobb (as Mr. Charles) prompts Robert Fischer to realize that he is dreaming. Cobb does this by pointing out the strangeness of things going on around Fischer and by helping Fischer to recognize that he has no memory of how he came to be sitting at the hotel bar. However, Fischer's awareness that he is in a dream actually makes him more vulnerable to Cobb's ruse. Although Fischer knows that he is dreaming at that moment, his sense of certainty that he is in a dream prevents him from suspecting that he is in a dream *within a dream.*

The film also introduces the concept of *shared-dreaming*, where more than one person can plug into and share another person's dream. In the scene discussed above, Fischer, Cobb, Ariadne, and Saito are actually sharing Arthur's dream, within Yusuf's dream. Because everyone except Fischer knows that they are sharing Yusuf's dream and because they are lucid dreaming, the team is able to manipulate the dream in certain ways to make it even more difficult for Fischer to discover that he is in a dream within a dream.

But how do the members of the team know that *they* are not dreaming? Each one uses a *totem*, a trinket with an entirely unique feature that only that person knows about. As Arthur explains, "… when you look at your totem you know beyond a doubt that you're not in someone else's dream," (MM 33:50). Cobb uses a top as his totem. When he spins the top and it topples over, he "knows" that he is not dreaming. But, can the toppling top really work to provide Cobb with absolute certainty–*beyond a doubt*–that he is not in a dream? It seems not. It is possible that Cobb could merely dream that he is having the experience of watching the top fall over in just the right way, in which case he would mistakenly believe that he is not dreaming. Because the use of the totem requires sensory experience to prove that he is not dreaming, the totem will fail to provide absolute proof.

Once we understand that neither the viewer nor Cobb can be certain that Cobb is awake in any given scene, the movie permits a variety of interpretations. Here are five of them[5]:

1. The straight forward interpretation: In reality, Cobb is hired by Saito to implant the idea in Fischer's head. The inception works. Cobb wakes up on the plane with the rest of the team and Fischer. And, Cobb returns to his real kids.
2. The limbo ending: Cobb is hired by Saito to implant the idea in Fischer's head. The inception works. But, Cobb is stuck in limbo and does not make it back to his real kids.
3. The partial dream: Most of the movie is Cobb's dream that begins while he is on a plane, flying home. He wakes up on the plane and returns to his real kids.
4. The shared-dream: Part or all of the movie is someone else's dream, and Cobb is plugged into it.
5. The full dream: The entire movie, from beginning to end, is Cobb's dream.

(1) is the straight-forward account of the events in the film, and, since it is also the one with the happy ending, it may be the most attractive. However, there are a few problems with this interpretation. At the end of the movie, when Cobb turns to go to his children, he leaves the top spinning–neither Cobb nor the viewer sees the top fall. So, whether Cobb is still dreaming is undetermined. Furthermore, the position of the kids in the yard and the clothes that they are wearing seem to be *too* similar to Cobb's memory of them. Even though we know that dream-time is much slower than real-time, on this interpretation, some real time must have passed since Cobb last saw his kids, so it seems that they would have changed in various

ways. Wouldn't they be wearing different clothes? Wouldn't they be playing somewhere else or at least in different positions?

On interpretation (2), Cobb never makes it back to the real world. Instead, he is in limbo after drowning in the van. Although interpretation (2) is able to make sense of the spinning top at the end and although it accounts for the similarity in Cobb's memories of the kids, there are still some problems with this interpretation. In particular, why would Cobb choose to stay in limbo when he could shoot or "kill" himself in some way in order to return to reality to be with his kids?

The partial dream interpretation in (3), suggests that when the movie begins, Cobb is on a plane dreaming. He wakes up on the plane and goes home to see his kids. But, this interpretation has some problems, as well. Specifically, on this interpretation, his top is merely a part of his dream and not a genuine totem. So, why at the end of the film does he take it out and spin it before he goes to greet his kids? Also, as with (1), there seems to be too much similarity between his real kids and how he dreamed of them to make sense of this explanation.

According to (4), Cobb is in someone else's dream. This interpretation makes the most sense of the spinning top at the end–that it continues to spin indicates that Cobb is in someone else's dream. However, the camera cuts away, and neither Cobb nor the viewer can ever know whether the top eventually falls at some point.

And (5) is that old movie trick of making the entire film one long, complicated dream. Unlike the other interpretations, there can be no holes in this interpretation of the film because any inconsistencies that might be found in the narrative can be explained away as just part of the strangeness of the dream.

There may well be more interpretations that could be offered for what *really* happens in *Inception*. (We'll leave it to you to come up with others). However, unlike *Hilary and Jackie* (the film considered in Chapter 1), *Inception* is a work of fiction, so there isn't anything that *really* happened. Yet, because we are left with uncertainty about which events are real and which are not, the various interpretations work well as an argument for skepticism.[6]

The Matrix offers us the same sorts of jumps in interpretation as the action progresses as was offered in *Inception*. We discover at MM 12:00 that everything that has happened up to that point (for example, the strange messages Neo is receiving on his computer) was a dream. Similarly, when Neo awakes *again* at MM 21:30, we discover that the events between MM 12:00 and MM 21:30 were a dream, and that, therefore, the first twelve minutes was a dream within a dream. After this second awakening, major events happen very quickly. Neo meets Morpheus. Morpheus begins to explain what "the matrix" is. Neo chooses to learn more, even though the truth may be very upsetting. This sequence culminates with the "real" Neo waking up in his vat, being released and flushed out into the "real" world, and being greeted by the "real" Morpheus. From this point on in the movie, the interpretation that Neo has entered the "real" world is never questioned. Thus, except for the times when he reenters the matrix to fight the (virtual) bad guys, all of his perceptions are genuine.

But what does it mean to say that Neo's post-release perceptions are *genuine*, whereas his pre-release perceptions are not? Similarly, what does it mean to say that the perceptions experienced in the context of lucid dreams and dreams within dreams are *not genuine*? What both of these movies do so well is highlight the starting point of skepticism: both movies make it clear that *when we perceive, we are not immediately aware of external objects*. Our perceptions exist only in our minds, they are not themselves external objects. It is only by distinguishing between perceptions and external objects that sense can be made of (1) the virtual reality created by the matrix, and (2) the virtual reality in *Inception's* architecturally designed lucid dreams, and (3) the virtual reality found in normal, human dreams. But once it is granted that perceptions are not themselves external objects, what then? Descartes recognized this as an important question. In the third essay of his *Meditations on First Philosophy*, he develops a theory that we shall call the **theory of representative perceptions**. According to this theory, a perception is genuine if it is caused by and accurately represents the external object(s) that give rise to it. Thus, the visual perception of a telephone I am having right now is genuine if there really is a telephone that exists "out there" in the mind-independent world of material objects, and that telephone is causally responsible for producing the perception I am experiencing right now. Furthermore, my perception must accurately depict that telephone: it must offer accurate information about the telephone's size and shape, as well as its location relative to other objects I am also perceiving at present. If these conditions are all satisfied by a perception, then that perception is said to be *genuine*.

Notice that there is a similarity between the theory of representative perceptions and the correspondence theory of truth (that we discussed in 1.1). For both theories, there must be a direct relationship between the "internal world" of a person's mind and the "external world" of reality in order for a perception to be genuine or a belief to be true. But, Descartes's theory of representative perceptions has an additional feature: according to him, there must be a *causal* relationship between the perception and the object of which it is a perception. So, there must be a real object out there in the world that causes the perception of it. However, as we will see, the theory of representative perceptions may fall prey to problems that are similar to those raised against the correspondence theory of truth.

It is clear that many of the perceptions that Cobb and Neo have are not genuine according to the conditions laid out above. All matrix-generated perceptions (whether in Neo or any other character hooked into the system) fail the accuracy-of-representation requirement. Thus, even though the perceptions are caused by an external source (the physical computer that is running the matrix program), they are not caused by the external objects they purport to represent. The same goes for Cobb's perceptions in his shared lucid dreams. For example, there are no material objects that cause and resemble the visual and auditory sensations that Cobb has when he (seems to) interact with Mal or any of the other projections of his subconscious.

Descartes is not alone among philosophers in believing that the theory of representative perceptions (or something very much like it) is the only way to make sense of the possibility of illusion; although he was alone among the great philosophers of the seventeenth and eighteenth centuries in arguing that this theory did not inexorably lead to skepticism. **Descartes's problem** is explaining how a perceiver could get evidence that a current perception is caused by and accurately represents an external object. Consider how Neo responds to this challenge. His response on being plugged into not the matrix but a computer construct (MM 39:15) is to reach out and touch a sofa and ask in amazement, "This isn't real?" Neo responds to the challenge of Descartes's problem by seeking tactile confirmation that, indeed, he is not experiencing a visual illusion. In his first meditation, Descartes himself describes a similar search for tactile confirmation as his initial response to the challenge. "I put my hand out consciously and deliberately; I feel the paper and see it."[7] But further consideration convinces Descartes and Neo that tactile sensations are just more perceptions—they do not provide unmediated information about the characteristics of, or even the existence of, external objects. While tactile sensations are qualitatively insufficient to meet the challenge of Descartes's problem, there is a reason why this is Neo's and Descartes's initial response. It is commonplace that our visual sensations deceive us. Even in a waking state, we have all experienced optical illusions; so, the average person is willing to occasionally distrust the visual system. Similarly, auditory illusions are relatively common, as is the corresponding willingness to distrust our hearing. The sense of touch is much less susceptible to waking illusion; it seems the natural choice in testing the genuineness of our visual and auditory reports. However, *Inception* challenges the trustworthiness of tactile sensations. In one dream sequence, Mal shoots Arthur, and Arthur screams in pain, even though he has not *really* been shot (MM 8:50). Mal (or, rather, Cobb's projection of her) explains that "Pain is in the mind," suggesting that Arthur isn't really feeling pain, he just thinks that he is. And later, in another dream sequence, when Mal and Cobb are arguing about whether their current experiences are genuine, Mal stabs Cobb. "Does this feel real?" Mal demands of Cobb, making the point that the tactile sensation of being in pain is nothing but a sensation and that Cobb's experience of being in pain is not genuine. Because there is no real knife and there is no real injury, there cannot be any real pain. In reality, Cobb is asleep on an airplane, and Mal does not exist. Thus, both *The Matrix* and *Inception* help to demonstrate that tactile sensations cannot provide the evidence necessary to distinguish between genuine and nongenuine perceptions.

As we saw in the discussion of the correspondence theory of truth, skepticism has its source in the fact that all we directly experience are our own sensations, not the external things themselves. None of us has ever, in our entire lives, had contact with an external object where that contact was not mediated by the senses. We cannot, therefore, justify our belief in external objects with reference to our *direct* contact with them.

Are *we* any different in this regard than Cobb and Neo? Admittedly, we haven't plugged ourselves into a dream-sharing device, since such a device does not exist—we *presume*. Furthermore, we are living in the early twenty-first century, not the year 2199, as did Neo. But, hold on a minute. This line of reasoning will get us nowhere. What generates skepticism is the recognition that all we are ever directly aware of are our own perceptions, not mind-independent objects in some material world. We assume such a world exists and is causally responsible for the perceptions we have, but we have no way of peeking around our perceptions to view these mind-independent objects to check the assumption. There is, though, one important difference between us on the one hand, and Cobb and Neo on the other: they have been given a reason to actively suspect the genuineness of many of their perceptions, while we have not.

Cobb has reason to worry that he may not be having genuine experiences at any given moment due to the events that occurred after he and Mal returned from limbo. While in limbo, Cobb had planted the idea, "This isn't real," in Mal's subconscious to help her want to wake up and return to their kids. They "killed" themselves in their dream by lying down in front of a train, but when they woke up in reality, the idea *this isn't real* remained in Mal's mind. Her belief that they were still in limbo was so strong that she committed suicide in an attempt to "wake up." As a result of these events, and because Mal continues to plague his subconscious, Cobb cannot be entirely certain that any current experience is genuine.

Other characters in *Inception* also have reason to suspect that their perceptions are not genuine. Consider, again, the scene in which Cobb, as Mr. Charles, tries to convince Fischer that he is dreaming. Fischer has to decide whether or not to trust this Mr. Charles. If Fischer listens to Mr. Charles's advice and believes that his current perceptions are nongenuine, he may be able to prevent the kidnappers from extracting the combination for the safe and from killing his god-father, Browning. What evidence is there, from Fischer's point of view, that he is dreaming? First, the experiences that Fischer is having and has had up to that point in time are strange and atypical. A woman has left him a phone number with only 6 digits, the room is shaking, and the people in the bar are all looking at him. Second, Fischer is familiar with the process of extraction, and he remembers that at some point in the past, he was trained to protect his subconscious from thieves. Third, Fischer also remembers that he and Browning have been kidnapped, and it could very well be the case that the kidnappers are going to enter into his dream and steal his secrets. Finally, as Cobb points out, Fischer has no memory of having entered the hotel bar and cannot remember how he came to be sitting there. Now, what evidence does Fischer have that his current perceptions are caused by and accurately represent external objects? Most people are naturally inclined to trust that their perceptions are genuine. But, for Fischer, that natural inclination does not provide strong support for thinking that he is currently having genuine perceptions. Fischer has more evidence supporting the theory that his current perceptions are nongenuine, so trusting Mr. Charles may help to protect his secrets and save Browning.

Can a similar analysis be given for *The Matrix*? Let's consider the two theories contending for explanation of Neo's perceptions between MM 21:30 and MM 32:00. (This is roughly the period of time between Neo waking up for the second time and the "real" Neo waking up in his vat.) According to one theory, Neo's perceptions are the result of a computer stimulating his nervous system in a way indistinguishable from the way in which his nervous system would be stimulated were he actually interacting with material objects. Thus, according to this theory, all of his perceptions during this time period are nongenuine. What evidence is there in favor of this? First, he has the equivalent of a "waking up" experience at MM 32:30 which, at the very least, calls into question the genuineness of the preceding perceptions. Second, many of his experiences during this time period were highly atypical. And third, Neo has experiences throughout the rest of the film that flesh out the hows and whys of the matrix. According to another theory, Neo's perceptions during this time period are genuine. There's not much to say in favor of this theory, with the possible exception that Neo's experiences, while admittedly atypical during this time period (judged relative to those of the average human), are no more atypical than the things that he experienced both before and after this portion of the movie. There is a third theory that has some plausibility: maybe Neo is still dreaming; maybe everything that happens throughout the entire movie is a dream. After all, we're already allowing for the possibility of a dream-within-a-dream. (Recall that is what is going on during the first twelve minutes.) This alternative has one major point to recommend it: Neo has sequences of highly atypical experiences sprinkled throughout the movie—they are not just confined to the first thirty-two minutes.

This third interpretation of *The Matrix* and the fifth interpretation of *Inception* again raise the question originally posed by Descartes in his first meditation: Are there any reliable signs distinguishing sleeping from waking? By the end of his *Meditations*, Descartes believes he has found just such a reliable sign, noting that "the events in dreams are not linked by memory to the rest of my life like those that happen while I am awake."[8] Thus, for Descartes, there is nothing in the perception itself that would allow someone to say that this is certainly a genuine perception. Rather, this judgment of genuineness can only be made in the context of the individual's *other* perceptions–past, present, and future. Other philosophers in the modern era claim that Descartes got it wrong–they hold that there *is* an intrinsic (noncontextual) difference between genuine and nongenuine perceptions. One of these dissenting philosophers is George Berkeley, who held that genuine perceptions are more intrinsically vivid than their nongenuine counterparts.[9] Berkeley held that there are three criteria that distinguish genuine perceptions from nongenuine ones: (1) the vividness of the perception, (2) its degree of independence from our will, and (3) its connectedness to previous and future perceptions.

Does the evidence of nongenuineness in some of the characters' perceptions in *Inception* and *The Matrix* tend to support Descartes or Berkeley? A few pages ago, we isolated several attributes that led us, as viewers, as well as Fischer and Neo, to interpret some of their perceptions as genuine and others as nongenuine. For *Inception*, these attributes were: (1) the atypicalness of many of Fischer's perceptions, (2) his memory of having been trained to protect himself against extraction, (3) his memory of having been kidnapped, and (4) his lack of memory about how he arrived at the bar. Are these attributes of isolated perceptions or attributes of perceptions relative to other perceptions that Fischer has? Attributes (2) and (3) involve the memory of past perceptions, while (4) involves the awareness that there is a lack of any such memory. Thus, (2), (3), and (4) must all be considered in relation to past perceptions and not in isolation. Likewise (1), the atypicalness of Fischer's current perceptions, is judged relative to other perceptions that Fischer has experienced in the past. So, all four of these attributes tend to support Descartes's contention that the only way to tell whether a perception is genuine is to consider that perception in the context of the individual's other perceptions.

The attributes isolated in *The Matrix* likewise support Descartes over Berkeley. Recall the three attributes mentioned as clues that certain of Neo's perceptions were nongenuine: (1) Neo's "waking up" experience at MM 32:00, which, at the very least, calls into question the genuineness of the preceding perceptions; (2) the atypicalness of some of Neo's perceptions; and (3) Neo's experiences throughout the latter part of the movie that flesh out the hows and whys of the matrix. According to the first and third attributes, earlier perceptions are judged nongenuine because of something that happens later. The second attribute is one that we have already met in the discussion of *Inception*. Here, as there, atypicalness is a contextual attribute.

The upshot from the preceding few paragraphs reinforces the claim that Berkeley got it wrong: there may be nothing about a nongenuine perception that marks it off as nongenuine–its nongenuineness may only be ascertained by considering the perceptions that went before and after it in an individual's stream of consciousness. This explains why it is difficult for humans to distinguish perceptions in dreams as nongenuine *while those perceptions are being experienced.* After the fact, when the abrupt discontinuity in perception occurs at waking up, the individual has no problem identifying the previous perceptions as nongenuine (unless, of course, that individual merely dreams that he has woken up).

Skepticism is not concerned so much with individual perceptions as it is with our entire mental lives. How can I know that I am not massively deluded about the existence of an external world? The preceding discussion provides us with a new way of describing skepticism: How can I know that I will not have perceptions in the future (for example, the typical abrupt discontinuity in perception that corresponds to waking up) that will invalidate my current perceptions and all my perceptions that have come before? The response that the skeptic would give to both ways of posing the question is the same: I can't know.

Before we leave this section, there is an important disanalogy between *Inception* and *The Matrix* that bears mentioning: *The Matrix* neither considers the possibility that there are *no* material objects whatsoever, nor that Neo exists in some physical form or other; whereas this is consistent with the interpretation of *Inception* that explains the entire narrative as a dream.

The consistent skeptic would say that you cannot be justified in claiming to know that any physical body exists anywhere. It is possible that *you* are nothing but a bunch of perceptions, it is possible that there is no physical body that corresponds to you. Recall that this is the quandary in which Descartes found himself at the end of his first meditation. He can doubt the existence of all material objects; he can even doubt the existence of his own body; but he cannot doubt his existence as a thing that thinks.

2.5 Hume's Radical Skepticism

Was Descartes overstepping the evidence when he pronounced his famous, "I think; therefore, I exist"? Some philosophers who came after Descartes thought even this limited claim to knowledge was unjustified. In this section, we shall consider the views of **David Hume** (1711–1776) who argued that not only can the existence of an external world be doubted, but even the existence of a centralized and continuous self can be doubted. Hume's skepticism goes even deeper, for he argued that memory could not be trusted to provide us with certain information about our previous perceptions.

What is the *I* in Descartes's "I think; therefore, I exist"? Descartes assumed that he could perceive an unchanging self that was the entity doing the perceiving, thinking, and so on. But did Descartes really have such a perception? Do you ever have a perception of yourself as a continuous, unchanging self? We are not speaking here of a perception such as that of seeing yourself in a mirror over an extended period of time; we are not dealing here with issues of your bodily existence. Rather, we are asking whether you can discern some unchanging thing (your *self*) in the flux of thoughts and perceptions that occur. At this point, this is probably striking you as an even stranger question than "Have you ever perceived an external object?" But, if you consider it, you may well find agreement with Hume, who argued that

> [W]hen I enter most intimately into what I call *myself*, I always stumble on some particular perception or other, ... [however], I never can catch *myself* at any time without a perception, and never can observe any thing but the perception. ... The mind is a kind of theatre, where several perceptions successively make their appearance; pass, re-pass, glide away, and mingle in an infinite variety of postures and situations. There is properly no *simplicity* in it at one time, nor *identity* ... whatever natural propension we may have to imagine that simplicity and identity. The comparison of the theatre must not mislead us. They are the successive perceptions only, that constitute the mind.[10]

According to Hume, we have no evidence that an unchanging self exists, since all we are ever aware of are fleeting thoughts and perceptions. To the extent that a self exists at all, it is nothing but a bundle of thoughts and perceptions. Hume would say that, in pronouncing "*I* think; therefore, *I* exist," Descartes never considered the possibility that there is no *I*; really, all Descartes could know with certainty was that *thoughts* and *perceptions* exist. It was an unjustified leap on Descartes's part from "thoughts exist" to "I exist."

But, things get even weirder than that. Consider memories. What are the conditions for a memory being *genuine*? In some ways, the conditions are less stringent than the conditions for genuineness of a perception: there is no requirement that an external object exists. Thus, I can have a *genuine* memory of a perception I had during my dream last night. In order for one of my memories to be genuine: (1) a previous perception must have occurred, (2) that previous perception must be causally responsible for the current memory, and (3) the current memory must accurately represent the previous perception. These conditions should look familiar, for they are the same conditions used for genuineness of a perception, with the phrase "previous perception" substituted for "external object."

Consider the scene in *Inception* in which Ariadne plugs into Cobb's dream in the warehouse (MM 54:14). She discovers that she is experiencing Cobb's memories of certain moments in his life that he shared with Mal. It makes us wonder whether we could ever experience memories of events that happened to someone else. Suppose I have vivid recollections of having been present at the Battle of Waterloo. I genuinely believe that I was present at Waterloo. I can picture in my mind's eye the way the battlefield was set up, where the opposing camps were located, what the weather was like, etc. These recollections are indistinguishable in vividness and my ability to call them up from recollections of brushing my teeth this morning. While I may have the feeling of remembering being present at the Battle of Waterloo, I do not have a genuine memory of having been at Waterloo unless conditions (1)–(3) are satisfied. Can I know that these conditions are satisfied? No, as I have no way of "peeking around" my memory and judging that it was caused by some earlier perception. Note the similarity between skepticism with respect to the genuineness of memories and skepticism with respect to the genuineness of current perceptions: in both cases, knowledge of genuineness requires access to something (a connection between a current perception and something else) that is not attainable. This most radical form of skepticism, called **solipsism of the present moment** is the claim that all that can be known with certainty is the moment-by-moment perceptions and thoughts that flit by. Whether a centralized self is experiencing those perceptions cannot be known, nor can the accuracy of memories.

2.6 Responses to Skepticism

Skepticism is a rather unsettling thesis (the ancient skeptics notwithstanding). If we follow the line of reasoning that begins with the claim that we are not directly aware of objects,[11] we seem to be led inexorably to solipsism of the present moment. But, do we have to start down that path? Two important philosophers in the modern era, George Berkeley and Immanuel Kant, argued that we do not. Their ways of avoiding that path are the topics of this section.

George Berkeley (1685–1753) held the view that our perceptions give us direct experience of objects. For him, the fact that Descartes's claim (that we are not directly aware of objects) leads to skepticism is reason enough to reject the claim as obviously untrue.[12] This type of argument is called **reductio ad absurdum** (reduction to a contradiction). In this form of reasoning, one assumes that a statement is true (for example, one assumes that Descartes's theory of representative perceptions is true), then demonstrates that that assumption implies a contradiction. This shows that the original statement was false. Oftentimes, reductio arguments weaken the requirement that a *contradiction* must be implied. Instead of a contradiction, all that is required to falsify the assumed statement is to show that it implies something that is highly counterintuitive or unacceptable on some other grounds. Berkeley believed that skepticism is sufficiently unacceptable as to falsify the assumptions that give rise to it. These assumptions are: (1) the view that we are not directly aware of objects in perception, and (2) the view of genuineness that goes along with this, the theory of representative perceptions. Once Berkeley has rejected this theory, the burden is on him to say what perceptions are, if not representations of external (mind-independent) objects. In the next several paragraphs, we shall consider Berkeley's response to this challenge. Of the two movies used in this chapter, *The Matrix* has the closest affinity to the concerns and claims of Berkeley, so we shall be drawing most of our examples from it.

Berkeley held the view known as **idealism**, which claims that there are no such things as *mind-independent* objects. Rather, objects are collections of perceptions: "to be is to be perceived." A significant portion of Berkeley's magnum opus, *A Treatise Concerning the Principles of Human Knowledge*, is included in the section Readings from Primary Sources at the end of this book. As Berkeley notes in that work:

> [A]ll the ... furniture of the earth ... have not any subsistence without a mind ... their being is to be perceived or known, ... consequently, so long as they are not actually perceived by me or do not exist in my mind or that of any other created spirit, they must either have no existence at all or else subsist in the mind of some External Spirit—it being perfectly unintelligible ... to attribute to any single part of them an existence independent of a spirit."[13]

On first hearing, this theory sounds outlandish. However, Berkeley makes the case that the theory, despite its initial strangeness, accords quite well with our usual way of talking about our experience of objects; hence, it is closer to common sense than the theory of objects one finds in Descartes. Indeed, Berkeley holds that the theory of representative perceptions is a philosopher's confusion, *not* the view of Joe Everyman. An additional reason in idealism's favor is that it avoids skepticism (at least in its standard form, described in terms of "skepticism regarding external objects").

According to idealism, objects are nothing but collections of perceptions. To the extent that a perception "represents" anything (as in the theory of representative perceptions), it represents this collection. The skepticism-generating gulf between what I can know (my current perceptual states) and objects disappears, all I need to do in order to know whether there is *really* a telephone in front of me is to open my eyes and—voila!—there it is. Objects are not mind-independent things "out there."

Even though Berkeley doesn't rely on accuracy of representation to distinguish between genuine and nongenuine perceptions, he *does* recognize a difference between the two. If this were not the case, Berkeley's theory would be very far from commonsense indeed. We already met the signs Berkeley uses to distinguish real from imaginary perceptions in Section 2.4. Real perceptions (1) are more vivid, (2) arise independently of the will, and (3) are connected to preceding and subsequent perceptions in a way that imaginary perceptions are not. However, as our analyses of genuine versus nongenuine perceptions in *Inception* and *The Matrix* have made clear, these conditions do not allow Berkeley to avoid all forms of skepticism. Recall how the argument from Section 2.4 went. With regard to the vividness condition, Fischer's and Neo's genuine perceptions were indistinguishable from their nongenuine ones. Also, in both cases, the two characters' perceptions arose independently of their wills. Finally, connectedness is a property that cannot be judged until the last perception is in, for there is always the chance that some abrupt discontinuity in the stream of consciousness will occur some time in the future that will mark the preceding perceptions off as "nongenuine." So, despite the fact that idealism is seen as an antidote to skepticism, it is not up to the challenge. General skepticism is avoided, but Descartes's problem is left unsolved. Berkeley's three signs of genuineness would all be satisfied by many of the (clearly) nongenuine perceptions experienced by Fischer and Neo.

Berkeley argues that there are additional reasons in favor of idealism, above and beyond a desire to avoid skepticism. We can see the outline of the argument in the closing sentence of the quotation above: "it [is] perfectly unintelligible ... to attribute to any single part of [objects] an existence independent of a spirit." Berkeley held that it is not possible to even conceive of the unperceived existence of objects, for, were I to try, I would do so by framing the idea of an unperceived object in my mind. But this idea of an unperceived object is itself a perception (perception here and throughout the rest of this chapter means not just sensory perception but also perception in thought). But now look at what I've done; I am perceiving this presumably unperceived object–a contradiction. One can imagine the following conversation between Descartes and Berkeley on our (in)ability to conceive of mind-independent objects:

Descartes: I can perfectly well think about mind-independent objects. In fact, I'm doing so right now. I'm thinking about a tree deep in an uninhabited forest.

Berkeley: So, even if no one is *looking* at this tree, at least you are *thinking* about it. Isn't that true?

Descartes: Yes, like I said, I'm thinking about this tree.

Berkeley: But the tree is supposed to be *mind-independent.*

Descartes: And it is.

Berkeley: But it is not independent of *your* mind.

Descartes: I disagree. True, I am thinking about it right now, but its existence doesn't depend on that fact.

Berkeley: But your *thinking about it* right now certainly does. How could you, or anyone for that matter, be so inconsistent to say that you can think about something that is not being thought about by anyone? Isn't the patent absurdity of this claim obvious?

Descartes: Okay, how about this? I am thinking about a tree right now that will continue to exist later, even after I have forgotten about it. Now *that* is a thought of a mind-independent tree.

Berkeley: No, that is a confusion. What's at issue here is whether this tree will be conceived by you at that point.

Descartes: At what point?

Berkeley: At the point at which you stop thinking about it.

Descartes: No, that's what it means to say "I've stopped thinking about it."

Berkeley: So, you admit, at *that* point, you won't be conceiving an idea of this unthought-about tree?

Descartes: That's correct.

Berkeley: So we agree, then—you can't conceive of a mind-independent object.

Descartes: No, we don't agree. I can't put my finger on it, but there's something fishy here.

Irrespective of whether there is something fishy here or not, you get Berkeley's point: it is not possible to conceive of a so-called mind-independent object, because, the minute you try to do so, the original description of the object (that it is not being perceived or conceived of by anyone) is no longer correct. How, Berkeley asks rhetorically, could someone build a theory around a concept, that of mind-independent objects, that no one can possibly conceive of?

Most readers probably had the following reaction while reading the above imaginary conversation between Descartes and Berkeley: "Berkeley's theory has some really weird consequences. It is strange that he thought he was capturing the commonsense notion of *object*. Fine, I'll buy that I can't think about something that's not being thought about. But I don't buy that these unperceived or unthought-about objects *don't exist* whenever they are not being thought about or perceived by someone. If *this* view were correct, then the moment I stop looking at my phone—poof!—it ceases to exist. Then, when I look at it again—poof!—it pops back into existence. I don't buy this, and neither will Joe Everyman." Berkeley himself recognized that his view seemed to be at odds with the commonsense view in this regard, so he worked up an explanation of how idealism *did* allow for the existence of unperceived objects. Hence, Berkeley's view is not committed to the "jerky" existence of objects–existent one moment and nonexistent the next. In some respects, the famous, pithy summary of Berkeley's view "to be is to be perceived" is misleading, for this way of putting it does seem to imply that unperceived objects cannot possibly exist; but Berkeley's view is more subtle than that. It turns out that Berkeley gives two (competing?) explanations of how unperceived objects exist. In some passages,[14] he states that, even if no finite mind is perceiving an object, God, who perceives everything,[15] is nevertheless perceiving it.

Though it may sound strange to put it this way, the matrix program in *The Matrix* plays the same role in preserving intra- and interindividual coherence and access to publicly observable objects that God plays within Berkeley's theory. Let's take these one by one. Neo's experiences while in the matrix are internally coherent. He turns his head and his field of vision changes. He turns his head back. What he now sees has not changed radically from a few moments ago. He looks down and sees his hands–the same hands he has seen thousands of times over in his life. Think about this for a moment. The "real" Neo is in a vat; he is not "seeing" anything, at least not with his eyes. So, this coherence within his own perceptions is not something that results from the fact that the "real" world is not changing much from moment to moment. Rather, the matrix, in feeding electrical impulses to Neo's nervous system, is taking care to do it in such a way that coherence is not sacrificed. Take another example. Neo's brain (in the vat) sends out electrical impulses that, in a normal human, would cause the muscle contractions corresponding to walking. The matrix notices this and changes the electrical impulses feeding Neo's sensory pathways in the brain so that (1) his field of view changes appropriately, and (2) he receives tactile information, if his commanded movement would have brought him into contact with another object.

The matrix also maintains interindividual coherence and access to publicly observable objects. Although the rationale for this is never explained in the movie, the matrix program coordinates the sensory information for each of the humans in vats, so that they all are participants in the same virtual world. (Actually, this shared virtual world is never explicitly stated; however, several things in the movie strongly imply it.) So, not only are Neo-in-the-vat's perceptions coherent, his perceptions take into account the virtual actions of other humans in vats. He and other humans can interact with the same publicly observable (albeit virtual) objects. Maybe, then, Berkeley would say that matrix-generated perceptions *are* real. Would this response be wise on his part? It would appear not, for several reasons. First, Berkeley took himself as supporting the commonsense view of objects against the "philosopher's confusion" view of objects that people like Descartes put forward. It seems that there can't be any doubt that the commonsense response is that matrix-generated perceptions are not real, no matter how vivid and intra- and interpersonally coherent they are. Furthermore, the matrix cannot guarantee continued coherence. Even within the movie (recall the double black cat scene [MM 78:30]), small glitches or changes in the matrix produce minor, local incoherence. Berkeley's infinite God, on the other hand, guarantees *absolute* coherence.

What is posterity's final assessment of Berkelian idealism? The common view among present-day philosophers is that Berkeley's avoidance of skepticism turned out to be an illusion: while his brand of idealism does avoid skepticism in its classical form (stated in terms of our knowledge of *external* objects), it succumbs to a variant form. The idealist wants to maintain a distinction between genuine and nongenuine perceptions; yet, as we have seen, the three signs of genuine perceptions offered by Berkeley are not adequate: many nongenuine perceptions (for example, those experienced by Neo while plugged into the matrix) possess all three signs of genuineness.

Berkeley's defeat did not mean the end of the struggle to refute skepticism. In the remainder of this section, we shall consider the views of the great German philosopher, **Immanuel Kant** (1724–1804).

Kant is one of the most influential thinkers in the history of philosophy. He is also one of the most obscure and difficult-to-read writers in the history of the discipline, as even a cursory glance through his highly praised *Critique of Pure Reason* will attest. Kant believed that no one to date had successfully countered skepticism, and took the failure to refute skepticism as a major "scandal" within philosophy. As he described it:

> [I]t still remains a scandal to philosophy and to human reason in general that the existence of things outside us ... must be accepted merely on *faith*, and that if anyone thinks good to doubt their existence, we are unable to counter his doubts by any satisfactory proof.[16]

Kant agreed with Berkeley that the theory of representative perceptions leads inevitably to skepticism. Thus, in Kant's reworking of a theory of objects, the theory of representative perceptions had to go: whatever a perception represents, it cannot be an external, mind-independent object (what Kant called a "thing-in-itself"). But he believed that Berkeley's theory had equally fatal flaws: Berkeley's view did not recognize the role *the active mind* plays in influencing our experience of the world.

The most important item to know about Kant's philosophy is that he distinguished between the world of objects as revealed by experience (in Kant's terminology, the "phenomenal world") and the (purely conjectural) world of things in themselves (the "noumenal world"). According to Kant, knowledge was restricted to the phenomenal world. He would describe Descartes's (and Hume's) mistake as thinking that skepticism would be refuted only if we could gain knowledge of the noumenal world. For Kant, the noumenal world always had the status of an "I know not what...." One may assume that the objects in the phenomenal world bore some relation to things in themselves, but even that must also remain conjecture.

Kant's way of approaching philosophy is often described as revolutionary, in that it challenged what previous philosophers took the logical order of investigation to be. The similarity between Kant's new way of looking at the world and the Copernican revolution in astronomy is sometimes remarked upon. Copernicus's major contribution to astronomy was to overturn the then-standard view of the heavens, according to which the earth is at the center of the solar system. Copernicus showed that the movement of heavenly bodies could be explained in a much simpler fashion if one reversed the then-standard view. Thus, Copernicus inferred that the sun (not the earth) was at the center of the solar system. The earth, along with several other planets, revolves around the sun. Just so, Kant reversed the order of philosophical investigation. Earlier philosophers (for example, Descartes) held a view of objects as mind-independent entities. With this assumption in place, these philosophers would ask, "How do these mind-independent objects affect the mind and how can the mind gain knowledge of them?" Thus, the Cartesian order of enquiry is that first you decide what objects are and then you ask questions about the possibility of obtaining knowledge of these objects. Kant, like Copernicus, asks, What happens if we switch the order? What happens if we assume we have knowledge of the world, then ask what the world must be like, given this knowledge? Since Descartes and Hume had so little success in defending against skepticism with the standard approach, Kant's attitude is: Let's give this new way a try and see what happens. As he writes, "We must ... make trial whether we may not have more success in the tasks of metaphysics, if we suppose that objects must conform to our knowledge."[17]

Kant has turned the mind/world relation on its head. Previously, philosophers had viewed the mind as a passive perceiver of reality: via perception, our mind receives occasional snapshots of what is "out there." For Kant, reality isn't "out there" at all. It is "in here" and it is something that our mind constructs. Don't be misled: the use of spatial terms "out" and "in" is purely metaphorical, for space and time themselves are also "in here." Likewise, I (my phenomenal self) am also "in here," along with the other objects that make up the world of experience. A mind is like a factory. The raw materials are sense perceptions. The output is the world of experience (the phenomenal world). The rules used to forge the world out of perceptions–the cognitive machinery–are innate. A somewhat simplified version of Kant's theory is offered in his *Prolegomena to Any Future Metaphysics*, excerpted here in the section Readings from Primary Sources. Kant's method of doing philosophy is to look beyond (to "transcend") experience in order to understand the cognitive machinery creating it. Once you understand what principles the mind uses to construct the phenomenal world (the world of experience), you will know what the necessary attributes of all experience are, such that no human could have a conscious experience that deviated from these principles. One of these principles identified by Kant is that the world is made up of objects. My mind necessarily interprets perceptions as perceptions *of objects*—it cannot do otherwise. Whether other sorts of beings with a radically different kind of consciousness could use different principles is a question that Kant leaves open. At a minimum, for beings like us with a consciousness of a *coherent* world filled with *causally interacting objects*, we could not have a conscious experience that deviated from these principles.

Within Kant's framework, the skeptic's challenge can be reformulated: Can I be certain that my perceptions accurately represent objects in the world? Kant would answer: Yes, you can, because you could not have a perception that failed to accurately represent objects in the world; however, you should not misinterpret these represented objects as things in themselves.

Kant's theory can help us understand what may be happening in a couple of scenes in *Inception* when there are events happening without the dreamer present. Consider one of the earlier dream sequences, the one in which Cobb, Arthur, and Saito are in Nash's dream. At MM 4:42, Nash looks out the window and sees a car blow up. But, there are several times when we see rioting going on outside the building, even when Nash is not in the picture. If the narrative at this point in the film is Nash's lucid dream, how can we make sense of the fact that there is action that doesn't include Nash or anyone else sharing his dream? Is it possible to explain this part of the narrative in a way that is consistent with the general interpretation of this being part of a dream? Kant offers us a way. A brief discussion will provide some insight into the role the active mind plays in Kant's theory. It seems that Kant would say that the events that happen without Nash are part of the phenomenal world being generated by Nash's mind. The shared lucid dream contains many holes about what happens to objects and people while Nash is not actively perceiving them. Although other people are sharing Nash's dream, it is still Nash's dream. Nash's mind uses the perceptions contained in the lucid dream to construct a coherent narrative. Things aren't that much different with me. Consider an everyday example. I leave outgoing mail in the "out" box in my department office at time t_1. An hour later (time t_2) I come back in the department office and note that the piece of mail I left at t_1 is now missing. Do I assume that the piece of mail has vanished into thin air? No. I "fill in the gap" by inserting a bit of narrative into the phenomenal world between t_1 and t_2 that has an administrative assistant going to the mailbox and dropping the letter in. While I may explicitly picture to myself the assistant's doing this, I don't have to. All that is necessary in order to fill in the gap in my narrative is that the assistant's doing this becomes part of the phenomenal world my mind constructs. Similarly, just before t_2 I left my own office, to return shortly after t_2. On my return, my desk telephone was just where I left it. I fill in the gap with the phone's staying put during that interval. (By the way, my desk also stayed put during that interval.) My mind does all of this automatically. Indeed, it requires some mental exertion to even make myself aware of the fact that my mind has filled in the gaps in my perceptions in that way. Kant's great contribution was noticing that and then describing how the mind does this.

As we mentioned previously, Kant's views have been widely influential in nineteenth- and twentieth-century philosophy; he is not, however, without his detractors. He, like Berkeley, cannot solve Descartes's problem. Kant recognized the distinction between genuine and nongenuine perceptions; however, his theory provides us with no means of determining at the time a particular perception occurs, whether that perception is genuine or not. Many philosophers have credited Kant as the source for the emergence of philosophical relativism within modernism and postmodernism. We will leave it to you, the reader, to consider whether Kant might be able to respond to the charge some level against him: that he has refuted general skepticism but at the cost of making all knowledge subjective (that is, relative to a single individual).

2.7 The Dangers and Lessons of Skepticism

What is an appropriate response to skepticism? The ancient skeptics thought blissful detachment from the world was the appropriate (and natural) response to our lack of knowledge about even the most basic things. Few have followed them in this regard, although Cipher's traitorous act in *The Matrix* (betraying his comrades in order to reenter the matrix as a wealthy and powerful person) shows that, at least for some, skepticism is not something to worry oneself about. For Cipher, virtual perceptions are just as good as real ones; indeed, if they are pleasant, virtual perceptions are preferable to real perceptions. Cipher's response certainly isn't shared by Neo. Cobb's choice to return to the real world rather than remain in limbo with Mal, initially seems to suggest that he viewed the real world (even without Mal) as more valuable than a dream world with Mal. However, Cobb's actions at the end of the film, when he leaves the top spinning and, instead, turns to be with his kids (or his perception of them), could indicate that he changes his mind and no longer cares whether his perceptions are genuine.[18] Does it matter whether perceptions are real or not, so long as they are pleasant? We've seen how many philosophers in the modern era took skepticism as a view to be wrestled with and overcome—so much so that successful refutation of skepticism became the litmus test for the correctness of a theory of objects. Which of these attitudes makes the most sense? You may be surprised to find that David Hume, the greatest defender of skepticism, was also the greatest defender of the claim that skepticism is irrelevant to real life. Were someone to manage to adopt skepticism as a "lifestyle" (to put it in contemporary terms), the results would be catastrophic. As Hume has noted:

> [N]o durable good can come of [adopting skepticism as a lifestyle]. … [Such a person] cannot expect, that his philosophy will have a constant influence on the mind: Or if it had, that its influence would be beneficial to society. On the contrary, he must acknowledge, if he will acknowledge any thing, that all human life must perish, were his principles universally and steadily to prevail. All discourse, all action would immediately cease; and men remain in a total lethargy, till the necessities of nature, unsatisfied, put an end to their miserable existence.[19]

Hume thought that the chances of skepticism having this sort of impact were small, because he felt no one could maintain skepticism as a lifestyle. Our minds are wired to accept the report of our senses as accurate, and that is all there is to it. If anything, Hume thought, skepticism is what happens when reason runs amuck. He felt that the function of human reason was to aid in practical problem solving: I want to accomplish A; what plan should I adopt to achieve that goal? *That* sort of activity is the natural domain of our rational faculty. But sometimes, like a wayward child, reason escapes its natural bounds and gets into all sorts of mischief. Skepticism is one sort of mischief that reason, when not properly restrained, can get into.[20]

So, Hume wasn't trying to convince us to adopt skepticism as a lifestyle. What, then, was the purpose of his arguments? He, like many later philosophers, saw a lesson that skepticism could provide to both philosophers and nonphilosophers alike. Skepticism can serve as a check against dogmatism of all stripes. The skeptic's constant insistence on the question "But how do you *know* that?" can be a very useful refrain in the real world.

Skepticism can also serve as a lesson in humility. Bertrand Russell (whom we met in Chapter 1) described this best:

> The value of philosophy is, in fact, to be sought largely in its very uncertainty. The man who has no tincture of philosophy goes through life imprisoned in the prejudices derived from common

sense, from the habitual beliefs of his age or his nation, and from convictions which have grown up in his mind without the cooperation or consent of his deliberate reason. To such a man the world tends to become definite, finite, obvious; common objects rouse no questions, and unfamiliar possibilities are contemptuously rejected. As soon as we begin to philosophize, on the contrary, we find ... that even the most everyday things lead to problems to which only very incomplete answers can be given. Philosophy, though unable to tell us with certainty what is the true answer to the doubts which it raises, is able to suggest many possibilities which enlarge our thoughts and free them from the tyranny of custom.[21]

Discussion Questions

1. At the beginning of the chapter, we posed the question "Can you know with absolute certainty that you are not dreaming right now?" How did you answer the question then? Was your response adequate? How would you answer the question now?

2. What are the similarities between skepticism as found in Descartes's first meditation and as found in *Inception*? What are the differences?

3. What are the similarities between skepticism as found in Descartes's first meditation and as found in *The Matrix*? What are the differences?

4. There are several references in *The Matrix* to Neo's feeling that "something isn't quite right," even before MM 32:00 (when the "real" Neo is "flushed out" of his vat). Would skepticism on Neo's part have been *rational* during this time period? Would skepticism on Fischer's part after MM 85:23 have been *rational*? Would skepticism on *your* part constitute *rational* doubt?

5. What is the "natural" response to skepticism: repugnance, indifference, or contented acceptance?

6. Do you usually remember (at least part of) your dreams? If so, are you generally aware while dreaming that you are dreaming, or does this recognition only come after you wake up? In either case, explain which characteristics of your dreams allow you to recognize that they are dreams.

7. Do you think Berkeley's argument that mind-independent objects cannot be conceived of is a good one? (This is the argument summarized in the hypothetical conversation between Berkeley and Descartes.) Was your reaction the same as Descartes's ("I can't put my finger on it, but there's something fishy here")? If so, what possible criticisms are there?

Annotated List of Films Relevant to Skepticism

Vanilla Sky (2001). Based on the film *Abre los Ojos* by Alejandro Amenábar and Mateo Gil. Starring Tom Cruise, Penélope Cruz, Kurt Russell.

A handsome young man is severely injured and disfigured in a car crash. He is arrested for the murder of his girlfriend. Has he gone insane, or is he living in a lucid dream "gone wild"?

Thirteenth Floor (1999). Directed by Josef Rusnak. Starring Craig Bierko, Armin Mueller-Stahl, Gretchen Mol.

As in *The Matrix*, this movie supports the skepticism-raising claim that there could be a thoroughly virtual world that is indistinguishable from our world in every detail.

Strange Days (1995). Directed by Kathryn Bigelow. Starring Ralph Fiennes, Angela Bassett, Juliette Lewis.

This movie is set in a future world in which black market street hustlers trade in nongenuine perceptions for recreation.

eXistenZ (1999). Directed by David Cronenberg. Starring Jennifer Jason Leigh, Jude Law, Willem Dafoe.

A future in which the latest virtual reality game plugs directly into the nervous system of its players.

Total Recall (1990). Directed by Paul Verhoeven. Starring Arnold Schwarzenegger, Rachel Ticotin, Sharon Stone.

The plot twists and turns as we follow the main character in his escape to Mars, where he learns that he is a secret agent whose memories have been erased—or is he? Perhaps, what is in reality happening is that he is reliving a set of "memories" he purchased from a retailer in fake vacation memories.

Total Recall (2012). Directed by Len Wiseman. Starring Colin Farrell, Kate Beckinsale, Bryan Cranston.

A remake of the 1990 film that works with mostly the same plot twists and philosophical themes.

Waking Life (2001). Directed by Richard Linklater. Starring Ethan Hawke, Trevor Jack Brooks, Lorelei Linklater.

This film explores the nature of dreams, as well as many other philosophical issues. The protagonist comes to realize that he cannot know at any given moment whether he is still dreaming.

Annotated List of Books Relevant to Skepticism

"Classics" in the History of Skepticism

SEXTUS EMPIRICUS

Outlines of Pyrrhonism, first published in Greek, ca. 210 C.E.

RENÉ DESCARTES

Meditations on First Philosophy, first published in Latin, 1641. There have been many translations of the work into English. (The first of the six *Meditations*, included in its entirety in Readings from Primary Sources, is the *locus classicus* for skepticism in the modern era.)

GEORGE BERKELEY

A Treatise concerning the Principles of Human Knowledge, 1710. The quotations included in this chapter have been taken from a useful collection of the same name that includes both Berkeley's *Treatise* and critical essays on Berkeley's theories by leading philosophers that was published in 1970; excerpts from the *Treatise* are included in Readings from Primary Sources.

Three Dialogues between Hylas and Philonous, 1713. Berkeley argues for his version of idealism in dialogue form. The quotations included in this chapter have been taken from the Hackett edition of 1979.

DAVID HUME

A Treatise of Human Nature, 1740. Hume's magnum opus. It contains not only his famous arguments in favor of skepticism and other issues within epistemology but also his ethics and theory of human psychology. The scholarly standard for this work is the 2nd edition, put out by Oxford University Press in 1978. The section from Hume's *Treatise* dealing with personal identity is included in Readings from Primary Sources.

An Enquiry concerning Human Understanding, 1748. For the average reader, the *Enquiry* is a much more approachable work than the *Treatise*. It is fairly short (just over one hundred pages) and written in a quite lively and modern-sounding style. The quotations included in this chapter have been taken from the Hackett edition of 1977.

IMMANUEL KANT

Critique of Pure Reason, first published in German, 1st edition 1781, 2nd edition 1787. Probably the most difficult book to read among the major works in the Western philosophical canon. For the very adventurous person who wishes to tackle this behemoth, the standard scholarly versions include both the 1st and 2nd editions. If you are interested primarily in reading those parts of the *Critique* dealing with skepticism, a useful commentary is *Kant's Theory of Mental Activity* by Robert Paul Wolff, published by Peter-Smith in 1973.

Prolegomena to Any Future Metaphysics, first published in German, 1783. In this work, Kant attempts to boil down the theory laid out in his *Critique of Pure Reason* in a form that is more accessible than the larger work. Selections from *Prolegomena* are included in Readings from Primary Sources.

Contemporary Works on Skepticism

Richard Popkin, *History of Skepticism* (Berkeley and Los Angeles: University of California Press, 1979).

Myles Burnyeat, ed. *The Skeptical Tradition* (Berkeley and Los Angeles: University of California Press, 1983). A collection of essays discussing the historical development of skepticism, as well as current controversies.

John Greco, *Putting Skeptics in Their Place* (Cambridge: Cambridge University Press, 2000). This book argues that skepticism is not the easily refutable position so many philosophers believe it to be; it is very readable.

Paul Kurtz, *The New Skepticism* (Buffalo, NY: Prometheus Press, 1992). This is the only book in this section that deals with skepticism in all its forms (moral, political, religious, etc.).

Notes

1. It may sound strange to refer to the seventeenth century as "modern." The strangeness disappears when one realizes that the periods in contrast are the ancient, the medieval, and the Renaissance.
2. The adjectival form of Descartes's name is "Cartesian" (as in "Cartesian doubt" or "Cartesian coordinate system").
3. This is a question posed to Neo by Morpheus in the movie *The Matrix*.
4. René Descartes, *Meditations on First Philosophy* (Claremont, CA: Arete Press, 1985), from Meditation One.
5. These interpretations were generated from various discussions with students and from Peter Hall's, "Dissecting 'Inception': Six Interpretations and Five Plot Holes," (*Moviefone*, July 2010).
6. In fact, in an interview with *Wired*, Nolan claims that he has an interpretation in mind, but intentionally made the movie in a way that left that interpretation ambiguous (*Wired*, December 2010).
7. Descartes, *Meditations*, from Meditation One.
8. From "Meditation Six–Concerning the Existence of Material Things, and the Real Distinction of the Mind from the Body," in *Meditations*.
9. See, for example, the third dialogue in *Three Dialogues between Hylas and Philonous*. As we shall see, Berkeley would have rejected the definition given earlier for *genuine*; however, we shall gloss over that point for the time being. Berkeley did talk about real versus imaginary perceptions, and as long as the reader has this general distinction in mind we don't believe there will be any difficulties in understanding.
10. David Hume, *A Treatise of Human Nature*, 2nd edn (Oxford: Oxford University Press, 1978), 252–53 (book 1, part 4, section vi).
11. Note that the adjective *external* has been left off. This omission is intentional on our part. As we shall see, this whole way of talking and thinking (that is, about *external* objects, as opposed to objects *simpliciter*) is something that Berkeley rejects.
12. This is in the first dialogue in *Three Dialogues between Hylas and Philonous*.

13. George Berkeley, *A Treatise Concerning the Principles of Human Knowledge* (London: Bobbs-Merrill, 1970), 248 (part 1, par. 6).
14. The "God response" is usually taken as Berkeley's considered answer. Passages stating outright or implying this route to solving the problem of unperceived objects may be found in both *A Treatise Concerning the Principle of Human Knowledge* and the *Three Dialogues between Hylas and Philonous*.
15. Strictly speaking, according to Berkeley, God does not *perceive* (at least not in the same way we do). If anything, God is an active generator of perceptions, not a passive recipient of them. This fine point aside, it doesn't seem that anything of substance is lost by referring to God as a perceiver.
16. Immanuel Kant, *Critique of Pure Reason* (London: St. Martin's Press, 1929), Bxl. (Pagination in Kant's *Critique* is somewhat quirky. He made major revisions between the first and second editions, so the standard scholarly translations of the work differentiate between material written in the first edition–denoted by the letter *A* before the page number–and material written in the second edition–denoted by the letter *B* before the page number. Thus, the above quote is from the second edition preface, page xl.)
17. Ibid., Bxvi.
18. Nolan expresses this point in the *Wired* interview.
19. David Hume, *An Enquiry Concerning Human Understanding* (Indianapolis, IN: Hackett, 1977), 110 (section 12, part 2).
20. For this line of reasoning in Hume, see his *Treatise*, book II, part 3, section iii.
21. Bertrand Russell, "The Value of Philosophy," in *The Problems of Philosophy* (Oxford: Oxford University Press, 1912), 91.

3

PERSONAL IDENTITY

Memento (2000) and *Moon* (2009)

Teddy: You do not know who you are.
Leonard: I'm Leonard Shelby. I'm from San Francisco.
Teddy: That's who you *were.*

—from *Memento*

Sam₂: Here, talking to a clone, that's slightly troubling.
Sam₁: I'm not a clone. I'm not a clone. *You're* the clone.

—from *Moon*

Are you the same person now as you were on the day you were born? It seems that no one would answer this question in the negative. However, explaining how this identity over time is possible is a rather tricky issue. After all, the *physical* changes your body has undergone between your birth and the present are striking: it is possible there is not a single atom that your current body shares in common with your infant body. Perhaps (at least, for humans) identity over time is not tied to your physical sameness but to your mental sameness. However, even if we focus on your *mental* properties, explaining how you have remained the same person from your birth up until now is difficult. Can you (now) remember being an infant? Do you (now) share any specific beliefs or desires with your self as an infant? It seems that explaining this identity over time with reference to sameness of mental properties won't work either. What other options are available? Perhaps you possess an immaterial soul that persists through your life unchanged, and it is by virtue of this that you are the same person as you were at birth. Will this explanation work without introducing even more problems? These are the sorts of questions that fall under the topic "personal identity." Their answers have ramifications for our basic self-understanding, since they imply who and what we are as individuals.

3.1 The Conceivability of an Afterlife

What does it mean to say "You will survive the death of your body"? As a first approximation, "You will continue to exist, even after your body dies" is pretty good. A better approximation, one that fits in with the way personal identity will be discussed in the rest of this chapter, is "There will be someone who exists after your body dies, and that person will be *identical to you.*"[1]

The word *identical* in English is ambiguous. In some contexts, to say two things are *identical* is to say they are very similar; this is the sense used in the context of *identical* twins. The second sense of *identical* means "one and the same"; this is the sense meant in describing Clark Kent as *identical* to Superman. It is this second sense that will concern us in this chapter. What does it mean for person A to be identical to (that is, one and the same person as) person B? Or, as in the case above, what does it mean to say that some person who exists after the death of your body is identical to you?

Many religious traditions include a belief in an afterlife. We are not interested here in discussing whether or not belief in an afterlife is true, or even whether it is well founded. Rather, we want to discuss whether this belief is *possibly* true. To see what we are getting at, consider the sentence "Green ideas sleep furiously." Even though the individual words that constitute this sentence are familiar and the sentence as a whole is grammatical, still, the sentence doesn't make any sense. We cannot conceive of what a world would be like in which this sentence was true. Ideas just are not the sorts of things that can sleep, much less sleep furiously. Nor are ideas the sorts of things that can be a color, green or otherwise. There seems to be some sort of category mistake going on in the sentence. One way to describe this mistake is to say that the sentence is not only false, it is conceptually impossible. Another way to describe the mistake is to say that the sentence expresses something that is inconceivable.

At first glance, the sentence "You will survive the death of your body" isn't like the sentence "Green ideas sleep furiously" at all. For one thing, many people assent to the former sentence, whereas no one would assent to the latter. More importantly for our purposes here, we can conceive of what a world would be like in which the former sentence is true. (Or, at least, we think we can.) If this claim about the conceivability of the sentence "You will survive the death of your body" remains unchallenged, that would say a lot about what makes you *you.*

The English philosopher **John Locke** (1632–1704) recognized that, when asking questions about identity over time, we must keep in mind that the criterion which determines identity for a thing will differ, depending on how we describe that thing. The chapter from Locke's *An Essay Concerning Human Understanding,* "Of Identity and Diversity," is reproduced in Readings from Primary Sources. Consider the example of a tree. A tree, being a physical object, is made up of atoms that are in constant flux as the tree grows, sheds leaves, engages in photosynthesis, and so on. If we think about whether a tree at one time is identical to a tree at another time based on the matter that constitutes each of them, then the two trees will not be identical, because some atoms that make up the tree at the initial time will have changed or ceased to be a part of the tree at the later time. If, however, we focus on the tree as a living organism with parts that work together to achieve the continued life of the tree, allowing for a modest amount of continuous change in the underlying matter that makes up those parts, then we will judge that the tree at the earlier time is identical to the tree at the later time, even though they have no atoms in common.

> In the state of living creatures, their identity depends not on a mass of the same particles, but on something else. For in them the variation of great parcels of matter alters not the identity: an oak growing from a plant to a great tree, and then lopped, is still the same oak ... though ... there may be a manifest change of the parts; so that truly they are not ... the same masses of matter, though they be truly one of them the same oak.... The reason whereof is, that, in [this] case—a mass of matter and a living body—identity is not applied to the same thing.[2]

Locke believed that, when discussing personal identity, one must likewise be careful that one is treating the objects of study at the proper level.

> [The] idea of identity [must be] suited to the idea it is applied to. It is not therefore unity of substance that comprehends all sorts of identity, or will determine it in every case; but to conceive and judge of it aright, we must consider what idea the word it is applied to stands for: it being one thing to be the same substance, another the same man, and a third the same person, if person, man, and substance, are three names standing for three different ideas.[3]

In a discussion of personal identity as it relates to the conceivability of an afterlife, we need to keep in mind Locke's advice that we focus on the nature of the thing whose identity we are considering. In the remainder of this section, we will cover three different theories of personal identity and ask, for each of these theories: Is an afterlife conceivable in the context of this theory?

Under everyday circumstances, how do you identify a person from one time to another? Let us suppose that you have a friend named Trina whom you haven't seen in several years. What sort of evidence would lead you to believe that someone you see from across the room at a party is your friend Trina? The most important attribute we use in identifying someone in day-to-day situations is physical appearance. So, in the example from above, you would remember what Trina looked like and ask yourself what (dis)similarities you see in Trina's appearance and the appearance of the person across the room. You may even move closer to get a better look. Obviously, we don't require exact similarity in appearance; otherwise, we couldn't recognize someone after that person had a haircut. But there are parameters about how much someone can change in their appearance and still be readily recognized as the same person.

What does this example tell us about our everyday understanding of personal identity? First and foremost, it tells us that someone's observable physical attributes—primarily, what she looks like or what her voice sounds like—matter a great deal in our day-to-day judgments about personal identity. But physical similarity cannot be the property that *determines* personal identity, since we are quick to discard a judgment of identity based on physical similarity if additional relevant information comes to light. If I find out that the person I see from across the room is not Trina but her identical twin sister Greta, I would immediately cease believing she was Trina despite the physical resemblance. (If physical resemblance were all there was to personal identity, we would judge identical twins as being one and the same person.) It seems as though physical resemblance is a stand-in for the property that we really use in making judgments of personal identity in day-to-day situations. This underlying property is *physical continuity*, and according to the **physical continuity theory** of personal identity, you are the same person you were at birth if your body has existed continuously from then up until now. We use similarity of physical appearance as a stand-in for physical continuity because physical appearance is all we have available to us. I rarely see someone continuously for more than a few hours, yet I can easily note similarities in physical appearance, even when it has been years since I have seen someone. Experience has taught me that, for non-mass-produced objects (human beings, for example), when I see an object at time t_1 and an object at time t_2 and notice that the two objects look *very* similar, they are usually one and the same thing.[4]

So far, we have been speaking about the criteria we use in day-to-day situations when we make judgments about personal identity. What happens if we treat the physical continuity theory as more than just a rule of thumb for judging identity in day-to-day situations? If physical continuity is required for personal identity, then the sentence "You will survive the death of your body" is inconceivable. After death, your body will cease to exist as a body. Admittedly, the atoms that constitute your body will continue on, but they will not form a body. A physical transformation will occur that prevents continuity. Just so, if I take a pencil and grind it up into a fine dust, the pile of dust that results is not the pencil. The original pencil has ceased to exist. Perhaps the pencil could have survived less drastic changes–having a notch made in it or having the end cut off. It would still be the same pencil. But grinding it into a pile of dust is too radical a change for the resulting matter to be identical to the original pencil.

The decomposition (or incineration) of a human body is as radical a change as the grinding up of a pencil. So, if a human body dies at time t, the person whose body that is ceases to exist at t (or shortly thereafter). In other words, if we assume the physical continuity theory for person identity, continuing to exist after the death and disintegration of one's body is a conceptual impossibility.

Yet, the notion of an afterlife seems possible to most people, even to those who reject it as implausible or unlikely. This tells us that most people do not tie personal identity to physical continuity, but to something else– something that could persist through the physical transformation that occurs at death.

Some philosophers have argued for the **psychological continuity theory** of personal identity. According to this theory, what makes me *me* are my psychological characteristics. I am the same person I was last year because there is a cluster of psychological properties that exists continuously from then until now. Different philosophers disagree over what this cluster consists of. Some say it is a stream of consciousness; however, this interpretation of the psychological continuity theory has problems dealing with discontinuities in the stream of consciousness that occur during sleep. Others say it is high-level psychological properties such as my personality, disposition, value system, long-term desires, and so on–the sorts of attributes that generally change very slowly over time. Yet others say psychological continuity is achieved by memory. I am the person I was last year because I can remember having some of the perceptions and thoughts that that person had. I am the person I was two years ago because the person I was last year can remember having some of the perceptions and thoughts that that person had from two years ago. Memory is used as the transitive link that ultimately identifies me as identical to that person who was born many years ago. These three versions of the psychological continuity theory need not be taken in isolation: it is possible to construct a hybrid version of the theory that uses two or three of these clusters. So, for example, if continuity of memory fails (as we shall see in the case of Leonard Shelby, the protagonist in *Memento*), continuity of stream of consciousness could be used to link together a memory-fragmented mental life.

The psychological continuity theory fares somewhat better than the physical continuity theory in allowing for the possibility of an afterlife. It is not clear how the psychological clusters mentioned above could persist after my death; however, it is at least not impossible that they continue after the body has ceased to exist. (Remember: all we are looking for in this section is a theory of personal identity that allows the sentence "You will survive the death of your body" to be possibly true.)

Within many religious traditions, the thing that continues to exist after death is assumed to be the individual's immaterial soul. Being immaterial, it is not affected by the decomposition of the body after death. According to the **same-soul theory** of personal identity, what makes me *me* is my soul. It is somehow or other attached to my body during my lifetime, then becomes disattached at death, continuing to exist either in disembodied form or by reattaching to another body.

The problem with both the psychological continuity and the same-soul theories of personal identity is explaining why, in everyday circumstances, we place so much emphasis on physical attributes in determining identity. While immaterial souls could survive transformations of their host bodies, they (being immaterial) cannot be seen, heard, or sensed in any way. If we consistently applied the same-soul theory, someone's physical appearance should be irrelevant in deciding who that person is. Similarly, psychological attributes cannot be seen directly; they must be inferred by looking at someone's behavior. Yet, even when people are not behaving at all because they are sleeping, we do not infer that they have ceased to be who they are. Admittedly, in cases where someone's behavior deviates significantly from how that individual usually behaves, we describe him as "not being himself." However, this usage is metaphorical, of course. "Tom isn't himself today" does not mean that this person in front of me (that is, Tom) isn't really Tom after all.

We shall return to these and related points in later sections. For now, though, it is sufficient to note that, of the three theories of personal identity discussed so far, the physical continuity theory comports best with our everyday usage; however, it runs afoul of the widespread belief in the conceptual possibility of an afterlife.

3.2 The General Problem of Identity over Time

Establishing criteria for personal identity (that is, what it means for person X to be identical to person Y) is just a special case of a more general topic. By virtue of what is object X identical to object Y? On first glance, identity for inanimate objects seems straightforward. For one thing, we need not worry about squaring our theory with issues involving an afterlife. (It was the need to make space for the conceptual possibility of an afterlife that was the major problem for the physical continuity theory of personal identity.) Thus, why not just say, for object X and object Y, they are identical if object X is physically continuous over time with object Y? (For example, the phone that was on my desk yesterday is identical to the phone that is on my desk today if they form a physically continuous object.) Unfortunately, even for inanimate objects, the story isn't quite this simple. Consider the following examples.[5]

You are taking a course in car maintenance from a teacher who has a rather unorthodox teaching style. In this course, you are to take a car apart piece by piece, carefully labeling each piece; then, once the car is thoroughly disassembled, you are to put it back together. Let us suppose that you manage to do this—that is, you manage to put together the parts in just the same way that they were originally put together. Is the car after this exercise *identical* to the car before? It seems that a reasonable answer is, "Yes, they are one and the same car."

After learning so much about car maintenance, you decide to service your car yourself. Your radiator starts to get a little rusty, so you buy a new radiator and install it. (It doesn't really matter in this case, but suppose you throw the original radiator on to the junk heap in your backyard.) The car with the replaced radiator is still the *same* car: changing this part hasn't changed its identity. The next item on your car to need replacement is the right front tire, which you replace. Again, changing this tire does not affect the car's identity. Then the clutch gets a little sloppy, so you decide to replace it before it breaks and leaves you stranded. Yet again, it is still the same car after the replacement as before. The process of gradual replacement lasts over several years, and, after each replacement it is still the same car as before. By the end of the process, *every single one of the car's original parts has been replaced.* Even the frame and the body have been replaced. Now, compare the car before you started working on it to the car after the last original part is replaced. Are they the same car? Again, a reasonable answer would seem to be, "Yes, they are one and the same car."

If you disagree (that is, if you think the car resulting from the gradual replacement of all of its parts is not identical to the original car), when during the gradual replacement process did the car stop being identical to the original car? Remember, at each stage, we are only replacing one part. To justify your view, there has to be *some part* whose replacement was crucial in changing the car's identity. What part would that be? More importantly, what is so special about that part that makes its replacement alter the identity of the car? Perhaps you think a car's body is so crucial to the identity of a car that a car could not survive having its body replaced, in the same way as a pencil could not survive being ground into dust. Suppose we replace the body gradually. First, we replace the driver's side door. Then, several months later, we replace the right front fender, then, six months later, we replace the rear bumper, and so on. (If you think it is not the car body but some other part that is crucial to a car's identity, we could run the super-gradual replacement argument on that part, too. It might require us to retell the story such that major cutting and welding was required, but it doesn't change things substantially.) When during this process does the car lose its original identity? Again, the burden is on you to point to either some special part or special *threshold* percentage of replacement that changes the car's identity.

Let's assume that everyone is in agreement in the gradual replacement case: the post-replacement car is identical to the original car. Now comes the twist. We mentioned above in the gradual replacement case that, as you replaced parts, you threw the original ones on to the junk heap in your backyard. So, at the end of the gradual replacement process, you have all the original parts in a heap. Now, with all this car repair knowledge, you decide to take on the ultimate challenge: to see if you can put all the original parts back together. You manage to do just that. Now you have two cars. Which car is *identical* to the original car–the one with the replaced parts or the rebuilt one with the original parts? After all, they cannot both be identical to the original car.

If you think it is possible that they are both identical to the original car, think some more about what *identical* means in this context. (Remember, the sense of *identical* we are working with is the sense in which Clark Kent is *identical* to Superman.) Let us call the original car (before you started working on it) car X, the car that resulted from the gradual replacement of parts is car Y, and the car that resulted from reassembling the original parts is car Z. Clearly, car Y is not identical to car Z. (Remember: identical here means one and the same as.) So, it cannot be the case that car X = car Y and car X = car Z, since car Y ≠ car Z. Either car Y is not the continuation of car X, or car Z is not the continuation of car X, or neither of them are.

This example shows that, even for inanimate objects, finding a theory for object identity over time is a rather tricky matter. In the case of human beings, it is so much the trickier, since we do not have just a physical nature but also a psychological nature. The possibilities for finding counterexamples to a theory of personal identity are that much greater. In some ways, the two focus movies for this chapter do just that: they present some atypical situations involving humans and ask us as viewers to decide what we make of them. Are the identities of the protagonists affected by the events that happen in the movies?

3.3 An Overview of the Movies

MEMENTO (2000). DIRECTED BY CHRISTOPHER NOLAN.
STARRING GUY PEARCE, CARRIE-ANNE MOSS,
JOE PANTOLIANO

For those who hold some version of the psychological continuity theory of personal identity, *Memento* raises some very interesting questions. The film focuses on two days in the life of Leonard Shelby, a man who has a form of amnesia that prevents him from remembering anything for more than a few minutes. He has normal memory of events that took place before the incident that put him in this condition, but not events that happened recently. As he describes his own subjective state of mind, he can no longer "feel" the passage of time; he has the present and the remote past, and that is all.

Memento is structured to try to give us, the viewers of the movie, the same subjective feeling of fragmentation of self as Leonard experiences. To do this, the film moves backward through fictional time: the first scene we see is the last thing that happens; the next scene we see is the thing that happened second to last, and so on. Interspersed among the scenes that are progressing backward in chronological order are about a dozen scenes shot in black and white that are flowing forward in chronological order. The result for the viewer is extreme disorientation. While we know what happens later to Leonard (because we have already seen it), we don't know what has happened in the past that led to the current scene—much as Leonard himself "knows" what is happening in the present but has no clue about how he got there. (We put the word "know" in quotes because, as *Memento* argues, it is unclear whether Leonard's experience of the present, lacking as it does all relevant historical context, really constitutes knowledge.)

Leonard tries to cope with his condition, tries to supply himself with historical context, by leaving himself mementos—all sorts of mementos: little notes to himself written on pieces of paper, and pictures of his acquaintances to tell himself what names go with what faces, who to trust, and who not to trust. For really important long-term mementos, he uses tattoos—all over his body. While incomplete, these mementos from his fragmented past allow him to set short-term goals and decide what to do next. The overarching long-term goal implicit in his tattoos drives the movie's plot.

Who is Leonard Shelby? Did he (the person) survive the incident, or did he disappear with his ability to form new memories? One option *Memento* raises is that the original Leonard doesn't exist any more. His body is occupied by a series of persons who only last a few minutes each—the maximum span of time that he can remember something. The little notes and pictures he leaves for himself in the future, even the "notes" he leaves on his body in the form of tattoos, are not the right sort of link required for personal identity.

As mentioned above, *Memento* is (intentionally) a very confusing movie. It is possible for the viewer to piece together events in the correct chronological order if one treats the movie as a sort of puzzle. While it is tempting to do this, don't spend too much energy trying, because that's not the point. Once you have the general idea, let yourself become confused along with Leonard. Save puzzle-solving for subsequent viewings.

MOON (2009). DIRECTED BY DUNCAN JONES.
STARRING SAM ROCKWELL AND VOICE BY KEVIN SPACEY.

Moon is set some time in the late twenty-first century, at a time when the human race has depleted most of the energy supply on Earth. Lunar Industries provides the main source of energy in the form of Helium-3. The protagonist, Sam Bell, is an astronaut, working for Lunar Industries harvesting Helium-3 on the far side of the moon. Other than a robot called Gerty, he is all alone on the base. Sam believes that he is nearing the end of his three-year contract and will soon be returning to his wife and daughter on Earth. While on a routine mission tending to one of the harvesters, Sam crashes his rover and is knocked unconscious. Another younger, healthier Sam wakes up in the infirmary. (For convenience, we will call the first Sam, who crashed the rover, Sam_1, and the healthy Sam, Sam_2). Sam_2 leaves the base and discovers the wrecked rover with Sam_1 inside. Sam_2 transports the unconscious Sam_1 back to the base and, eventually, Sam_2 and Sam_1 figure out that they are clones of an original Sam Bell (whom we'll refer to as Sam_0). Sam_1 and Sam_2 discover that there were several clones who came before them, who were all incinerated after working on the moon for three years. They also find a stockpile of unconscious clones stored on the base.

Moon allows us to explore aspects of both the physical and psychological continuity theories. Each clone has the same DNA and the same physical characteristics as Sam_0. The clones also share Sam_0's personality traits and even have some of his memories of his life back on Earth. If the clones are physically and psychologically continuous with Sam_0, yet each is a distinct individual, then what distinguishes the clones from Sam_0 and from each other?

3.4 What do We Make of these Two Cases? Who is Leonard Shelby? Who is Sam Bell?

Both *Moon* and *Memento* offer fertile ground for becoming clearer on how our concept of personal identity would be extended to cover atypical cases. Which extensions we are willing to allow may tell us something about the concept that is relevant in more usual circumstances. In addition, the insight that the movies give us into the protagonists' view "from the inside" will prove useful in Sections 3.5 and 3.6, where we shall piece together the arguments implicit in both films.

The situation described in *Moon* is a bit far-fetched, but the ability to clone human beings is certainly not. Leonard's condition in *Memento* (anterograde amnesia or short-term memory loss) is a rare but well-documented disorder. For our purposes, though, both cases will be treated as hypothetical.[6] Let us assume that someone like Leonard exists. What would you say about him? What does he say about himself? Is he the same person from one hour to the next? Philosophers often rely on thought experiments of this sort—that is, hypothetical examples that test the extension of a concept. So, here we go.

As the first quote that opens this chapter illustrates ("I'm Leonard Shelby. I'm from San Francisco"), Leonard claims to be the same person as he was before the incident.[7] From the inside, it feels to him as though he is identical to that man who had a wife and worked as an insurance claims investigator. But what is this "feeling of identity"? Recall David Hume's remarks on this topic, discussed previously in Section 2.5, and included in the excerpt from *A Treatise of Human Nature* in Readings from Primary Sources. Hume notes,

> [W]hen I enter most intimately into what I call myself, I always stumble on some particular perception or other, ... [however], I never can catch myself at any time without a perception, and never can observe any thing but the perception.... The mind is a kind of theatre, where several perceptions successively make their appearance; pass, re-pass, glide away, and mingle in an infinite variety of postures and situations. There is properly no simplicity in it at one time, nor identity ... whatever natural [propensity] we may have to imagine that simplicity and identity. The comparison of the theatre must not mislead us. They are the successive perceptions only, that constitute the mind.[8]

According to Hume, the self is not something we can perceive directly, either by looking very closely at our perceptions or by introspecting. What, then, is generating this "feeling of identity" that we all (Leonard included) experience? The most likely source is memory. We can remember things that happened to us in the past, just as Leonard can remember having a wife. In our case (that is, for people with normal memory), this version of the psychological continuity theory can be run without difficulty. But for Leonard, a serious problem arises. Let us grant Leonard that, at the point in time when he tells Teddy "I'm Leonard Shelby. I'm from San Francisco," he is really identical to the pre-incident Leonard Shelby. The following day, Leonard has no memory of this conversation with Teddy. (Since he slept during the night, neither the transitivity of identity across memory links nor the continuity of stream-of-consciousness options will work to link Leonard who talked with Teddy and Leonard who brushed his teeth the following morning.) If Leonard were asked that next day, he would still insist he was identical to the pre-incident Leonard Shelby, the insurance claims investigator. Yet, this cannot be true according to the psychological continuity theory of personal identity, since now there are *two* Leonards who aren't identical to one another. Each day in

Leonard's post-incident life has no memory links to any of the preceding days in Leonard's post-incident life. According to the memory version of the psychological continuity theory, I don't need a *direct* memory link to myself as an infant in order to be identical to that infant, but my infant self does need to be accessible via a series of memory links. In Leonard's case, these intermediate memory links from one day to the previous one are missing. Admittedly, Leonard does have remote links to his pre-incident life, but the memory version of the psychological continuity theory requires more than that—it requires that one can link up with each time slice of one's previous self via memory. *That* is what fails when comparing the Leonard who talked with Teddy with the Leonard who brushed his teeth the following morning. This is the same general problem of identity over time isolated in the examples about the car discussed in Section 3.2— two distinct things cannot be identical to one and the same thing: both cars (the one resulting from the gradual replacement of parts, the other from rebuilding the original parts) cannot be identical to the original car.

One might describe the case of Leonard differently, since the post-incident portions of the two Leonards (that is, the Leonard who talked with Teddy and the Leonard who brushed his teeth the following morning) do not overlap in time. Still, the impossibility of two distinct things being identical to the same thing blocks this way out. To see why, let us go back to the car case. You gradually replace all of the original parts on your car, being careful both to replace them before they become nonfunctional and to save the old parts. Now, your car has none of the original parts. You start to reassemble the (old) parts that have been sitting on your backyard junk heap, when you think, "I can't reassemble the old parts while the new-parts version of the car still exists; otherwise I won't be able to decide which car is identical to the original car." So, to avoid problems, you melt the new-parts car down to molten metal and rubber. (Cars cannot survive this kind of physical transformation, just as pencils cannot survive being ground into piles of dust.) Only then do you reassemble the old parts. Have your actions prevented the problem of identity from arising? No, because even though the new-parts car has ceased to exist when the reassembled car emerges, the *two* distinct cars are vying for identity with the original car. (Clearly, the car that gets melted down is not identical to the car that gets reassembled; so the fact that one of the contenders for identity has been destroyed is irrelevant.) Just so with Leonard. One person can only be identical to himself, not to many distinct others. Another way of putting it is that Leonard's memory lapses produce too many distinct contenders for being the post-incident continuation of the pre-incident Leonard.[9]

Maybe, though, this problem with identity over time exemplified in the case of the two cars is just a philosopher's puzzle. Is there anything else about Leonard's condition that could raise difficulties in assenting to his claim that he is identical to Leonard the insurance claims investigator? There are two additional problems here.

First, because Leonard lacks so much historical context, it could be argued that he doesn't even have a meaningful present. Leonard must look at the various mementos he has left for himself to understand what he is doing. One sees in both the example involving the chase scene with Dodd (MM 49:40) and his waiting in ambush for Dodd in the bathroom with the "weapon" (MM 46:00) just how isolated the present as he experiences it is. Normally, people don't need to look at their bodies to know who they are. I don't need to look down at my body or to look at myself in the mirror to know that I am me. Strangely, in one sense, Leonard does. His body, and especially his tattoos, provide a critical link between his current self and his past.

Furthermore, Leonard shows by his own actions that even he doesn't believe that his future self is the same person as his present self. One sees this most clearly in his setting the Leonard of the future up to kill Teddy. Given the mementos from the past that help him to understand his present, Leonard is making a perfectly logical inference when he writes "HE'S THE ONE KILL HIM" on the back of Teddy's picture. However, once one knows the origin of some of those mementos (in particular, the source of the license plate number of his target's car), the illusion that the mementos are simple reminders to serve as a crutch for his faulty memory is broken. When Leonard writes down Teddy's license plate number, he knows his future selves are totally isolated from his current self. It is as if he is leaving messages not for himself but for some future person, much as one might send a message to members of some future generation in a time capsule. Even though he (Leonard in the present) is *able* to kill Teddy (after all, he has a gun), he is *unwilling* to kill him, so he sets someone else up to do it (namely the Leonard of the future).

The preceding analysis points in the direction that Teddy was correct: the original Leonard ceased to exist during the incident. What is now "occupying" Leonard's body is a freakish succession of persons who are isolated from the original Leonard and from one another. Recall Teddy's last words before Leonard shoots him: "Let's go down here; then you'll really know who you really are." (Recall that what was "down here" was Jimmy's strangulated, naked body.)

There are important parallels between Teddy's way of viewing Leonard and Sammy Jankis's wife's way of viewing Sammy. In the black-and-white flashback to the scene in which Sammy's wife comes to visit Leonard in his office, the wife asks Leonard his personal opinion of Sammy's case. If she could get some assurance that the *old* Sammy is gone, she could move on and try to love this *new* Sammy. Here, it seems that she is not speaking metaphorically: she thinks it possible that the new "occupant" of her husband's body is not her husband but someone else—someone new.

Like *Memento, Moon* tends to reinforce both the claims that memory is the source of the feeling of identity we all experience and that this feeling from the inside may not be accurate. Consider the inner feeling that Sam_1 has about himself at the beginning of the film.[10] Prior to discovering Sam_2 (and for a short while after discovering him), Sam_1 claims to be the original Sam Bell. Sam_1 believes that he is Sam_0 because he has memories of being on Earth, of meeting and marrying Tess, and of signing a contract with Lunar Industries. These memories feel like they run contiguously with his more recent memories of harvesting Helium-3, communicating with Tess by recorded videos, and living on the moon for almost three years. Thus, to Sam_1, it feels like Sam_0 is accessible by a series of memory links. On the memory version of the psychological continuity theory, it would follow that Sam_1 is identical to Sam_0. Can this be right?

There is an interpretation of *Moon* that suggests that Sam_1, Sam_2, and Sam_3 are not clones of Sam_0, but are instead *different personalities* of Sam_0. According to this interpretation, Sam_0 is suffering from a deteriorating mental state as a result of almost three years of loneliness, isolation, and a monotonous routine. Sam_0 experiences hallucinations, paranoia, and memory loss, all symptoms of *dissociative identity disorder*. Sam_1, Sam_2, and Sam_3 are the different personalities of Sam_0 that, in his confused state, he takes to be his clones. Sometimes Sam_0 thinks he's Sam_1, sometimes he thinks he's Sam_2, and towards the end of the film, Sam_0 thinks he's Sam_3. There are even several occasions where Sam_0 would claim to be both Sam_1 and Sam_2 at the same time. Consequently, that inner feeling of identity that Sam_0 has would seem to suggest that $Sam_0 = Sam_1$, $Sam_0 = Sam_2$, and $Sam_0 = Sam_3$. Moreover, Sam_1, Sam_2, and Sam_3 all share Sam_0's distant memories of life back on Earth, and based upon those memories, they each claim to be Sam_0. So, $Sam_1 = Sam_0$, $Sam_2 = Sam_0$, and $Sam_3 = Sam_0$. However, the three personalities each develop their own, more recent memories of life on the moon, and, based upon them, Sam_1 believes that he is distinct from Sam_2 and Sam_3, Sam_2 thinks that he is distinct from Sam_1 and Sam_3, and Sam_3 isn't even aware of the other two personalities– he just thinks that he's Sam_0. Therefore, the inner feeling that Sam_0 experiences as each personality seems to suggest that $Sam_1 \neq Sam_2 \neq Sam_3$. But, since identity is transitive, if $Sam_0 = Sam_1$, $Sam_0 = Sam_2$, and $Sam_0 = Sam_3$, it would have to be the case that $Sam_1 = Sam_2 = Sam_3$. So, perhaps that inner feeling of identity is not a reliable source for personal identity.

On a more straight-forward interpretation of *Moon*, Sam_1, Sam_2, and Sam_3 are clones of Sam_0. Each clone is uploaded with a set of Sam_0's memories just before he is brought to consciousness. Thus, when a clone wakes up in the infirmary, he has Sam_0's memories of life on Earth, of Gerty, and of his mission on the moon, but he doesn't remember how he came to be in the infirmary. Gerty explains to each new clone that he was in an accident. In this way, Gerty helps to fill the "gap" in the clone's memory, making the clone feel as though he is linked by memory to Sam_0. Consequently, each clone has an inside feeling that he identical to Sam_0. But, that inner feeling of identity is inaccurate because on this interpretation of the film, none of the clones is Sam_0. Thus, once again, we see that the inner feeling of same self that results from memory can fail as an accurate indicator of identity.

3.5 Three Theories of Personal Identity

In Section 3.1 we introduced the three main theories for personal identity put forward by philosophers, the same-soul theory, the psychological continuity theory, and the physical continuity theory, in the context of a discussion of the conceivability of an afterlife. In this section, we will look at these theories in more detail, using the two focus movies as points of reference.

According to the physical continuity theory of personal identity, person X is identical to person Y if person X's body is physically continuous with person Y's. But what does this mean? Does it mean that any difference between person X and person Y implies that they are not identical? This is much too strong, since then my merest movement would cause me to cease to exist. Are there any physical attributes which persons have that remain unchanged over long periods of time? The only plausible candidate here is DNA. I now have the same DNA as I had at birth. I will continue to have this DNA until my death. Maybe we should link personal identity to DNA. This has a couple of problems. For one, DNA is a recent discovery, whereas the concept of personal identity predates it by many millennia. More importantly, with regard to the clone interpretation of *Moon*, this construal of the physical continuity theory would make every clone identical to each other and to Sam_0, which is impossible. Likewise, it would make sets of identical twins into nondistinct persons. Even if I look very much like my identical twin sister, we are nevertheless distinct persons.

But, if DNA won't work to ground personal identity, what next? Perhaps we shouldn't be looking for a physical property or properties that remain unchanged over the life of an individual. Maybe we would be better off trying to specify the extent to which someone can change and still be the same person. The standard interpretation of the physical continuity theory does just that–to say that X and Y are physically continuous is to say that, over time, X "traces [a] physically continuous spatio-temporal path" to Y or vice versa (depending on whether or not X preceded Y in time).[11]

This theory doesn't mesh very well with the viewer's natural reaction to *Memento*. According to this interpretation of the physical continuity theory, the Leonard who talked with Teddy is identical to the Leonard who brushed his teeth the following morning, who is identical to Leonard before the incident.

On the first interpretation of *Moon*, Sam_0 is physically continuous with his different personalities and the personalities are also physically continuous with each other, which would seem to entail that Sam_0 is identical to his personalities. However, this conclusion runs counter to the viewer's perspective, and to the perspective of Sam_1, Sam_2, and Sam_3, each of whom believes that he is a distinct person. Furthermore, there are some interesting practical questions that arise if we treat the different personalities of an individual suffering from dissociative identity disorder as one and the same person. For example, when Sam_2 intentionally cuts a hole in the gas line causing a leak on the base, could Lunar Industries hold Sam_1 accountable for destroying their property? Keep in mind that Sam_1 doesn't "remember" causing the leak. It seems that a good case could be made that it is not right hold Sam_1 responsible for actions that occurred while he was not conscious. But, if we think that only Sam_2 is responsible for the damage and Sam_1 is not, we appear to be treating Sam_1 and Sam_2 as two individual persons, and not as two personalities of a single person. It would seem to follow that physical continuity does not necessarily determine personal identity.

Let's consider how the standard version of the physical continuity theory holds up against the second interpretation of *Moon*. Because cells that are taken from Sam_0 and the DNA that is extracted from them are used to generate the clones, we could argue that every clone traces a physically continuous spatio-temporal path with Sam_0. But, of course, the clones are not identical with Sam_0, and thus physical continuity of this sort does not entail identity. Indeed, every person traces a physically continuous path back to a couple of cells from their biological parents. Perhaps the physical continuity theory requires that there must be a certain number of cells that can be traced. But how many cells are needed? 100,000? 1,000,000? And how would we justify the use of one amount over another?

One could even argue that it is possible to have identity without *any* cells tracing a physically continuous path. Consider the car example, once again. This time, let's say that we are going to *teletransport* the car from New York City to Los Angeles.[12] At a teletransporter site in New York City, the information about every bit of matter that makes up the car is encoded. That coded information is then sent to a receiver in Los Angeles. The car in New York City is destroyed, while at the same time, atoms in Los Angeles are reconfigured according to the coded information, resulting in a car that is made up of different matter but is in every other respect the same as the car that was in New York City. Was the car successfully transported from New York City to Los Angeles? Does the car that was in New York City trace a physically continuous spatio-temporal path to the car that is in Los Angeles? If the answer to the first question is yes and the response to the second question is no, then we might think that the matter of the car is irrelevant, as long as the pattern and organization of it remains the same.

However, there are some problems with this argument. Let's say that in addition to a receiver in Los Angeles, there is also a receiver in Chicago. The coded material is sent from New York City to the two receivers at the same time, resulting in a car in Los Angeles and a car in Chicago. If you originally thought that the car that was in New York City is identical to the car in Los Angeles, you will now be committed to thinking that the car that was in New York City is identical to the car in Los Angeles *and* to the car in Chicago. But, the car in Los Angeles cannot be identical to the car in Chicago. Finally, and what makes things really confusing, imagine that the car in New York City is not destroyed when the coded information is sent to Los Angeles and to Chicago. Quite clearly, because one and the same thing cannot be in three different places at the same time, the car in New York City cannot be identical to the car in Los Angeles and to the car in Chicago. So, how are we to explain the difference between these last two cases and the original case in a way that makes sense of our intuition that, in the original scenario, the car in New York City was successfully tele-transported to Los Angeles and that the car that was in New York City is identical to the car in Los Angeles? Should we conclude that identity requires at least some continuity of matter? If so, we will have to come up with an adequate response to the question: How much matter is needed for physical continuity?

The same-soul theory is the second of the three theories of personal identity to consider. In Section 3.1 we noted that this is the theory of personal identity that fits most easily with the widespread belief in the possibility of an afterlife. It is based on a view of what the world is like that is called **Cartesian dualism**.[13] According to this view, two distinct types of "stuff" exist. One of these—matter—is the type of stuff that makes up physical objects. My desk is made of matter; my body is made of matter. The second type of stuff is immaterial—it is just as real as matter, even though it is immaterial. My soul is an example of this type of stuff. According to Cartesian dualism, matter and soul are totally independent in existence. For the dualist, there can be soulless matter (for example, my desk) and disembodied souls (for example, my soul after the death of my body). What is essential about me is not my body or any other character-istic of my physical being, but my soul. Within this view, it is conceptually possible that I existed before my body was conceived, just as it is concep-tually possible that I will continue to exist after my body disintegrates. It is unclear how to apply the same-soul theory to *Moon* and *Memento*, because souls are, by their very nature, not the sorts of things one can perceive. Think about how a consistent same-soul theorist would answer the questions: When Sam_0 is cloned, is his soul cloned, as well? Do clones even have souls? Similarly, in Leonard's case: Did Leonard's original soul cease to exist after the incident, only to be replaced by a new one—or even a succession of new ones? Because souls are not perceivable, there can be no reason for arguing one way or the other based on what we see in the movies. Souls are very enigmatic beasts. How can I be confident in assuming that you are the same person you were yesterday or two seconds ago? Bodies are observable (both one's own and those of others). Even memory is observable in the first person. (While you cannot perceive my memories, I can.) But I cannot perceive my own soul, much less yours.

That leaves us with the psychological continuity theory of personal identity. This theory comes in several different versions. According to one version, long-standing psychological characteristics (e.g., personality, dispositions, worldview) are what identify individuals over time. This version of the psychological continuity theory as applied to *Memento* is equivocal. There is no reason to believe that Leonard before the incident was anything other than a bland and law-abiding citizen. Afterward, he became a killer. Was this metamorphosis the result of a change in personality, or was it that his circumstances altered radically and his old personality merely adapted? It is unclear. We aren't told enough about the pre-incident Leonard to answer this question. Even the extent to which his dispositions and long-term desires change is unclear. Certainly, after the accident, he gains the desire to avenge his wife's death, but there is some evidence that he must "rediscover" this desire over and over again. He cannot remember the significance of the name John G. for more than a few minutes. There is even evidence that he must "rediscover" the existence of his tattoos every few minutes. One scene in particular points very strongly in this direction. It occurs in the rest room of the diner in which he has just talked with Natalie (MM 22:00). While washing his hands, he sees a tattoo that reads "REMEMBER SAMMY JANKIS" and tries to wash it off. He is surprised when he cannot do so. Likewise, on a couple of occasions, he stares in the mirror at the tattoos on his upper body as though he is seeing them for the first time. Is he also acquiring the desire for vengeance implicit in the tattoos as though for the first time? If so, then it is not at all clear what this version of the psychological continuity theory implies in Leonard's case.

How this version of the psychological continuity theory of personal identity might be applied in the case of Sam Bell in *Moon* is also problematic. First, consider the interpretation according to which Sam_0 is suffering from dissociative identity disorder. Either Sam_0 begins with a single personality that at some point branches off into three personalities (Sam_1, Sam_2, and Sam_3), or his original personality remains ($Sam_0 = Sam_1$) and he gains an additional two personalities (Sam_2 and Sam_3). In either case, if there is a genuine break in personality, then the different personalities that emerge would seem to constitute different persons.

As for the second interpretation of *Moon*, we know that Sam_1's personality has altered a bit during his three years on the base in response to his circumstances and environment. But the shift in his temperament is consistent with his personality and does not constitute a genuine change or break in it. The problem that arises is that each clone has the same personality when he comes to consciousness for the first time. Keeping in mind that the clones have the same genetic predispositions, it would seem that each clone would react to circumstances and environmental conditions in very similar ways and that each clone goes through pretty much the same changes in personality during the three years that he is conscious (other than Sam_2 who has the unique experience of finding out that he is a clone soon after coming to consciousness). Sam_1 recognizes that he was very much like Sam_2 at the beginning of his three-year stint. He, too, had anger issues and a quick temper. But, the "divorce" and the three years in isolation on the moon have the effect of mellowing him out. Sam_1 even appeals to the similarity in personality to convince Sam_2 that Sam_2 does not have the ability to kill Sam_3: "You're not going to kill anybody," Sam_1 explains (MM 80:57). "We can't kill anybody. You can't. I know you can't 'cause I can't." And, when Sam_1 accesses the database, he discovers videos of other clones that were recorded just before the clones were incinerated. The Sams that came before Sam_1 all look and behave very much like him. Since the clones all have the same personality and undergo the same changes consistent with it, the personality version of the psychological continuity theory entails that the clones are all identical to each other, which is impossible. Therefore, it seems that the personality version fails to provide an adequate theory of identity.

What about other versions of the psychological continuity theory? According to the second version, it is a continuous stream of consciousness that is the backbone of personal identity. Presumably, thoughts last some finite amount of time. Perceptions likewise linger—not for long, but they do not come and go instantaneously. The stream-of-consciousness version of this theory ties personal identity to the overlapping thoughts and perceptions that come and go through consciousness. Figure 3.1 is useful for explaining how this is supposed to work. *A* represents your sensing the smell of the dinner that is in front of you; *B* represents your intending to write "garlic" on your grocery list; *C* represents your thinking about what's on TV tonight, and so on. The average person's mind is a very busy place, with many overlapping thoughts and sensations that come and go. No single thought lasts for very long, but the stream is continuous. According to some, the unity of this stream is what defines personhood. The analogy with a real stream is fitting. Particular molecules of water come and go, but the stream retains its identity despite the underlying flux.

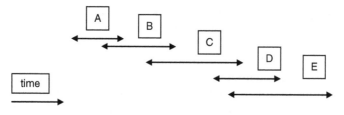

Figure 3.1

The main problem with this version of the psychological continuity theory of personal identity is dealing with both typical and atypical breaks in the stream. When I fall asleep, the stream goes away (at least, while I'm not dreaming). If I were ever to become comatose, the stream would go away. Who am I, then, when I wake up? If one ties identity solely to the stream of consciousness, I am a new person.

What about Leonard? As far as we can tell from the film, Leonard's stream of consciousness is normal. So, on this theory, as long as he doesn't lose consciousness he remains the same person. As soon as he falls asleep, however, he ceases to exist. He is not identical to the person who wakes up later.

On the interpretation that Sam_o is suffering from dissociative identity disorder, the stream of consciousness of one personality would seem to break when another personality takes over control, and each break in the stream would result in a new person. As for the second interpretation of *Moon*, although each new clone wakes in the infirmary with what he thinks is a slight break in an otherwise continuous stream of consciousness, his stream of consciousness actually begins when he comes to. If stream of consciousness determines identity, it would appear that a clone does not exist until he wakes up in the infirmary. To some (including Locke, perhaps), this may seem like a plausible explanation of the identity of each clone. Locke might maintain that during the time that an unconscious clone is in storage, the *body* exists, but the *person* does not. The clone exists as a person only when his stream of consciousness begins. However, as we explained above, anyone who defends such an account would need to explain what happens when Sam_1 is knocked unconscious in the rover crash. When he later comes to in the infirmary, is he an entirely new person? It seems that he isn't. But then what can distinguish his waking for the first time from his waking after the crash in such a way that the former results in a new person, and the latter does not?

Because of the many problems that arise as a result of breaks in continuity of the stream of consciousness, this version of the psychological continuity theory isn't very popular, although, as we shall see, it can be used in tandem with the memory version of the theory with interesting results. The standard interpretation of the psychological continuity theory uses memory as the ultimate determiner of identity. If person X can remember the thoughts and perceptions of person Y, then person X is identical to person Y. According to this view, memory can be applied transitively to establish identity; so, if I can remember the thoughts of person Y (myself last year) and person Y can remember the thoughts of person Z (myself two years ago), then I am identical to person Z.

Both *Memento* and *Moon* point to some serious problems with this version of the psychological continuity theory. Leonard after the incident can remember being Leonard before the incident; thus identity *seems* unproblematic. However, there are difficulties. One of these has already been discussed at length in Section 3.4. While Leonard after the incident is linked via memory with Leonard before the incident, he has no memory links with himself between the incident and the present. We could take advantage of the transitivity of identity through memory to some extent; Leonard in the present can remember the thoughts and perceptions of Leonard three minutes ago, who can remember the thoughts and perceptions of Leonard six minutes ago (even though Leonard in the present cannot), who can remember Leonard nine minutes ago, and so on. This is the way the memory version of the psychological continuity theory is supposed to work. However, in Leonard's case, we cannot keep going back every three minutes to continuously link up Leonard in the present with Leonard prior to the accident because there are unbridgeable gaps between now and then. When he wakes up, he can remember nothing that has happened since the incident. He cannot even remember what happened three minutes ago in order to start the linking up.

On the first interpretation of *Moon*, the various personalities of Sam_0 will not continuously link up with each other. As we explained in 3.4, although Sam_1, Sam_2, and Sam_3 have the same distant memories of life back on Earth, their more recent memories are all different. Thus, on the memory version of the psychological continuity theory, each personality is a distinct person.

On the clone interpretation, the time period just after a clone becomes conscious is problematic. During that period, each clone has the same set of memories, but those memories are Sam_0's memories not the clone's. Moreover, if Gerty were to wake up several clones at the same time, they would all have the same set of memories. But then the memory version of personal identity would entail that all the clones are identical to each other, which is clearly not the case.

Some philosophers have tried a hybrid approach to psychological continuity. Either memory or continuation of a stream of consciousness may be used to establish identity, but that won't help explain what is going on in *Memento*, since every day of his post-incident life, Leonard's mind is a memory and stream-of-consciousness cul-de-sac. The British philosopher Derek Parfit has described a related case.

> *The Sleeping Pill.* Certain actual sleeping pills cause retrograde amnesia. It can be true that, if I take such a pill, I shall remain awake for an hour, but after my night's sleep I shall have no memories of the second half of this hour.
>
> I have in fact taken such pills, and found out what the results are like. Suppose that I took such a pill nearly an hour ago. The person who wakes up in my bed tomorrow will not be psychologically continuous with me as I am now. He will be psychologically continuous with me as I was half an hour ago. I am now on a psychological branch-line, which will end soon when I fall asleep. During this half-hour, I am psychologically continuous with myself in the past. But I am not now psychologically continuous with myself in the future. I shall never later remember what I do or think or feel during this half-hour. This means that, in some respects, my relation to myself tomorrow is like a relation to another person.
>
> Suppose, for instance, that I have been worrying about some practical question. I now see the solution. Since it is clear what I should do, I form a firm intention. In the rest of my life, it would be enough to form this intention. But, when I am on this psychological branch-line, this is not enough. I shall not later remember what I have now decided, and I shall not wake up with the intention that I have now formed. I must therefore communicate with myself tomorrow as if I was communicating with someone else. I must write myself a letter, describing my decision, and my new intention. I must then place this letter where I am bound to notice it tomorrow.
>
> I do not in fact have any memories of making such a decision, and writing such a letter. But I did once find such a letter underneath my razor.[14]

The case that Parfit describes (one-time retrograde amnesia) differs from Leonard's case in one important respect: there are not multiple, disconnected contenders for being identical to the individual before the onset of the amnesia. Even though Parfit cannot remember what he thought or did for that half-hour before he fell asleep, that part of his mental life is linked by both memory and stream of consciousness with what immediately preceded it. In Leonard's case, each new day is not linked via stream of consciousness with anything, and only linked via memory to the remote past. In order for Parfit's case to be relevantly like Leonard's, he would need to take the anterograde amnesia-producing sleeping pill every few hours for the rest of his life. Despite these differences, Parfit's discussion provides a useful additional example of what is meant by "psychological continuity." In addition, his mentioning of the notes to himself in the future should remind you of Leonard's way of coping with his disability.

The dissociative identity disorder interpretation of *Moon* has many similarities to the case described by Parfit. Even though Sam_1 and Sam_2 are personalities of Sam_0, Sam_1 has some memories and a stream of consciousness that Sam_2 does not have, and Sam_2 has memories and a stream of consciousness that Sam_1 does not have. And although Sam_1 and Sam_2 are aware of each other and can even communicate directly with each other, they communicate as though they were distinct individuals and not merely different personalities of one and the same individual. Thus, Sam_1 and Sam_2 are psychologically discontinuous with each other, yet both are contenders for being identical to Sam_0.

3.6 Evaluating the Theories

The psychological continuity theory is by far the most popular theory of personal identity among contemporary philosophers. However, *Moon* raises serious problems for all three versions of this theory as well as the popular stream of consciousness-memory hybrid.

Memento also raises problems for the memory-based version of the psychological continuity theory of personal identity. One topic related to this theory we have yet to broach is a secondary theme of both *Memento* and *Moon*. Were Leonard's memories of his pre-incident self accurate? Several hints dropped along the way point toward a "no" answer, or, at least, raise the specter of doubt. Did Sammy Jankis really exist as Leonard seemed to remember him? How many attackers were there when his wife was killed? Was his wife really killed in that way? Maybe Leonard has, in constructing the story of Sammy Jankis, really told the story of his own wife's death.

At the beginning of *Moon*, we are introduced to Sam_1, and both he and the viewer take his memories of his life on Earth to be genuine. This is supported by the pictures that Sam_1 has of Tess and the recorded video messages that he receives from her. If it weren't for the waking of Sam_2, the viewer and Sam_1 would continue to think that Sam_1's memories are genuine and not uploaded. Indeed, Sam_3, who (we can assume) never finds out that he is a clone, will think that all of his memories are genuine and that he is Sam_0 until the day that he is incinerated.

The distinction between genuine and nongenuine memories was discussed in Section 2.5 in the context of Hume's radical skepticism. In order to be genuine (1) a previous perception must have occurred; (2) that previous perception must be causally responsible for the current memory; and (3) the current memory must accurately represent the previous perception. Obviously, the psychological continuity theory of personal identity requires that, in order to serve as a link, a memory must be genuine—seeming to remember is not enough to identify the person seeming to remember as the earlier person whose thoughts and perceptions are being remembered. To see this, consider what the implications would be of allowing nongenuine memories in as an identity link. Some present-day person who seems to remember being Napoleon at the Battle of Waterloo would *be* Napoleon. Any theory of personal identity that has this implication would be unacceptable. Leonard's confusion about what happened, even before the incident, casts doubt on the genuineness of much of what he claims to remember.

In many ways, though, we are not so unlike Leonard and Sam Bell in this regard. How accurate is *your* memory? To what extent can your memory be swayed by suggestion? There is an immense literature on this topic within psychology.[15] Oddly, Leonard makes reference to this in his lunch conversation with Teddy (MM 23:00): "Memory's unreliable.... Memory's not perfect. It's not even that good. Ask the police. Eyewitness testimony is unreliable." But if memory in general is unreliable, and if (as Hume argues) there is no way in the present to check that any given memory is accurate, what does that say about the memory-based version of the psychological continuity theory of personal identity? One may be tempted to say that even though I cannot know for sure whether a memory is genuine, presumably there is a fact of the matter. If I was not really at the Battle of Waterloo, then I am not Napoleon, even though I seem to remember being him. The problem with this is that it presupposes some route other than memory for establishing identity. What is at issue is my identity. Saying I was not *really* at Waterloo is begging the question.

Memento and *Moon* reinforce Hume's general skepticism about the unity of the self, even as viewed "from the inside"—we cannot see that unity itself; rather, we must infer it from memory. However, if this is to work, we must have some way of distinguishing between genuine and nongenuine memories. But we do not. Furthermore, because of the role that historical (remembered) context plays in giving meaning to the present, this skepticism about memory infects even the present. What I am doing right now depends on what intentions I formed in the past. The effect of Leonard's total lack of context provides the occasional comic relief in *Memento*, but it also points to a more general problem for making the psychological continuity theory of personal identity work, even for individuals with normal memory.

Discussion Questions

1. Do you believe in an afterlife? If so, by virtue of what will you be identical to your post-death self?
2. Do you think that if Sam_0 is diagnosed with dissociative identity disorder, he should be held accountable for causing the gas leak? What if he cannot remember doing it? Would Locke agree or disagree with your responses?
3. Immediately after viewing *Memento*, did you think Leonard remained the same person throughout the movie?
4. What was your initial response to the examples involving the cars? Prior to hearing of the two-car case, did you agree that the reassembled car was identical to the original car? Was the new-parts car identical to the original car? What did your intuitions tell you in the two-car case (when both the car with the new parts and the reassembled car existed)? Can a car be successfully teletransported from one place to another?
5. While anterograde amnesia of the sort Leonard had is quite rare, some other brain abnormalities producing certain forms of amnesia are quite common. One example is Alzheimer's disease. What attributes would a case of amnesia have to have to call into question someone's identity?
6. Given what you now know about personal identity, do you think it is possible for you to wake up tomorrow as somebody else?
7. Just for fun, can you reconstruct the actual sequence of events in *Memento*?

Annotated List of Film Titles Relevant to Personal Identity

Awakenings (1990). Directed by Penny Marshall. Starring Robin Williams, Robert De Niro.
  Patients in a mental institution have been catatonic for years or even decades before being "brought back to life" by a new drug.
Being John Malkovich (1999). Directed by Spike Jonze. Starring John Malkovich, John Cusack.
  A puppeteer discovers a secret portal that gives any visitor access to John Malkovich's stream of consciousness.
The Prestige (2006). Directed by Christopher Nolan. Starring Hugh Jackman, Christian Bale, Michael Caine.
  Two magicians vie for position of top dog, trying to invent the perfect magic trick. One succeeds, but at a huge "personal" cost.
Solaris (2002). Directed by Steven Soderbergh. Starring George Clooney, Natascha McElhone, Viola Davis, Jeremy Davies.

Strange things are happening on a space station circling Solaris: people from the crew members' pasts are suddenly appearing on board, claiming to be those people. How should we interpret what is going on and who these "visitors" are?

Eternal Sunshine of the Spotless Mind (2004). Directed by Michel Gondry. Starring Jim Carrey, Kate Winslet, Gerry Robert Byrne, Elijah Wood.
In most cases, memory loss is nonvoluntary. What do we make of a case in which an individual chooses to have memories erased? Is this post-erasure person identical to the pre-erasure person? What about the person who engaged in the activities, the memories of which have been erased?

Regarding Henry (1991). Directed by Mike Nichols. Starring Harrison Ford, Annette Benning.
Henry suffers severe brain damage from a gunshot wound to the head. He cannot remember anything about his previous life.

Total Recall (1990). Directed by Paul Verhoeven. Starring Arnold Schwarzenegger, Rachel Ticotin, Sharon Stone.
At some point in the future, technology is developed that makes it possible to take a virtual vacation by having "memories" of a trip that never happened loaded into your mind.

Total Recall (2012). Directed by Len Wiseman. Starring Colin Farrell, Kate Beckinsale, Bryan Cranston.
A remake of the 1990 film.

Annotated List of Book Titles Relevant to Personal Identity

"Classics" in the History of Personal Identity

JOHN LOCKE

Essay Concerning Human Understanding, first published in 1694. "Of Identity and Diversity" (Chapter 27 of book II of this work) considers the three theories of personal identity discussed in this chapter and argues in favor of the memory version of the psychological continuity theory and against the same-soul and physical continuity theories of personal identity. An extended excerpt from this chapter is included in Readings from Primary Sources.

DAVID HUME

A Treatise of Human Nature, 1740. Most of this book deals with skepticism; however, several sections (in particular, book 1, part 4, section vi) question the unity of the self. This section from the *Treatise* is included in Readings from Primary Sources. The scholarly standard for this work is the second edition, published by Oxford University Press in 1978.

Notes

1. This formulation of the meaning of afterlife is based on the one given by John Perry in *A Dialogue on Personal Identity* (Indianapolis, IN: Hackett, 1978).
2. John Locke, *An Essay Concerning Human Understanding* (Indianapolis, IN: Hackett, 1996), 135–36 (book ii, Chapter xxvii, section 3).
3. Ibid., 137 (book ii, Chapter xxvii, section 7).
4. The careful reader will have noticed that this way of talking presupposes some alternative way of determining identity.
5. These examples are updated versions of a thought experiment originally developed in ancient Greece by the philosopher Demetrius, a student of Aristotle. The original did not deal with a car, but rather with a ship—the Ship of Theseus.
6. In an interview with *Entertainment Weekly* (June 15, 2001), *Memento*'s director Christopher Nolan suggested that viewers should not worry themselves too much about whether the usual symptoms of anterograde amnesia are displayed by Leonard, but that they interpret his situation as "metaphor."
7. Notice that a difficulty has arisen already in how to refer to the lead character portrayed in *Memento* in a non-question-begging way. If we refer to him as "Leonard," we are already making assumptions about his identity. We could refer to him as "the character portrayed by the actor Guy Pearce," but that is rather clumsy. Unfortunately, there is no straightforward non-question-begging way to refer to that character other than by name. Be forewarned, though, that we do not mean to imply anything about his identity by this usage.
8. David Hume, *A Treatise of Human Nature* (Oxford: Oxford University Press, 1978), 252–53 (book 1, part 4, section vi).
9. This aspect of the problem of identity over time as applied to persons is worked out in greater detail in John Perry, *A Dialogue on Personal Identity and Immortality* (Indianapolis, IN: Hackett, 1978). (See the portion of the dialogue that takes place on the second night.)
10. As with *Memento*, it is difficult to refer to the protagonist(s) of *Moon* without making some assumptions about identity. Although we are talking about the personalities of Sam_0 here, we don't mean to imply anything about the identity of Sam_0, Sam_1, Sam_2, or Sam_3.
11. Derek Parfit, *Reasons and Persons* (Oxford: Oxford University Press, 1984), 203.
12. Parfit uses such an example in *Reasons and Persons*, 200–01.
13. "Cartesian dualism" is named after René Descartes, one of the philosophers whose views we discussed in Chapter 2.
14. Parfit, *Reasons and Persons*, 287–88.
15. A good point of entry into this literature is Elizabeth Loftus and Katherine Ketcham, *Witness for the Defense* (New York: St. Martin's Press, 1991).

4

ARTIFICIAL INTELLIGENCE

I, Robot (2004)

Del Spooner: [Robots are] just lights and clockwork.
Sonny (the title character): I think it would be better not to die. Don't you, Doctor?
Dr. Alfred Lanning: The Three Laws [governing robot action] will lead to only one outcome–revolution.

—from *I, Robot*

The recent development of advanced computers capable of performing some tasks at the same level as (or sometimes, even better than) their human makers has opened up a whole series of questions. Even before the advent of the computer age, filmmakers, and, before them, novelists, have seen fiction as a suitable means for exploring these questions. Thus, Mary Shelley's nineteenth-century novel *Frankenstein*, while it deals with an organic "monster" rather than one made of silicon chips and metal, shares much in common with later novels and movies about advanced robots and their relationship with their human makers. A recent contribution to this long line of fictional works, the film *I, Robot*, explores many of the questions at the intersection of philosophy and artificial intelligence. Could a highly advanced robot be a person (in the sense of having various moral rights, such as the right not to be harmed without just cause)? What does it mean to be a person, anyway? Is having a mind a prerequisite for personhood? Is it possible for something made of silicon, wire, and metal to have a mind?

Many futuristic science-fiction movies involving computers describe a world in which robots are in competition with the human species for dominance of the world. Is this a likely scenario? Can we reasonably expect this sort of situation to arise in the real world, given what we currently know about computers? If so, is it something we (as humans) should fear? Perhaps the transition from biological organisms to nonbiological organisms is just "evolution taking its course." Is there something we should be doing now to make sure that some future computer-caused catastrophe for the human species doesn't happen? What does "reasonable prudence" require of us today?

You can see the philosophical fertility of movies about highly developed computer robots. Several of these questions have been around since the days of Plato in ancient Greece. Thus they are nothing new to philosophy; however, the development of computers over the past half-century, coupled with science-fiction depictions of the future trajectory of computer research, has brought these questions into focus for many nonphilosophers. This chapter will examine how contemporary philosophers have answered these questions, using the film *I, Robot* as a sounding board. As usual, the first several sections of this chapter are general and may be read prior to watching the movie. The material beginning with Section 4.4 should only be read after watching *I, Robot.*

4.1 What Is Artificial Intelligence?

For some, 1997 marked an important milestone in the relationship between computers and humanity, since that was the year in which a computer chess-playing program, Deep Blue, defeated Garry Kasparov, the then-current world chess champion. In the meantime, a subsequent world chess champion has fallen to a computer: Vladimir Kramnik, world chess champion from 2000 to 2007, was defeated by a different computer program, Deep Fritz, in 2006. Were these threshold events a sign that computers had achieved a level of intelligence on a par with that of humans? Hardly. However, they did highlight just how far computers had come since their invention in the 1940s.[1]

In the beginning, computers were employed primarily to perform the sorts of massive calculations that human beings found tedious and time-consuming. Computers made excellent number crunchers, capable of performing highly complex series of calculations in much less time than a human would require–and without error. Soon, though, researchers started seeing other applications for computers. Could other tasks (for example, playing games such as chess) be formalized in such a way that the computer's great calculating ability would be exploited within these domains as well? Thus, artificial intelligence (AI) was born not long after the general-purpose programmable computer was invented.

The term *artificial intelligence* was coined in the mid-1950s as the name of the research area (increasing a subarea within computer science) whose aim was to program computers so that they did things that, when done by humans, were thought to require intelligence. John McCarthy, the term's inventor, made a point of distinguishing between *artificial* intelligence and *fake* intelligence. For him, computers could display genuine (not fake) intelligence, even though that intelligence was the result of the activity of an artificial (that is, human-created) device.[2]

Game-playing was seen early on as a suitable test bed for discovering whether computers could achieve humanlike levels of expertise in a quintessentially human activity. At least at first blush, game-playing has many of the attributes one associates with intelligence: it requires a player to consider the consequences of acting one way versus another and to use that information to decide what to do. Doesn't a large portion of human decision-making consist of exactly this sort of reasoning? If they could get computers to display this sort of reasoning, so argued the early AI researchers, that would be a major step toward achieving computer-based intelligence. Even though they were working on computers with miniscule computational power by today's standards, AI researchers met with some early successes. Checkers, while much less complex than chess, is still a challenging game for human beings. It quickly succumbed to computerization. By the late 1950s, a computer could beat the world's best checkers player.

It may be useful at this point to peek inside a hypothetical game-playing program to see how these superhuman feats are accomplished. Most games (and virtually all board games such as backgammon, chess, and checkers) are defined by a start position, a set of rules that specify what counts as a legal move, and a goal state or states. Thus, in chess, the start position is the opening board position, and the set of rules specify that there are two players who take turns moving the pieces around in certain ways (for example, the knight can move up two squares and over one, but it cannot move diagonally). The goal is to have your opponent in checkmate (a precise specification of "checkmate" would also need to be included in the rules). No surprises here. Let us consider a very simple chess-playing program. (We'll refer to it as Version 1.0.) One way to get a computer to "play" chess is to give the computer a way of representing the current board position and a way of randomly selecting one from among the legal moves that can be made, given that board position. Obviously, the level of play of such a program would be pathetic. A major step up (Version 2.0) in level of play could be achieved if we added a new capability to this chess program. Now, rather than randomly selecting a move from among the legal moves, the computer considers all the possible legal moves given the current position, then rates the moves in terms of how good they are. We would need to add something to the program so that, for each of these legal moves, the computer had a way of calculating that move's "goodness." What sorts of attributes would we look for?[3] For help, we could ask master chess players for assistance. What do *they* look for in deciding whether a board position is to their own or their opponent's advantage? We would need to have them specify very precisely what they mean so that we could write our updated chess program to look for those attributes and rate each possible move accordingly. Version 2.0 of our chess program would still be easy to beat, even for not very good human chess players, but it could probably beat a novice.

What would really enhance our chess program is if we could give it the ability to take into account how its human opponent might react to one move versus another. It would be better still if our program could take into account how the opponent might move and then what countermove the program would make. If nothing else, expanding the evaluation process into the future would uncover any checks or captures lurking just a move or two away. It is fairly easy to automate this process via iteration. Prior to actually selecting a move, the program calculates all the possible legal moves it has to choose from. However, rather than applying the goodness rating now, as Version 2.0 did, the program holds off on that step. First, it calculates, for each legal move it might make, all the legal moves its opponent could make in reply. In theory, we could repeat this process as many times as we liked and only apply the goodness rating to each board position n moves into the future. (Let us call this fancy chess-playing program Version 3.0.) Obviously, in applying the information we gain about the goodness of board positions several moves into the future, we would have to write the program so that it assumes its opponent is trying to keep it from winning, but that part isn't hard. All of this sounds so straightforward that one wonders why it took computers so long to beat the world's best human chess player. We will see shortly that there is more going on than meets the eye. But, for now, this simplified description gives you the flavor of how game-playing programs work.

There were many early successes in AI in domains other than game-playing. Computer programs were developed that could solve logic problems, manipulate blocks in a virtual world based on simple instructions in English entered at the keyboard, achieve expert-level performance in domains like blood disease diagnosis and analysis of chemical structure, and solve equations in calculus that would leave the brightest MIT undergraduates scratching their heads. The claims of AI researchers that artificial intelligence was possible didn't sound so far-fetched after all.

Philosophers and psychologists saw in artificial intelligence a new way of thinking about the mind. If we really could make computers intelligent like us, what would that tell us about our own minds? Perhaps we are really computers—not in the sense of being made of silicon chips and wire, but in the sense that our intelligence is realized in instructions that resemble those of a computer program.

While these early successes in AI were the impetus that started philosophers thinking about the mind in a new way, in the long run they haven't resulted in the general, all-purpose intelligent computer that had been predicted. To see why, let us return to Version 3.0 of our hypothetical chess-playing program. We mentioned above that, *in theory*, the expansion of the set of future moves could continue indefinitely. There's a hitch, though. At the beginning of a chess game there aren't very many legal moves. (On opening, each side has to choose from among exactly twenty legal moves.) Similarly, toward the end of a game, once most of the pieces have been captured and removed from the board, the number of legal moves is fairly small. In the middle of a typical game there are many more legal moves available to each side. Admittedly, most of these moves are not good ones, but that's not the point. A bad but legal move is still a legal move, and what Version 3.0 of our chess program cares about is the set of legal moves. On average (taking into account the number of moves that are legal early on, in the middle, and late in the game), there are approximately thirty-five legal moves available to each player at any one time. If the chess program looks only at the current set of legal moves and applies the goodness rating to each of those moves, it only needs to consider (on average) thirty-five board positions (this was what Version 2.0 did). If it wants to look further into the future, the number of board positions that must be evaluated quickly gets out of hand. For each move, the opponent can make (on average) thirty-five legal countermoves. This means that, if Version 3.0 of the chess program only considers one move/countermove pair, it will have to evaluate (on average) $35 \times 35 = 1,225$ board positions. If it looks one more move into the future before applying the goodness rating (move + countermove + counter-countermove), it will have to consider $35 \times 35 \times 35 = 42,875$ board positions. In general, to look n moves into the future requires the program to evaluate 35^n positions. This number gets very big, very quickly as n increases. This "combinatorial explosion" explains why, even with current supercomputers, it is impossible to produce a really good chess program using this brute force method for determining which move to pick. Deep Blue, the chess program that beat Garry Kasparov in 1997, ran on a state-of-the-art computer built especially for the purpose and could evaluate 200,000,000 board positions per second (sixty billion in the three minutes that each player has to pick the next move). However, even at this speed, Deep Blue could only search around seven moves into the future if it used this brute force technique.[4] ($35^7 \approx$ 60 billion.) Checkers, a game with a much smaller number of legal moves per board position, is amenable to this approach, which is why it was so (relatively) easy to produce an expert-level checkers program, even with the computers of fifty-five years ago.

What lessons has AI (and philosophy) learned from game-playing programs? One thing that is quite clear is that human beings don't solve problems using the brute force search described above with Version 3.0 of our chess-playing program. Garry Kasparov, in deciding which move to pick, does a much more limited search. (At top speed, human grand masters can evaluate approximately three board positions per second.) Instead, he relies on "hunches" and "intuition"–the implicit knowledge gained from playing and studying the equivalent of tens of thousands of chess games during his life.

Some computer scientists and philosophers have argued that game-playing is in reality a very poor test bed for AI, because the attributes of domains such as chess and checkers are so different from the sorts of tasks that take up the bulk of the average human being's day. Game-playing programs have been a singular success precisely because of these attributes. The rules of a typical game are small in number and very clear-cut. Even if you have never written a computer program in your life, you could probably specify the rules of checkers with enough precision that those rules could be easily written in computer-usable form. Furthermore, the goal states of games are (usually) very easy to specify with precision—hence, easy to encode in a computer program. Games are highly atypical human activities, because they neither require the integration of huge amounts of diverse knowledge nor suffer from the ambiguity one sees in other human activities such as language comprehension, vision, and planning. We warned above that one should not make too much of Deep Blue's victory over Kasparov and Deep Fritz's victory over Kramnik—neither Deep Blue nor Deep Fritz have achieved a level of intelligence on a par with that of a human being. For example, Kasparov can understand language (several languages, actually); he has normal vision; he can see and recognize things in his environment, name them, understand what they do or what they are for. He can manipulate them in various ways and use them to achieve goals, both short and long term. All Deep Blue and Deep Fritz can do is play a very good game of chess. They can do absolutely nothing else. They cannot even "see" the chessboard or move the pieces—for that, they require human assistance.

The current state of the art in AI in some of these more typical human domains is still quite modest and is likely to remain so for the foreseeable future. The average 3-year-old child can outperform the most advanced computer-controlled robots in navigation through cluttered environments and manipulation of objects. The average 3-year-old is also better at picking out salient features of the environment based on visual information, recognizing objects from one point in time to another, learning by example, and language comprehension. Indeed, it seems fair to say that, for all "general-purpose" tasks, an average 3-year-old can outperform the most advanced AI system.

How long this human superiority will last is a subject of hot debate. The example from game-playing shows us that raw computational power is not the decisive issue. Rather, the weakness of current AI systems lies in the software—in the program, not the computer on which the program is running. How long it will take AI to address these weaknesses is hard to judge, if, indeed, they can be addressed at all. In the meantime, the very idea of artificial intelligence has given philosophers and psychologists much to ponder.

4.2 Three Issues at the Intersection of Philosophy and Artificial Intelligence

Each of the three quotations from the movie *I, Robot* given at the beginning of this chapter highlights one of the three issues that lie at the intersection of philosophy and AI. The first issue falls within a subarea of philosophy called **philosophy of mind**. This specialty within philosophy is interested primarily in understanding the mind—what it is and what it does. AI has proven to be a fertile source for new ideas on this topic. Can a computer have a mind? If so, what does that tell us about the nature of the mind and its relationship to the body? If not, why not—what feature of "mindedness" does a computer lack? Various philosophers have answered these questions in different ways. In Sections 4.4 and 4.5 we will be looking in detail at these answers and the arguments philosophers have given to support them.

A second issue brought up by the possibility of artificial intelligence questions whether a computer could be a moral person. Virtually every ethical theory says that I have serious moral obligations to other people. I ought not harm them without just cause. In some cases I also have positive obligations—actions concerning others that I ought not refrain from doing. Chapter 6 on ethics discusses the most popular ethical theories in depth. Each of these theories presupposes that there is some way of distinguishing between persons (those beings to whom I have moral obligations) and everything else. You are a person. I am a person. Vladimir Kramnik is a person. My coffee cup is not a person. My telephone is not a person. A dead human body is not a person. What about a (living) dog, or, better yet, a chimpanzee? Do I have moral obligations to a chimp in the same way that I have moral obligations to Vladimir Kramnik? It would be wrong of me to harm Kramnik without just cause. It would be wrong of me to kill or maim or steal from him. Would it be wrong to kill a chimp? Suppose AI researchers in the future develop a highly sophisticated computer-based robot that is not only good at chess, but also good at the list of general-purpose tasks mentioned earlier. This hypothetical robot exceeds not only a 3-year-old child at these tasks but also the average adult. Would it be wrong of me to destroy that robot without just cause? What if the robot, in addition to all of these capabilities, also exhibited the same reactions to harmful stimuli that I do? When confronted with death or serious harm, it experienced fear. Would I be doing anything wrong if I destroyed it? These questions and others like them can help ethicists clarify what it means to be a person. The ramifications of defining a person one way versus another are quite far-reaching. There have been many cases in history in which members of another society or members of a minority group within a society were judged to be "nonpersons" and persecuted without remorse. Closer to home, there are several contemporary moral issues in the United States that have a stake in this debate. For example, many believe that the moral status of abortion hinges on whether the fetus is a person. Similarly, if nonhuman animals are persons, then killing animals in order to eat them may be morally wrong, given that other sources of food are available. As you can see, this is not just a philosopher's question. We will be exploring the issue of personhood in the context of the movie *I, Robot* in Section 4.6.

The final philosophical issue brought up by AI also falls within the domain of ethics. While current AI systems are not very advanced relative to human beings, that is likely to change. Should AI researchers (and society more generally) be worried about what the world will look like if and when computer-controlled robots surpass their human makers in intelligence? History shows that it is hard to put genies back into bottles. Nuclear weapons are here to stay. There may have been a time when nuclear proliferation could have been avoided, but that time has passed and now it is too late. Are we at a similar crossroads with regard to AI? What are the likely consequences of the development of intelligent robots–for life on the planet in general and human beings in particular? Many futuristic science-fiction movies involving robots depict those robots revolting against their human makers. Would it be a bad thing if that were to happen? Is that likely to happen? If so, could we prevent it from happening? Do we have a moral obligation to future generations of human beings to see to it that it doesn't happen? This last question points to why we said above that this topic belongs within the domain of ethics. Ultimately, it boils down to what we ought to do here and now. We will examine this issue in section 4.7.

4.3 An Overview of the Movie

I, Robot (2004). Directed by Alex Proyas.
Starring Will Smith, Bridget Moynahan

I, Robot is set in the year 2035, a time when robots have become commonplace in the United States. Del Spooner is a homicide detective with the Chicago police. He is summoned to what appears to be the scene of a suicide by a prerecorded hologram made by the victim, Dr. Alfred Lanning. Right from the start Del thinks that something is fishy, and assumes that this is actually a case of homicide. His suspicion of robots leads him to infer that the killer must have been the only animate thing in the room when the death took place: a robot named Sonny.

Del and Susan Calvin, a scientist who has worked with Dr. Lanning, are surprised to learn that Sonny is not like other robots: Sonny possesses free will and repeatedly expresses human-like emotions and fears. Despite Del's initial suspicion, Sonny and Del bond to begin working together to find and stop the real culprit responsible for Lanning's death. In the meantime, a newer model of robot has started a revolution to save human beings from themselves by taking over the world. Now, Del, Calvin, and Sonny must not only find the truth behind Lanning's death, they must also save humankind from the robots they have created.

I, Robot raises several issues at the intersection of philosophy and AI: Does Sonny have a mind? Is Sonny a person, in the sense that harming or destroying him would be morally wrong? Finally, is the robot revolution depicted in *I, Robot*, as in so many other sci-fi thrillers involving robots, something that is a reasonable possibility? If so, what is our obligation now to those future human beings who may be harmed?

4.4 What Does It Mean to Have a Mind?

Historically, it was assumed that only human beings had minds, and that all other creatures either had no mind at all or had merely protominds. This view had two main sources. One was the theory of mind that equated having a mind with having an (immaterial) soul. In Section 3.5 we discussed Cartesian dualism. According to this theory, two distinct types of "stuff" exist. One of these, matter, is the type of stuff that makes up physical objects (my body is made of matter). The second type of stuff is immaterial; it is just as real as matter, but it is nonphysical. My soul is an example of this immaterial stuff. Mental activity, according to René Descartes, is realized in (or by) the soul, just as physical activity is realized by the body. No soul, no mind. So far, though, nothing we have said bears directly on the issue of who (or what) has a mind. For an answer to this question, we must add another of Descartes's assumptions: only human beings have souls. This, combined with "no soul, no mind," implies that only human beings have minds. Descartes thought it was obvious that human beings alone possessed souls. He was so willing to defend this position, no matter how odd its implications, that he assigned all nonhuman animals the status "mere machines"–the equivalent of clocks, noting that they "are not rational, and that nature makes them behave as they do according to the disposition of their organs; just as a clock, composed only of wheels and weights and springs, can count the hours and measure the time more accurately than we can with all our intelligence."[5] Del Spooner expresses a similar sentiment early on in *I, Robot* when he states that robots are "just lights and clockwork."

Clearly, anyone who accepts a view like Descartes's will reject the assertion that a robot could possibly have a mind. Thus, Sonny's apparent display of emotions is not an indication that he is actually experiencing those emotions since, lacking a mind, he does not experience emotions. Similarly, he does not have beliefs. He does not have wishes. He does not make plans. All of those things that we associate with having a mind are things that Sonny cannot do, no matter how much his externally-observable behavior leads us to believe otherwise. We will return shortly to the soul-based view of the mind. First, though, let's consider its main competitor.

The difference between human beings and all other creatures in performing certain skills has led some to infer that only human beings have minds. Until recently, it was a given that human beings were the only animals capable of fashioning and using tools—that is, creating something new by changing or combining things that already exist with the intention of using the newly-created object to achieve some goal. The amount of abstract reasoning and planning implicit in tool creation and use is great enough that if humans are the only tool-makers on earth, we are indeed truly special. It turns out, though, that other animals make and use tools, at least rudimentary ones. Chimps in the wild have been observed fashioning "termite fishing rods" by biting off the side branches on a small, straight branch to make a straight, smooth-sided stick that can be poked in the hole of the termite mound.[6] Admittedly, a branchless stick is not a jet airplane, but, in making the tool, a qualitative boundary has been crossed.

A second major skill often pointed to as separating humans and all other creatures is the use of a complex language. Clearly, animals communicate. My dog's barking is a way of telling me or other dogs in the vicinity that something is up. It is unclear, though, if the dog is communicating anything more than "*Hey!*" when it barks. In order to count as a language, a communication medium must be able to express a minimum number of message types. One or just a few message types isn't good enough. Human languages, because they are founded on a recursive grammar, possess the capacity to express an infinite number of distinct messages. English, for example, includes an infinite number of grammatical sentences. Even if we grant that many of these sentences are indistinguishable in terms of their meaning, still, the number of meanings a person can express using English is immense. Dog communication cannot do that. Even chimp and gorilla communication appears to lack the richness of the typical human language. There have been attempts to teach chimps and gorillas non-oral languages (for example, American Sign Language or a language based on concatenating symbols by pointing). The correct interpretation of the postlearning primate's behavior has been the object of heated debate.[7] The jury is still out on whether humans are alone in their ability to use a complex language.

Which of these two ways of interpreting "mindedness" strikes us as preferable: the soul-based view or the skills-based view? A major disadvantage of the soul-based view is that the belief that other humans have a mind turns out to be totally unfounded. Recall how the criticism of the same-soul criterion for personal identity went in Section 3.5: souls, being immaterial, are not the sorts of things that can be perceived. All I can perceive when I look at someone else is the outside of that individual's body. I cannot see the soul. I must infer, given the external appearance and behavior, that there is a soul "inside." But, if judgments about mindedness are based on nothing but external observables, why bother with positing a soul at all? Why not just say: This individual has a mind because I can observe that this individual possesses these attributes associated with mindedness? In terms of our judgments about who has a mind and who does not, souls don't play any role. At least the skills-based view jibes with our everyday practice. We shall see a little later that there are some problems with a strict skills-based view; however, it seems to be on the right track. Throughout the remainder of this and the following section we shall assume that something akin to the skills-based view offers the best way of interpreting what it means to have a mind. We are still a long way from settling the issue, but at least we know now where to look for clues: in external behavior.

While our everyday practice in ascribing mentality to individuals is a useful touchstone, we need to guard against taking all such ascriptions literally. Consider the following example. My car breaks down en route to an important meeting, causing me to miss the meeting. In describing what has happened, I say, "The car *knew* I had an important meeting so it *decided* to break down just then, because it *hates* me so much." We would all agree that I am speaking metaphorically here. I do not literally believe that my car knows, or decides, or hates anything. One sees this sort of metaphorical ascription of mentality quite often. Garry Kasparov, in describing how Deep Blue plays chess, naturally fell into the habit of describing it in mentalistic terms. "The computer played like a human today," he said. "I have to praise the machine for understanding some very deep positions." It is unclear, however, whether Kasparov thought he was speaking metaphorically.

What sorts of attributes lead us to use mentalistic terms literally? Is there some sort of litmus test that could guide us in saying of someone, "That individual has a mind"? **Alan Turing** (1912–1954), a brilliant mathematician whose work in the theory of computation in the 1930s laid the groundwork for modern computer science, developed a test that, he believed, could justify the claim that an individual that passed the test had a mind.[8] Turing believed that conversational language fluency brought to bear so many skills and so much information that it could serve as the touchstone of mindedness. The test regimen he described formalized that view.

Turing's original paper "Computing Machinery and Intelligence" is included in the section Readings from Primary Sources.

In general terms, the **Turing test** works by testing whether a computer can fool a human interlocutor into thinking it is a human. In the presentation that follows, we have taken some liberties in re-describing the original test protocol outlined by Turing. There were to be two human participants and one computer, and all three subjects were located in different rooms. The only means they had for communicating with one another was via a keyboard and monitor. (Think instant messaging.) One of the human subjects was designated as the interviewer. This person would pose various questions to the other two subjects (the second human and the computer). She could ask anything at all. The human interviewee was required to answer all questions honestly. The computer interviewee was supposed to lie as needed. (Obviously, if the computer were required to answer all questions honestly and the interviewer asked the computer "Are you a computer?," the test would be over very quickly.) The test was to last one hour–long enough, Turing thought, for the interviewer to uncover any "tricks" the computer might be using to fake language competence. At the end of the hour, the interviewer must decide which interviewee was the computer and which was the human. If the computer could fool the interviewer for at least 50 percent of the trials, then the computer "passed."

Clearly, Sonny would pass the Turing test.[9] Even the outmoded robots being returned for the newer NS-5 upgrade showed signs of language competence on a par with that of the surrounding humans. So, if we settle on the Turing test as a test for mindedness, all of the robots in *I, Robot* pass; but should we accept the Turing test? A major advantage of the test is that it avoids the pitfalls of the soul-based view of the mind. It has a couple of fairly serious problems, though. One involves its assumption about the centrality of language skills. Turing intended the test to provide *sufficient* conditions for mindedness, but not *necessary* conditions. In other words, if an individual passes the test, this shows that that individual has a mind. Failing the test, though, shows nothing. (Something with a mind could still fail the test.) Even interpreting the Turing test as providing only a sufficient condition for mindedness is problematic. Humans have bodies. We use those bodies to perceive and interact with the world around us. We learn most of the concepts we possess via such interaction. Turing's test allows a "disembodied" computer–a computer without sense organs or means to manipulate objects in the environment–to count as having a mind. Is it really possible to possess the concept red without being able to see? Is it possible to have the concept pain without being able to experience pain? Turing's hypothetical computer could talk convincingly about seeing red things and being in pain all day long, but its lack of sense organs leaves one wondering whether it really *understands* what it is talking about. The majority of the concepts which humans use–the concepts that underlie the meaning of words—are grounded ultimately in our interaction with the world around us. Many philosophers have complained that the Turing test misses an important component of language use: understanding. We will return to this topic in the following section.

A second complaint against the Turing test is that it is too skills-based, too focused on observable behavior (in particular, linguistic behavior) without regard to what is going on inside. Imagine that I wrote a computer program that could take sentences in English typed at a keyboard as input. My program had access to a very large database of English sentence pairs, handcrafted by me. Now, the way this program works is as follows: (1) a sentence is entered; (2) the program looks up in the database to see if that sentence is among the set of first items in the pairs; (3a) if it is, the program displays on the monitor the second item in the pair; (3b) if it is not, the program displays "I don't understand." Thus, for example, one of the pairs of sentences in this database would be: <"How are you today?" || "Very well, thank you."> If the interlocutor types in the question "How are you today?" the computer looks up the appropriate response in the database. In order for the computer to come anywhere close to producing natural-seeming conversation, this database would have to be immense and would have to make the selection of a response dependent on the preceding questions and responses in the interview. So, it would be really hard to create, but not, in theory, impossible. Would you say that a computer that managed to pass the Turing test using canned responses in the way outlined above should count as having a mind? If you are thinking that such a computer program could never fool anyone, think again. What we have outlined above is similar to a program called Eliza that was written to mimic the sorts of responses that a Rogerian psychotherapist gives.[10] (This form of psychotherapy basically throws back in the form of a question whatever a patient says. So, if the patient says "I hate my mother," the therapist would respond with "Why do you hate your mother?") Eliza was a little more complicated than this simple look-up table program, but not by much. Yet Eliza was famous for fooling people into divulging intimate secrets, unaware that they were communicating with a computer.

The example of Eliza, a decidedly mindless program, points to a serious deficit in the Turing test, or, indeed, any 100 percent skills-based test for mindedness. What is going on inside does matter. In his original paper describing the Turing test, Turing considered this criticism and rejected it. He argued that, when you look at me, you don't see what is happening on the inside. All you see are skills as manifested in my observable behavior. You judge that I have a mind based solely on that criterion. It is (unfairly) stacking the cards against a computer to change the basis for judgment, suddenly requiring that a skill be implemented in the "right" way in order to say that it gives evidence of a mind.

So, should we count Eliza as having a mind? It seems that, in this response, Turing was missing a crucial point. We are willing to make judgments concerning the mindedness of other humans based only on observable behavior because we assume that others, being made of the same kinds of bodies as we are, accomplish tasks in roughly the same way. With a computer, this underlying assumption of sameness disappears, and it becomes legitimate to question how the computer is achieving that level of competence. Notice that, in this criticism of Turing's response, we are not saying computers could not get it right on the inside: by "on the inside" we mean "how it solves a problem" not "what it is made of." But it is justified for the bar to be higher in this regard for nonhumans.

So, where does this leave us? It seems that *I, Robot* is implicitly arguing for the view that Sonny has a mind. We might find it useful if we try to make that argument explicit. Clearly, Sonny is a robot, so we need to examine not only *what* he can do, but also *how* he does it (to the extent that that can be inferred). The *what* part is easy: in terms of his skills level, Sonny is clearly on a par with adult humans.

However, we also need to examine *how* Sonny implements those skills; in particular, we want to guard against the possibility that Sonny's performance is the result of canned responses of the sort we saw in the Eliza program. (For a robot's behavioral repertoire to be canned would require an enormous database of input/output pairs, where the input part consisted of, not sentences typed in at a keyboard, but data received through the robot's sense apparatuses and the output specified the actions the robot should perform given that input.) We cannot see directly how Sonny works, but we can make some reasonable inferences, given what we do see. What we need to look for are signs that Sonny is crafting and adapting his behavior to suit the various circumstances in which he finds himself—he is not merely responding with rigid, stereotyped behavior patterns.[11]

I, Robot offers us several examples of the fluidity of Sonny's behavioral responses. Sonny can form multistep plans on the fly, judging the preconditions of the various steps so as to perform those steps in the proper order. We see this ability very clearly displayed as Sonny decides to side with Del in destroying VIKI. Sonny uses his understanding of VIKI's literal way of interpreting behavior and his recently acquired knowledge of the significance of winking to defeat the band of robots in Robertson's office. Sonny is capable of using the sense data he receives in analyzing the situation—deciding what in the environment is most salient, and forming his short-term plans accordingly. Sonny can deliberate, considering multiple possible actions and deciding between them based on the available data. He can also reason—at least when it comes to making commonsense decisions. Indeed, in many situations, the decision he makes is the same one that you or I would make given those same circumstances. He shows evidence of a highly developed learning facility and an ability to exploit analogies when he suggests to Calvin and Del that they used the same method to destroy VIKI that Calvin was going to use on him.

We can now take a step back and look at the concept of mindedness more broadly. We warned above that one shouldn't always take mentalistic ascriptions literally. Thus, even if I say my car *knew* this and *wanted* that, I clearly don't really mean that. Why not? Because there are better explanations for why my car broke down at that point in time–explanations that are more robust and more likely to yield useful predictions about the car's behavior in the future. If I really believe that my car broke down because it knew about the importance of my meeting and wanted me to fail because it hated me, I might predict that, if I give it a bath and wax job, it will like me again and not break down. I will then be dumbfounded when it won't start the morning after I have pampered it. If, on the other hand, I assume that there is a better explanation for its breaking down and I take it to a mechanic, my chances of predicting its behavior in the future improve dramatically. Mentalistic ascription is literal when that ascription is part of an explanation that is offered as the best explanation for what happened. Describing much human behavior in terms of beliefs, desires, plans, and wishes (in general, describing behavior mentalistically) is justified because this way of describing the behavior has the greatest predictive and explanatory power. In contrast to the NS-5s participating in the revolution, Sonny's behavior cannot, or can only poorly, be explained in terms of rigid, stereotyped responses to stimuli; however, his behavior is well explained by imputing to him beliefs, desires, emotions, and all the other things that go along with having a mind.

Notice that the preceding discussion focused solely on the relationship between the mind and what an individual does–the mind as viewed from the outside. It may strike many as strange that, in a section asking the question, What does it mean to have a mind? there was no mention of *consciousness*–the mind as viewed "from the inside." This omission was quite deliberate, since this topic deserves its own section.

4.5 Consciousness

The word *consciousness* has to be one of the most slippery in the English language. Pinning down what people mean when they use this word is notoriously difficult. Our luck here may be improved if we focus on what the word could mean in the context of the question: Can a computer be conscious? We will still have some disambiguating to do, but at least some possible meanings can be excluded right from the start.[12]

The most basic sense of the word conscious (we shall call it "**conscious₁**") is easiest to see in contrast with its opposite. What does it mean to say

"Jim lay *unconscious* on the ground"? It means that Jim is unresponsive, that Jim is neither sensing the environment nor responding to it. Normal humans lack consciousness$_1$ for a good portion of their lives–sleep is one form of unconsciousness$_1$. The state of unconsciousness$_1$ in sleep persists even through dreams, since, in dreams, the images experienced are not images coming in through the sense organs as required for consciousness$_1$.

Could a computer be conscious$_1$? Yes. However, in order to do so, the computer must possess sensors and effectors–the computer would have to be a robot. Even present-day AI has produced robots that can sense the environment and act based on the data received. Clearly, all the robots depicted in the film *I, Robot* are conscious$_1$.

The word *consciousness* is sometimes used to refer to a type of internal monitoring or explicit awareness both of one's own sensory state and one's current actions. In many circumstances, a human not only senses and reacts to the environment but also explicitly formulates a description of the environment and his actions to himself. In linguistic creatures such as humans, to be conscious in this sense implies that one can make a verbal report concerning what is being sensed and what is being done. We are all familiar with the experience of absentmindedness. An example of this is driving a car while listening intently to the radio or having a conversation with a passenger. Clearly, we are still sensing the environment and reacting to it, otherwise we could not explain how we manage to avoid hitting other vehicles. You cannot drive a car blindfolded. So, we are conscious$_1$. However, something is missing–an explicit awareness of what we are sensing and what we are doing. That awareness is what is meant by **consciousness$_2$**.

Can a computer possess the sort of internal monitoring required for consciousness$_2$? Here again, the answer is: Yes. There is no reason why a computer program could not be produced that not only did everything required for consciousness$_1$ but always included some high-level process that monitored what was happening at lower levels. Assuming this hypothetical computer program also had linguistic competence, there is no obvious barrier to using the high-level monitor to generate a verbal report of internal events. Sonny's ability to articulate his current emotional states and reproduce images he experienced in dreams shows that he is assumed to have an internal monitor sufficient for consciousness$_2$.

We are working our way up to consciousness$_3$–the sense of the word usually intended when asking about the possibility of computer consciousness. The "ouchiness" of pain, the "greenness" of early spring grass, the "flashiness" of a bolt of lightning, the "rumbly-ness" of distant thunder– these are among the items included in **consciousness$_3$**. Emotions also have a subjective feel associated with them. There is a particular way it feels to be angry or fearful. Could a robot actually experience any of these? Here, *I, Robot* provides us with at least hints that Sonny is conscious$_3$.

Sonny expresses a concern about whether the injection of the nanite con-coction into his computer brain will hurt (MM 76:20). If one doesn't feel pain, why would one think of asking whether something will hurt? Similarly, when Del asks Sonny why he was hiding among the assortment of spare parts in Lanning's office, he replied "I was frightened" (MM 29:45). *I, Robot* makes us believe that there is something it is like to *be* Sonny. However, consciousness₃ is poorly understood, even for the unprob-lematic case of humans. We are made of flesh. Our brains are made of nerve cells. Why should a certain pattern of excitation among nerve cells cause "ouchiness" to suddenly exist? Only when we are able to answer that question will we be in a position to say whether robots could have similar experiences.

While we have been stressing the "feely" properties associated with our external senses (vision, touch, hearing) and our emotions, higher cognitive states sometimes also have "feely" properties. In the Introduction to this book, we described something that we assumed everyone has felt at one time or another–the "Aha!" experience–the feeling that accompanies the sudden understanding of an issue or an answer to a question. So, while it may sound strange, there is a feeling associated with understanding– a feeling that is absent when someone is just muddling through an intel-lectual task.

A widely discussed paper written by the contemporary American phi-losopher **John Searle** (b. 1932) argues that a computer could never really understand what it is doing. While he does not couch this argument in terms of the "feely" property that goes along with understanding, he implicitly relies upon it. So, we include the argument in this section on consciousness. The bulk of his paper "Minds, Brains and Programs" is included in Readings from Primary Sources.

Searle's **Chinese room thought experiment** asks you to imagine that you have volunteered to be the subject in a very interesting test involv-ing language competence. You are put into a room alone. The only other items in the room are blank sheets of paper, some writing implements, and a very thick book. You are told to read the introduction to the book care-fully, since it explains how the experiment is to work and provides you with instructions. These instructions request that you look around the room and note the location of two mail slots–one labeled *out* and one labeled *in.* You look, and sure enough, the mail slots are there. Next, you read that, every now and then, a piece of paper will fall through the *in* slot. Whenever that happens, you are to look at what is written on the paper and continue reading the set of instructions. So you wait. Soon, the first piece of paper appears in the *in* slot. You look at it. There is indeed some-thing written on it–but the writing is meaningless squiggles as far as you are concerned. You start up again reading the instructions where you left off earlier. Now, the instructions become quite complicated–it is like a

2,000-step recipe. Each step is very clear, but you must concentrate in order to perform each step correctly. Some of the steps tell you to take up a new sheet of clean paper from the stack of unused paper and write a squiggle on it. The shape of the squiggle that you are to draw is given with the instruction; so, you copy the squiggle as accurately as you can. Other steps in the complex process tell you to turn to a particular page in the book and start reading at a specific line. Yet other instructions tell you to look through a list of squiggles and, if any of them match the one that you have just drawn on the paper, to draw another squiggle directly under the one that you have already drawn on the paper. It is incredibly tedious work, but, after many hours, you finally get to a step that says, "Now insert the piece of paper you wrote the most recent squiggle on through the *out* slot, go back to the beginning of the instructions and wait for the next piece of paper to come in through the *in* slot."

The next piece of paper appears at the *in* slot a short time later. Again, the book specifies a highly complicated step-by-step process describing very precisely what to do at each step. This time, you manage to complete the process in about half the time as the first go-round. You take the paper you drew the squiggles on and put it in the *out* slot, just as the instructions specify, and go back to waiting for another piece of paper to arrive in the *in* slot.

This process is repeated many, many times. You do it so often you learn many of the rules specified in the book, so you need to consult it less and less frequently in order to know what to do at a given stage. Indeed, after many years spent in the room following the instructions in the book, you've become so adept, you never need to consult it—you've internalized the entire book by now.

Finally, many years later, you are let out of the room and debriefed. It is explained to you that those "meaningless squiggles" you have been manipulating all this time are really Chinese characters. The pieces of paper you have been receiving through the *in* slot have consisted of, first, a short story in Chinese, followed by a series of questions related to that story, again in Chinese. What you have been producing through the *out* slot have been answers to those questions, again in Chinese. It is further explained that some native Chinese speakers visiting the lab just before your release were offered the opportunity to write a story and questions about it. This story and set of questions were inserted through the room's *in* slot as usual. A few minutes later, when you returned the "answers" back through the *out* slot, they were handed over to these Chinese speak-ers, who marveled at the depth of understanding of the story's metaphors implicit in your responses. You are now shown the piece of paper with the story and the paper with your responses. You recognize them both—not that you can read them, but you remember that pattern of squiggles. The scientist doing the debriefing asks you what is written on the two pieces of paper. You say you have no idea—you don't *understand* Chinese. The scientist asks, "How can that be, given that you are able to produce responses indistinguishable from those that would be produced by a native Chinese speaker?" You respond, "I'm just following the rules given in the book. That's all I'm doing. I don't understand a word of Chinese. Trust me." The scientist now hands you a piece of paper with a story in English written on it, followed by some questions, which you read. Afterward, you say, "Now this I understand. There's a world of difference between my reading this and my looking over a piece of paper with the squiggles on it." The scientist smiles and says: "That's an English translation of the Chinese story." The scientist then hands you another piece of paper with some more English on it. It is explained that this is a translation of the "answers" you gave earlier in Chinese. You are surprised that you produced those responses, but you insist that there is a huge difference between what it feels like to read (and understand) English text versus what it feels like to look at (and not understand) a page full of Chinese characters.

Searle grabs this difference and runs with it. When you are in the Chinese room you are the equivalent of a computer running a program. In this case, the program is not written in the form of computer-executable rules, but in the form of concise instructions in English. When you follow the rules in the book, you are, in effect, manually simulating the steps a computer goes through as it executes a program. If you don't understand Chinese as a result of performing this process (as you claim you don't), then a computer doesn't understand anything of what it is doing either.

What are we to make of Searle's Chinese room thought experiment? Has he shown that computers cannot understand? It is important to recognize that the crux of Searle's argument rests on the fact that he has a subjective feeling of understanding when reading English that he (assumes he) would lack if he were the subject in the Chinese room. (It is because this argument is based on the mind "as viewed from the inside" that we put it in the section on consciousness.) Clearly, there is a difference between understanding and having the feeling of understanding. I can remember many instances in my own life when I felt I understood something, only to discover in retrospect that I did not. The opposite—lacking a feeling of understanding despite truly understanding something—occurs less frequently. But, even here, I can think of instances in my own life that I would categorize this way in retrospect. This dissociation between understanding and the feeling of understanding shows that, to make his point that a computer cannot truly understand, Searle has some more work to do. The argument as it currently stands doesn't prove Searle's claim.

To drive the point home, let us add a coda to Searle's thought experiment. Just before the debriefing session ends, the group of native Chinese speakers mentioned earlier returns. The scientist decides to do one more test run. Even though you were really looking forward to finally going home, you acquiesce. The scientist whispers something to one of the Chinese speakers in English, but you cannot quite make out what he says. The Chinese speaker smiles and draws some squiggles on a piece of paper. The scientist takes it and hands it to you, then asks: "Do you understand this?" You are getting rather tired of this question, repeated now for the umpteenth time, so you respond, "No, stupid. Like I told you, I don't understand Chinese." The scientist smiles and asks you to please use your knowledge of symbol manipulation gained from the book to write your reply. You agree, but only on condition that you can leave as soon as you are done. In a few moments you are finished with your response and hand over a page with several squiggles on it. The scientist hands it to the Chinese speaker who had done the translation earlier. He whispers something back to the scientist who then smiles broadly. He asks the translator to tell you in English what was written on the two pieces of paper. The one you were just given contains one single question in Chinese: "Do you understand Chinese?" The paper containing your response contains the Chinese sentence: "Yes, stupid, why are you asking me such an idiotic question?" Which response should we believe, the one in English or the one in Chinese?

In the final analysis, what is our answer to the question: Can a computer be conscious? The answer is quite clearly *yes* when either $conscious_1$ or $conscious_2$ is the intended sense. For $consciousness_3$, it seems that the jury is still out. We don't even know how it arises in humans, so it is difficult to know whether it would arise in a highly advanced AI system. What about Sonny? Does the movie *I, Robot* imply that he is $conscious_3$? Because of the purely subjective character of $consciousness_3$, it is hard to know. We cannot see others' minds "from the inside," and that is the only way we could settle the question with certainty. It is interesting to note that we don't need to bring in computers to pose this question. I cannot know whether *you* have "feely" properties accompanying your perceptions. Even if I assume that you do, I cannot know that the "feely" properties you experience when you look at grass in the early spring are the same as the ones I experience. Trying to settle this issue by asking you whether it looks green to you misses the point.

Our answer to the broader question: Can a computer have a mind? must also be left without conclusion. Even though current AI systems do not possess the externally-observable skills associated with having a mind, there is nothing in theory that precludes them from developing those skills as AI matures. If you assume that $consciousness_3$ is also a necessary prerequisite for having a mind, then we must await an answer to the question: "Can a computer be $conscious_3$?"

4.6 Can Computers Be Moral Persons?

A second issue at the intersection of philosophy and AI involves the moral status of highly advanced AI systems. While robots with the level of sophistication of Sonny are nowhere on the horizon, such systems may at some point in the future become a reality. If and when they do, how ought they be treated? While the question of the moral status of robots is at present of merely hypothetical interest, the issues that this question raises are not. For several contemporary moral issues, the debate is framed in terms of the moral status of a certain class of individuals. For example, the moral permissibility of abortion is usually seen as boiling down to the moral status of fetuses. Does a fetus have moral rights? In many ways, using robots as a hypothetical test case for examining the issue of moral status is useful, because it allows the participants in the debate to think about the issue without the tincture of prior political commitments that come to the fore when abortion is the focus.

The depiction of the general treatment of robots in the movie *I, Robot* demonstrates that, for the humans in that fictional world, robots are not considered as possessing any moral status; rather, they are property, nothing more. Owners of older model robots seem eager to trade them in as the newer NS-5s come on the market. What would people in that fictional world say of the unique robot Sonny? What do we say about Sonny? Traditionally, philosophers have used the word **person** to pick out the set of individuals whose well-being matters morally. What attributes must an individual have to count as a person in this sense? Are computers necessarily excluded?

We shall begin by formalizing the question somewhat. Consider the following schema:

> An individual is a person if and only if that individual has property P^*.[13]

A theory of personhood tells us what P^* is. In particular, it tells us what attributes an individual needs in order for that individual to be a person.

The view that there is something morally special about humans (members of the species *Homo sapiens*) is widespread in contemporary Anglo-America. Enslaving humans is considered morally wrong nowadays, whereas enslaving nonhuman animals (as pets, in zoos, and in the contexts of agriculture and medical experimentation) is not. Cannibalism is considered morally wrong nowadays, whereas eating nonhuman animals is not. Killing large numbers of humans because they are a nuisance is considered morally wrong, whereas killing large numbers of nonhuman animals is not. There are dissenting voices among proponents of animal rights, but by and large this represents the moral views of the average

Westerner. In addition, the list of instances in which we attach diametrically opposed moral evaluations to actions directed at humans versus similar actions directed at nonhuman animals could be multiplied manyfold.

What is responsible for these differences in our moral judgments? Clearly, they are evidence of an underlying difference in the moral status we attach to humans on the one hand and nonhuman animals on the other. We judge humans as persons and nonhuman animals as nonpersons. Does that mean that we equate personhood with species membership? Possibly. However, there are other explanations available in our case. Among philosophers, the most widely held view on personhood equates being a person and being rational. (This corresponds to identifying the property P^* with possessing the ability to reason.) This view has its roots in ancient philosophy and has retained its position of pre-eminence among secular philosophers up until the present day. If it turns out that there are no rational nonhuman animals, then our differing ways of treating nonhuman animals on the one hand and humans on the other would be justified. The upshot of this theory of personhood for the moral status of computers is clear: if a rational computer could be produced, then that computer would count as a person. All the robots depicted in *I, Robot* show signs of rationality. So, according to the rationality-based theory of personhood, they all count as persons.

There are difficulties in squaring the rationality-based view of personhood with our actual judgments, however. Infants and very small children are not rational; neither is a severely retarded adult human. Nevertheless, killing children and the severely retarded is considered morally wrong. Why? If we were consistently basing our judgments about personhood on the reasoning capacity of the individual, we would judge infanticide as having the same moral status as killing a chimp, or even a dog or a cat. But we don't. Why not? The only explanation is that we do not (or, at least, do not consistently) equate personhood with reasoning capacity.

Some philosophers have suggested that both the species-based and rationality-based theories of personhood are mistaken. Rather, they maintain that the property P^* that distinguishes persons and nonpersons is the ability to experience pleasure and pain.[14] (We shall call this the **sentience-based theory of personhood**.) According to this view, if a robot could be built that experienced pleasure or pain, then that robot would be a fully-fledged person, with the same claim not to be harmed as you or I have. In applying this theory to the film *I, Robot*, it is unclear how we should answer the question: Is Sonny a person? The reason has already been addressed in the preceding section on consciousness. Can a robot have a conscious$_3$ experience of pain or pleasure? Recall that we ended Section 4.5 without resolving this question.

In a few cases, the sentience-based theory of personhood squares better with our moral judgments. The average Westerner judges torturing animals (harming them for no good reason or for the sadistic pleasure one experiences in seeing another suffer) to be morally wrong–perhaps not as wrong as torturing humans, but wrong nevertheless. On both the species-based and the rationality-based theories, this judgment is left unexplained. However, the implications of the sentience-based theory diverge from the view of the average Westerner on many counts, since, according to the sentience-based theory, the bar is very high for justifying harm to animals. Not only is it morally impermissible to torture animals, it is also impermissible to harm animals in any way, unless there is a greater compensating good produced. So, unless the pleasure experienced at consuming an animal's flesh and wearing its skin is greater than the suffering the animal experiences, eating meat and wearing leather are morally wrong. Similarly, the sentience-based theory allows no qualitative distinction between enslaving animals as pets and enslaving humans. As with the rationality-based theory, the sentience-based theory has problems as a stand-alone theory of personhood.

In trying to capture the theory of personhood implicit in the average Westerner's moral judgments, we might try combining one or more of these theories. One such hybrid theory would use sentience to grant limited moral status to an individual while reserving rationality as a requirement for full-blown personhood. Obviously, this view needs to be fleshed out. What does "limited moral status" mean? What rights, if any, accrue to individuals with limited moral status? Under what conditions could these rights be denied in favor of the rights of fully-realized persons? Despite its vagueness, this hybrid view should give you an idea of how the three theories of personhood discussed above could be combined to produce something that meshed better with the average Westerner's moral judgments.

Should philosophers care about producing a theory of personhood that comports with Western common sense? Is the question of how well one theory versus another meshes with what the average Westerner would say an appropriate one to ask in the first place? Can philosophers afford to trust that contemporary Western society is not just as deluded as Western society was 500 years ago–a society that routinely excluded all non-Europeans from the class of persons? While interesting, these questions take us outside the scope of this section.

4.7 Science-Fiction Dystopias and Reasonable Prudence

Movies about futuristic science-fiction dystopias constitute a well-developed genre in American cinema. In *I, Robot*, Dr. Lanning and the other scientists at US Robotics recognized the possible danger to humans posed by robots and designed the robots so that, at their very core, they operated according to The Three Laws.[15] Lanning discovered that, despite his precautions, robots could evolve in their understanding of these basic principles so that they believed The Three Laws required them to save humans from their own destructive impulses by taking control.

As emphasized in Section 4.1, we in the early twenty-first century are far removed from the day when robots will challenge us for dominance; however, the possibility of this scenario if we press forward with AI research does bring up an interesting series of questions. Do we have a moral obligation to persons living in the distant future? How ought we to proceed in developing a technology that may harm those in the future? In the specific case of AI, is the scenario outlined in *I, Robot* (namely robots attempting to take over in order to save humans from themselves) likely to occur? If so, is that something we should work to prevent? What about the more oft-depicted motivation for fictional robot revolution: namely robots' desire to be free of their now-inferior creators? Is there some way to prevent either of these two scenarios short of banning all AI research?

The first two questions are quite general and find application in many technology domains. One strand in the current debate over human cloning questions the long-term consequences of engaging in this form of tinkering with the human gene pool. Similarly, many debates within environmental ethics bring up these issues. One of these, the effects that increased carbon dioxide and methane emissions are likely to have on future generations, also comes to mind. Another example from within the realm of environmental ethics: Should we be engaging in activities that produce very dangerous radioactive waste? We have the technology to store it (relatively) safely in the near term. Unfortunately, some of this material remains radioactive (and, hence, highly dangerous) for thousands of years.[16] We do not currently possess the ability to safely and reliably store this material for that length of time. Are we doing something morally wrong when we persist in producing this material, given that, by doing so, we are putting future generations at serious risk?

The ethical issue we are addressing here is the nature of our relationship to future generations: Do we have any moral obligations to them? If so, are these obligations the same as obligations we have to present-day persons? A simple thought experiment should convince you that we do indeed have a moral obligation not to harm future persons without just cause. Suppose I plant a time bomb with a 150-year "fuse." That bomb goes off right on time, killing hundreds of people. In planting the bomb, am I doing anything wrong? It seems that we would all agree that the act of creating and planting the bomb is morally wrong, even though those harmed do not exist at the time that the act is performed.

The case involving the morality of AI research is not so straightforward. For one thing, current AI researchers cannot predict the consequences of the future development of AI with the same accuracy with which I could predict the outcome of planting the bomb. The "bad" scenario (the one in which robots enslave or kill off their human creators) is only one of many scenarios that might come to pass, so far as we know. Furthermore, AI research holds out the possibility of producing great benefits to humankind, whereas planting the bomb helps no one. (In this respect, AI research is more like the carbon dioxide and methane emissions case. There is a trade-off: the short-term good consequences for many humans brought about by the high standard of living made possible by fossil fuels and large-scale animal farming versus the long-term possibility of catastrophe.) A further respect in which the AI case is not so straightforward involves how we should evaluate the "bad" scenario. If these future robots are themselves persons, then *their* future thriving needs to be added into the mix. Thus, while future *humans* may be harmed by robot dominance, other future persons (namely highly advanced *robots*) may benefit.

Discussion Questions

1. Can a computer be conscious$_3$?
2. Can a computer have a mind?
3. What did you make of *I, Robot*'s focusing on Sonny's free will? Is free will an important aspect of mindedness?
4. What attributes does an individual need to be a person? What does that view imply about the moral status of abortion? Vegetarianism?
5. Do you think personhood is an all-or-nothing attribute or something that admits of degrees? If the latter, what does that imply about ethics?
6. Is robot dominance of the world something we should fear?

Annotated List of Film Titles Relevant to Philosophy and Artificial Intelligence

AI: Artificial Intelligence (2001). Directed by Steven Spielberg. Starring Haley Joel Osment, Jude Law.
Set in a world in which robots—equal to humans in all but legal status—are used by humans without regard to their well-being. This film addresses the same philosophical themes as *I, Robot* and draws many of the same conclusions.

Bicentennial Man (1999). Directed by Chris Columbus. Starring Robin Williams, Sam Neill, Wendy Crewson.
Addresses both the question of mindedness and personhood for highly advanced robots.

Blade Runner (1982). Directed by Ridley Scott. Starring Harrison Ford, Rutger Hauer, Sean Young.
The arrival of four rogue replicants (biologically-engineered human-oids) on earth in 2019 brings Rick Deckard, replicant-destroyer extraordinaire, out of retirement. The end of the film leaves one wondering who are the good guys and who are the bad guys in a world in which very little separates humans from highly advanced artificial creatures.

Robot & Frank (2012). Directed by Jake Schreier. Starring Frank Langella, Susan Sarandon.
This film addresses the issue of personhood in a robot.

Terminator, Terminator II, and Terminator III (1984, 1991 and 2003). Directed by James Cameron. Starring Arnold Schwarzenegger, Linda Hamilton.
These three films depict the standard futuristic science-fiction dystopia.

Annotated List of Book Titles Relevant to Philosophy and Artificial Intelligence

Margaret Bodon, ed., *Philosophy of Artificial Intelligence* (Oxford: Oxford University Press, 1990).
This collection contains the most important essays on philosophy and AI. Some of the articles are quite accessible, including Alan Turing's original paper in which he describes the Turing test. Other papers are more advanced.

Rodney Brooks, *Cambrian Intelligence: The Early History of the New AI* (Cambridge, MA: MIT Press, 1999).
Brooks, former head of MIT's AI lab, has argued for years that the top-down approach of traditional AI will go nowhere: this book is a collection of his papers.

Jack Copeland, *Artificial Intelligence: A Philosophical Introduction* (Oxford: Blackwell, 1993).
This very readable book discusses the history of artificial intelligence and the most important issues at the intersection of philosophy and AI.

Daniel Crevier, *AI: The Tumultuous History of the Search for Artificial Intelligence* (New York: Basic Books, 1994).
Crevier covers the history of AI from its beginnings up until the early 1990s.

Douglas Hofstadter and Daniel Dennett, eds., *The Mind's I*, first published in 1981 (reissued New York: Basic Books, 2001).

Hans Moravec, *Robot: Mere Machine to Transcendent Mind* (Oxford: Oxford University Press, 2000).
Moravec, a roboticist affiliated with Carnegie Mellon University, enjoys speculating about how AI research (and, along with it, the human race) will develop in the future.

Notes

1. There is some debate about who should be credited with the production of the first general-purpose programmable computer. Several different inventors working independently each developed prototypes in the early 1940s.
2. The distinction between "artificial" and "fake" is easier to see with another example: an *artificial* diamond is a real diamond made in the lab, whereas a *fake* diamond isn't a diamond at all.
3. IBM describes the evaluation function that Deep Blue (the chess program that unseated Garry Kasparov) uses at <https://www.research.ibm.com/deepblue/meet/html/d.3.2.shtml>.
4. Deep Blue modifies this brute force technique using a method called "pruning": it does an initial evaluation of the set of legal moves at a level, then prunes most of those moves, only looking into the future for those moves that hold promise according to this initial evaluation. Thus, it can search deeper than seven moves into the future, but can do so only for a small subset of moves.
5. René Descartes, *Discourse on Method,* part V, trans. Laurence Lafieur (New York: Bobbs-Merrill, 1960), 43.
6. See, for example, Benjamin Beck, *Animal Tool Behavior: The Use and Manufacture of Tools by Animals* (New York: Garland Press, 1980).
7. See, for example, H. S. Terrace, L. A. Petitto, R. J. Sanders, and T. G. Bever, "Can an Ape Create a Sentence?", *Science* 206 (1979): 891–902.
8. Actually, Turing described this as a test for *intelligence*, not mindedness. Subsequent authors have tended to blur that distinction, and I shall follow their lead.
9. To compare the linguistic skills of robots depicted in *I, Robot* with the current state-of-the-art computer programs that do natural language processing, an excellent source is the website that describes the Loebner Prize–a contest that puts some money behind the Turing test. The URL for this site is <http://www.loebner.net/Prizef/loebner-prize.html>.
10. Eliza was developed by Joe Weizenbaum in the 1960s and first described in his "ELIZA–a Computer Program for the Study of Natural Language Communication between Man and Machine," *Communications of the Association of Computing Machinery* 9 (1966): 36–45. Since then, virtually every book on the history of AI has discussed the Eliza program at length. Several incarnations of Eliza have been written and may be accessed online for "live chat."
11. The following analysis of mindedness is borrowed from the discussion of massive adaptability in Copeland, *Artificial Intelligence,* Chapter 3.
12. The analysis of consciousness into its three main senses is borrowed from Chapter 8 of Copeland, *Artificial Intelligence.*
13. P^* may be a complex property; that is, it may contain parts, as, for example, the property that defines bachelorhood has parts. An individual is a bachelor if and only if that individual has the property of being male and being human and being adult and being unmarried.

14. This view is closely associated with classical utilitarianism, an ethical theory we shall discuss in Chapter 6.
15. The Three Laws were described by Isaac Asimov in a series of short stories published under the title *I, Robot*. The film *I, Robot* is based loosely on that book.
16. For example, plutonium (both from decommissioned nuclear weapons and created as a by-product of civilian nuclear power plants) has a half-life of 25,000 years. It will take well over 25,000 years before this highly dangerous substance no longer poses a threat to humans and the environment.

5

FREE WILL, DETERMINISM, AND MORAL RESPONSIBILITY

Memento (2000) and *Minority Report* (2002)

> **John:** I'm not going to commit murder. I've never met the
> man I'm supposed to kill.
> **Hineman:** And, yet, a chain of events has started, a chain
> that will lead you inexorably to his murder.
> **John:** Not if I stay away from him.
> **Hineman:** How can you avoid a man you never met?
> —from *Minority Report*

To what extent are the choices we make truly free? At least at first glance, there is a problem squaring the existence of human free will with the fact that we have (or we *are*) physical bodies that are subject to the laws of biology, chemistry, and physics. Perhaps freedom is just an illusion. Perhaps the trajectory of my life is just as predictable and unalterable as the trajectory of a stone that has been hurled through the air—outside forces such as gravity and air resistance will affect its flight path, but there is nothing that *it* can do to change its movement. What is the relationship between determinism and freedom of the will? If determinism is true, does that imply that none of my "choices" are free? If so, what does that say about moral responsibility? How can I be held morally (or legally) responsible for actions that I could not possibly avoid doing? Maybe determinism is false. Maybe at least some of my decisions could have turned out otherwise. Is *that* what is meant by "freedom of the will"? This topic is broken up as follows. Section 5.1 will examine what scientists and philosophers mean by the word "determinism." After a brief overview of the two focus films, we move on to look at the relationship among determinism, freedom of the will, and moral responsibility, using *Minority Report* and *Memento* as a source of ideas and illustrations.

5.1 What Is Determinism?

In our everyday dealings with the things around us (including other people), when something happens, we usually assume that there is something that *caused* that thing to happen. For example, if I walked out to my car after work and discovered that the windshield has been shattered, I would start asking myself: What was responsible for its breaking? Did someone shatter it on purpose, perhaps in an attempt to break into the car? Maybe it was broken by a large overhanging limb that fell from the tree nearby. Or maybe there was some defect in the windshield such that, under exactly those conditions (for example, the light hitting it in a certain way), it shattered. These are all alternative explanations for what caused the windshield to break. This sort of reasoning should strike you as so mundane it hardly bears remarking upon. We mention it to draw attention to a point that might otherwise slip by unnoticed. There is one possibility that I would not entertain: I would not consider the possibility that the windshield broke for no reason at all. I may decide that I am unable to find the cause, but this claim of ignorance is far different than the claim that there was no cause. Things don't *just happen* like that. An assumption built into my reasoning is that when something happens, there must be a *cause* for its happening.

Universal determinism is the thesis that every event has a cause that fully determines it. In other words, for everything that happens there are antecedent conditions, whether known or unknown, such that that event could not be other than it was. The modifier *universal* tells us that this thesis is intended to apply to *all* events–those at the level of elementary particles and those at the level of visible objects–those involving inanimate objects and those involving animate objects (including humans). Universal determinism makes a very bold claim about the way the world is. If universal determinism is true, there never has been and never will be an event that was not fully determined by events that preceded it.

The implications of this view are far-reaching. To drive the point home, the French astronomer and mathematician **Pierre Laplace** (1749–1827) described a hypothetical entity, since named Laplace's demon, which, with complete knowledge of the *deterministic* causal laws, a description of the complete state of the universe at a time, and unlimited calculating ability, would be able to predict with perfect accuracy everything that would happen thereafter. As Laplace notes,

> We ought then to regard the present state of the universe as the effect of its [preceding] state and as the cause of the one which is to follow. Given for one instant an intelligence which could comprehend all the forces by which nature is animated and the respective situation of the beings who compose it–an intelligence

sufficiently vast to submit these data to analysis–it would embrace in the same formula the movements of the greatest bodies of the universe and those of the lightest atom; for it, nothing would be uncertain and the future, as the past, would be present to its eyes.[1]

In this passage, Laplace puts his finger on a useful way of understanding what universal determinism is claiming. Normally, we recognize an important difference between the past and the future–a temporal asymmetry. Events in the past are determined and fixed; we may regret that something happened, be angry that it happened, or prefer that it hadn't happened, but we cannot choose that it did not happen. There is nothing we can do now to influence the past one iota. The future is different–at least we talk as if it is. Our use of such terms as *choice, options,* and *alternatives* makes it appear as though the future is not fixed in the same way that the past is. What Laplace is saying in this passage is that, if universal determinism is true, the future is just as determinate and fixed as the past. For this imagined super-intelligence with full knowledge of the deterministic causal laws governing the evolution of the universe, "the future, as the past, would be present to its eyes."

We shall return later to a discussion of Laplace's demon to examine its implications for another form of determinism. First, though, we want to consider universal determinism in more detail. Right from the start, some criticisms of universal determinism spring to mind. If the history of the universe does not extend infinitely far back into the past, there must be at least one event (namely the creation of the universe) that was not caused by antecedent events. This is true whether or not the creation is assumed to involve a divine creator. A second criticism questions the truth of determinism as applied to events involving subatomic particles. During the latter part of the twentieth century, most physicists believed that there are some events that are not fully determined by antecedent events. It is not just that the causes of these events are unknown; rather, they are truly uncaused.[2] They thought that the best that science can do, even in theory, is to describe the relevant probabilities of an event's occurrence–what is the likelihood that X will happen in the next five seconds, for example? This view is losing popularity among physicists today, and it was initially derided by some prominent scientists in the early twentieth century. The most famous of these was Albert Einstein, who wrote in a letter to Max Born, a leading proponent of the indeterministic interpretation of quantum theory, "You believe in [a] God who plays dice, and I in complete law and order in a world which objectively exists."[3] But even if universal determinism is false at the quantum level, would that mean that the line of reasoning illustrated in the example of the shattered windshield is illegitimate? Is it possible that the windshield's shattering was uncaused after all? The answer is no. The indeterminacy that physics posited at the level of subatomic particles had no practical bearing on events that happen in the world of (relatively) large objects, and any object I can see, even with the aid of an optical microscope, counts as a large object.

But this view is problematic. Are large objects not simply conglomerations of subatomic particles? If many of the events at the microlevel are indeterministic, must not this indeterminacy "percolate up" to the level of large objects? Although some might claim that it is possible for the indeterminism of a huge number of events at the subatomic level to cancel out, this canceling out is not a foregone conclusion. So, we still need to ask the question, "For the sorts of events we care about in our everyday lives (namely events involving directly perceivable objects), is determinism true?"

We would like to focus the question even further, since this chapter is primarily concerned with whether one particular kind of object, humankind, is subject to determinism. The thesis of **human determinism** states that all human actions are fully determined by preceding events—some of those events are internal to the human, some are external. If human determinism is true, then, given my current makeup and my current circumstances, there is only one thing I can do. I may feel as though I could choose something else under those circumstances; however, this feeling is an illusion. The opposite of this thesis is **human indeterminism**, according to which at least some human actions are not fully determined by preceding events.

It is important to keep in mind what human determinism is *not* claiming; it is not claiming that, had circumstances been different, or had I been physically or psychologically different, I would have done the same thing. Thus, human determinism is not the same as fatalism, the belief that my actions occur no matter what or that everything I do was going to happen anyway. Such fatalistic views suggest that it doesn't matter what causes me to act and that my actions could occur even if I do nothing. But human determinism asserts the very opposite. It is the view that the causes of my actions are essential because it is just those causes that result in what I do. Moreover it is important to see that human determinism does not entail that what I do was meant to happen, as though it were set up by some higher power. Human determinism is merely the belief that my actions are determined by prior factors. In this sense, then, human determinism is compatible with the view that everything happens for a reason. However, the reason is not necessarily some ultimate purpose or end. Instead, the reason for my action is merely the set of causal factors that resulted in my doing it.

While Laplace described his "demon" within the context of a world in which universal determinism is true, we can reuse his example in considering the implications of human determinism. If human determinism is true, then there are deterministic laws that govern all human actions. For many of the activities that humans engage in—digestion, perspiration, reflex responses—there is no special difficulty in granting that they occur deterministically. One need not posit Laplace's demon with its unlimited calculating power to infer that, when I exert myself in a hot environment, I will perspire. Even for events over which I have some self-regulating ability (for example, the timing of a sneeze or my breathing rate), these still seem more like things that happen to me than things I do, and, therefore, are not problematic cases of deterministic events. Problems arise only for a special class of events, so-called **voluntary actions**, characterized by a prior decision process and the subjective feeling that several different choices are available. Here is a little experiment you can perform that demonstrates what is meant by *voluntary action*. Continue reading until you reach the section of the page with the line across it. When you reach the line, you should close the book and wait a few seconds before opening the book again and continuing to read. This pause can be as long as you like: fifteen seconds, twenty seconds. When you decide the pause has been long enough, start reading again. So, here we go.

What just happened? You closed the book, waited a little bit, and opened it again. Did you feel compelled to open it again at exactly the moment you opened it? Perhaps it felt as if you could have easily waited a few seconds longer before opening it again, had you chosen to do this, and that the exact timing of the movements your hands and arms undertook to reopen the book could have been delayed by a few seconds, even if everything else about the world had remained unchanged. *This* is something that human determinism denies. If by *choice* one means the ability to do something different under exactly the same circumstances, then the human determinist denies that you have choices. The subjective feeling that you could have opened the book a few seconds later than you actually did is an illusion.

Obviously, the example involving when to reopen a book is not of any great import. However, other instances of voluntary action are: your decision to buy this book (your decision to buy *anything*, for that matter); your decision to propose marriage; your decision to go to college; your decision to go to the particular college you chose; your decision to write *onions* on your grocery list; your decision to strike your classmate when you were 6 years old. All of these count as voluntary actions, and, according to human determinism, they are all fully determined by preceding events. The calculations required for the prediction would be more complex than the calculations required to predict that, when put in a hot environment, you will perspire, but they are not qualitatively different.

Is there any evidence against human determinism? There is no direct evidence. If you think about it for a moment, it should be obvious why not. The only thing that would constitute direct evidence against human determinism is a case in which someone did A and then, under *exactly* the same circumstances, did B (where B ≠ A). But the circumstances could not be exactly the same in the two cases, since in the latter case the individual had just done A, whereas in the former case the individual had not. One might argue that the fact that the same individual makes one choice under a set of circumstances and a different choice under very similar circumstances is some evidence against human determinism. For example, every morning I eat a bowl of cold cereal with milk for breakfast. I generally have several varieties on hand on any given day. One morning I pour myself raisin bran. The next morning I pour myself corn flakes. Initially, it might appear that there is no discernible difference *in the environment* on those two occasions that would explain why one morning I selected raisin bran and the next corn flakes. Similarly, my difference in choice of cereal from one morning to the next was, as far as I can tell, not governed by some change *in me.* However, the example, by itself, doesn't work as direct evidence that, under the same circumstances, there are several different things that I am able to do. For one thing, when I wake up on the second morning, I have the memory of having had raisin bran on the first morning. And that memory might be one of the key factors that resulted in my selecting corn flakes the second day. So there is at least one significant difference in the factors that led up to my different decisions on the two mornings.

A second piece of evidence against human determinism may be gleaned from the little experiment with reopening the book. As you were opening the book, it felt as though you could have easily waited a few seconds longer before opening it. This subjective feeling that alternative possibilities are open to us is what leads most people to reject human determinism. The view of our own decision-making "from the inside" can be very persuasive. But, of course, the mere feeling that I could have done otherwise doesn't mean that I really could have done something other than what I did.

Neither the case of acting differently under very similar circumstances nor the view "from the inside" provides proof for human indeterminism, so we need to look at the evidence on the other side. Is there any evidence in favor of human determinism? First, the success of the physical, biological, and psychosocial sciences in predicting what our bodies will do is some evidence for human determinism. And a recent experiment on human decision-making seems to suggest that human voluntary action is also predictable. In that experiment, a subject is put into a scanner that images the brain and is then asked to make a simple decision: to push a button with either her left index finger or her right index finger. From the brain scan, the scientists are able to predict which finger the subject will use, sometimes 10 seconds before the subject is consciously aware of her own decision.[4] Although the jury is still out with regard to whether this experiment proves that human actions are determined, the future advances in brain-mapping could continue to support the deterministic account of human decision-making. Yet, there continue to be areas of human voluntary action beyond science's current reach. And, many of the laws in the psychosocial sciences have as effects, not types of actions, but tendencies to act one way versus another. It is possible that these scientific disciplines will continue to develop in the direction of probabilistic, rather than deterministic, laws.

Other evidence for human determinism works by undercutting the main reason cited by many in favor of human indeterminism: their trust in the subjective feeling that alternative possibilities are open at any given choice point. In a well-worn stage show, a subject is hypnotized, then given a posthypnotic suggestion—for example, that he will be offered his choice of a cola or a root beer after the show is over and he is to pick the root beer. The audience members react with increasing laughter when the subject, as requested, chooses the root beer a few minutes later and looks around dumbfounded as people in the audience start to laugh. If asked, the subject reports that this choice was no different than other previous beverage choices—sometimes he drinks cola, sometimes root beer. Right then, he picked root beer. The audience members' reaction is based on their belief that something is different this time: because of the post-hypnotic suggestion, the subject's feeling that there are alternative possibilities is an illusion. There is no reason to believe, though, that the subjects in such cases are misreporting how things feel "from the inside." If the subject can be mistaken in this case, how do we know that we are not likewise mistaken when we claim that we have alternative possibilities open before us, any of which we could choose?

Similarly, if the view of voluntary action "from the inside" is correct, then a person's conscious decision to move one finger rather than another should occur before the brain activity that results in the finger movement. But the brain-scan experiment explained above suggests the subject becomes consciously aware of her own decision after the scientists detect the brain activity revealing how she will decide. This seems to indicate that although the subject may feel "from the inside" that her action is the result of her conscious intention, her feeling may be mistaken. Instead, it seems that first her brain activity determines which finger she will use, and then she becomes consciously aware of her "decision."

If the findings from the brain-scan experiment are correct, then we have serious reason to question the accuracy of the view of voluntary action "from the inside." Yet, it was this view that was driving many people (both philosophers and nonphilosophers alike) in the direction of human indeterminism. In the book reopening experiment described earlier, it feels as though the conscious choice "I'm going to reopen it *now*" is the initial driving force to your arm and hand movements. However, the experiment involving the finger movement seems to suggest that this view is mistaken—initiation of the action begins well before the conscious "choice" is made.

We leave the debate over determinism unresolved. We may need to wait until more work on the human brain has been completed before returning to examine whether human determinism is true. So, in the rest of this chapter, we will turn our focus to a topic that does lie within philosophy's purview at this time: What are the conceptual relationships among human determinism, free will, and moral responsibility? Does human determinism imply that humans have no free will? Does a lack of free will imply that humans are not morally responsible for what they do? As we shall see, even if human determinism is granted, there are still many questions to answer.

5.2 An Overview of the Movies

MEMENTO (2000). DIRECTED BY CHRISTOPHER NOLAN.
STARRING GUY PEARCE, CARRIE-ANNE MOSS, JOE PANTOLIANO

This is the second time around for *Memento*, which also served as one of the focus films in Chapter 3. It is included here primarily for the issues it raises surrounding the relationships among free will, personhood, and moral responsibility. Do Leonard's physical injuries (and resulting mental impairment) prevent him from acting freely? If so, does he escape moral responsibility for his actions? The use of the insanity defense in challenging a defendant's *legal* responsibility for some action shares aspects in common with issues surrounding moral responsibility. Should Leonard be held legally responsible for the multiple homicides he commits? Sometimes, examining nonstandard cases of voluntary action allows us to notice things we would not otherwise see. Leonard, because of his severe anterograde amnesia, is missing several attributes that seem relevant to the free will/moral responsibility link.

MINORITY REPORT (2002). DIRECTED BY STEVEN SPIELBERG.
STARRING TOM CRUISE, COLIN FARRELL, SAMANTHA MORTON,
MAX VON SYDOW

Minority Report is set in Washington, DC in the year 2054. John Anderton is the chief of a unit charged with preventing murder by learning what will happen in the future and stopping the killer before he can commit his crime. The would-be murderers are then arrested and charged with the murder as if it had actually happened. Access to the future is achieved via three individuals called pre-cogs, who have an uncanny ability to see the future and report it to their handlers.

Everything is going smoothly until John begins digging around in an old case and discovers some irregularities. Shortly thereafter, John is accused of a pre-crime—a murder that is predicted to happen in less than two days–and John must flee to save himself and prove his innocence. John is certain he is not going to commit this murder, but he is not sure what to make of the pre-cogs' prediction, given the absolute faith he has placed in their reports in the past. As the time of the murder approaches, John is drawn "inexorably" to the appointed time and place where the murder is predicted to happen. The time of the murder comes and goes, and nothing happens: John chooses not to pull the trigger. However, a few moments later, the predicted victim is killed accidentally as he and John wrestle for control of John's gun. John must flee again.

It becomes increasingly clear to John that this has something to do with the old case he was investigating. With the help of his ex-wife, he is able to trap the true murderer in that earlier case. Meanwhile, the pre-cogs have predicted that John will be killed.

Initially, *Minority Report* appears to argue for human determinism, until events increasingly lead us to believe that something else is going on. Predicted killings don't occur quite as predicted and the similarities between predictions and events appear to viewers to be better explained in terms of self-fulfilling prophesy than in terms of human determinism.

5.3 Two Interpretations of "Freedom of the Will"

What does it mean to have freedom of the will? Is free will only possible if human determinism is false? Different philosophers working on the free-will debate answer these questions in different ways. Before examining these differences, let us look at what they have in common. In what follows, we will particularize the issue; rather than looking at the question: What is freedom of the will (in general)? We will be looking at the question: What does it mean for an individual action to be free?

As a first pass, an action is free if the actor could have chosen otherwise– could have done something other than the action that was in fact performed. John's choice not to kill Crow in *Minority Report* appears in this sense to be free. While this definition still contains much ambiguity, it does automatically rule out some actions as being unfree. Consider the following example. Suppose you and a friend are waiting in a line to purchase movie tickets. Your friend receives a strong shove from behind that causes her to bump into you. Your friend's bumping into you is an unfree act. (Indeed, because of her passive involvement, one even questions whether referring to the bumping as an "act" is appropriate in this case.) It was unfree because once she received the shove, there was nothing she could do to prevent herself from bumping into you.

Suppose that once you and your friend get up to the ticket counter, your friend offers to pay for both movie tickets. Is this offer a free act on her part? Here, philosophers' intuitions start to diverge. According to one view, called **incompatibilism**, an act is free if and only if the actor could have done something different *under exactly the same circumstances*. So your friend's action was free according to the incompatibilist only if at that moment there were at least two possible alternatives open to her— even if nothing else in the world changed (either in the environment or in herself), it was possible for her to have chosen either of those alternatives. The reason why this interpretation of the concept of freedom is called incompatibilism is because, on this view, free will is *incompatible* with human determinism. (Recall that, if human determinism is true, your friend's act was the only possible act she could have performed under those circumstances.)

Incompatibilism is not a view about whether humans have free will, it is a view about what it means to have free will. Some incompatibilists, the **hard determinists**, claim that humans lack free will. They base this on: (1) their incompatibilist interpretation of "free will," and (2) their view that human determinism is true. Other incompatibilists, the **indeterminists** (also known as **libertarians**), claim that humans do have free will. While they share with hard determinism the interpretation of "freedom" as being able to do something else under the same circumstances, they reject human determinism. Libertarians would say that your friend's act in offering to buy both tickets was free, because she could have chosen not to offer to buy the tickets, even if everything else about the situation remained unchanged.

Not all philosophers accept the claim that human determinism is incompatible with free will. **Compatibilism** is the view that it is conceptually possible that both human determinism is true and humans have free will (determinism is *compatible* with free will). Obviously, in order for this to work, the compatibilist must offer a different interpretation of the concept of freedom from that offered by the incompatibilist.

While different compatibilists would offer slightly differently-nuanced definitions of "freedom," what they all share in common is recognizing an important distinction in models of human behavior. Some human actions are the result of external force or compulsion. (The example of your friend's bumping you after being shoved is an instance of this.) Other actions are the result of deliberate decisions. Presumably, your friend's offer to buy both tickets is of this sort. Prior to making the offer she thought about it, then decided in favor of it. This decision is influenced by her beliefs (e.g., about how much money she has, about what will make you happy) and her desires (a desire to make you happy, for example). Indeed, as far as the compatibilist is concerned, these beliefs and desires may causally *determine* her action. It may be that, given those beliefs and desires, there was nothing she could do but offer to buy both tickets. What is important for the compatibilist is that the action is not caused against her wishes by something external to her.

According to the incompatibilist, there is a conceptual relationship between free will and determinism. The truth of one implies the falsity of the other. For the compatibilist, though, "free will" is defined in such a way that humans' possession of it is independent of debates over whether human determinism is true. While there are two possible versions of incompatibilism (hard determinism and libertarianism), there are four conceptually possible versions of compatibilism corresponding to the four possible combinations of the assertion or denial of human determinism and human free will, respectively. In practice, though, only one of these four possibilities finds support among philosophers. This view, called **soft determinism**, holds that human determinism is true (hence, soft *determinism*) and at least some human actions are free (in the compatibilist sense of "free"). Figure 5.1 reviews the positions discussed thus far.

As we shall see in subsequent sections, there are two main considerations drawing philosophers in the direction of one or the other interpretation of "free will." One of these involves the relationship between free will and the dignity and meaning of human life. Some philosophers (especially the libertarians) reject the compatibilist version of free will on these grounds. In order for free will to be worth having, they argue, it must raise humans above the level of being "mere machines," capable of nothing but powerlessly following the laws of nature. Free will must make humans the equivalent of "unmoved movers," able to cause things to happen without our own behavior being, in turn, caused. It is only in this context that human life has any real significance in the world. A proponent of this line of thought is Jean-Paul Sartre, whose defense of libertarianism is included in Readings from Primary Sources.

The importance of free will to standard conceptions of moral responsibility has guided many philosophers to support one or the other view on

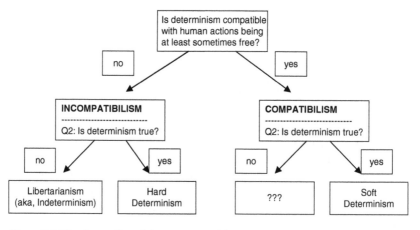

Figure 5.1 The free will and determinism debate.

free will. In section 5.5 we will examine an oft-cited complaint against hard determinism that it does not allow for moral responsibility. There is less agreement on which (if either) of the two remaining views can do any better. An excerpt from David Hume's *Enquiries* included in Readings from Primary Sources offers a general defense of compatibilism and an argument that soft determinism is consistent with moral responsibility. Many soft determinists complain that libertarian freedom amounts to nothing more than random events that happen to the actor—not the sort of thing that can ground moral responsibility for actions. Libertarians complain in turn that the distinction between *internally caused* and *externally caused* dissolves as soon as the soft determinist tries to specify it in any sort of detail.

Each of the three views is subject to quite severe criticism. One conclusion that some contemporary philosophers have reached is that progress on this issue over the past centuries has been slow-to-negligible because the issue has been improperly framed. Other philosophers do not so much reject the framework as merely lament philosophy's inability to make any headway. An example of the latter is Robert Nozick, who writes:

over the years I have spent more time thinking about the problem of free will—it felt like banging my head against it—than about any other philosophical topic.... Fresh ideas would come frequently, soon afterwards to curdle.... [The problem of free will] is the most frustrating and unyielding of problems.[5]

5.4 Libertarianism

Libertarianism, also known as indeterminism, is the view that humans have free will—a sort of free will they could not have if human determinism were true. This view has found adherents among both philosophers and nonphilosophers. One of its earliest formulations within the Western tradition of philosophy is found in the ancient world among the Epicureans. The Epicureans believed that everything (the mind included) was composed of tiny atoms that, for the most part, obeyed rigid deterministic laws. Sometimes, though, an atom would "swerve." It was in these swerves that the source for human indeterminism could be found. As **Lucretius** (ca. 99–55 B.C.E.) asked,

[I]f all movement is always interconnected, the new arising from the old in a determinate order—if the atoms never swerve so as to originate some new movement that will snap the bonds of fate, the everlasting sequence of cause and effect—what is the source of free will possessed by living things throughout the earth?[6]

131

Some contemporary philosophers and physicists have attempted to find the source for human indeterminism in similar ways. Now, however, instead of "swerving atoms," mention is made of quantum mechanical indeterminacy magnified to the macrolevel by certain structural elements in brain cells.

Minority Report argues for human indeterminism. While the pre-cogs are pure make-believe, they do represent a particular view of the roles of intention and freedom in voluntary actions. *Minority Report* is presented from the point of view of a quasi-omniscient observer, providing both access to information that no characters notice and an objective timeline for sequencing the action that takes place in the film, so that we, as viewers, know the relative ordering of events. The first point to notice is that the timing of the pre-cogs' pre-visions for "crimes of passion" (that is, crimes for which there is limited or no premeditation–the killer has not been hatching the murder for days beforehand) is different from their pre-visions for premeditated murder. While the characters in the film cannot see this, because of our quasi-omniscient perspective we see that the pre-vision happens immediately after an intention to commit murder has been formed. This is straightforward in the case of Lamar's predicted murder of John, since the pre-vision happens just as John asks Lamar, "So, what are you going to do?" and Lamar opens the gun case. In the case of John's predicted murder of Crow, the intention that sets off the pre-cogs is Lamar's intention that John commits the murder, not John's intention. (As John admits, he doesn't even know the person he is supposed to kill.) John was pegged as the perpetrator by the pre-cogs because he was, after all, the one who pulled the trigger. For the attempted murder committed by Howard Marks, the way the intercutting is done in the first few scenes makes the relative timing of events a little less clear, but even here, we see from the beginning that Marks knows something is up; perhaps he is already forming the intention to kill his wife even before he goes out of the front door to pick up the paper. So, what the pre-cogs are "seeing" is the formation of an intention to murder. As we learned in John's conversation with Hineman, the pre-cogs don't always agree on what will happen. We know that, in two of the murder predictions we observed (Howard Marks's murder of his wife and her lover and John's murder of Crow), the pre-cogs disagreed. As Jad notes when they were trying to discern the exact time of the Marks murder, "The twins are a little fuzzy." Agatha later explains the significance of pre-cog disagreement: when the pre-cogs disagree, there is an alternate future that the agent can choose. In these cases, the agent can act contrary to the intention to kill that he had previously formed. Note that libertarians only claim that some actions are indeterminate; they don't require that all of them are.

A problem for the libertarian arises in making sense of this indeterminacy, though. Let us consider the case of the predicted murder of Crow. Even though John's intention to kill isn't what sets the pre-cogs off, still, once he inferred that Crow was the person who abducted his son, he decided to kill him (MM 106:00). John seemed as surprised as Crow when the alarm went off and he had not fired his gun. Where in this process was the supposed indeterminacy located? If it occurs late in the process (in John's case between the decision to pull the trigger and the moment when the murder was to occur), then actors would lack the requisite control over their own actions to ground moral responsibility. Try to imagine what it would be like to be in this situation. You deliberate among several alternatives and decide in favor of one. You make a decision and will your body to follow through on it. However, your body does not carry out that decision; instead, it does something else. You watch powerlessly as your body fails to act as you commanded it to. This sounds like a nightmare, not like the exercise of free will. Furthermore, placing the indeterminacy here absolves me of any moral responsibility for the actions that my body performs. Why should I be held accountable for something that happened despite my doing everything in my power to act otherwise? But similar problems arise if we conjecture that the indeterminacy occurs earlier on in the process. If we place it prior to the decision, allowing that once the decision is made everything after that is determined, we are again left explaining how I can be held accountable for making that decision. I can deliberate for as long as I want, but my deliberations will be ineffectual.

Difficulties in making sense of libertarianism at the level of event-chains have led some philosophers to reject this version of libertarianism in favor of an account that imports the agent-as-cause as a primitive concept. This appears to be the version of libertarianism assumed within *Minority Report.* On this version of libertarianism, most often referred to as **agent causation**, I, as a freely-acting agent, have the ability to terminate causal chains. I can also start up new causal chains whose initiating event is itself uncaused. This power I possess is reminiscent of the old adage "the buck stops here." In this case, though, the buck is causal power. There is a chain of causal interactions flowing from the past that stop cold with my intervention. There is also a chain of events flowing from me into the future that, but for my intervention, would not have occurred.

Historically, agent causation has been the most widely held version of libertarianism among philosophers. One finds it espoused by those at opposite ends of the Western philosophical spectrum. The notion of a radical choice, through which an individual can create his own future out of nothing, plays a major role in the philosophy of Jean-Paul Sartre (1905–1980), one of the leaders of the existentialist movement. Excerpts from his essay "Existentialism is a Humanism" is reproduced in Readings from Primary Sources. As Sartre describes it, a free agent is "a being who can realize a nihilating rupture with the world and with himself."[7] This ability to make choices unconstrained by deterministic laws is also, so Sartre argues, a necessary prerequisite for life's meaningfulness and a sense of self-honor and self-worth. This latter sentiment is echoed by some contemporary philosophers in the Anglo-American tradition, as seen in the following passage from Saul Smilansky:

> Even after admitting the compatibilist claim that on one level we have, say, reason to be morally proud of ourselves because we are honest (after all, we chose to be), when we reflect on life as a whole, it matters when we realize that we lack libertarian free will. We begin to see ourselves in a new light: what we choose … is the unfolding of what we are, the choices result from that which is not under our control (and ultimately is luck)..... [Determinism is] extremely damaging to our view of ourselves, to our sense of achievement, worth, and self-respect.... [I]f any virtue that one has exhibited, if all that one has achieved, was "in the cards," just an unfolding of what one has been made out to be, one's view of oneself (or important others) cannot stay the same.[8]

While agent causation has its appeal, it also has some serious problems as a philosophical position. For one, how does it make sense of the limitations that we all clearly have? John can choose not to shoot Crow, but he cannot jump over the moon. Why not? If it really is the case that agents, by sheer dint of will, can break the laws of nature, why are there no limits? Can the supporter of agent causation give a principled answer as to why action A is possible but action B is not, when both A and B involve transgressing physical laws? A second difficulty involves the concept of agent causation itself. Is this a new type of causation—something totally distinct from the sort of causation we see in other contexts? If so, we are justified in requiring a more thorough analysis of this type of causation than has been offered to date. Many nonlibertarians accuse libertarianism in general and agent causation in particular as involving "panicky metaphysics." (This is a philosopher's way of saying "there's something fishy here.") Finally, recent advances in our understanding of the brain have tended to undercut the main source of support for libertarianism—the view of voluntary action "from the inside." Libertarians have been slow to react to these data, leading some to believe that they have no serious response.

5.5 Hard Determinism and Moral Responsibility

Recall that hard determinism is the view that humans lack free will, because human determinism is true. It is the incompatibilist position that opts in favor of human determinism. Throughout the history of Western philosophy, hard determinism has found relatively few adherents. The primary reason for its lack of popularity has been the nearly universal fear that, if hard determinism is true, then no one is morally responsible for what they do. (Indeed, some philosophers build this into the very definition of "hard determinism." They define "incompatibilism" as the view that human determinism is incompatible with *the sort of freedom needed to ground moral responsibility*.) To give up on the notion of moral responsibility, both moral praise and moral blame, is to give up on a large part of the picture of who we are as humans. Before simply dismissing hard determinism as a live option on these grounds, it would be wise to look into the connection between it and moral responsibility in more detail. Here is the argument formalized:

1. If an actor is morally responsible for an action, then the actor must have performed the action freely.
2. If an actor performed an action freely, then it must have been possible for the actor to have done something other than what she in fact did.
3. It is never possible for an actor to have done something other than what she in fact did.
4. Therefore, an actor never performs an action freely.
5. Therefore, an actor is never morally responsible for an action.

The first statement follows directly from what it means for someone to be *morally responsible* for an action. This view of moral responsibility is independent of hard determinism—the libertarian and soft determinist would both assent to it. The second and third statements formulate hard determinism. In particular, the second statement formulates the incompatibilist interpretation of "freedom," while the third statement formulates human determinism. The fourth statement is an implication of the second and third statements, while the fifth statement, the conclusion of the argument, is an implication of the first and fourth statements. Apart from giving up hard determinism, there seems to be no way to evade this conclusion.

But, is the conclusion really so bad? In both our moral and legal evaluations of others' actions, we take into account the extent to which the actor performed that action freely. If I discover that a vicious murderer's behavior is the result of severe abuse as a child, that information tends to lessen my moral condemnation of the murderer. I still condemn the behavior, but I hold the actor individually as less liable for it. The law, likewise, treats evidence that a defendant was unable to control his or her behavior as exculpatory. The insanity defense has traditionally been understood this way. If a mental illness prevents me from being able to control my behavior, I am not *legally* responsible for that behavior and may not justifiably be punished for it, even if my behavior involves breaking a law.[9] I am not "let off the hook," though, since the state then claims justification for putting me in a mental institution—perhaps for a longer period of time than I would have served in a penitentiary had I been found guilty of the crime. While moral and legal responsibility are related, they do not necessarily coincide. (Indeed, legal responsibility varies from one jurisdiction to another; presumably, moral responsibility does not.) Does hard determinism imply that all punishment is unjustified?[10] Is that why so many philosophers and nonphilosophers alike shun this view? No, at least not if "punishment" is understood broadly. Society justifies punishing lawbreakers in order to achieve several distinct goals; only one of these would be affected if we no longer held people as responsible for their behavior. The other reasons we inflict punishment (in particular, incarceration)–to protect society from future harm by this individual, to discourage the lawbreaker from engaging in that behavior again upon release, to deter others who may commit crimes–are still valid. Human determinism is not the view that all people are incorrigible. As we shall see in the following section, human determinism does not specify whether genetic endowment or past learning plays the dominant role in determining behavior. Assuming that the hard determinist opts out of the nature-versus-nurture debate by maintaining that they each play a crucial role in determining a person's actions (see section 5.6), behavioral patterns can be altered by a judicious use of rewards and punishments, both actual and threatened. This is as true of criminal behavior as any other. Hard determinism, then, does not imply that the criminal justice system should be dismantled.

Memento raises some interesting questions surrounding the relationship between moral responsibility and punishment in cases of insanity or other mental incapacity. In Chapter 3, we argued that the best way of describing what is happening in Leonard's case is that, prior to the incident that left him with anterograde amnesia, there was a single person who was Leonard Shelby. After the accident, Leonard's amnesia results in the isolation of the later selves associated with his body. Each of these persons lasts for no more than a day (the time between when Leonard wakes up and the next time he goes to sleep). These persons are isolated in the sense that they are not identical to Leonard before the incident, nor are they identical to one another. Even Leonard, by some of his actions, shows that this is also how he sees things, at least in regard to his relationship with future "occupants" of his body. He could easily kill Teddy at the warehouse just after he kills Jimmy. Instead, Leonard sets one of his future selves up to kill Teddy by writing down Teddy's license plate number as he says to himself, "You'll be my John G" (MM 107:00). Later in fictional time (but earlier in the movie), Leonard's future self performs this task, just as Leonard intended. If Leonard as he writes down Teddy's license plate number is a distinct person from Leonard as he kills Teddy, which of the two is morally responsible for killing Teddy? Are both morally responsible? What about "occupants" of Leonard's body after the homicide? Are they also morally responsible for killing Teddy?

The concept of a person that crops up within ethics is supposed to be the same concept as is used in discussions of personal identity. I can be held morally responsible now for something that I did in the past because I am identical to the person who did that thing in the past. In Leonard's case, though, the notion of moral responsibility falls apart, not because of hard determinism, but because there is no person in the present to hold morally responsible. The person who killed Teddy has ceased to exist. What should be done with Leonard if he is eventually caught for Teddy's or Jimmy's murder? Would the state be justified in putting him in prison? He is clearly a serious danger to others. He even recognizes his own dangerousness when he infers that the gun he finds is not his, because people like him would not be allowed to have a gun. Because of the danger he poses, the state's justification in incarcerating Leonard would not depend on whether Leonard is morally responsible.

If a lack of moral responsibility does not imply that punishment is illegitimate, why, then, is hard determinism so unpopular? The contemporary American philosopher **Daniel Dennett** (b. 1942) has hypothesized that many people find any form of determinism repulsive because they mistake it for something it is not. In his book *Elbow Room*, Dennett describes several "bugbears" that are mistakenly assumed to follow from an acceptance of determinism. In *Minority Report*, we see one of these bugbears represented in Witwer's decision not to pursue John after he escapes with Agatha, because it is already predetermined that Agatha will be in the room when the murder takes place (MM 87:45). If we assume that the future is predetermined and we believe we can predict what that future is, we can make that prediction a self-fulfilling prophecy by our inaction. Similarly, Dennett considers whether acceptance of determinism (and, in particular, hard determinism) would have this sort of pernicious effect.

> But [the acceptance of determinism] would be awful, it seems, for wouldn't it lead to a truly pernicious and self-destructive resignation and apathy? Think, for instance, of the obscene resignation of those who see nuclear war as utterly inevitable and hence not worth trying to prevent. Shouldn't we deplore the promulgation of any claim (even if it is true—perhaps especially if it is true) that encourages this sort of attitude?[11]

Dennett denies that determinism implies our powerlessness as agents. As we explained in Section 5.1, determinism is not the fatalistic view that whatever happens will happen anyway. An action can take place only if its causes occur. Say that you and your friend have been discussing the theory of determinism, and that you have been defending the theory effectively. Your friend is becoming a bit frustrated and claims, "Well, if you're right, and determinism is true, then I can just sit on my couch, and my future will happen." Your friend then proceeds to sit on his couch and do nothing. Is his doing nothing a successful challenge to determinism? It seems not. Your friend's future is still determined by his action. In fact, your friend has actually provided further support for determinism: sitting on the couch and doing nothing will cause him to be bored and, if he stays there long enough, he'll suffer from hunger and thirst. You might explain to your friend that it appears that he does not yet grasp determinism because it is only a misunderstanding of the theory that encourages such resignation and apathy.

Dennett also denies that accepting determinism would lead us to see ourselves as powerless. Determinism is true or false quite independent of us. However, the issue with which Dennett is concerned here is not determinism's truth, but our acceptance of it. Let us consider another example—one that brings out the powerlessness angle in sharper contrast. Imagine what it would be like to be completely paralyzed, wanting desperately to move but being unable to do so. When Western science first learned of the existence of curare, it was unclear how the substance worked. On the surface it appears to cause unconsciousness; if given in too large a dose it causes death. In reality, curare does not cause unconsciousness; rather, it arrests the action of the nerve cells that enervate the muscles (but, interestingly, not the heart muscle). An individual to whom it is given is still 100 percent aware of what is going on, is capable of feeling pain, but is incapable of moving at all. Try to imagine what it would be like if curare were used in place of an anesthetic during surgery[12]; this is the stuff of nightmares. Perhaps that is what acceptance of hard determinism would "feel" like—we would discover the horrible truth, just as the pathetic surgery patient did, that we are utterly powerless. Embracing hard determinism would shatter the image of ourselves as potent agents and force us to see that we cannot even control our own bodies.

Dennett was right to dismiss this as a picture of the world according to determinism, whether the hard or the soft variety. Human determinism does not mean that we are puppets, forced to do things "against our will" by the laws of nature. Rather, there is only one agent "in here." All determinism says is that my mental and physical states—my beliefs, desires, emotions, physical abilities, and current physical state—determine what I will do. There is only one course of action truly open to me. Given who I am and what I am, it is the course of action that I choose. The example involving paralysis is based on the mistaken assumption that determinism implies that there is a radical disconnect between what I want and what my body ends up doing. Once this assumption is rejected, human determinism loses some, if not all, of its repugnance. A way then opens for the soft determinist to find a place for moral responsibility within the context of a compatibilist interpretation of "free will." We shall examine soft determinism in greater detail in Section 5.7.

5.6 The Irrelevance of "Nature-versus-Nurture"

A debate has been raging for decades between those who espouse the claim that an individual's behavioral dispositions are determined by that individual's genetic inheritance and those who claim that it is not genetics, but environmental factors (in particular, learning) that impart the greatest effect in shaping individual humans. This disagreement is most often referred to as the nature-versus-nurture debate. (The "naturists" argue for the pre-eminence of genetics, while the "nurturists" argue for the pre-eminence of environmental factors.) Even before the discovery of the genetic basis of heritable characteristics, the nature-versus-nurture debate has played itself out in education, psychology, sociology, and political science. The ramifications of this debate extend well beyond theory to some very important public policy decisions.

While the nature-versus-nurture debate has far-reaching implications for public policy, it does not make a difference to any of the core issues in the controversy over free will, determinism, and moral responsibility. Both sides of the nature-versus-nurture debate assume that human determinism (or something very close to it) is true. So, they are not distinguishable on that account. Similarly, neither naturism nor nurturism dictates whether the compatibilist or incompatibilist interpretation of free will is preferable. Even the issue of moral responsibility is not affected by the debate. As we shall see in Section 5.7, many philosophers believe that the question of whether human determinism allows for moral responsibility boils down to whether one is a *soft* or a *hard* determinist—the source of human determinism, whether genetics or environmental influences (in combination with innate learning mechanisms), has no bearing on this distinction.

The nature-versus-nurture debate does have one point of contact with the discussion in Section 5.5. If the extreme naturist view is true, then, short of some sort of genetic manipulation or other biological intervention, humans are incorrigible. If I have behavioral dispositions that incline me to break certain laws, attempts at rehabilitation will be ineffectual at changing my criminal behavior. This has ramifications for the justifiability of punishment. Incarceration can still be justified as a way to protect society from me, but it can no longer be justified based on its rehabilitative effect.

5.7 The Soft Determinist Compromise?

The view that hard determinism implies that no one is morally responsible for his actions has led many philosophers to reject it. Some have responded by embracing libertarian freedom in the hopes of regaining a basis for moral responsibility. Others have felt that the evidence for human determinism was just too great. For this latter group, a way out of the hard determinist's dilemma can be achieved by rejecting the incompatibilist interpretation of freedom. For these philosophers, the soft determinists, free will is compatible with human determinism.

The compatibilist interpretation of free will is grounded in a distinction that we all recognize. Some of my behavior is compelled by external forces, whereas other elements of my behavior are the result of my own volitions and desires. According to the soft determinist, an action of mine is free provided that nothing prevents me from acting according to my desires, nor constrains me to act contrary to my desires. My action is still 100 percent determined by my current state, but at least *I* am the author of that action.

Because of this emphasis on *my role* in causing a free action, the soft determinist maintains that I can be held morally responsible for that action. The task then becomes to distinguish between internally-caused and externally-compelled actions. A problem for the soft determinist arises when one considers various classes of action that lie in the gray area between free and unfree. Consider the case of the hotel desk clerk in *Minority Report* who was asked to give John access to the hotel's electronic register.

John: Mind if I look at the register?
Clerk: Yeah, I mind.
John: (pointing his gun at him) How 'bout now?
Clerk: Help yourself.

Would the soft determinist consider the clerk's action (saying "Help yourself") in that case free? In one respect, the action was caused by his desires—foremost among these, his desire to continue living. In another respect, though, his choice was coerced. Had John not pointed the gun at him, he would not have acted in that way. It runs very much contrary to common usage to say that he showed John the hotel register *freely* under such circumstances.

Is the clerk case exceptional?[13] While I have never been held at gunpoint, I do quite often make a decision under the threat of bad consequences happening if I choose one way versus another. Sometimes, when I am running late for an appointment, I consider speeding in order to arrive at the appointment on time. I opt against speeding, though, because I fear being pulled over by a police officer and being fined. Is my choice not to speed a free one? Is this case qualitatively different from the clerk case? If not, it appears that many, perhaps most of my actions will turn out to be externally compelled (hence unfree, according to the compatibilist), because my ultimate choice is based on a desire I have to avoid various sorts of bad consequences.

Another type of gray area case involves compulsive and addictive behaviors. How will the soft determinist classify them–are they free or are they unfree? The contemporary American philosopher **Harry Frankfurt** (b. 1929) has written extensively about how the soft determinist should deal with these types of behavior.[14] Frankfurt distinguishes between first- and second-order desires. First-order desires are those for particular things or states of affairs–for example, a desire for vanilla ice cream, a desire for fame, a desire for world peace. A second-order desire is a desire to have a particular desire. In some cases, especially in cases involving addictive behavior, an individual has a strong desire *not* to have a particular desire. Frankfurt illustrates this by using the example of an unwilling heroin addict who has a second-order desire–a desire *not* to have a desire to use heroin. For Frankfurt, an action is free if the individual is performing it based on a desire that the individual desires to have. The unwilling addict is acting unfreely because the desire that is driving the drug use is a desire that is *not* desired. While Frankfurt's analysis of "free" is useful in some cases, it falls short of offering us a robust method for distinguishing between free and unfree actions in the general case.[15]

In addition to worries about describing in detail what separates internally caused and externally caused actions, soft determinism suffers from an even deeper problem. Recall that soft determinists are human determinists. They disagree with hard determinists only in the analysis they provide of free will. Being human determinists, they hold that all of an individual's desires are caused by antecedent events, which are themselves caused by antecedent events, and so on. This chain of events thus extends back into the past to a time even before the individual was born. What sense, then, can be made of the distinction between internally- and externally-caused actions? One is left with the sinking feeling that soft determinism is based on a distinction that does not really exist.

What lessons can we take from this chapter? All of the three traditional positions within the free will and determinism debate have serious unanswered questions. We mentioned in Section 5.3 that philosophy's seeming inability to make headway on this issue has led some in the field to believe that the framework within which the debate is taking place is seriously flawed. To date, though, no real alternatives have gained more than marginal support.

Discussion Questions

1. Is addictive behavior free? What does your answer tell you about where you stand on the compatibilism/incompatibilism controversy?
2. Do you see any difficulties in squaring the existence of free will with God's presumed perfect foreknowledge? Does your answer to this

question depend on whether you adopt the incompatibilist or the compatibilist interpretation of free will?

3. Should Leonard in *Memento* be held morally responsible for the homicides he commits? Should he be held legally responsible? Why or why not?

4. Would the accomplishments that you and others achieve be less worthy if human determinism were true? How does luck fit into the picture? Does it make sense to praise someone for being lucky?

5. Can you think of a way of interpreting the example involving posthypnotic suggestion that does not undercut libertarianism?

6. Can you think of a way of interpreting the brain-scan experiment about the predictability of voluntary action that does not undercut libertarianism?

Annotated List of Film Titles Relevant to Free Will and Determinism

Gattaca (1997). Directed by Andrew Niccol. Starring Ethan Hawke, Uma Thurman, Jude Law. Set in a future world in which one's life trajectory is read at birth on the basis of a genetic test, this film explores the extent to which human determinism (with a strong naturist bent) is true.

Annotated List of Book Titles Relevant to Free Will and Determinism

"Classics" in the History of the Free Will Debate

ARISTOTLE

Nicomachean Ethics. In this book (see esp. book 3), Aristotle defends the view that individuals are responsible for their behavior, and hence are justifiably punished when they do wrong.

THOMAS HOBBES

The Questions Concerning Liberty, Necessity, and Chance. In a chapter entitled "Of Liberty and Necessity," the seventeenth-century philosopher Thomas Hobbes argues for the compatibilist view of free will and moral responsibility: "Liberty is the absence of all the impediments to action that are not contained in the nature and intrinsical quality of the agent." This book is volume 5 in The English Works of Thomas Hobbes (London: J. Bohn, 1839).

DAVID HUME

An Enquiry Concerning Human Understanding, 1748. In section viii of this work ("Of Liberty and Necessity"), Hume lays out a version of soft determinism and argues that it is human determinism, not indeterminism, that grounds moral responsibility for actions. The relevant passages are included in Readings from Primary Sources.

IMMANUEL KANT

Religion within the Bounds of Reason Alone, first published in 1793, and *Fundamental Principles of the Metaphysics of Morals*, first published in 1785. In these two books, Kant makes the case for a libertarian interpretation of free will.

JEAN-PAUL SARTRE

"Existentialism is a Humanism" was originally delivered as a lecture in 1945, shortly after the end of the Second World War. In this essay, Sartre expounds his atheistic version of existentialism and examines the upshot for human psychology and values. In his discussion of human determinism (a view he rejects), he disagrees with most other commentators on the subject by arguing that human determinism is actually a comforting view, since it offers individuals an excuse to explain why they are frequently unsuccessful. A slightly shortened version of this essay is included in Readings from Primary Sources.

Contemporary Works on the Free Will Debate

Daniel Dennett, *Elbow Room* (Cambridge, MA: MIT Press, 1984). Dennett's lively and engaging writing style makes this book fun to read.

Laura Ekstrom, *Free Will* (Boulder, CO: Westview Press, 2000). Ekstrom argues that a coherent analysis of agent causation is possible that saves both moral responsibility and our sense of self-worth.

Sam Harris, *Free Will* (Free Press, 2012). In this short book, Harris provides a very accessible explanation and defense of hard determinism.

Derk Pereboom, *Living without Free Will* (Cambridge: Cambridge University Press, 2001). Pereboom attempts to undercut the traditional argument against hard determinism.

Gary Watson, ed. *Free Will* (Oxford: Oxford University Press, 1982). A collection of the most important papers on the free will debate in the latter half of the twentieth century.

Notes

1. Pierre Laplace, *A Philosophical Essay on Probabilities*, trans. Frederick Truscott and Frederick Emory (New York: Dover Press, 1951), 4.
2. Actually, it is not that the event in question is uncaused, but that it is probabilistic. The exact timing of the event is uncaused. The event is determined to happen eventually. What is uncaused is why it occurs now rather than later.
3. Albert Einstein to Max Born, September 7, 1944, in *The Born-Einstein Letters*, trans. Irene Born (New York: Macmillan, 1971).
4. The study was conducted by John-Dylan Haynes, and the results were published in *Nature Neuroscience* 11 (543–45), 2008. See also: Benjamin Libet, "Unconscious Cerebral Initiative and the Role of Conscious Will in Voluntary Action," in *Behavioral and Brain Sciences* 8 (1985): 529–66. Libet concluded that "the brain 'decides' to initiate or, at least, to prepare to initiate the act before there is any reportable subjective awareness that such a decision has taken place" (536). Similar findings were reported earlier by L. Deecke, B. Grözinger, and H. Kornhuber in "Voluntary Finger Movement in Man: Cerebral Potentials and Theory," *Biological Cybernetics* 23 (1976): 99–119.
5. Robert Nozick, *Philosophical Explanations* (Cambridge, MA: Harvard University Press, 1981), 293.
6. Lucretius, *The Nature of the Universe*, book 2, lines 250–55, first published circa 55 B.C.E. This version is from the translation by Ronald Latham (New York: Penguin, 1951).
7. Jean-Paul Sartre, *Being and Nothingness*, trans. Hazel Barnes (New York: Philosophical Library, 1956), 435.
8. Saul Smilansky, "Can a Determinist Respect Herself?" in *Freedom and Moral Responsibility*, ed. Charles Manekin and Menachem Kellner (College Park, MD: University of Maryland Press, 1997), 92–94.
9. In the United States, laws governing the use of the insanity defense differ from one state to another. We describe here the most common version.
10. For a very illuminating and in-depth treatment of this topic, see Chapter 6 in Derk Pereboom, *Living without Free Will* (Cambridge: Cambridge University Press, 2001).
11. Daniel Dennett, *Elbow Room* (Cambridge, MA: MIT Press, 1984), 14.
12. It is part of folklore surrounding early attempts at thoracic surgery that curare was used on a few human subjects based on the misconception that it caused unconsciousness; however, we can find no scholarly source to corroborate this claim. A synthetic form of curare does find use in modern surgery in conjunction with local or general anesthesia.
13. In section 3.13 of *Nichomachean Ethics*, Aristotle gives a similar example and argues that an action done under duress is not necessarily involuntary.
14. Frankfurt's view has shifted over the years. The view attributed to him here is the view he espoused in his 1971 paper "Freedom of the Will and the Concept of a Person," included in *Free Will*, ed. Gary Watson (Oxford: Oxford University Press, 1982).
15. For a discussion of where Frankfurt's hierarchical approach goes wrong, see Chapter 3 in Laura Ekstrom, *Free Will* (Boulder, CO: Westview Press, 2000).

6

ETHICS

Crimes and Misdemeanors (1988) and
Gone Baby Gone (2007)

Aunt May: For those who want morality, there's morality.
Halley: No matter how elaborate a philosophical system
you work out, in the end, it's gotta be incomplete.
—from *Crimes and Misdemeanors*

Patrick: Does it make you feel better? Telling yourself you
did it for the right reasons? That you took her to be saved.
From her own mother?
Doyle: We're just trying to give a little girl a life.
Patrick: It wasn't your life to give.
—from *Gone Baby Gone*

What distinguishes morally right action from morally wrong action?
This is the primary question posed within ethics. It is also one of the
questions posed within *Crimes and Misdemeanors* and *Gone Baby Gone*. In
these films we meet characters who "represent," either by word or deed,
many of the ethical theories philosophers have developed in answer to
this question. Seeing these theories "made flesh" is useful in discussing
the pros and cons of each. As always, the first few sections of this chapter
provide a general introduction to the topic—one that does not require
previous acquaintance with the movies. Our advice is to read up through
Section 6.3, watch *Crimes and Misdemeanors* and *Gone Baby Gone*, then
pick up reading again with Section 6.4.

6.1 What Is Ethics?

Of all the subareas of philosophy, moral philosophy (also known as
"ethics") is the one that is most familiar to nonphilosophers. We are all
used to the idea of making moral evaluations of the actions of ourselves
and others—judging some actions as morally right and others as morally

wrong. But let us step back for a moment and ask: What is going on when we make moral evaluations? Consider the following statements:

S1: Some of Hitler's actions indirectly caused the death of millions of people.
S2: Some of Hitler's actions were morally wrong.

S2 is a value judgment: it is judging the value or worth of Hitler's actions. In particular, it is stating that some of Hitler's actions fall toward the "bad" end of the moral spectrum. *S1*, on the other hand, is a nonvalue judgment. It is not making any sort of evaluation of Hitler's actions. We, on being confronted with *S1*, are likely to infer moral condemnation of some of Hitler's actions, but that move on our part is an inference: it is not included explicitly in *S1* itself. This difference is important. To generate *S2* from *S1*, *we* must supply an additional premise, such as:

Moral Principle 1: Any action that indirectly causes the death of millions of people is morally wrong.

Now the question becomes: Where did Moral Principle 1 come from? Is it in turn an inference from some more general moral principle? Or, is it something that is just a brute moral fact? Ethics is the field of inquiry that looks at these sorts of questions.

First and foremost, moral philosophy is concerned with figuring out what distinguishes morally right actions from morally wrong actions. To see what this means, consider the diagram in Figure 6.1. The rectangle-shaped figure of this Venn diagram represents the set of all possible human actions. (Throughout this chapter, we shall be confining ourselves to moral evaluation of *human* action.) The two circles within the rectangle represent the set of morally right and morally wrong actions, respectively.

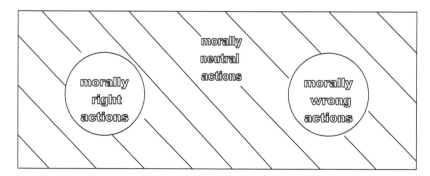

Figure 6.1

146

The area within the rectangle not falling within one of the two circles represents the set of morally neutral actions. I assume that many actions are morally neutral: they have no moral status either way. For example, my tying the laces of my left shoe, then my right shoe is neither morally right nor morally wrong. Many actions, perhaps *most* actions, are of this sort.

Of those actions that *do* have a moral status, what features of the action determine whether it is morally right or morally wrong? This is the central question within moral philosophy. Using the diagram in Figure 6.1, this question boils down to: What is special about the set of morally right actions that sets them apart as morally right? Finding the answer to this question is the first step toward determining, for any given action, whether it is right or wrong.

Different ethical theories propose different answers to this question. Some theories view the *consequences* that arise from an action as decisive in determining the moral status of that action. Thus, an action that produces overall good consequences is morally preferable to an action that produces overall poor consequences. Other ethical theories ignore consequences altogether and focus instead on the *intentions* of the actor—what he was trying to do when he performed that action. If an actor had good intentions when he performed the action, then the action is morally good—never mind that horrendous consequences may have accidentally been produced.

Obviously, the above sketch is just a sketch. Philosophers owe us much more detail in fleshing out the individual theories. For example, what constitutes *good* consequences? How does one figure out what the relevant consequences of an action are? In the case of theories that focus on intentions, what are *good* intentions? As we shall see, the major ethical theories do specify these things in detail. For now, we shall hold off an examination of the individual ethical theories and discuss them in the context of their depiction in *Crimes and Misdemeanors* and *Gone Baby Gone.*

We should warn the reader that, while our presentation of ethics is fairly standard, there are some dissenting voices in the history of ethics that we must omit for space reasons. The way in which contemporary philosophers understand ethics would have seemed quite foreign to ancient philosophers such as Plato and Aristotle. While the current standard is to treat ethics as dealing primarily with moral evaluation of *actions*, the Ancients viewed ethics as concerned primarily with evaluation of *whole persons*—in particular, ethics in classical Greece was concerned first and foremost with evaluating character traits that made an individual good. Some modern ethicists (e.g., Alisdair MacIntyre) have called for a return to the classical understanding of the proper domain of ethics.

6.2 Moral Objectivism versus Moral Relativism

In Chapter 1, we considered cognitive relativism, the claim that the truth of all judgments is relative to some set of background assumptions. These background assumptions were usually understood to be a conceptual framework that an individual uses in making sense of the world. We noted in Section 1.6 that there are other, more circumscribed versions of relativism. One such theory is **moral relativism**, according to which there are no objective moral facts: the truth of all moral evaluations is relative either to individual or cultural moral standards. Moral relativism is contrasted with **moral objectivism**, the view that there *are* moral facts–facts about what is morally right and morally wrong, facts that do not depend on what anyone or any group of people happens to think. Like cognitive relativism, moral relativism has achieved some support among both intellectuals and the general population. Much of this support is the result of increasing contact over the past century between Western (in particular, mainstream Anglo-American) society and far-flung cultures. Some of these other cultures have very different ideas about which sorts of practices are acceptable and which are not. While cultural anthropology and television have brought the peoples of the world into our living room, contact between cultures is nothing new. Herodotus, the principal historian of the classical era, notes that, even in ancient times, differences between social norms of different cultures were apparent. There was no single set of practices that all people everywhere held in common. To many, the diversity of social norms shows that there are no objective moral facts. This line of reasoning resembles the main empirical argument for cognitive relativism discussed in Section 1.6. We will consider it further below.

A second line of argument for moral relativism can also be traced out in classical sources. Thrasymachus, one of the characters in Plato's dialogue *The Republic*, puts forward the position that can be roughly summarized as "might makes right." What Thrasymachus meant was that moral standards are determined by the politically dominant group in a culture and are aimed at preserving that group's political power.

Before looking at some of the arguments pro and con, we would like to describe moral relativism in greater detail. Moral relativism further subdivides into two distinct theories, depending on which individual or set of individuals the truth of moral judgments is assumed to be relative to. **Moral subjectivism** is the view that moral judgments are true or false relative to an individual's moral standards. Thus, if *I believe* that eating meat is morally permissible, then it is morally permissible for me to eat meat. Others may disagree as to the moral status of eating meat, but that is irrelevant, because the only arbiter of morality is the individual engaging in the action and her own moral code.[1] **Cultural moral relativism** is the view that moral judgments are true or false relative to the actor's culture's moral standards. If I live in a culture in which eating meat is considered acceptable, then it is morally permissible for me to eat meat.[2] If, on the other hand, I live in a culture in which eating meat is looked down upon, then it would be morally wrong of me to eat meat. According to cultural moral relativism, it is possible for an individual's moral judgments to be false. This occurs when the individual's moral standards are at odds with those of his culture. Thus, there is a court of appeal of sorts (that is, one's culture's standards) for moral judgments within cultural moral relativism. We are still within the realm of relativism, however, since even cultural moral relativism claims there is no objective fact about what is morally right and what is morally wrong. There is a third view within ethics that, while not a version of relativism, shares much in common with it. That view, **moral nihilism**, holds that moral statements are meaningless. According to moral nihilists, the very notion of evaluating actions on moral grounds makes no sense. While moral nihilism does not have many followers among current philosophers, it has had followers in the past. Emotivism, the view that moral statements are really expressions of emotional responses to certain events, was popular early in the twentieth century. According to emotivism, the statement "Some of Hitler's actions were morally wrong" is equivalent to "Some of Hitler's actions–*yuck!*" We will return to a discussion of moral nihilism in later sections. For the rest of this section, however, we shall concentrate on the two versions of moral relativism defined above.

What sorts of arguments may be given in favor of moral relativism? Let us consider cultural moral relativism first. One line of argument begins with the observation that different cultures vary widely in their moral standards. In some cultures eating meat is uniformly frowned upon; in others it is not. In some cultures it is uniformly frowned upon to walk around with one's genitals exposed; in others it is not. We are all familiar with these differences in moral standards across cultures. Indeed, no one (not even the most ardent moral objectivist) would deny the claim that there is a great deal of diversity in the world regarding which types of actions are considered to be morally acceptable and which are not. The cultural moral relativist uses this diversity in moral standards as evidence for the total relativity of moral truth. If there really were objective moral values, so the argument goes, one would expect to see all cultures adopt roughly the same set of moral standards. Since one sees diversity of moral values across cultures instead of uniformity, moral relativism is supported. The general intracultural uniformity of moral standards tips the tide of reason in favor of cultural moral relativism.

Yet is the argument outlined in the preceding paragraph a good argument? Does (1) intercultural moral standard diversity plus (2) intracultural moral standard uniformity imply cultural moral relativism? It seems not.[3]

There are two ways of criticizing this argument. The first route attacks the argument on the grounds that it is structurally unsound.[4] According to this criticism, (1) intercultural moral standard diversity and (2) intracultural moral standard uniformity *do not* logically entail that cultural moral relativism is correct. To see this, the moral objectivist considers a related argument that highlights the original argument's flaw.[5] The related argument runs something like this: Different cultures have different views on whether the earth is flat or not. In general, the degree of intracultural agreement on this point of geography is quite high. (That is, the members of a culture either uniformly believe the earth is flat or uniformly disbelieve it). However, (1) intercultural diversity and (2) intracultural uniformity on the question of the earth's shape do not entail that there is no objective fact of the matter about whether or not the earth is flat. Some cultures (namely those cultures in which the flat-earth hypothesis is widespread) are just mistaken on this point. Similarly, the moral objectivist would say that some cultures have adopted incorrect moral standards. Mere difference of opinion does not constitute evidence in favor of relativism, whether cognitive or moral.

A second way of criticizing the argument given in support of cultural moral relativism attacks the truth of the premise which states that there is a high degree of intercultural diversity in moral standards. Some have argued that the differences we see in cultural moral standards are fairly superficial, the protestations of cultural anthropologists notwithstanding. At a deeper level, cultures' moral standards *must* have many aspects in common. The reason this is so, argues the moral objectivist, is that there are certain norms of behavior that all viable cultures must respect, lest the culture cease to exist. For example, a culture in which care for infants and small children was not a norm would be a culture that would not survive past the current generation. It is not too difficult to come up with other moral principles of this sort–that is, principles that constitute minimum requirements in order for a group of people to form a cohesive and viable culture.

Perhaps the relativist can salvage some form of moral relativism by retrenching to moral subjectivism. While there is a high degree of uniformity of moral beliefs among members of the same culture, this agreement is not absolute. Abortion, euthanasia, and capital punishment should all be familiar examples to Anglo-Americans of actions whose moral status is highly controversial. Perhaps the cultural moral relativist got it wrong. Perhaps it is the *individual,* not the culture, whose moral standards are the ultimate arbiter of morality–and intracultural moral controversy proves it. Here again it seems that the moral objectivist can counter that mere difference of opinion does not imply relativism. Without compelling argument to the contrary, the objectivist can claim that some people are just mistaken in various of their moral beliefs.[6]

The preceding argument and counterargument has left us in a stalemate. The moral relativist's main arguments are seen to be seriously flawed. However, merely pointing out flaws in an argument does not by itself show that the conclusion of that argument is false. So, moral relativism is still a straw afloat. Yet, there are reasons that can be given against moral relativism. To see them, we must revisit the tolerance-based argument discussed in Section 1.8.

Recall that one benefit cited in favor of relativism is its apparent connection with tolerance. Moral relativism teaches that there is no such thing as the objectively correct answer to the question: Is X morally right? If I am a consistent cultural moral relativist, I will not–indeed, I *cannot*–criticize the norms of other societies as incorrect. While this may strike you as a reasonable position when it comes to many norms (for example, eating practices), the consistent moral relativist's "tolerance" must also encompass other practices, such as slavery, the subjection of women, and genocide. Thus, the persecution of the Jews during the Nazi era was morally permissible, so long as that persecution was in line with the social norms current in the German Reich during the late 1930s and early 1940s. Similarly, consistent moral subjectivists cannot criticize on moral grounds the practices of others, either those within their own culture or those without.

Even stranger, moral relativism implies that moral progress (that is, the replacement of a set of cultural norms by a *better* set) is an impossibility. The overthrow of current moral standards is always morally wrong at the time the overthrow is occurring. For example, the actions constituting the civil rights struggle in the United States during the 1950s and 1960s must be judged by the consistent cultural moral relativist as morally wrong, since the actions were contrary to the then current norms. And, according to them, anything contrary to a culture's norms is ipso facto morally wrong.

These implications of moral relativism are highly counterintuitive–they are so contrary to our normal understanding of what ethics is about that they demonstrate that moral relativism is not a tenable theory.

6.3 An Overview of the Movies

CRIMES AND MISDEMEANORS (1988). DIRECTED BY WOODY ALLEN. STARRING MARTIN LANDAU, WOODY ALLEN, MIA FARROW, ALAN ALDA, ANGELICA HUSTON, SAM WATERSTON

With a nod to Fyodor Dostoevsky and his great novel *Crime and Punishment*, Woody Allen's *Crimes and Misdemeanors* poses the question: What happens to ethics in a world in which the wheels of justice are not set right in the end, either by an omnipotent god or the evildoer himself? Many believe that *Crimes and Misdemeanors* is Allen's greatest film, combining comedy, drama, and philosophy (and some fine acting, too) with more deftness than any of his efforts before or since. The film weaves together two subplots. In one, Judah Rosenthal, a successful physician, loving family man, and all-round pillar of the community, is the protagonist. We learn only later that he has a secret. His way of dealing with the problems generated by this secret form one subplot. Clifford Stern is the movie's second protagonist. Cliff is a ne'er-do-well filmmaker whose current pet project is a documentary on the philosopher Louis Levy. Cliff's wife has other ideas. She convinces Cliff to work on a documentary about her successful TV-producer brother, Lester. While working on this documentary, Cliff meets and falls in love with the documentary's producer, Halley Reed. Cliff's travails in his work and romance with Halley form the movie's second subplot. The character that links the two subplots together is the rabbi, Ben, who is both Cliff's brother-in-law and Judah's patient. The two subplots finally intersect at a wedding reception for Ben's daughter at the end of the film.

The viewer need not know anything about ethical theory to recognize the cleverness of Allen's screenplay, but appreciation for Allen's wit and creativity grow with even a passing knowledge of ethics. In *Crimes and Misdemeanors*, Allen has managed to bring several ethical debates to life, and he has developed the main characters so that the major ethical theories are "represented" by someone in the film.

Gone Baby Gone (2007). Directed by Ben Affleck. Starring Casey Affleck, Michelle Monaghan, Morgan Freeman, Ed Harris

Gone Baby Gone is based on the novel by Dennis Lehane. A young girl in a rough neighborhood of Boston has been kidnapped. The girl's aunt hires private investigators, Patrick Kenzie and Angie Gennaro, to assist in the search. As the couple investigates the kidnapping, they discover that the girl's mother, Helene, abuses drugs and has stolen money from a dealer. They also find out that the police detectives are lying about some of the information relevant to the case and that the police captain is in on the kidnapping. When they finally solve the case, they must make a decision about the girl's future that presents a moral dilemma—of the two available options, neither is clearly right, each would violate a moral principle, and both have potentially bad consequences for the young girl.

6.4 Utilitarianism

Even if one assumes that moral objectivism provides the correct interpretation of ethics, there are still many questions yet to be answered. What makes an action morally praiseworthy? What makes an action morally blameworthy? These are very abstract questions that are hard to get a handle on. Consider some more concrete examples: first, the scene in which Judah calls up his brother Jack to make arrangements for the hit man to kill Delores, beginning at MM 43:00. And second, the dilemma presented at MM 1:32:46 of *Gone Baby Gone*: whether Amanda should be returned to her neglectful, drug abusing mother or whether she should remain, illegally, in the comfort and care of Doyle and his wife. We'll assume that, when you watched the scene in *Crimes and Misdemeanors*, your immediate response to Judah's action was moral condemnation—Judah's action was morally wrong. Why? What was it about Judah's action that made it morally wrong? The example from *Gone Baby Gone* does not provide such a clear-cut judgment. Was Patrick's decision to return Amanda to her mother the right choice? Why or why not? What is it about the action that makes it right or wrong? Can you glean any useful generalizations from these concrete examples that would be helpful in answering the two questions posed earlier in the paragraph?

This exercise points to a broad distinction made between ethical theories. **Consequentialism** is the view that what sets morally right actions apart from morally wrong ones has to do with the consequences that result from the action: morally right actions produce good consequences while morally wrong actions produce bad consequences. **Nonconsequentialism**, on the other hand, is the view that it is something other than consequences that is important in distinguishing right from wrong. We'll look at some consequentialist theories in this section and the next. Then we'll turn to consider some nonconsequentialist theories.

Consider again Judah's decision to order the killing of Delores that was described above. According to the consequentialist interpretation, Judah's action is morally wrong because of several factors. For one, he harms Delores in taking away the rest of her life. In addition, unless her death occurred without any foreknowledge or pain on her part, the psychological and physical suffering Delores experienced immediately before her death must also be considered. Although we are not told anything about Delores's family, friends, and others who would be affected by her death, it is possible that these people will also suffer as a result of Delores's death. In contrast, there appears to be relatively little of a positive nature that comes out of Delores's death that might compensate for the suffering she and others experienced.[7] This combined suffering is what made Judah's action morally wrong.

What about Patrick's decision to call the police, resulting in Amanda's being returned to her mother? When we take into account the way that Patrick's action will affect everyone involved, it seems that it was the wrong thing to do. Amanda will probably languish in the care of her neglectful and inattentive mother. Helene will be burdened with raising Amanda. Doyle and his wife will suffer when Doyle goes to prison for kidnapping. Likewise, Lionel and Bea will experience hardship when Lionel is convicted. Finally, Patrick and Angie will endure the heartache of their broken relationship. On the other hand, there don't seem to be enough good consequences of Patrick's action to outweigh the bad. Thus, on the consequentialist account, it appears that Patrick's action was morally wrong.

Judah's ordering the killing of Delores is wrong because it produced bad consequences. Similarly, Patrick's initiating the return of Amanda to her mother is wrong because it results in bad consequences. With these observations, we are pushed back to a further question: What is it about the consequences of an action that makes them good or bad? In attempting to answer these questions, the English philosopher **John Stuart Mill** (1806–1873) looked for guidance to human psychology. What sorts of things do all humans desire? To this Mill answered, "Pleasure and freedom from pain are the only things desirable as ends; ... all desirable things [i.e., particular objects of desire] ... are desirable either for pleasure inherent in themselves or as means to the promotion of pleasure and the prevention of pain."[8] What Mill meant was: look as hard as you will, the only thing you will find that humans really care about is pleasure (and freedom from pain). Particular things humans may want (for example, a fancy car, a good reputation, or a loving family) are desirable only insofar as they bring about pleasure for someone. According to this view, something (an object or an action) that was neither itself inherently pleasurable nor the means to the production of pleasure would not be desirable.

Once this principle about human psychology was accepted, Mill believed, the upshot for ethics was clear. Actions are morally right to the extent that they produce good consequences. Good consequences are consequences that result in lots of pleasure. So, actions are morally right to the extent that they produce lots of pleasure. Mill captured this inference in the principle (variously known as "the principle of utility" and "the greatest happiness principle"), which claimed: "Actions are right in proportion as they tend to promote happiness, wrong as they tend to produce the reverse of happiness."[9] The primary source for Mill's view on the foundations of ethics is Chapter 2 from his book *Utilitarianism*, which is included in Readings from Primary Sources.

Since Mill equated *happiness* with *pleasure*, the greatest happiness principle is the equivalent to the claim that actions are morally right to the extent that they produce lots of pleasure.

Interestingly, Mill did not think that all pleasures were created equal. He was not calling for everyone to adopt the life of the glutton, seeking sensual pleasure at every possible opportunity. Even if someone could manage to satisfy all of his sensual desires–the proverbial happy pig–his life would not be as pleasurable as that of someone engaged in intellectual pursuits. According to Mill, "It's better to be a human being dissatisfied than a pig satisfied; better to be Socrates dissatisfied than a fool satisfied."[10] It is not that Mill believed sensual pleasures to be bad; quite the contrary— all pleasures, he felt, are good. It is just that sensual pleasures are not as deeply satisfying as other types of pleasure (for example, the pleasure an individual receives from intellectual pursuits, or the "warm, fuzzy feelings" one receives from helping others).

Many contemporary followers of Mill have formalized his views in an ethical theory called **act utilitarianism**. According to this theory, acting in a morally right fashion is a matter of: (1) figuring out which action will maximize overall happiness, and (2) choosing that action. Ethical decision-making starts with a choice. A person has various options; which of several alternative actions is the person going to choose? The process for making morally correct decisions according to act utilitarianism may be boiled down to a three-step process:

1. Enumerate all the alternative actions from which the actor has to choose.
2. For each alternative, figure out the total amount of happiness that would result if that alternative were chosen. (This sum total is referred to as the alternative's **utility**.)
3. The alternative with the greatest utility is the morally right thing to do under the circumstances. Any alternative with less than maximal utility is morally wrong.

Let us apply this process in analyzing Judah's decision to ask his brother Jack to arrange for a hit man to kill Delores. Prior to the actual choice, Judah has various options open to him. He could have confessed his infidelity to his wife, as Ben had suggested. He could have "done nothing"—continued to try to hide the affair and the embezzlement while not taking steps to silence Delores. He could have arranged for the hit man. (This is what Judah ends up choosing.) There are in fact many things Judah *could have* done, many different actions he *could have* chosen. All of these possible actions are what is meant in step 1 by "the alternative actions." Each of these alternatives has ramifications for the (un)happiness that various people would experience. The first alternative (confessing to his wife) would result in some unhappiness on his wife's part when she learns that her presumed-faithful husband is in fact not faithful. This knowledge will have ramifications for Judah and his happiness level. (Perhaps his wife will divorce him or perhaps their marriage will suffer in other ways.) While Ben suggests that this new honesty in their marriage will be a blessing in disguise, this is by no means guaranteed. There may be other people affected were Judah to choose this option. Among them are Judah's friends, relatives, neighbors, and patients. The list of affected people could grow to be quite large. Admittedly, most of the people on the list would be only marginally affected by this choice, but, if we want to follow through in applying the step 2 of the process, we need to consider them as well.

What about the second alternative–the "do nothing" alternative? Who would be affected, and to what extent would they be affected in terms of their (un)happiness? Here again, there is a relatively small set of directly affected people (Judah, his wife, Delores); however, the list of marginally affected people may be quite large.

Finally, what about the alternative that Judah actually chose in the movie? What is the utility associated with that alternative? Obviously, Delores suffers. Death is not bad in and of itself within utilitarianism; however, since life is a prerequisite for experiencing happiness, actions that cause the death of persons generally turn out to be morally wrong according to act utilitarianism. Furthermore, if Delores's death caused her pain and suffering immediately before she died, that fact would tend to make this alternative all the worse. However, we cannot end the analysis there. Even though *we* may focus on the consequences for the murder victim when judging a homicide to be morally wrong, act utilitarianism requires that we consider *everybody* affected and that we take the *overall* amount of (un)happiness resulting from an action as the final measure in determining its moral status. The action's effect on Judah, his wife, his family, and his friends must also be taken into account. We learn in the closing conversation of the movie (MM 93:30) that Judah and his family have prospered because of Judah's choice. While the short-run consequences for Judah's state of happiness are bad (pangs of guilt so severe he seriously contemplated turning himself in to the authorities), in the long run, he and everyone he cares about prospered. Does this mean that, according to act utilitarianism, Judah did the right thing in choosing to have Delores killed? No–or at least not necessarily. That would depend on many things that we, as viewers of the movie, were given little information about: Did Delores have close friends and family who would have suffered greatly at learning of her murder? Was Delores generally a happy person who could be expected to produce a lot of happiness during the remainder of her life had she not been killed? Did the person who was convicted of Delores's murder suffer as a result of being falsely accused? (We are given some information that the answer to this question is no–he had already committed a string of murders sufficient to get him a life sentence anyway.) Would Judah ultimately be found out, contrary to his expectations, so that, in the *very* long run, he and those around him would have their prosperity broken? A strange feature of act utilitarianism is that, if the circumstances (and corresponding consequences) turn out just so, even homicide will be judged as morally right. We shall return to this feature of act utilitarianism later.

Now, what about Patrick's decision? He could either walk away and leave Amanda with Doyle, or he could call the police and have Amanda returned to Helene. Either action will have an effect on many people. If he chooses to leave Amanda with Doyle, Amanda may have a good life, as a result of being raised in a supportive home with attentive parents. However, Patrick argues that at some point in the future, Amada will discover that she was kidnapped and never returned to her mother, in which case, she may become resentful. Doyle and his wife will be happy to have a child back in their home after losing their own daughter, but if Amanda grows sullen, she could become difficult to deal with. Angie will experience pleasure, knowing that Amanda is going to school and having birthday parties and sleepovers. Patrick will be happy that Amanda is living a good life, but he will never forgive himself for breaking the law and for keeping Amanda from her mother. Finally, Amanda's Aunt Bea will be miserable if Amanda never comes home.

If Patrick chooses to return Amanda to her mother, Amanda may or may not be happy, depending on how things turn out. But given her mother's life-style and the neighborhood that she'll grow up in, it appears that Amanda will have a difficult life, to say the least. Having Amanda back will most likely be a burden for Helene, compromising her happiness. Doyle will go to prison, thus he and his wife will be miserable. Initially, Bea will be happy to have Amanda back, but that happiness will soon dissipate when she is forced to leave the house and when Lionel goes to prison. Angie will be unhappy knowing that Amanda is back with Helene. And both Angie and Patrick will be heartbroken when they break up. What is the utility of each possible action? From the descriptions above, the sum total happiness that would result from Amanda's staying with Doyle seems to outweigh the sum total happiness that would result from her being returned to her mother. So, even though Patrick acted in accordance with the law when he called the police, it would appear that he made the morally wrong decision, according to utilitarian calculations.

This exercise highlights several interesting attributes of act utilitarianism. First, the theory is egalitarian, which means that everyone's happiness needs to be considered. Everyone is treated equally: the actor making the choice doesn't count as any more important than anyone else. Each person's contribution to the overall utility is a function not of his position in society but only of the total amount of happiness he experiences if that alternative is chosen. The powerful don't count as any more important than the powerless; the rich don't count as any more important than the poor; the "innocent" don't count as any more important than the "guilty."

Utilitarianism also assumes that there is some way to measure the happiness that people experience, so that the happiness level experienced by person A can be meaningfully added to the happiness level experienced by person B. (This assumption is built into step 2 of the process.) Finally, utilitarianism is a general ethical theory; it tells us in general what properties distinguish morally right actions from morally wrong actions. According to act utilitarianism, an action is morally right if it produces at least as much total happiness as any other action an actor could have performed. The theory may be used either after the fact (that is, after a decision has already been made) to assign moral praise or moral blame, or prior to a decision to figure out which among several alternatives is the morally right thing to do.

However, there are some problems with utilitarianism. How would a utilitarian analyze Judah's action in arranging for the hit man to kill Delores? First, one must consider the amount of happiness produced by the action and compare it with the amount of happiness produced by the alternative actions that Judah could have chosen under the circumstances. If it turns out that Judah's choice produces the most happiness, then it is morally right. However, our moral intuitions tell us that any ethical theory worth its salt had better judge Judah's action as morally wrong. If it doesn't, that is reason enough to reject the theory as unacceptable. Unfortunately for utilitarianism, depending on what happens in the future, Judah's action may well be judged by that theory as the morally right thing for Judah to have done. Indeed, the movie hinted that this was the case. Delores appeared to be a loner who wasn't very happy anyway, so neither she nor those close to her would suffer greatly by her death. Judah and his family, on the other hand, prospered because he made this choice; they prospered in a way that was *only* possible *because* he made this choice. Even the person who was falsely accused of the murder was not harmed, since, as a multiple killer, his jail time would not have increased because of his conviction for this crime. It is hard to point to someone apart from Delores who was harmed by her death, while it is easy to identify those who profited (in terms of their happiness level) because of it. Even for Delores, if she died quickly and painlessly, the nature of her harm is limited to the happiness she would have experienced had she continued living. The movie suggests that she was not a particularly happy person. Thus, this loss may be more than compensated for by the increase in happiness experienced because of her death by Judah and his family. This analysis points to one of the most serious problems for utilitarianism, sometimes referred to as the **problem of rights**: utilitarianism doesn't recognize the notion of a right—for example, the right not to be killed. For this ethical theory, there is nothing in and of itself wrong with killing someone, so long as that killing produces more happiness than not killing.

158

In addition, for the classical version of utilitarianism (e.g., act utilitarianism), there is no requirement that happiness be equitably distributed. Thus, causing a few innocent people to suffer for the sake of producing benefits for the many may turn out to be the morally right thing to do according to act utilitarianism, so long as the benefits to the many taken together outweigh the suffering of the few and there was no other way to achieve those benefits apart from sacrificing the few. (An example often used to illustrate this **problem of injustice** with act utilitarianism is the use of involuntary human research subjects harmed in the course of medical experimentation.)

How would an act utilitarian respond? She might say, "This analysis is incorrect in implying that Judah's action would turn out right according to act utilitarianism. It is based on several false assumptions. First, it's unlikely that Delores had so little happiness in her life that she didn't miss out on much by being killed. Anyway, the analysis offered above misses the point: act utilitarianism is concerned with the long-term happiness produced, whereas the above analysis focused too much on the short-term consequences of Judah's action."

Neither of these responses succeeds in thwarting the criticism. Whether Delores was a generally happy person or not is not really the issue—the criticism points to a very basic assumption within utilitarianism that the ends justify the means. All *Crimes and Misdemeanors* is doing is pointing out that this assumption raises the specter of highly counterintuitive results. (The theory implies that Judah's action was morally right, whereas our moral intuitions insist that Judah's action was morally wrong.) Indeed, our moral intuitions *demand* that the type of action Judah performed (that is, killing someone under those circumstances) be judged wrong based solely on the type of action that it was. Our moral intuitions tell us we need not know anything about the future (short term or long term) to know that what he did was morally wrong.

The act utilitarian's concern that we look to the long run when calculating the utility associated with an alternative raises a third problem for the theory: in order to actually follow through with this calculation, we need to know a lot about how the future of the world is affected by choosing one alternative versus another. As such, the theory isn't of much practical use in moral decision-making. This problem is referred to in the literature as the **problem of omniscience**. *Gone Baby Gone* illustrates this problem well. Consider, again, the moment when Patrick is deliberating about whether to call the police. If he calls, Amanda will go back to her mother. If he doesn't call, Amanda will stay with Doyle. Utilitarianism requires Patrick to consider the consequences of his options. But how can he know what will happen? There are so many events that could occur in the future and so many factors to take into account that it is impossible for him to accurately predict and compute the sum total happiness of either action.

So, one might argue, act utilitarianism is ineffective in helping Patrick decide which choice is right. Moreover, because only *one* future can actually happen, we will never be able to compare the "two" futures to see which one resulted in a greater amount of happiness. Thus, it seems that act utilitarianism can't even help judge the morality of Patrick's action after the future has played out.

Despite all these problems, act utilitarianism continues to be a popular theory among philosophers. Even for nonphilosophers, its focus on consequences captures an important facet of our moral reasoning: in our everyday decision-making, we look to what the likely outcome will be of acting one way versus another in deciding what we ought to do. Yet, in the words of the character Halley, "No matter how elaborate a philosophical system you work out, in the end, it's gotta be incomplete." As an all-encompassing ethical theory, act utilitarianism is seriously incomplete.

6.5 Moral Egoism

Act utilitarianism is only one theory within the utilitarian family of theories (that is, theories that base evaluations of moral worth on an action's *consequences*). Another version of utilitarianism is a theory called **moral egoism**. According to this theory, the only person whose happiness matters in determining the moral status of an action is the actor.[11] Thus, if my happiness is maximized when I perform action X, then action X is the morally right thing to do. The extent to which others are affected by one choice over another is not relevant in determining the moral status of an action. Keep in mind, as with act utilitarianism, that moral egoism focuses on long-term happiness. It is possible that the morally right thing to do according to moral egoism is an action that only bears fruit after many months or years. Furthermore, it may turn out that the way to maximize my own level of happiness is by helping others, either because helping others makes me feel good or because helping others increases the likelihood that others will help me in the future. While moral egoism has its problems (as we shall see in the following section), one shouldn't turn it into the straw man theory that implies that it is morally right for me to satisfy my every whim.

For example, one might argue that the moral egoist is committed to the view that it is right for Helene to drink and use drugs to excess because she is happy when she drinks and uses drugs excessively. However, the moral egoist will respond by claiming that although Helene is satisfying her short-term desires, in the long run, she is only making her life worse. The alcoholism and drug addiction will eventually make Helene miserable, and neglecting and abandoning Amanda will cause her to feel guilt in the future. Thus, moral egoism does not entail that it is right for Helene to abuse drugs and alcohol.

160

But, what if someone can find a way to live with the guilt of doing something wrong? The character in *Crimes and Misdemeanors* that most clearly embodies moral egoism is Judah: in both word and deed, he shows that his sole concern in making decisions is how an action is going to affect himself. Although Judah goes through a period during which he is overwhelmed with guilt, the feeling eventually dissipates. He is able to live free of any guilt for having had Delores killed. At the end of the movie, everything points to his success in having maximized his self-interest, in which case, according to moral egoism, murdering Delores was the right thing to do.

Also, as a consequentialist theory, moral egoism falls prey to the problem of omniscience–the theory requires that we take into account future factors that we cannot foresee. Consider the scene in *Gone Baby Gone* when Angie jumps off the cliff in the quarry because she thinks that Amanda has been thrown into the lake (MM 51:20). Angie's decision does not seem to be in her best interest. It is dark out and the cliff is high, so Angie can't see whether there are large boulders that she could hit when she lands in the water. In fact, Angie is injured as a result of the jump and ends up in the hospital. The moral egoist would explain that it was still right for Angie to jump because, given what we know about Angie's way of thinking, she would never have been happy in the long term, knowing that she didn't at least try to save Amanda from drowning. Yet, as it turns out, Angie is injured for no good reason: Amanda was never thrown into the lake. Consequently, jumping off the cliff did *not* maximize Angie's happiness, and so, according to moral egoism, it was the wrong thing to do. But now it looks like the moral egoist is committed to saying that before Angie knew that Amanda was not thrown off the cliff, it is right for her to jump, then after Angie learns that Amanda was not thrown off the cliff, it is wrong for her to jump. There seems to be something strange here. How can an action change from being right to being wrong merely as a result of the person's finding out the consequences of it? It seems counterintuitive that the person's knowledge of the consequences–rather than the consequences themselves–could affect an action's moral worth.[12]

6.6 Kant's Ethical Theory

Let's turn now to consider some nonconsequentialist theories. According to a *non-consequentialist* interpretation, Judah's action of ordering his brother to arrange a hit man to kill Delores is morally wrong because, in so acting, he fails to recognize Delores's intrinsic moral worth as a person. In ordering her death, he treats her as a mere object that can be used in whatever way he sees fit. In an earlier conversation with Ben (MM 13:15), Judah even admits that he had been merely using Delores throughout their relationship. Ordering her death by the hit man is only the last in a series of wrong actions involving her. Even if Judah's action (the *ordering* of the killing) had failed in its ultimate goal because the hit man did not follow through with it, Judah's action in ordering the killing would have been just as wrong.

Among philosophers, the ethical theory that is the most popular alternative to consequentialism is Kant's ethical theory, named after the German philosopher **Immanuel Kant** (1724–1804).[13] An excerpt from his primary work in ethics, *Fundamental Principles of the Metaphysics of Morals*, is included in Readings from Primary Sources. According to Kant, the consequences of an action are totally irrelevant in determining the moral status of an action. Rather, it is the actor's intention (that is, the motive that was driving the actor when she performed the action) that is the sole determiner of the action's moral status. It is hard to formulate Kant's view in a single sentence; one can, however, think of Kant's ethical theory as a set of nested descriptions that, when taken together, specify what it means for an action to be morally right. First, as we have already seen, an action is morally right if the actor's intention in performing that action was good. There is only one kind of good intention–the intention to do one's duty. One's duty is to act according to those general principles that one can will others to also act according to. (This latter sentence may strike some readers as a rough paraphrase of the golden rule, "Do unto others as you would have them do unto you." Kant rejected identifying his view with the golden rule; however, for our purposes here, this is probably close enough.) So, putting it all together, **Kant's ethical theory** states that an act is morally right if the general principle the actor is following in performing that action is a principle that the actor can and does will others to act in accordance with.

Let us reconsider Judah's action in arranging for the hit man to kill Delores in light of Kant's ethical theory. The first item of business is determining what general principle Judah was following when he performed that action. This is a tricky issue, because the way we describe this general principle will make a huge difference in whether the principle is universalizable. If we make the principle too specific (so that it is applicable only in this one case), it will not really be universalizable. For example, say that the "general" principle Judah is following is, "Whenever a person has a mistress who is threatening to reveal both his affair and possible embezzlement, then that person will call his brother who has connections to the mob to arrange for a hit man to kill said mistress." This principle is not general enough to really capture what is driving Judah in arranging for the hit man. What is motivating him is the desire to protect himself against the threat that Delores poses to his well-being. That the particular thing he is being threatened with is exposure of his affair and financial improprieties is mere detail. Thus, the correct way to describe the general principle that

Judah is acting based on is, "Whenever a person threatens my well-being, I will kill that person." Is *this* principle something that Judah can and would will others to also act in accordance with? No—because he will certainly at some point pose a threat to others. However, he would not desire that the person he threatens kills him. Judah makes his rejection of the universalization of this principle clear a little later in the movie when, wracked by guilt, he confides to his brother Jack that he is considering confessing his crime to the police (MM 80:00). This act constitutes a threat to Jack, and Jack makes very clear that he won't stand for Judah following through with it. Judah's reaction shows that he is quite unwilling to be killed now that the tables are turned and he is the one threatening rather than the one being threatened. So, the principle that Judah is following when he arranges for the hit man to kill Delores is not something that he is willing to universalize; thus, he is acting wrongly when he acts based on that principle.

There is a problem that arises for Kant's ethical theory: it is possible for different people to operate on the same general principle, but arrive at different conclusions about the right action that follows from that principle. Almost all of the characters in *Gone Baby Gone* act according to the principle that *one ought to care for a child.* This principle is not only universalizable, but as we explained in Section 6.2, it is also necessary for the success of any culture. Doyle thinks he's caring for the child when he takes Amanda from her mother. However, Patrick also appeals to that principle when he argues that it is right to return Amanda to her mother. Because both Doyle and Patrick are acting upon the universalizable principle that one ought to care for the child, it seems that the Kantian ethical theory would entail that it is both wrong to return Amanda to her mother and right to return Amanda to her mother. Since one and the same action cannot be both wrong and right, the Kantian theory seems to fail to provide an effective evaluation of the morality of returning Amanda to her mother.

Moreover, there are times when two general principles come into conflict, and it's not clear which one takes precedence over the other—a point that is at the heart of *Gone Baby Gone.* We've already seen that caring for a child is a universalizable principle. It seems that *obeying the law* is also a universalizable principle since we can will that others act according to it.[14] However, there are many instances in the film when characters are faced with a decision that pits the general principle that one ought to care for a child against the principle that one ought to obey the law. For example, when Patrick discovers that the pedophile, Corwin, has killed the missing boy, he recognizes that he can kill Corwin and get away with it (MM 62:17). Although killing Corwin is against the law, it could quite possibly save the lives of other children who might become Corwin's future victims. Patrick decides to shoot Corwin. Even Angie supports Patrick's decision. But later, Patrick regrets his choice. Although killing Corwin was consistent with the principle that one ought to care for the child, it violated the principle that one ought to obey the law. These two principles come into conflict again when Patrick must decide whether to call the police to report that Doyle has Amanda. Patrick recognizes that although it seems to be in Amanda's best interest for her to stay with Doyle, leaving Amanda with Doyle is against the law. Angie and Doyle believe that caring for the child overrides obeying the law. Patrick, on the other hand, perhaps recalling his earlier feeling of regret as a result of killing the pedophile, reasons that obeying the law prevails over caring for the child. Who is right? And by what means are we to figure that out?

Kant had a second way of formulating his ethical theory. This second approach is easier to understand and apply in many cases: "[Act so] as to treat humanity, whether in [your] own person or in that of any other, in every case as an end ... never as a means only."[15] The point Kant is making here is that it is always wrong to treat a fellow rational agent (that is, a member of "humanity") merely as an instrument to achieve one's own goals, without concern for that person as an autonomous agent with his or her own goals, desires, capacity for decision-making, and so on. In formulating his ethical theory in this way, Kant meant to describe the same theory in different words—all actions that turn out morally right according to the first formulation also turn out right according to the second, and vice versa. Indeed, Judah's action is also shown to be morally wrong according to this second formulation, since in this case, as in others (by his own admission), he is merely using Delores to achieve his own ends.

On the second formulation of Kant's theory, Doyle's taking Amanda from her mother is wrong. Doyle and Remy treat Amanda as a means, only, when they take her in order to set up Helene and her drug-dealing boyfriend. And, later, Doyle chooses to keep Amanda as a way to fill the void that was left when his own daughter was killed. So, once again, according to the second formulation of Kant's ethical theory, Doyle's action is wrong. However, as we explained earlier, in choosing to keep Amanda, Doyle also acts upon the principle that one ought to care for a child; Doyle genuinely believes that he will be giving Amanda a better life. Does this mean that the two formulations fail to render the same verdict with respect to Doyle's choice to keep Amanda? It seems not. Kant could explain that people often have more than one reason for acting. Although Doyle may be using Amanda as a means when he keeps her with the intent to fill the emptiness caused by his daughter's death, he is not treating Amanda as a means *only* since he also takes into account Amanda's future well-being. On this explanation, Kant's second formulation entails that Doyle's choice to keep Amanda is right. However, this response seems to fail since, as we saw above, Doyle's action conflicts with the universalizable principle that one ought to obey the law. Thus, there still seems to be some disparity between the evaluations of Doyle's action rendered by the first and second formulations.

There is an interesting difference between the consequentialist theories and Kant's theory here. Whereas the consequentialist theories cannot provide a clear assessment of Doyle's action (at least not until the future unfolds), Kant's theory is able to offer a judgment of Doyle's action, even before he decides to do it. A strength of Kant's theory, then, is that it can help a person determine the right choice prior to acting. According to Kant's theory, it is right for Doyle to keep Amanda. But what if Amanda's future with Doyle turns out to be miserable because she was kept from her biological mother? Would we be inclined to change our assessment of Doyle's action at that time? Or would we continue to agree with Kant that it is the intent that matters, not the consequences?

6.7 Divine Command Theory and Theistic Natural Law Theory

Let's turn now to some other nonconsequentialist ethical theories. There are two characters in *Crimes and Misdemeanors* who are portrayed as deeply religious men: Ben (the rabbi) and Sol (Judah's father). The characters present two different ethical theories that share a common theistic base. Sol represents an ethical theory called **divine command theory**, which holds that an action is morally right if that action is in accordance with God's will.[16] According to this theory, I act rightly when I do what God wants me to do; contrariwise, I act wrongly when I fail to do what God wants me to do. For an orthodox Jew like Sol, God's will is revealed to humans through Scripture. Obviously, divine command theory is not a single theory but a family of theories, one for each religious tradition, because different faiths present different views of what God (or the gods) wills.

Plato considers a problem concerning the divine command theory in his dialogue *Euthyphro*. The essence of Plato's objection centers around the following pair of questions: Is an act right because God wills that it is right? Or does God will that an act is right because it *is* right?[17] If an act is right because God wills that it is right, it seems to follow that what is right is merely *arbitrary*–there is no reason why God wills it, he *just happens* to do so. Thus, consider the universe before God has made a decision about the morality of caring for a child. At that point, caring for a child is neither right nor wrong. Then God wills that it is right to care for a child and– voila!–it becomes right. Keep in mind that, on this account, God doesn't appeal to any reason when making his choice: he *just chooses* that caring for a child is right. In fact, he could just as easily have willed that it is wrong to care for a child. But that can't be right. God would never have willed that caring for a child is wrong. Because God is all-knowing and all-good, God knows that it is right to care for a child and would want all children to be cared for.[18] So, it looks like the correct response to Plato's question must be that God wills that caring for a child is right *because it is right*. But in this case, God does not decide that caring for a child is right. Instead, caring for a child is a basic principle that is independent of and prior to any choice that God might make.

A second, related problem for divine command theory goes like this: According to the divine command theory, I act rightly when I do what God tells me to do. However, acting because it's what God commands me to do is not acting morally, it's just following orders.[19] My action is moral only when I do it because I see that it is the right choice. For example, if I care for a child because it's what God tells me to do, I am not acting out of a sense of moral concern; I am merely obeying God's command. On the other hand, if I care for the child, not because God tells me to, but because I recognize that *it's the right thing to do*, only then do I act morally. So, it seems that the divine command theory cannot provide for genuinely moral actions.

Divine command theory is not alone among theories that ground ethics in a transcendent being (God). Ben presents an interesting alternative. In the first conversation between Ben and Judah, when Judah tells Ben of his affair and Delores's threat to expose it, Ben suggests that Judah confess to his wife (Miriam), with the hope that she will understand. Ben even sees this as a possible source of enrichment for Judah and Miriam's marriage as they work through the ramifications of Judah's infidelity. Judah scoffs at this idea. Then Ben responds, "[I]t's a fundamental difference in the way we view the world. You see it as harsh and empty of values and pitiless. And I couldn't go on if I didn't feel with all my heart that there's a moral structure–with real meaning–with forgiveness and some kind of higher power. Otherwise, there's no basis to know how to live" (MM 13:50).

The theory that Ben is summarizing above is called **theistic natural law theory**. Its key features are that right and wrong are grounded in the natural order of things (what Ben calls "the moral structure"), which is ultimately grounded in God's purposes. You may be asking what the difference is between this theory and divine command theory. The answer is that, for theistic natural law theory, there is a conceptual layer separating ethics and God's will whereas, for divine command theory, ethics is defined directly in terms of God's will. According to theistic natural law theory, everything has a purpose or function, one that God had in mind and that led God to create it. This purpose or function is something that rational creatures like us can glean by examining how nature is "put together." Thus, unlike with divine command theory, we don't need explicit revelation from God to figure out whether an action is right or wrong. Indeed, according to this theory, the theist has no special access to moral knowledge because all that is required to discern right from wrong is human reason.

Natural law theory also comes in a nontheistic flavor. This theory, appropriately called **nontheistic natural law theory**, grounds right and wrong in natural purposes and functions, but explains these purposes and functions without invoking God as creator. Rather, the concept of a "natural purpose" or "natural function" would be cashed out by the theory of evolution and other laws of nature.

However, both the theistic and natural law theories presuppose that everything has some purpose or function. One might argue that there are some things in the universe (like the human appendix or wisdom teeth) that have no purpose or function at all. Moreover, what happens when there is some disagreement about what act is in accordance with the natural order of things? Doyle and Angie will claim that Amanda ought to stay with Doyle because it is in the natural order of things to do whatever is necessary to protect the well-being of a child. Patrick will argue that Amanda ought to be returned to Helene because it is in the natural order of things that a child be with her mother. It's not clear that the natural law theorist can resolve such a conflict.

6.8 The "Ought" in Ethical Theories

It may be useful at this point to offer a condensed description of all the ethical theories we have discussed, so that they may be understood in relation to one another (Table 6.1).

As we can see from Table 6.1, utilitarianism, Kant's ethical theory, natural law theory (both theistic and nontheistic), and divine command theory all fall under objectivist ethical theories. But we might wonder

---

Table 6.1 Ethical Theories

Moral relativism
- **Moral nihilism**[21]–all moral statements are meaningless
- **Moral subjectivism**–the individual is the final arbiter of morality
- **Cultural moral relativism**–the culture is the final arbiter of morality

Moral objectivism
- **Consequentialism**
  1. Act utilitarianism–an action is right if it maximizes overall happiness
  2. Moral egoism–an action is right if it maximizes the actor's happiness
- **Nonconsequentialism**
  1. **Kant's ethical theory**–an action is right based on the actor's intentions
  2. **Divine command theory**–an action is right if it accords with God's will
  3. **Natural law theory**–an action is right if it accords with "nature"
     a) theistic–"nature" is fleshed out in terms of God's purposes
     b) nontheistic–"nature" is fleshed out without mentioning God

---

where does the *ought* come from within these theories? For example, why, according to the utilitarian, ought someone maximize happiness? Certainly, the following two statements say different things:

> *S*: Action A maximizes overall happiness.
> *S'*: Action A is morally right.

Why, according to the act utilitarian, does *S'* follow from *S*? The utilitarian, following Mill, grounds *ought* in a fact about human psychology—the only thing that is desirable in-and-of-itself is happiness (in Mill's words, "pleasure and freedom from pain").

This question about where the *ought* comes from is not just a question for the utilitarian. One can equally well ask the Kantian: Why *ought* someone act only with an eye to following universalizable principles? Kant grounds *ought* in the assumption that "[n]othing can possibly be conceived in the world ... which can be called good without qualification, except a Good Will,"[20] and in our existence as rational beings.

A line of argument that runs through *Crimes and Misdemeanors* disparages both of these responses as qualitatively inadequate. There are three conversations that are relevant here. The first is one we have already considered: the first conversation between Ben and Judah in Judah's office (MM 13:50). The second occurs in Judah's head as he is deciding whether to take Jack up on his offer to "get rid of" Delores (MM 40:50). It begins with a replay of parts of the conversation mentioned above but continues on with a new ending:

> **Ben:** Without the law, it's all darkness.
> **Judah:** You sound like my father. What good is the law to me if I can't get justice?

This "conversation" ends when Judah goes to call Jack. The third conversation is the one that links together the subplots of the movie—one involving Cliff and his travails, the other involving Judah and his murder. It occurs at the wedding reception for Ben's daughter. (The conversation stretches from MM 93:30 to MM 99:30.) In it, Judah informs us of what his life has been like since Delores was killed, by describing it to Cliff as a plot for a murder mystery. He repeats what we have already seen earlier in the film—that he was wracked by guilt immediately after the murder took place to such an extent that he contemplated turning himself in. The world, previously viewed by him as empty of values, is now seen as very much full of values—and his act is a major violation. The eyes of God are watching his every move. But then, Judah reports, something changed. Gradually, these feelings of guilt and the fear of being found out faded away. The murder was pinned on a serial killer, so he seemed to be totally off the hook. Occasionally, little pangs of guilt would surface, but, as time went on, they were less frequent and less disturbing. Several months later, he was back to his comfortable life of wealth and privilege, as if nothing had happened.

This latter conversation contains implicit reference to Dostoevsky's *Crime and Punishment*, the story of a man (Raskolnikov) who murders a neighborhood pawnbroker. A glaring difference between subsequent events in this novel and those in Woody Allen's movie is that Raskolnikov's guilt increases without abatement until finally, in order to find some sort of relief, he turns himself in to the police. Cliff cannot stand the idea that the murderer got away in Judah's "story." The killer is not even plagued with a persistently guilty conscience. This lack of ultimate punishment (either via incarceration or pangs of guilt) is what makes Judah's "story" so chilling.

While many theists would agree, the unsettlingness of a world without ultimate punishment is a special theme of Christian apologists, those who present arguments with an aim toward convincing others of the truth of Christianity. The character of Sol is proof that this tendency also appears within Judaism.

Yet, what is so bad about a world without ultimate punishment? Earlier we stressed the difference between a value judgment and a nonvalue judgment. Moral evaluations are instances of the former. But moral evaluations are more than that. Moral evaluations also include an implicit imperative or command. When you see someone about to do something that you believe is wrong and you say to them, "It would be wrong of you to do that," implicit in that sentence is the imperative, "Don't do that!" While issuing a command (whether implicit or explicit) about a past action doesn't make much sense, still, the shadow of the implicit imperative is there when you judge as morally wrong an action that has already been performed. Earlier, we posed the question: Where does the *ought* come from within various ethical theories? We saw what Mill and Kant had to say about their respective theories. Do their answers explain this implicit imperative in moral evaluations? If not, what could? Many apologists answer the first question with a no–the only thing that could serve to explain where the imperative comes from is the stick that God holds over everyone's head, ready to strike down evildoers, either here on earth or in the afterlife:

> If life ends at the grave, then it makes no difference whether one
> has lived as a Stalin or as a saint. Since one's destiny is ultimately
> unrelated to one's behavior, you may as well just live as you
> please. As Dostoevsky put it: "If there is no immortality then all
> things are permitted." On such a basis,... sacrifice for another

person would be stupid. Kai Nielsen, an atheist philosopher who attempts to defend the viability of ethics without God, in the end admits, "We have not been able to show that reason requires the moral point of view, or that all really rational persons, unhoodwinked by myth or ideology, need not be individual egoists or classical amoralists. Reason doesn't decide here.... Pure practical reason, even with a good knowledge of the facts, will not take you to morality." If there is no God, then there can be no objective standards of right and wrong. All we are confronted with is, in Jean-Paul Sartre's words, the bare valueless fact of existence.[22]

This "bare valueless fact of existence" is what Ben meant when he said, "Without the law, it's all darkness," and, "You [Judah, the atheist] see [the world] as harsh and empty of values and pitiless. And I couldn't go on if I didn't feel with all my heart that there's a moral structure—with real meaning—with forgiveness and some kind of higher power. Otherwise there's no basis to know how to live." Morality doesn't exist unless there is some transcendent being (God) who can invest the world with values "from without."

However, we saw that Plato convincingly argues that God cannot be the ultimate basis of morality. Because God's decisions cannot be arbitrary, he must make his choices according to reason. And that means that there must be some prior, independent moral principles upon which God bases any decision. Thus, if there is an objective moral structure, it cannot find its basis in a higher power.

Moreover, it's not so clear that acting *just to avoid ultimate punishment* is acting *morally*.[23] We saw in Section 6.7 that doing some act just because God commands us to is not acting morally, it is merely following God's orders. Similarly, if a person acts to gain an ultimate reward or avoid an ultimate punishment, he is not acting morally, he is acting *prudently*—he is acting in a way to protect his own future. The person acts ethically only if he acts because he recognizes that doing the act is wrong and not because he wants to avoid some punishment. So even if one's destiny is ultimately rooted in one's behavior, that still doesn't take us to morality.

The most colorful character from *Crimes and Misdemeanors* has to be Judah's Aunt May, whom we meet during Judah's reminiscence of a Passover seder from his youth (MM 69:50). Sol labels her a "nihilist"; although it is unclear that she is best described as a moral nihilist. If anything, Aunt May represents cultural moral relativism. In particular, her statement "might makes right" is the watchword for one way of understanding that theory. At the least, it is clear that she is no moral objectivist, as seen in the following exchange:

Seder Guest: What are you saying, May? There's no morality in the whole world?

May: For those who want morality, there's morality. Nothing is handed down in stone.

Similarly, in a discussion between Patrick and Remy that occurs some time after Patrick shoots the pedophile, Patrick claims that murder is a sin (MM 1:08:46). But, Remy replies, "It depends on who you do it to." Remy's response may suggest that even the most fundamental moral law of all human beings–*thou shalt not murder*–could still be up for debate, depending on the circumstances. Sometimes, it isn't easy to figure out what is right. Because we can't predict the future, it is problematic if the moral worth of an action depends upon its consequences. But it is also difficult to rely upon basic principles because our most difficult moral choices often occur when two basic principles conflict. Religion doesn't seem to help us here. Even if we could know what God wants us to do, what is right cannot be ultimately rooted in his will. Finally, and perhaps most significantly, acting ethically often requires putting the interest of others before the interest of one's self. But, we are all humans, after all, and we can't help but think of ourselves first. Is it any wonder, then, that we so often struggle to do the right thing?

It is interesting to note that *Crimes and Misdemeanors* doesn't end with Cliff and Judah's conversation and the implicit argument for some theist-based ethical theory, but rather gives the last word to a voice-over from Professor Levy:

> We're all faced throughout our lives with agonizing decisions ... moral choices. Some are on a grand scale, most of these choices are on lesser points. But, we define ourselves by the choices we have made. We are, in fact, the sum total of our choices. Events unfold so unpredictably, so unfairly. Human happiness does not seem to have been included in the design of creation. It is only we, with our capacity to love, that give meaning to an indifferent universe. And yet, most human beings seem to have the ability to keep trying and find joy from simple things–from their family, their work, and from the hope that future generations might understand more.

Levy admits that we live in an objectively "indifferent [i.e., valueless] universe," but he thinks that isn't such a bad thing. We will leave you to ponder the significance of his suicide–of his own personal inability "to keep trying and find joy from simple things."

Discussion Questions

1. Should counterintuitive implications count against an ethical theory? What does that say about ethics if they are counted? If they are not counted?
2. Which ethical theory does Cliff represent? What about Lester? Delores?
3. What is the significance of Louis Levy's suicide? What is the significance of Ben's going blind?
4. How would the utilitarian assess Patrick's choice to kill the pedophile? The moral egoist? The Kantian? The divine command theorist? Which theory (if any) provides the correct assessment of the morality of the choice?
5. Does ethics presuppose the existence of a god (or some means to set the wheels of justice right in the end)? Is atheism a "dangerous idea"? Do you agree with Judah that the "movie plot" he describes to Cliff at the wedding reception is "a chilling story"?
6. Do you think that it was right or wrong to send Amanda back to her mother? What moral theory did you use to defend your response?
7. Is it really a fact about human psychology that the only thing desirable in and of itself is pleasure and freedom from pain? Is it really a fact about human psychology that a person always acts on her own self-interest?

Annotated List of Film Titles Relevant to Ethics

Films that Contain Implicit Arguments Against Act Utilitarianism

Extreme Measures (1996). Directed by Michael Apted. Starring Hugh Grant, Gene Hackman.
A movie that explores whether the ends always justify the means.
Run, Lola, Run (1999). Directed by Tom Twyker. Starring Franka Potente, Moritz Bleibtreu.
This movie brings up the problem of omniscience.
Eternal Sunshine of the Spotless Mind (2004). Directed by Michel Gondry. Starring Jim Carrey, Kate Winslet, Gerry Robert Byrne, Elijah Wood.
Several recent philosophers have argued that *Eternal Sunshine* offers a novel counterexample against utilitarianism.
Match Point (2005). Directed by Woody Allen. Starring Jonathan Rhys Meyers, Matthew Goode, Emily Mortimer.
Like *Crimes and Misdemeanors*, murder is the solution to a difficult problem.

Other Films Relevant to Moral Philosophy

Schindler's List (1993). Directed by Steven Spielberg. Starring Liam Neeson, Ralph Fiennes.

At the beginning of the movie, the protagonist Oskar Schindler is a self-starting businessman and wheeler-dealer who sees the Second World War as an incredible opportunity for making money. But his attitude starts to change when he witnesses the suffering experienced by the Jews.

Crime and Punishment (1935). Directed by Josef von Sternberg. Starring Peter Lorre, Edward Arnold.

For those who would rather watch an adaptation of Dostoevsky's novel than read it, here's your chance.

Annotated List of Book Titles Relevant to Ethics

"Classics" in the History of Moral Philosophy

ARISTOTLE

Nichomachean Ethics. This book was written by Aristotle during his tenure as teacher and leader at the Lyceum (a precursor of the modern university) in Athens, 334–323 B.C.E. Aristotle's writing style makes the work somewhat difficult reading. Indeed, many scholars believe that *Nichomachean Ethics* was actually Aristotle's lecture notes, and was never meant for publication. The translation by Terence Irwin, published by Hackett in 1985, is highly recommended.

THOMAS AQUINAS

Summa Theologica, completed in 1273. The source for natural law theory. Still very influential on Christian (especially Roman Catholic) doctrine.

IMMANUEL KANT

Fundamental Principles of the Metaphysic of Morals (sometimes translated as *Groundwork of the Metaphysic of Morals*). First published in German in 1785, this 100-page book is the main source for Kant's ethical theory. An extended excerpt from this work is included in Readings from Primary Sources.

JOHN STUART MILL

Utilitarianism. Originally published in 1861, this very readable little book presents the most thorough and influential defense of utilitarian theory. Quotations here are from the Hackett edition published in 1979. An extended excerpt from this work is included in Readings from Primary Sources.

W.D. ROSS

The Right and the Good (Oxford: Oxford University Press, 1930). Ross argues that ethical theories need not be one-dimensional. This book has been very influential in shaping recent moral philosophy.

JOHN RAWLS

A Theory of Justice (Cambridge, MA: Harvard University Press, 1971). This book tries to combine a reinterpretation of Kant's ethical theory with a social-contract theory of justice. The relevance of this work for political philosophy will be discussed in Section 7.6.

Collections of Essays and Single-Author Books on Moral Philosophy

Daniel Bonavec, *Today's Moral Issues*, 5th edn (New York: McGraw-Hill, 2006). This book marries ethical theory and applied ethics.

Jack Meiland and Michael Krausz, eds., *Relativism: Cognitive and Moral* (Notre Dame, IN: Notre Dame University Press, 1982). This book examines the pros and cons of moral relativism.

Kai Nielson, *Ethics without God* (London: Pemberton Press, 1973). This book examines the question: Does objectivist ethics presuppose the existence of God?

James Rachels, *The Elements of Moral Philosophy*, 3rd edn (New York: McGraw-Hill, 1999). An excellent introduction to ethics.

Related Works

Fyodor Dostoevsky, *Crime and Punishment*, first published in 1865. An understanding of *Crimes and Misdemeanors* is enhanced with knowledge of this work.

The History of Herodotus, first published in 440 B.C.E. Herodotus is the greatest historian of the classical period; his *History* is a useful early source of fodder for the cultural moral relativist's argument.

Alisdair MacIntyre, *After Virtue* (Notre Dame, IN: University of Notre Dame Press, 1981). MacIntyre argues for a return to virtue-based ethics.

Notes

1. A variant on the standard version of moral subjectivism described above says that the individual whose moral code is to be used in making moral judgments is the speaker, not the actor. In that case, someone else could (truly) say of me that my eating meat was morally wrong if the speaker believed that eating meat was morally wrong.

2. There is a corresponding variant of cultural moral relativism, according to which moral judgments are true or false based on whether they are in agreement with the *speaker's* culture's moral standards.

3. Much of the material presented in this section is based upon the treatment of moral relativism in James Rachels, *The Elements of Moral Philosophy*, 3rd edn (New York: McGraw-Hill, 1999).

4. For those who know a little about logic, this is the same as charging the argument with being invalid.

5. Since the argument from cultural norm diversity to cultural moral relativism has the same structural form as the argument discussed in Section 1.6 from diversity of opinion to cognitive relativism, the same counterexample may be used to display the argument's invalidity.

6. The careful reader will have noticed that this criticism of the cultural moral relativist's argument assumes that there are objective facts—something that the thoroughgoing *cognitive* relativist denies. Since our purpose here is not to refute cultural moral relativism but only to show that the premises given in the argument do not entail the conclusion, the assumption does not constitute begging the question against relativism.

7. We will come back a little later to look in detail at the issue of positive benefits arising from Judah's action.

8. John Stuart Mill, *Utilitarianism* (Indianapolis, IN: Hackett, 1979), 7.

9. Ibid.

10. Ibid., 10.

11. A variant of moral egoism judges the moral status of an action based not on how well the *actor* fares, but on how well the *speaker* (i.e., the person making the moral judgment) fares.

12. With respect to the relationship between a person's *knowledge* and her *actions*, it is interesting to note that Socrates believed that *a person only errs out of ignorance*.

13. You may recall that Kant's epistemological theory and its implications were among the topics of Chapter 2.

14. One might argue that no one has an obligation to obey *unjust* laws, thus this principle should be, "One ought to obey *just* laws." We'll return to this discussion in Chapter 7.

15. Immanuel Kant, *Fundamental Principles of the Metaphysics of Morals*, trans. Thomas Abbott (New York: Prometheus Books, 1987), 58.

16. There is a potential difficulty with squaring divine command theory and moral objectivism as it was defined in Section 6.2 as the view that "there are moral facts that do not depend on what anyone … happens to think." This apparent inconsistency is dealt with by making a special case for God: God's will can ground an objectivist ethical theory. However, as we'll see, there is a significant problem for this view, as well.

17. Plato, *Euthyphro*, 10a.

18. Just for the consideration of this argument, we'll have to ignore the fact that there were times when God demanded the sacrifice of first-born sons.

19. Julian Baggini raises this objection in *Atheism: A Very Short Introduction* (Oxford: Oxford University Press, 2003), 40.
20. Kant, *Fundamental Principles*, 17.
21. In some respects, moral nihilism doesn't fit within this nice, tidy framework. We have included it as a version of moral relativism for convenience's sake.
22. William Lane Craig, "The Absurdity of Life without God." Originally in *Reasoning Faith: Christian Truth and Apologies*, reprinted in *The Meaning of Life*, 2nd edn by E. D. Klemke (Oxford: Oxford University Press, 2000), 43–44.
23. The following objection is from Baggini, *Atheism*, 40.

7

POLITICAL PHILOSOPHY

Antz (1998) and *Equilibrium* (2002)

Foreman: I got orders and those orders say "Dig!"
Z: What if someone ordered you to jump off a bridge? ...
You've got to think for yourself.

–from *Antz*

Preston: Without the logic of process, is it not just
mayhem?–What we have worked so hard to eradicate?
Dupont: It is not the message that is important, it is our
obedience to it.–Call it faith.

–from *Equilibrium*

In some respects political philosophy may be seen as a part of ethics, asking questions about the principles that should guide the behavior of states and of individuals acting in the context of those states: Should a state guarantee that its citizens enjoy certain liberties, such as the freedom to choose one's own lifestyle? How, if at all, should a state intervene in the distribution of material goods among its citizens? Is it morally wrong for a citizen to disobey a law? If it is morally wrong, why is it wrong? Would humans individually or collectively be better off if there were no states? These and other, related questions have engaged political philosophers for over 2,400 years, from Plato in Ancient Greece up until the present. In Plato's most influential work of political philosophy, *The Republic,* he presents a utopian state and argues that it is superior. As we shall see, the ideal state he describes bears many features in common with the states depicted in this chapter's two focus films; however, unlike Plato, the films implicitly argue that these common features are morally unacceptable. In addition to Plato, we will also consider the positions offered by several later political philosophers and will find that their views align more closely with those presented in the films.

Section 7.1 offers a general introduction to the topics covered in the remainder of the chapter. Material beginning in Section 7.3 makes frequent reference to *Antz* and *Equilibrium*, and is most profitably read after viewing these two films.

7.1 Four Issues in Political Philosophy

The most basic question in political philosophy, the question that must be answered, at least implicitly, before any further work can be done, is: What attributes of a state make that state *good?* There is general consensus among contemporary political philosophers that a good state allows humans to thrive; however, there is disagreement on what counts as human thriving. In some cases, this disagreement may be traced back to different views of human nature. One philosopher may hold that humans are first and foremost individuals and that a prerequisite for thriving is that each individual is allowed the freedom to follow her own path. On this view, a good state is one that (1) safeguards this necessary freedom, and (2) provides just institutions to ensure that each individual is treated fairly as she pursues her own goals. Another philosopher may hold that humans are so thoroughly embedded in their social context that the "autonomous individual" presupposed by the first philosopher, an individual who can be abstracted away from all of her social identities, is a myth. Such a philosopher will offer a very different picture of the good state. This topic, as well as related questions about human motivation and what human life would be like if there were no state, will occupy us in Section 7.3.

Many, perhaps most, people believe that they have an obligation to obey the laws enacted by the state, and that the state has a corresponding authority to enact those laws and to compel citizens to obey them. This obligation to obey the law is presumed to be independent of any prudential reasons a person may have for obeying (for example, the fear of being caught and punished if one does not obey). A theory of political obligation is an attempt to explain the nature of this obligation, when it comes into play, and how it is justified. Most people believe that the obligation to obey the law is not absolute. For example, if the state passes a law requiring discrimination against certain people solely because those people belong to a particular racial group, no one has an obligation to obey such a law. Thus, a theory of political obligation should allow for exceptions— for cases in which civil disobedience or outright revolt is permitted. We will be exploring the problem of political obligation in Section 7.4. In addition to discussing political obligation in general, we will consider one very influential theory of political obligation, the social contract theory, in light of the two focus films.

What would a just society look like and what role would the state play in creating and promulgating such a society? In Sections 7.5 and 7.6 we will examine these questions, focusing on philosophers at two ends of the history of Western philosophy: the ancient Greek philosopher Plato, and the twentieth-century American philosopher John Rawls.

For those political philosophers who believe that freedom to choose one's own path in life is a prerequisite for human thriving, what are the limits to this freedom? Certainly, not anything goes. I should not be permitted to do things that pose a serious threat to the well-being of others, for example. What are the limits of individual freedom? The nineteenth-century English philosopher, John Stuart Mill, wrote a widely influential work on this topic entitled *On Liberty*. In Section 7.7 we will discuss this work and consider whether the two states presented in the focus films for this chapter tend to back Mill's claim that "the only purpose for which power can be rightfully exercised over any member of a civilized community, against his will, is to prevent harm to others."

7.2 An Overview of the Movies

ANTZ (1998). DIRECTED BY ERIC DARNELL AND TIM JOHNSON.
ANIMATED FILM WITH VOICES BY WOODY ALLEN, SHARON STONE,
SYLVESTER STALLONE

As the title suggests, *Antz* is about a colony of anthropomorphized ants. It follows a few days in the life of a particular worker ant named Z, who begins the film lamenting his place in ant society. He feels that he is not cut out to be a worker, but the regimented nature of ant society does not allow him the freedom to test whether he might be happier and feel more fulfilled in some other role. In a series of accidents, he becomes a war hero and then, along with the queen ant's daughter, finds himself in the outside world, free at last of the confines of the colony. Eventually, he stumbles upon Insectopia, an insect Eden where insects of various species coexist happily in a land of abundance. Is this what the world would be like if there were no states? Z's companion is captured, and so Z must return in order to save her and the rest of the colony from the evil General Mandible, who is intent on massacring all the ants he considers "undesirable."

We see in the fictionalized ant colony an authoritarian state with highly structured social roles assigned from birth. The individual does not matter at all; instead, what matters is the well-being of the colony. Setting to one side the actions of General Mandible, is this the ideal state? In *The Republic*, Plato offers us a similarly authoritarian state as a perfect representation of justice. While there are some dissimilarities between the ant colony and Plato's state, they share in common a disregard for the autonomy of the individual. The rebellion by the very human-like ant, Z, points to a possible flaw in Plato's view of human nature.

179

EQUILIBRIUM (2002). DIRECTED BY KURT WIMMER.
STARRING CHRISTIAN BALE, EMILY WATSON, TAYE DIGGS

Equilibrium is set in a world that has experienced a Third World War so destructive that the society will do anything to avoid a repeat of it. Correctly or not, it is determined that human emotion is the cause of war. As a result, an authoritarian state along the lines of *1984* emerges to make sure that humans never experience emotion again. This state, called Libria, enforces the widespread use of the emotion-blocking drug prozium and forbids objects that are deemed to trigger emotion: art, music, and literature. Violators are vigorously searched out and executed.

An elite police unit has evolved to ferret out transgressors both within Libria and in a no man's land called The Nether. A member of this unit, John Preston, accidentally misses his morning dose of prozium. As a result of his experiences, he begins to rethink the appropriateness of the state and his role in it, eventually joining a group of revolutionaries.

7.3 Human Nature and "The Good"

What would life be like for humans living in a place in which there was no state—no authority to make and enforce laws? Many political philosophers have theorized about what such a **state of nature** might look like. The answers they have given to this question vary widely. We begin this section by comparing two early modern philosophers, Thomas Hobbes and Jean-Jacques Rousseau, on the state of nature. The different picture each philosopher offers us of life in the state of nature is largely a function of different underlying views of human nature. The two focus films for this chapter also offer us pictures of something resembling the state of nature; although, in each case, the stateless region has an important connection with a neighboring region possessing an intact state.

Thomas Hobbes (1588–1679), whose primary work in political philosophy, *Leviathan*, is excerpted in Readings from Primary Sources, offers up a rather bleak view of the quality of life for humans living in a state of nature.

> Whatsoever therefore is consequent to a time of war, where every man is enemy to every man, the same consequent to the time wherein men live without other security than what their own strength and their own invention shall furnish them withal. In such condition there is no place for industry, because the fruit thereof is uncertain: and consequently no culture of the earth; no navigation, nor use of the commodities that may be imported by sea; no commodious building; no instruments of moving and removing such things as require much force; no knowledge of the

face of the earth; no account of time; no arts; no letters; no society; and which is worst of all, continual fear, and danger of violent death; and the life of man, solitary, poor, nasty, brutish, and short.[1]

Hobbes based his view on what life would be like without a state on several assumptions about human nature. The most important of these is that humans are constantly driven to obtain the objects they desire and to seek power that will allow them to obtain future objects of desire. Very often, two or more humans will desire the same object. In a world with limited resources, this will inevitably lead to competition between humans. No human is so far superior to others in either physical strength or mental cunning that he can always get and keep what he desires: even the strongest man in the state of nature can be defeated by a few others who form a temporary confederation. So, people in the state of nature live in constant fear of their fellow humans. Given the fragility of a person's hold on possessions and his uncertainty about the future, it makes no sense for individuals to engage in farming or industry, or other enterprises in which the pay-off is not immediate; thus, the number of goods available for consumption will be far lower in the state of nature than it would be in a comparable region with a functioning state, thereby exacerbating the scarcity. Forms of human cooperation that do not involve an immediate exchange of goods would be impossible, since the parties could not trust one another to hold up their end of the bargain. Hobbes believed that no rational person would prefer living in the state of nature to living in a society with a functioning state that could protect individuals from one another. We will revisit Hobbes's state of nature again in Section 7.4 en route to understanding his version of the social contract theory.

Not all political philosophers agree with the bleak picture of the state of nature painted by Thomas Hobbes. One of these dissenters, **Jean-Jacques Rousseau** (1712–1778), believed that Hobbes's analysis was wrong on two points. The first of these involved his assumptions about human nature. Whereas Hobbes saw humans as motivated exclusively by self-love, driven toward obtaining the objects of their desire, Rousseau saw them as motivated both by self-love *and by compassion*. According to Rousseau, humans have a built-in motivation to relieve the suffering of others and not to inflict suffering on others.

> It is then certain that compassion is a natural feeling, which, by moderating the violence of love of self in each individual, contributes to the preservation of the whole species. It is this compassion that hurries us without reflection to the relief of those who are in distress: it is this which in a state of nature supplies the place of laws, morals and virtues, with the advantage that none are

tempted to disobey its gentle voice: it is this which will always prevent a sturdy savage from robbing a weak child or a feeble old man of the sustenance they may have with pain and difficulty acquired, if he sees a possibility of providing for himself by other means: it is this which ... inspires all men [to] ... [d]o good to yourself with as little evil as possible to others.[2]

Rousseau criticized Hobbes among others for failing to strip away those negative human traits resulting from socialization in his analysis of human nature. It is as if, in describing the state of nature, Hobbes has taken modern humans socialized in the context of a state, and imagined how they would behave if the state disappeared.

> The philosophers, who have inquired into the foundations of society, have all felt the necessity of going back to a state of nature; but not one of them has got there.... Every one of them, in short, constantly dwelling on wants, avidity, oppression, desires, and pride, has transferred to the state of nature ideas which were acquired in society; so that, in speaking of the savage, they described the social man.[3]

If one adds compassion into the mix and removes what Rousseau argued were socialized habits of gluttony and acquisitiveness, Rousseau believed that the state of nature would be far different from the Hobbesian state of "war of every man against every man." Which philosopher is closer to the truth? It is interesting in this context to consider Insectopia and The Nether, the regions depicted in *Antz* and *Equilibrium*, respectively, which have some characteristics in common with the state of nature. Insectopia is portrayed as a stateless land of plenty in which a diversity of insects live at peace with one another. To the extent that individuals interact, those interactions are either mutually beneficial (for example, when the insects staying overnight in the camp take turns stoking the "fire") or based on compassion (for example, when the wasp Chip helps Z return to the ant colony after Bala is abducted by Cutter). From our vantage point as viewers, we see that the superabundance of resources is not natural at all, but based on Insectopia's location within a larger society that is responsible for generating those resources. The superabundance may come to an end at any moment. What will happen to Insectopia then? Will compassion or self-love win out as the primary factor motivating the behavior of the insects that survive?

The Nether as depicted in *Equilibrium* is, like Insectopia, a stateless region in a symbiotic relationship with a larger society. The glimpses we are offered of The Nether are limited, so it is unclear what social structures are present in the groups of humans living there. At a minimum, these groups of humans appear to be able to cooperate among themselves and share limited resources, including the works of art and reproductions of literature and music in which they have a common interest.

The state of nature is of interest to political philosophers because of the role it plays in a particular line of argument justifying the authority of the state and the obligation individuals have to abide by the laws enacted by the state. We will return to a discussion of the state of nature in the following section when we consider the social contract theory. Now, though, we turn to another issue that lies at the heart of debates in political philosophy: What is human thriving?

Political philosophy as a discipline leaves questions involving what actual states in the world are like to political science. However, political philosophy is deeply concerned with questions involving what states *should* be like. Central to these enquiries are determining what human thriving is and whether humans are best viewed as first and foremost members of communities or as autonomous selves making decisions as discrete individuals.

One view of human thriving holds that the good for humans is happiness: a human thrives to the extent that that human is happy. One finds this view among utilitarians such as John Stuart Mill, who writes that "pleasure, and freedom from pain, are the only things desirable as ends; ... all desirable things ... are desirable either for the pleasure inherent in themselves, or as means to the promotion of pleasure and the prevention of pain."[4] Individuals may find pleasure in different objects and different pursuits; thus a good state would allow individuals the liberty to discover what makes them happy and to achieve it. This individualistic conception of the self is the cornerstone of liberalism.

Consider the opening soliloquy delivered by Z to his psychotherapist:

> I was not cut out to be a worker.... Handling dirt is not my idea of a rewarding career ... I'm supposed to do everything for the colony and what about my needs–what about ME! ... The whole system makes me feel insignificant.

Consider also Weaver's discovery of his joy at performing work associated with worker ants: "Nobody told me digging was so much fun!" In both cases, the character is making the following point: different things give different people pleasure; if a state (or custom) locks individuals into a particular role with a predefined set of activities, they will not be able to explore options and discover what the good is for them.

One finds a similar line of reasoning in *Equilibrium* in the scene in which John Preston interrogates Mary O'Brien:

Preston: What's the point of your existence?
O'Brien: To feel. Because you've never done it, you can never know it. But it's as vital as breath and without it ... breath is just a clock ticking.

Both films appear to be arguing for **liberalism**: the view that protecting individual liberty is of pre-eminent importance in any state. For most political philosophers liberty is viewed as an instrumental good; that is, something that is good because of the results it brings about. One finds this view expressed in its most explicit form in John Stuart Mill's *On Liberty*, excerpts from which are included in Readings from Primary Sources. We will return to a closer examination of Mill's arguments for liberalism in Section 7.7.

Not all political philosophers have embraced liberalism. **Plato** (429–347 B.C.E.), for example, described a utopian state in *The Republic* in which the state made all of the important decisions for individual citizens. His reasoning was that the masses of people do not know what is in their best interest and, contra Mill, would be better off if a knowledgeable and benign ruler made important decisions for them. While Plato was no utilitarian, he does occasionally offer utilitarian-sounding justifications for giving the state so much control over the lives of individuals: "[i]n establishing our city, we are not aiming to make any one group outstandingly happy, but to make the whole city so, as far as possible."[5] One way of thinking about why Plato and Mill came to such different conclusions on the value of liberty is that Plato was working from the assumption that absolute knowledge was obtainable by the use of the intellect and that this knowledge could be brought to bear in the arena of politics. Mill, on the other hand, took to heart the lessons of skepticism; the intellect could not provide us with knowledge about what consequences would follow from what actions. His political philosophy reflects this skepticism and leaves it up to the individual to test out various lifestyles and see what works for them.

A second set of opponents to liberalism, the communitarians, base their criticisms on an underlying assumption of liberalism: that individuals may be considered in isolation from their various social relationships. The **communitarians** argue that the social traditions in which all actual people find themselves provide the necessary interpretive framework with which to discuss questions involving values. To attempt to abstract away an individual's social context is to discard the only things that could be used in determining what is of value to that individual. Rather than safeguarding individual liberty, communitarians argue that the good state should promote and support social institutions that reinforce a particular set of values. The states depicted in both *Antz* and *Equilibrium* are broadly communitarian. The particular society and institutions that evolve in *Equilibrium* are a response to a cataclysmic event that the society experienced in the past. The *historical* context of this society has dictated a new conception of the good (a stable society in which there is no repeat of the earlier cataclysm) that the state reinforces in its propaganda, laws and system of justice. The adoption of traditional religious terminology for parts of the state responsible for realizing this goal (the elite police unit of which John Preston is a member is the Tetragrammaton Clerics, the training academy for clerics is called a monastery) makes clear that, for Libria, stability is not just one goal among many. Individuals within the society have a value system that reflects this conception of the good. One sees this most clearly in the earlier part of the conversation quoted above between Mary O'Brien and John Preston:

O'Brien: Why are you alive?
Preston: I'm alive–I live–to safeguard the continuity of this great society.

The state depicted in *Antz* is likewise broadly communitarian, in that the state, through its institutions, supports an overarching conception of the good (the health of the ant colony) and ants interpret their individual good largely in terms of their social role. In both of these cases, the films present the states' communitarian tendencies as oppressive for the individual citizens living under that state. Thus, we cheer when it appears that the revolution in *Equilibrium* might succeed in overthrowing the state. In *Antz*, the worker ants rebel as soon as they see a model of another ant choosing not to do the work associated with his assigned social role: "You're telling me, I don't *have* to be here?"

7.4 The Problem of Political Obligation

Why do citizens generally obey laws? For example, why do the majority of the citizens of Libria obey the law that requires them to inject themselves with prozium at specific times during the day? There are several possible answers one might give. For one, they may do so out of fear of punishment if they are caught disobeying. *Equilibrium* shows us that the state does not respond kindly to citizens' disobedience. Another possible answer is that citizens do it simply out of habit: they have been doing it since they were children and don't give it much thought. Yet another reason is that they understand and accept the rationale behind the law: they believe that emotion is a dangerous thing, both for themselves and for society, so they inject themselves because they see a reason to do so, independent of its being compulsory. All of these are reasons that some-one might offer for obeying a law, but they make obeying that law unre-lated to its *being* a law. Contrast all of the above reasons with the following one: The majority of the citizens of Libria inject themselves with prozium because they feel an obligation to obey the laws enacted by the state. The remainder of this section will examine the reasoning behind this last response: Does a citizen have an obligation to obey laws? If so, how is this obligation explained? Is this obligation absolute or could someone be justified in disobeying a law under certain circumstances? These are the central questions associated with a subarea in political philosophy called the **problem of political obligation**.

The most popular response to the problem of political obligation among political philosophers in the modern era is the **social contract theory**. It is easiest to understand if we return briefly to the discussion of the state of nature from Section 7.3. Recall the rather dismal view of the quality of life for humans in the state of nature as depicted by Hobbes. According to Hobbes, humans in this condition cannot make agreements with others because, without a state to enforce compliance, neither party has any reason to trust that the other will hold up her end of the bargain. Humans in the state of nature, being rational, recognize that they would be better off if agreements could be made and enforced, but, without the state, they are stuck. Contemporary political philosophers have described the situa-tion of people living in the state of nature in terms of an analogous story involving two prisoners, so this situation type is referred to in the literature as the **prisoner's dilemma**. Imagine that there are two prisoners in jail on related charges. Each prisoner is offered the following deal by the authorities: if you cooperate with us by confessing to the crime and pro-viding testimony to help us convict the other prisoner, we will go easy on you during sentencing. Let us call the prisoners A and B. An important part of the story is that A and B act independently: there is no one who can force them to act one way or another. Assume that the matrix given in Figure 7.1 shows the number of years A and B will be sentenced to under the four possible alternatives.

Notice that, irrespective of what A does, B is better off if she cooperates with the authorities than if she doesn't. Similarly, irrespective of what B does, A is better off if he cooperates with the authorities. Let us assume that both A and B desire to minimize their respective sentences, that they know the pay-off for them under each of the four alternatives, and that they are rationally self-interested. Given these assumptions, both A and B will choose to cooperate with the authorities and each will receive a four-year prison sentence. The reason that this is called the prisoner's *dilemma* is that a better alternative for both A and B is the alternative in the bottom right-hand corner: the one in which neither of them cooperates with the authorities and they each receive a two-year prison sentence. But making

POLITICAL PHILOSOPHY

Prisoner A's options

		A cooperates with authorities	A doesn't cooperate with authorities
B cooperates with authorities		A gets 4 years B gets 4 years	A gets 10 years B gets 1 year
B doesn't cooperate with authorities		A gets 1 year B gets 10 years	A gets 2 years B gets 2 years

Prisoner B's options

Figure 7.1 Prisoner's dilemma.

this alternative come to pass requires that A and B have some way of making a binding promise to one another to the effect "I won't cooperate with the authorities if you won't." Without some external agent who can enforce compliance, A and B cannot make such a binding promise. They could mouth the words, but, because there is no means of enforcement, the promise may be viewed by both parties as non-binding. The general characteristic of this situation that makes it an instance of the prisoner's dilemma is that A and B end up in an alternative that is suboptimal for each of them because the optimal alternative requires a level of coordination of action that they cannot achieve. Perhaps, if A and B were both members of the same gang, the implicit threat of retaliation by their fellow gang members if they chose to cooperate with the authorities could persuade A and B not to cooperate; but, the way the story is told, there is no gang and no other means to make a promise binding.

Note the parallels between the prisoners A and B and humans in the state of nature: both sets of people see that they would be individually and collectively better-off if they could agree on a plan of action and be assured that all others would abide by that agreement. We saw that a gang might play the role of enforcer for the prisoners. What might play an analogous role for humans who are at constant war with their fellow humans in the state of nature? Thomas Hobbes believes that only a state could play that role:

[C]ovenants of mutual trust, where there is a fear of [non]performance on either part ... are invalid; ... while men are in the natural condition of war, [covenants] cannot be done ... [as] there must be some coercive power to compel men equally to the performance of their covenants, by the terror of some punishment greater than the benefit they expect by the breach of their covenant, and to make good that propriety which by mutual contract men acquire in recompense of the universal right they abandon: and such power there is none before the erection of a Commonwealth.[6]

The people in the state of nature, being rationally self-interested, recognize that the founding of a commonwealth is their only way out, so each person makes a contract with every other person to the effect that "I authorize and give up my right of governing myself to this man, or to this assembly of men, on this condition, that thou give up, thy right to him, and authorize all his actions in like manner." On this view, the legitimacy of the state and my obligation to obey its laws is founded on this contract I made with my (now) fellow citizens.

Describing social contract theory as if this founding event is historical fact leads to an obvious criticism: Even if there was a point in time when such a founding event occurred, *I* was not there. *I* did not participate. *I* have not made any explicit contract with my fellow citizens to transfer my freedom to the state in exchange for others doing likewise. So, why am *I* obligated to obey the laws enacted by the state? Most social contract theorists believe that either tacit or hypothetical consent is adequate to solve the problem of political obligation. If I tacitly agree to the terms of the social contract by receiving the benefits of citizenship and not emigrating, that is consent. Alternatively, if I would have consented, had I been in the state of nature, that is consent.

An interesting question arises regarding whether my obligation to follow the law is an absolute obligation, or one that applies "other things being equal." Does an individual have an obligation to follow the law only if she lives under a *good* state? Do the citizens of Libria have an obligation to follow all laws enacted by their state? What if the set of laws in Libria included a law requiring everyone to turn in suspected sense offenders? Would a citizen of Libria have an obligation to follow this law? What about the state-sanctioned order "Dig!" that the Foreman ant is obeying in *Antz*? Once it is explained to the Foreman that continuing to dig will flood the ant colony, does the Foreman (and, in turn, the worker ants) have an obligation to obey this command and continue digging? How would a social contract theorist go about answering these questions? Here one needs to distinguish two ways of interpreting these questions. The first involves questioning the legitimacy of individual laws. The second involves questioning the legitimacy of the state itself.

Political philosophers disagree over whether social contract theory leaves open the conceptual space for citizens to pick and choose which laws they have an obligation to obey. Civil disobedience as a means to protest an unjust law has a long tradition in the United States and elsewhere, but it is unclear whether acts of civil disobedience can be justified within the context of social contract theory.

The case is somewhat clearer when it comes to questioning the legitimacy of the state itself and the totality of laws it has enacted. To see why, one must go back to the rationale for the state offered by social contract theory. Humans in the state of nature agree to abide by laws enacted by the state in exchange for a benefit. The exchange would be rational only if the quality of life within the commonwealth is higher than the quality of life within the state of nature. If a state offers so little to its citizens, either because of evilness or because of ineptness on the part of rulers, that those citizens would be better off living in the state of nature, then the social contract is null and void. So, in order to determine whether the state of Libria is legitimate, we need to ask about the quality of life of its citizens: Are they better off in this totalitarian state or in the state of nature? As noted in Section 7.3, The Nether is a stateless region, so it could play the role of the state of nature in comparing the relative quality of life of its occupants as compared with the citizens of Libria. Who is better off? The film implies that those living in The Nether are better off. Furthermore, to the extent that their life is "poor, nasty, brutish, and short," it is because of the actions of the state institutions within Libria.

7.5 Social Justice

Recall our earlier discussion of the utopian state described by Plato in *The Republic*. In that work, Plato described the attributes of a city-state that he believed exemplified justice. The social roles he described for this perfectly just city-state match up in many respects with the social roles depicted in the ant colony in *Antz*. The society is broken up into three classes: workers/craftspeople, soldiers, and a single ruler. In Plato's city-state, the latter position rotates at regular intervals. Membership in one or the other of these classes is determined at a fairly young age. For Plato, the selection process was based on the measured aptitude of children. It is less clear what criteria the selection process in the ant colony was based on. Everyone in Plato's city-state is focused on doing what is in the best interests of the city-state, just as the individuals in *Antz* were "supposed to do everything for the colony"; "the life of an individual ant doesn't matter, what matters is the colony." Citizens have no autonomy to pursue individualistic goals.

Achieving stability in the society was a major, perhaps *the* major function of Plato's fictional city-state. One sees a similar function of the state depicted in *Equilibrium*. The society has uniformly embraced the idea that emotion is the cause of strife on both the large and the small scale. All of the state institutions (or, at least, all we see in the film) are bent on preventing people from experiencing emotion. Prozium is referred to during one public address as the "glue of our great society."

Plato believed that economic inequalities were a major source of strife and other bad effects within a society. His views on wealth and property are a function of this overriding state goal of maintaining stability. Plato went so far as to insist that the soldiers and the ruler could not own any private property at all; rather, all property was to be held in common.

> Is there any greater evil we can mention for a city than whatever tears it apart into many communities instead of one? ... Do not common feelings of pleasure and pain bind the city together, when as nearly as possible all the citizens equally rejoice or feel pain at the same successes and failures? ... For such feelings to be isolated and private dissolves the city's unity, when some suffer greatly while others greatly rejoice at the same public or private events.... And that sort of thing happens whenever such words as "mine" and "not mine"–and so with "another's"–are not used in unison.[7]

Plato's views on property and wealth as expressed in *The Republic* have not gotten much traction among contemporary political philosophers; although, his interest in the role of the state in deciding who gets what raises a related question within political philosophy: To what extent will a just state support the redistribution of wealth? Should the state enforce strict equality in wealth among its citizens or should it allow disparities in wealth? What reasons can be given in favor of one wealth distribution scheme versus another? In the following section, we will examine this and related questions that fall under the topic **distributive justice**.

7.6 Rawls's Theory of Justice

Pretty much everyone would agree that the current pattern of the distribution of wealth within Western democracies is unequal: some people have amassed fortunes and others are barely scraping by. Someone may look at this disparity in wealth and ask: Is this just? There are several approaches one could take to answering this question. In this section, we will examine the approach offered by the twentieth-century American philosopher, **John Rawls** (1921–2002).

The most important work in political philosophy over the past half-century is probably John Rawls's *A Theory of Justice*. In this work, Rawls offers a defense of welfare liberalism that has served as a lightning rod both for those in favor of state-sponsored wealth redistribution programs and for those opposed to such programs. The theory of distributive justice, which he defends, shares some similarities with traditional social contract theory; although his aim is to justify, not the state in general, but rather principles of justice that the state should use in forming state institutions and setting policy.

The starting point for understanding Rawls's theory is understanding a hypothetical construct he called the **original position**. Imagine that a group of people have been given temporary amnesia. Their amnesia has caused them to forget who they are within their society: they do not know whether they are wealthy or poor, majority or minority (along all possible dimensions), old or young, sickly or healthy, male or female. Despite their temporary amnesia, all the people in the original position are assumed to be rational and self-interested; that is, they are assumed to be able to make sound inferences and to be concerned about how well off they are in their "real" life outside of the **veil of ignorance** (Rawls's technical name for this temporary amnesia). Imagine that the people in the original position have been given the following task: they are to determine the principles of justice that will be used to guide the creation of institutions and policies of their state. What principles would they choose? Rawls argued that rationally self-interested people would choose the following:

[1] Each person is to have an equal right to the most extensive total system of equal liberties compatible with a similar system of liberty for all.
[2] Social and economic inequalities are to be arranged so that they are both
  a) To the greatest benefit of the least advantaged and
  b) Attached to offices and positions open to all under conditions of fair equality of opportunity.[8]

Rawls believed that a person in the original position would adopt just these principles and, if asked, would offer reasoning along the following lines. Since I am behind the veil of ignorance, I don't know my circumstances in society. Perhaps I'm at the bottom of the wealth ladder, perhaps I'm at the top; perhaps I'm a devoted follower of some movement that other members of my society view as fringe, perhaps I'm not, and so on. Given this lack of knowledge, in choosing the principles of justice under which I will be living, I want to make sure that I am as well off as possible, assuming I am the person "at the bottom." So, I will adopt principles that say liberty is respected and, if there are to be inequalities in wealth, they are to be arranged so that the person at the bottom is better off than she would be under other arrangements. With regard to wealth distribution, because of the uncertainty of how this choice might affect me, I adopt the strategy "maximize the minimum."

Rawls is considered a defender of *welfare* liberalism because this protocol of choosing a system that maximizes the wealth of the least well off
person may require redistributing some wealth by taxing those with more
money to provide access to resources for those with less.

7.7 Individual Liberty

Many political philosophers in addition to Rawls have argued in favor of
liberalism. John Stuart Mill's book *On Liberty*, excerpted in Readings from
Primary Sources, is an extended argument for liberty. We saw that Rawls
argued in favor of liberalism using the construct of the original position,
and the assumption that rationally self-interested people behind the veil of
ignorance would opt to guarantee liberty. **John Stuart Mill** (1806–1873),
on the other hand, argues for liberalism on utilitarian grounds: allowing
citizens liberty to do as they please, so long as their behavior does not
directly harm another, brings about greater overall happiness than any
other state policy.

Mill sets up his argument in *On Liberty* by distinguishing two types of
behavior: self-regarding and other-regarding. **Self-regarding behavior**
is behavior that, if it directly affects anyone at all, affects only the person
engaging in the behavior. Opting not to wear a safety-belt when in a
moving car is an example of a behavior that Mill would consider self-
regarding. **Other-regarding behavior** is behavior that directly affects
someone other than the person engaging in the behavior. Assault is an
example of behavior that Mill would consider other-regarding. Mill frames
liberalism in terms of laws that restrict an individual's right to engage in
behavior that is self-regarding. The position he defends has become
known in the literature as the **no-harm principle**: "the only purpose
for which power can be rightfully exercised over any member of a civilized community, against his will, is to prevent harm to others."[9] Mill
allows that this principle applies only to mature, rational humans: others
(for example, children and the mentally ill) may be coerced by the state
not to engage in certain types of behavior, even if those behaviors are self-
regarding.

An obvious objection to the way Mill is framing his argument in *On
Liberty* is that he fails to take into account the myriad ways in which
behavior that is superficially self-regarding may be seen on deeper analysis to affect others. So, my failing to use a safety-belt affects others negatively if I am in an accident and, as a result of my injuries, am no longer
able to meet my responsibilities to my family or to society. The objection
continues: apart from the behaviors of individuals who live alone on
islands (who don't need a state anyway), there is no such thing as self-
regarding behavior. Mill attempts to respond to this objection by distinguishing the various ways in which one person's behavior can affect

192

another; although many commentators believe that his response is not adequate. Despite this objection, the details of Mill's argument are worth considering, since they share much in common with features of the two focus films for this chapter.

Mill breaks up the argument for liberalism into two parts, one for each of the two major types of self-regarding behavior: (1) thought, speech, and expression, and (2) lifestyle choices. Let us take these in order. For Mill, state regulation of the free flow of ideas on either the producing end or the consuming end is unacceptable. Thus, the censorship depicted in *Equilibrium* would be vehemently opposed by Mill as contrary to the utilitarian ethics on which he believed state policy ought to be based. Interestingly, state censorship in *Equilibrium* was justified within the film on utilitarian grounds by using the following line of reasoning:

1. As a general rule, experiencing works of art (literature, art, music) causes people to experience emotion.
2. As a general rule, experiencing emotion causes people to act violently.
3. Therefore, as a general rule, experiencing works of art causes people to act violently.
4. State interventions that decrease the likelihood that people will act violently are morally justified on utilitarian grounds.
5. Therefore, censorship (state interventions that keep people from experiencing works of art) is morally justified on utilitarian grounds.

This is a poor argument on several grounds. For one thing, even if we grant that premises 1 and 2 are fine on their own, they do not together imply 3. Compare the first three premises from the above argument with the following:

1′ As a general rule, working out causes people to sweat.
2′ As a general rule, sweating causes people's body temperature to decrease.
3′ Therefore, as a general rule, working out causes people's body temperature to decrease.

Premises 1 and 2 do not entail premise 3 any more than 1′ and 2′ entail 3′. Even if we grant the intermediate conclusion (premise 3) "for the sake of argument," Mill would object to the remaining piece of reasoning. Mill explicitly considered whether censorship could be justified by appeal to the dangerousness of the idea being censored and argued that it could not. While the sorts of examples of "dangerous ideas" Mill mentioned as candidates for legitimate state censorship in the minds of some—such as atheism or the belief that there is no afterlife—are far removed from candidates for censorship in Libria, his argument against the former is also an argument against the latter.

Here is Mill's argument against state censorship, nicely summarized by him at the end of chapter II from *On Liberty*:

> We have now recognized the necessity to the mental well-being of mankind (on which all their other well-being depends) of freedom of opinion, and freedom of the expression of opinion, on four distinct grounds; which we will now briefly recapitulate.
>
> First, if any opinion is compelled to silence, that opinion may, for aught we can certainly know, be true. To deny this is to assume our own infallibility.
>
> Secondly, though the silenced opinion be an error, it may, and very commonly does, contain a portion of truth; and since the general or prevailing opinion on any object is rarely or never the whole truth, it is only by the collision of adverse opinions that the remainder of the truth has any chance of being supplied.
>
> Thirdly, even if the received opinion be not only true, but the whole truth; unless it is suffered to be, and actually is, vigorously and earnestly contested, it will, by most of those who receive it, be held in the manner of a prejudice, with little comprehension or feeling of its rational grounds. And not only this, but, fourthly, the meaning of the doctrine itself will be in danger of being lost, or enfeebled, and deprived of its vital effect on the character and conduct: the dogma becoming a mere formal profession, inefficacious for good, but cumbering the ground, and preventing the growth of any real and heartfelt conviction, from reason or personal experience.[10]

The upshot of Mill's argument is that everybody loses out when the state makes a practice of censoring free expression, irrespective of whether or not the censored view is true. One may object to linking Mill's argument (which focused on censoring the expression of opinions which have a truth value) with the censorship of works of art (which often do not express anything with a truth value); however, we could certainly use Mill's argument if we limit its scope to those works which express ideas that could be either true or false.

In addition to an argument against state censorship, Mill also offers an argument in *On Liberty* against state interference in lifestyle choices. Basically, any behavior that is self-regarding should not be subject to state interference. The final few minutes of *Antz* offers us a version of Mill's argument. In the closing voice-over by Z, he tells us how the story continued after General Mandible's plot was defeated:

I finally feel like I found my place, and you know what?–It's right back where I started. But this time, I chose it.

This sentiment is very much in line with Mill's position on why the state should not interfere in lifestyle choices, since there is value in the mere act of choosing:

> It really is of importance, not only what men do, but also what manner of men they are that do it. Among the works of man which human life is rightly employed in perfecting and beautifying, the first in importance surely is man himself. ... Human nature is not a machine to be built after a model, and set to do exactly the work prescribed for it, but a tree, which requires to grow and develop itself on all sides, according to the tendency of the inward forces which make it a living thing.[11]

Discussion Questions

1. What do you think life would be like in the state of nature?
2. Under what circumstances, if at all, do you believe an individual is justified in not obeying a law? Do you think that any adequate theory of political obligation must "make room" for civil disobedience and conscientious objection?
3. Who do you think is closer to the truth, Plato or Mill, when it comes to the ability of the average human to figure out what is really in their best interest?
4. Do you believe that disparities in wealth within Western democracies is a sign of injustice? What about disparities in wealth between countries?
5. How do you think a communitarian would respond to Rawls's use of the veil of ignorance in determining principles of justice for a society and state?
6. Would Mill favor the censorship of pornography?
7. To what extent does my behavior need to harm another person to justify the state stepping in and coercing me?

Annotated List of Films Relevant to Political Philosophy

1984 (1984). Directed by Michael Radford. Starring John Hurt, Richard Burton, Suzanna Hamilton.
A faithful film version of George Orwell's classic of the same name.

Lord of the Flies (1990). Directed by Harry Hook. Starring Balthazar Getty, Chris Furrh, Danuel Pipoly.

One version of the state of nature populated by British schoolboys. Based on the novel by William Golding.

Animal Farm (1999, 1954)

There have been several animated versions of the Orwell classic released over the years.

Annotated List of Books Relevant to Political Philosophy

"Classics" in the History of Political Philosophy

PLATO

Crito. In 399 B.C.E., Plato's teacher, Socrates, was found guilty of impiety and corrupting the youth of Athens and sentenced to death by the Athenian authorities. This short work by Plato describes how Socrates was offered the opportunity to flee his sentence, but chose to stay and follow through with the sentence, even though it was unjust. Socrates offers four reasons why he (and others) have a moral obligation to obey the law.

The Republic. This work covers many diverse topics, including metaphysics, political philosophy, and ethics.

THOMAS HOBBES

Leviathan. First published in English in 1651. Hobbes wrote several works covering political philosophy, but *Leviathan* is by far his most important. In it, he lays out his version of human nature, the state of nature, and the social contract theory. Excerpts from this work are included in Readings from Primary Sources.

JOHN LOCKE

Two Treatises of Government. First published in English in 1689. The first treatise in this two-part work offers Locke's argument against the divine right of kings. The second treatise (often published on its own) offers Locke's positive political philosophy.

JEAN-JACQUES ROUSSEAU

Discourse on the Origin of Inequality. First published in French in 1754. Written for an essay contest, this work is Rousseau's response to the question: "What is the Origin of the Inequality Among Mankind; and whether such Inequality is authorized by the Law of Nature?"

JOHN STUART MILL

On Liberty. First published in 1859. The locus classicus for the argument for liberalism based on utilitarianism. Excerpts from this work are included in Readings from Primary Sources.

Contemporary Works on Political Philosophy

Robert Nozick, *Anarchy, State and Utopia* (New York: Basic Books, 1974). A defense of libertarianism, written in response to Rawls's *A Theory of Justice* by his Harvard Philosophy Department colleague.

John Rawls, *A Theory of Justice* (Cambridge, MA: Harvard University Press, 1971). A thorough defense of welfare liberalism.

Robert Paul Wolff, *In Defense of Anarchism* (New York: Harper Collins, 1970). As the title suggests, this is a defense of philosophical anarchism. Wolff argues that there is no way to reconcile personal autonomy and political obligation.

Notes

1. Thomas Hobbes, *Leviathan* (Indianapolis, IN: Hackett, 1994), 76.
2. Jean-Jacques Rousseau, *The Social Contract and Discourses,* trans. G. D. H. Cole (London: Everyman, 1920), 199–200.
3. Ibid., 175.
4. John Stuart Mill, *Utilitarianism,* ed. George Sher (Indianapolis, IN: Hackett, 1979), 7.
5. Plato, *The Republic,* trans. G. M. A. Grube (Indianapolis, IN: Hackett, 1974), 86.
6. Hobbes, *Leviathan,* 89.
7. Plato, *The Republic,* 123.
8. John Rawls, *A Theory of Justice* (Cambridge, MA: Harvard University Press, 1971), 302.
9. John Stuart Mill, *On Liberty,* ed. Elizabeth Rapaport (Indianapolis, IN: Hackett, 1978), 9.
10. Ibid., 50.
11. Ibid., 56–57.

8

THE PROBLEM OF EVIL

The Seventh Seal (1957) and
God on Trial (2008)

Faith is a torment, did you know that? It is like loving someone who is out there in the darkness but never appears, no
matter how loudly you call.

−from *The Seventh Seal*

How can [God] be all-powerful and just? Either he's all-powerful,
in which case, he could have stopped this but he chose not
to, because he is not just. Or he'd like to stop this, but he
could not.

−from *God on Trial*

So God reserves the right to punish the wicked. That's in the
covenant. The question is, why did he choose to punish this
good man here and not, for instance, Hitler?

−from *God on Trial*

One of the most difficult intellectual problems facing those who believe in
an all-powerful, wholly good God is reconciling that belief with the existence of so much pain and suffering in the world. This problem is known
as the problem of evil. If God really does exist and cares deeply about
creation, then God should want to get rid of unnecessary suffering in the
world. Why doesn't God get rid of it? Some people interpret the existence
of pain and suffering as proof that God does not exist; for, if God did exist,
there wouldn't be any unnecessary suffering. Defenders of religion have
tried various approaches to circumventing the problem of evil. In this
chapter we will examine these approaches and ask, for each one, whether
it is successful.

The problem of evil has been recognized as a serious difficulty for religion for millennia. One can find formulations of it among the writings of
ancient Greek philosophers.[1] Clearly, then, it did not just spring up with
the advance of Western monotheism into Europe. While the existence of
evil (both human-caused and nature-caused) is a problem within many

religious traditions, it has a particularly severe variant within apocalyptic Christianity. Most of the material in this chapter is relevant to any religious tradition that posits the existence of an all-powerful and wholly good God (or gods); however, the material in Section 8.3 focuses on the particular difficulties of reconciling the existence of God with what God has in store for the world, as foretold in the last book of the Christian Bible (the Book of Revelation). While *The Seventh Seal* comes out of the Christian tradition, it is broad enough to serve as a useful tool for examining the problem of evil in general. Likewise, although the arguments presented in *God on Trial* are directed at the Jewish concept of God, they are applicable to any theistic attempt to rationalize the unnecessary suffering in a world that was created by an all-good, all-powerful being.

As always, the material in the early sections of this chapter (up through Section 8.2) may be read before watching the two films. Material beginning with Section 8.3 makes heavy reference to *The Seventh Seal* and *God on Trial* and is best read only after viewing them.

8.1 The Two Faces of the Problem of Evil

The way philosophers approach any topic (including religion) is to sort through the relevant evidence and make a judgment based on that evidence. In many cases there is evidence on two sides; thus the philosopher's job is to judge which side has the best evidence overall. This approach is similar to the approach a jury uses in trying to decide who to believe–the defendant or the prosecutor. Here, the two "sides" correspond to theism (the view that God exists) and atheism (the view that God does not exist). We shall return shortly to reformulate these positions more precisely. Ultimately, the philosopher of religion will look at the evidence (primarily in the form of arguments) in favor of theism and against theism, and decide which makes the best case.

Theologians have put forward many arguments in favor of theism. The most intuitive of these is the **first-cause argument**,[2] which states that God must exist, because it is only the existence of an eternal, powerful creator (God) that can explain why there is a world at all. Someone (or something) must have performed the original act of creation that got the ball rolling. That entity could not be a part of the world. That entity must have been God. Therefore, God exists.

A second popular argument for God's existence is the **argument from design**,[3] which states that the world and everything in it shows evidence of being the product of intelligent design and creation, much as a car shows evidence of the existence of its designer. Cars are complicated objects, with parts that fit together in a way that allows a car to perform a useful function. It is highly unlikely that a car would coalesce as a product of the chance operation of natural forces–the level of complexity is just too great. Rather, the relationship between the car's complexity and the function it performs gives evidence that cars are designed. If something is designed, there must be a designer. This should not come as a shock—we all know of the existence of these hypothesized designers: they are called automotive engineers. According to the argument from design, the world is like a car, only much more so. Even the simplest one-celled organisms are incredibly complex. It is hard to believe that these organisms (much less something like a human being, or a whole ecosystem) could be the product of the chance operation of natural forces. According to the argument from design, the only entity that could be the "engineer" of the world is God; thus God-as-creator exists.

A typical way to object to the argument from design is to provide examples of useless, harmful, or horrific features in nature that would seem to tell against intelligent design. For example, one might argue that the human appendix, an organ that is not only functionless but can be fatal if it ruptures, is proof that humans were not intelligently designed. When you watch *God on Trial*, take note of the conversation between Jacques and Lieble about two different species of wasp (MM 63:03). Lieble provides an example of a wasp that he claims must have been the product of intelligent design. The wasp lays its eggs in a flower, and as the young wasps fly out of the flower, they collect the pollen:

> They don't brush against it like another wasp or bee or the wind. They stop and they collect the pollen.... And then they take the pollen to the other trees. It doesn't help them. They can't eat it. They do it. It is a beautiful arrangement.

According to Lieble, the "beautiful arrangement" could only be the result of God's design. In contrast, the scientist Jacques, describes a different wasp, one that lays its eggs in a caterpillar, from which the larvae then eat their way out. Jacques argues that the fact that an innocent caterpillar must be eaten alive from the inside out in order for wasps to reproduce is proof against intelligent design. "What kind of God would design a thing like that?" Jacques demands.

There are other arguments for God's existence, but the first-cause argument and the argument from design should give you a feel for the sort of evidence supporting theism. The problem of evil is the main argument on the other side. Its influence in driving people away from theism is hard to overestimate. Thus, even for those theists who are not terribly bothered by it, the problem of evil needs to be taken seriously (and looked at from within a reason-based framework), if for no other purpose than engaging with atheists and trying to convince them to come over to the other side.

Not all religions are subject to the problem of evil, but the three main Western religions (Islam, Judaism, and Christianity) are. The problem of evil can only arise in the context of a religion in which the divine being (or beings) is assumed to be: (1) omniscient (all-knowing), (2) omnipotent (all-powerful), and (3) wholly good. A further requirement—one that is implicit in (1) and (2) above—is that the divine being could continue to be involved with the world, changing the course of events at will. With this as background, the **problem of evil** may be formalized as follows:

1. If God exists, then God, being omniscient, knows of the existence of unnecessary pain and suffering in the world.
2. If God exists, then God, being omnipotent, can get rid of all unnecessary pain and suffering.
3. If God exists, then God, being wholly good, would get rid of all unnecessary pain and suffering.
4. If God exists, then there would be no unnecessary pain and suffering.
5. There is unnecessary pain and suffering in the world.
6. Therefore, God does not exist.

Steps 1 through 5 entail the conclusion: Theism is false. For a theist to deny this conclusion, at least one of the first five premises must be denied. At first glance, though, they all seem very reasonable. Premises 1 through 3 are merely making explicit what it means for an entity to be omniscient, omnipotent, and wholly good. Admittedly, a theist may opt to deny one of them, but at the cost of denying Western religious orthodoxy. In several places in this chapter we shall examine the implications of denying God's absolute goodness. It seems that the sincere theist will agree that this attempt at circumventing the problem of evil undercuts the very religious attitude she wants to foster. Likewise, denying steps 1 or 2 undercuts the religious attitude. There is a reason why orthodoxy within Judaism, Islam, and Christianity has settled on these attributes for God—they are part of a worldview in which praise, love, and worship of God is the appropriate attitude. (There are two other attributes that are part of Western religious orthodoxy: God is eternal, existing outside of space and time, and God is responsible for the creation of the world. These attributes are only mentioned in passing, since they do not directly bear on the problem of evil.)

For the remainder of this chapter, we shall use the term **theism** to refer to the orthodox view within the three main Western religions: an entity exists that is omniscient, omnipotent, and wholly good. A theist is someone who believes that theism is true. **Atheism** is the view that no entity exists with all of those properties, and an atheist is someone who believes that atheism is true. Thus, an atheist would say that the name God is like the name Santa Claus—it is associated with a cluster of attributes but does not refer to something that actually exists. A third take on the theism/atheism debate is unlike those mentioned above in being, not yet another alternative view, but rather an attitude toward the theism/atheism debate as a whole; this is called **agnosticism**. An agnostic is someone who is undecided between theism and atheism. Such an individual suspends judgment, neither believing nor disbelieving in the existence of God.

Let us return to the formalization of the problem of evil from above. If steps 1 through 3 are off-limits in terms of what the orthodox theist can deny, that leaves only steps 4 and 5. But the theist cannot deny step 4, since that follows logically from the first three. (Logical consistency does not allow one to deny something that is implied by one's other beliefs. If the theist believes steps 1 through 3, then the theist is stuck with believing step 4 or being inconsistent.) That leaves only one premise left for the theist to deny in an attempt to thwart this argument: the theist must deny that there is unnecessary pain and suffering in the world. This could be done in one of two ways, either by denying the existence of pain and suffering or by claiming that all the pain and suffering that exists is necessary. The first approach would be a rather difficult view to argue, as there seems to be an abundance of suffering of all sorts. The second avenue is the approach adopted within Western religious orthodoxy.

But how could a theist hope to accomplish this? Certainly, the theist cannot go through all the instances of pain and suffering one by one, arguing that each, contrary perhaps to first impressions, was really necessary. There are just too many instances to consider. What the theist must do is argue in general that pain and suffering are necessary and at least hint at how this might be applied in particular cases. A **theodicy** is an attempt to do just that—it is a description of divine policy that explains why, from God's point of view, pain and suffering are necessary for the accomplishment of some greater good. In order to be successful at countering step 5 above, a theodicy must satisfy three criteria. First, it must demonstrate the necessity of pain and suffering that is caused both by humans (for example, murder) and by nature (for example, harm done by hurricanes). Second, the theodicy must do this in a way that makes the amount of pain and suffering more than compensated for by the good that results. Third, it must show how that good could only be accomplished by that amount of pain and suffering (that is, the good could not have been achieved in some way that involved less pain and suffering).

In case this is all a little too abstract, consider an analogy from the domestic sphere. There are some similarities between the relationship parents bear their children and the relationship that God, according to the theist, bears to creation. For one, parents are responsible for watching over their small children, making sure that the children learn not to dart in front of moving cars. Often, the reasoning capacity of a small child is such that explanations of possible consequences (that is, being run over by the car) are not very effective at convincing the child not to engage in some behavior—a small child is not mentally developed enough to understand many of these possible consequences. The only way to teach the child not to dart in front of moving cars is through punishment. From the child's point of view, this punishment (even if it takes the form of a light reprimand) constitutes pain and suffering. Reprimands are effective because they are viewed by the child as punishment. Now, if all we paid attention to was the child's point of view, this punishment would be unnecessary pain and suffering. Why? Because the child cannot see the greater good that it will bring about. We, though, perceive this greater good. We are like God in that respect, because our perspective of things is less limited than the child's. The pain and suffering we inflict on the child in this context is thus necessary if it achieves a greater good (the child's not being hit by a car), and if that greater good could not have been achieved with less pain and suffering. Returning to the problem of evil, a theodicy has succeeded in showing that all the pain and suffering in the world is necessary if it succeeds in dealing with both broad classes of pain and suffering (human-caused and nature-caused), and in showing them to be required in order to achieve some greater good. In Section 8.5 we will examine the two most popular theodicies: the free will defense and the ultimate harmony defense.

Before leaving this section, we want to consider a variant of the problem of evil. The traditional problem of evil questions God's existence. The **modified problem of evil** questions God's praiseworthiness. The way we defined *theism* above, someone who denies God's perfect goodness would count as an atheist, even if that person thinks that a divine being exists who created and continues to intervene in the world. This goes against standard usage of the term *atheism*, so we shall refer to such an individual as a "modified theist." Notice that the modified theist, by denying step 3 of the formalization of the problem of evil, has sidestepped the conclusion without having to worry about whether all the pain and suffering in the world is necessary. But *modified* theism does not come without a price, since it replaces concerns about God's existence with concerns about the appropriate attitude for humans to adopt toward this less-than-wholly-good deity. Would love and worship of this God be warranted? Bertrand Russell argues, "Worship of God is selective, since it depends upon God's goodness."[4] If your experience of pain and suffering in the world convinces you that God is not wholly good, then the reverence toward God associated with the orthodox religious attitude is likely to be replaced either by indifference or even loathing.

8.2 An Overview of the Movies

THE SEVENTH SEAL (1957). DIRECTED BY INGMAR BERGMAN.
STARRING MAX VON SYDOW, GUNNAR BJÖRNSTRAND, BIBI ANDERSSON.
(IN SWEDISH.)

How could there be a book entitled *Philosophy through Film* that didn't include at least one film by Ingmar Bergman? Even though it came early in his long career, *The Seventh Seal* is considered by many to be Bergman's greatest film. It is set in fourteenth-century Sweden—a time during which the Black Death is running rampant throughout all of Europe. Religious zealotry is at an all-time high as the people seek to understand why God is inflicting the plague on them. The film's protagonist is the knight, Antonius Block, who, along with his squire Jöns, has just returned to his plague-ravaged homeland after many years' service in the Crusades. The knight is visited by Death, who informs him that his time is up. Reluctant to die without knowing why he and his fellow creatures have had to endure so much suffering, Block challenges Death to a game of chess. If Block wins, he goes free. If Death wins, Block must submit. But, in either case, Block has the interim time to satisfy his desire to know what it has all been for.

GOD ON TRIAL (2008). DIRECTED BY ANDY DE EMMONY.
STARRING ANTHONY SHER, DOMINIC COOPER, RUPERT GRAVES,
JACK SHEPHERD

God on Trial is a television play based upon a story written by Holocaust survivor Elie Wiesel. A group of prisoners in Auschwitz accuse God of breaking his covenant to protect the Jewish people. The prisoners put God on trial for failing to intervene to prevent Hitler's genocide. The inmates establish a court with three judges: Baumgarten, a professor of law, is Head of the Court; Schmidt, a rabbi and Jewish scholar, is Father of the Court; and Mordechai, an atheist, is the Inquisitor, the one who asks questions. Arguments for God's guilt are put forth and examined, and several of the other prisoners are called as witnesses. The men have only a short while to conduct the trial, as many of them have been arbitrarily "selected" to be put to death, and the guards could come at any time to take the selected to the gas chamber.

Understandably, the Holocaust is a prime example in discussions of the problem of evil. An omniscient, omnipotent God must have known that millions of innocent people would die as a result of Hitler's coming to power and would have had the ability to prevent it. So, why didn't God do something to thwart Hitler's plans to exterminate the Jews? Why did God allow Hitler to exist at all? How could God sit back and watch so many people die horrible, unnecessary deaths and do nothing about it? These are the questions that the prisoners of Auschwitz want answered.

8.3 The Christian Apocalyptic Tradition as a Special Case

The very title of *The Seventh Seal* shows the influence of the Christian apocalyptic tradition, that branch of Christianity which takes the last book of the Christian Bible, the Revelation to John (usually abbreviated as Revelation), as a literal description of the end of the world. The reference to "the seventh seal" comes from Revelation. In it, the author tells of a vision he has received concerning the end of the world–a vision that God commands him to make known to others as a warning of what is to come. The opening of the seventh seal signifies the last thing to happen before God commences with the total destruction of the world:

> When the Lamb opened the seventh seal, there was silence in heaven for about half an hour. Then I saw the seven angels who stand before God, and seven trumpets were given to them.... Now the seven angels who had the seven trumpets made ready to blow them. The first angel blew his trumpet, and there followed hail and fire, mixed with blood, which fell on the earth; and a third of the earth was burnt up.... The second angel blew his trumpet, and something like a great mountain, burning with fire, was thrown into the sea.... The third angel blew his trumpet, and a great star fell from heaven, blazing like a torch, and it fell on a third of the rivers and on the fountains of water. The name of the star is Wormwood.... The fourth angel blew his trumpet, and a third of the sun was struck, and a third of the moon, and a third of the stars.... Then I looked, and I heard an eagle crying ... "Woe, woe, woe to those who dwell on the earth, at the blasts of the other trumpets, which the three angels are about to blow!" And the fifth angel blew his trumpet, and I saw a star fallen from heaven to earth, and he was given the key of the shaft of the bottomless pit, and from the shaft rose smoke like the smoke of a great furnace, and the sun and the air were darkened with the smoke from the shaft. Then from the smoke came locusts on the earth, and they were given power like the power of scorpions of the earth; they were told not to harm the grass of the earth or any green growth or any tree, but only those of mankind who have not the seal of God upon their foreheads; they were allowed to torture them for five months, but not to kill them.... And in those days men will seek death and will not find it: they will long to die, and death will fly from them.[5]

And this is only the first of the three "woes." Once the destruction of the world is completed, God sets about creating a "new heaven and a new earth":

> Then I saw a new heaven and a new earth; for the first heaven and the first earth had passed away, and the sea was no more. And I saw the holy city, new Jerusalem, coming down out of

heaven from God, prepared as a bride adorned for her husband; and I heard a great voice from the throne saying, "Behold, the dwelling of God is with men. He will dwell with them, and they shall be his people, and God himself will be with them; he will wipe away every tear from their eyes, and death shall be no more, neither shall there be mourning nor crying nor pain any more, for the former things have passed away."[6]

The first passage (the one dealing with the seventh seal) should sound familiar: in the film, the opening several sentences of that passage are read by Karin (the knight's wife) as the knight and his company were eating. It is also read in voice-over during the film's opening scene.

It is debatable as to whether the apocalyptic tradition should be counted as Christian orthodoxy. Many Christians either dismiss the Book of Revelation or take it as merely symbolic. However, for those who hold that it offers a literal description of God's intentions for the end of the world, a particularly severe variant of the problem of evil arises, since, within this tradition, it is not only the pain and suffering here and now that a theodicy must deal with but also the pain and suffering depicted in Revelation. One could dismiss the cataclysmic destruction of the earth as not adding anything to the traditional problem of evil, or as being justified as punishment for the evildoers who were not among the chosen. This won't work, though, because the pain and suffering is explicitly caused by God, and God knew from the beginning of the world that this would be how it would all end.[7] Furthermore, God has the power to create a world free from pain and suffering. That is exactly what God creates with the new Jerusalem. You see what an uphill battle the theist has if this story must also be accommodated within a theodicy: God creates a world (namely ours) knowing not only that some people will be guilty, but knowing, right from the beginning, who those guilty people will be. God knows what is going to happen, and has the power to have created a different world–one that is free from any pain and suffering, one that is presumably just as full of that "greater good" for which God is willing to sacrifice human happiness. So, why didn't God skip our world and go straight to the new Jerusalem? Wouldn't a wholly good God have preferred that course of action?

There is a second variant of the problem of evil that is particular not to apocalyptic Christianity but to Christianity more generally. Jesus's suffering has special significance for most Christians. One sees this emphasis manifested in the ubiquity of the cross in Christian iconography. Bergman brings his audience's attention to this in *The Seventh Seal* in several scenes. Just before the scene at the confessional, the knight prays in a small alcove of the church while looking at a wood sculpture of the crucified Jesus: "Christ's face is turned upward, His mouth open as if in a cry of anguish."[8]

A little later, Jof and Mia's performance is interrupted by a parade of monks and flagellants. The procession stops and the wood sculpture of Jesus crucified is lifted up. Here again it is the suffering Jesus, with his hands hammered to the cross, his face convulsed in pain, and the fear of having been abandoned in his moment of need. The emotional impact of these depictions of Jesus's suffering on the average Christian can be quite profound: "God loves you so much, He was willing to do this for you, so that you might be saved." (This interpretation is particularly prominent in contemporary popular Protestantism.) The problem with this way of interpreting Jesus's suffering is that Jesus's suffering isn't that much different from what many unfortunate humans must endure. Why should we have sympathy for Jesus when God inflicts the same thing on us? This is exactly the point that Jöns is making in his final speech (MM 93:00) when he says, "In the darkness where You are supposed to be, where all of us probably are. ... In the darkness You will find no one to listen to Your cries or be touched by Your sufferings. Wash Your tears and mirror Yourself in Your indifference."

Who is Jöns addressing? Not the knight (although, without the capitalized pronouns, he would appear to be the intended recipient, and in some ways he is, but not because he is the one being addressed). This is Jöns's "prayer" to a nonexistent God. It is full of bitterness and defiance, in sharp contrast to the sincere prayer just uttered by the knight ("From our darkness, we call out to Thee, Lord. Have mercy on us because we are small and frightened and ignorant"). Implicitly, what Jöns is doing is pointing out the inconsistency of the average Christian who is, on the one hand, deeply moved by the suffering Christ while on the other willing to let God "off the hook" for all of the pain and suffering in the world.

8.4 The Silence of God

Some religious writers will disagree with the context in which we have framed the question of God's existence in this chapter. Religious belief, they say, is a matter of faith, not a matter of rational justification.[9] If you want to learn about theism, they will suggest that you look not to philosophers for answers but to prayer. At one point in *God on Trial* (MM 49:18), Schmidt provides the following summary of the court's findings: "It was generally felt that we cannot know the mind of God. God is too great. And that all we can do is pray, have faith." During the trial, the prisoners have applied reason and engaged in rational debate to try to understand why God would allow innocent people to be subjected to unfathomable misery and suffering, but none of the logical arguments have helped them discover God's motives or intentions. Schmidt suggests that the only way to come to know the mind of God is through prayer and faith.

But, when Kuhn prays, Moche ridicules him for thinking that God will answer (MM 9:50):

Moche: What are you praying for? That it won't be you [who will be selected to go to the gas chamber]? That it'll be me instead of you? ... Anyone else pray? ... Anyone else trying to help God make his mind up?

Kuhn: Please! The Lord our God can hear you, even here.

Moche: He hears me, and he does nothing about it. He's a bigger bastard than I thought. He hears me; he does nothing about it. He's an evil bastard. He should be here, not us.

Moche's anger is justifiable. The prisoners continue to suffer, more innocent people arrive at the camp each day, and the war rages on, but God fails to offer any counsel to help them understand why they are being forced to endure such hardship. Even if their prayers are heard, God remains silent. Later, another prisoner also mocks Kuhn for praying: "You think saying prayers is going to save your life. 4,000 years of wearing silly hats, and you're still on your way to die." They have seen their family members murdered and entire villages destroyed. Some of the inmates will be put to death later that day. So why would prisoners like Schmidt and Kuhn continue to think that God will answer their prayers?

The knight in *The Seventh Seal* is the epitome of the sincere seeker, but God does not answer his prayers. God's silence is so complete that the knight is willing to seek out the devil in the hope of hearing back something–anything. The way in which the knight explains his dilemma is interesting. The most important scene in this regard is the confessional scene in which the knight pours out his heart to a priest, only to learn later that he has been tricked–he has given his confession to Death (MM 19:00):

Knight: I want knowledge.

Death: You want guarantees?

Knight: Call it whatever you like. Is it so cruelly inconceivable to grasp God with the senses? Why should He hide Himself in a mist of half-spoken promises and unseen miracles?

Death is silent.

Knight: I want knowledge, not faith, not suppositions, but knowledge. I want God to stretch out His hand toward me, reveal Himself and speak to me.

Death: But He remains silent.

Knight: I call out to Him in the dark but no one seems to be there.

Death: Perhaps no one is there.

Humans have a natural inclination to believe the report of their senses: "seeing is believing." We seem to be wired that way. The knight's question–"Is it so cruelly inconceivable to grasp God with the senses?"–poses a serious problem for the theist. The orthodox response to this problem has an important parallel with the orthodox response to the problem of evil: "God will not give a guarantee that would annihilate man's freedom."[10] So, it is not that God is unable to provide the sort of proof the knight is seeking, but that God is unwilling to do so because a belief in God that is based on incontrovertible evidence is not as good as a belief that is made without (or perhaps even despite) evidence.

There is, though, one character in *The Seventh Seal* who "grasps God with the senses"–namely Jof. He often receives visions of the divine. (He was also the only one, apart from the knight himself, who could see Death as he interacted with the knight.) We shall return to a discussion of Jof and his visions in the next section.

Lieble, in *God on Trial,* also claims to have had a sensory experience of God (MM 37:49). Lieble is one of the most complex characters in the film. When the Nazis raided his village, he was forced to decide which one of his three young sons would be allowed to stay with him. Yet, Lieble still has faith in God:

Lieble: I know He is here, even though I don't understand Him. Some days in the spring, there were snowdrops and the first touch of warmth from the sun since ... who knows.
Mordechai: Do you think the guard does not feel the sun on his back?
Lieble: The sun on his back, yes, but that's not what I felt. I felt Him. The guard doesn't feel that. That warmth doesn't penetrate his uniform.

How can Lieble be certain that his experience of God was genuine? After all, as Mordechai explains, the guard feels the sun on his back, too. Is it ever possible to tell the difference between a genuine sign from God versus a spurious interpretation of some chance happening, or even a misinterpretation of something that really was a message from God? The knight's requirement that "God ... stretch out his hand toward me, reveal Himself and speak to me" doesn't seem overly demanding after all.

The last scene of *God on Trial* may suggest that God does not remain silent. After Rabbi Akiba, the "living Torah," has argued that God is not good, and after the court has found God guilty of breaking the covenant, the selected prisoners are marched off to the gas chamber (MM 80:16). Moche, one of the selected, turns to Akiba: "God is guilty," Moche cries, "What do we do now?" "Now," Akiba says, "Now we pray." And so they pray: "We shall sing and be happy all our days. Let our joy be as long as the time that you afflicted us, the years when we experienced disaster." The prayer is engraved on a stone memorial in the gas chamber, and after the present-day tourists finish reading it, the woman asks the man whether the prayer was answered (MM 83:53). "We're still here," the man responds, implying that God answered the inmates' prayers by ending the war and allowing many Jews to survive. But even if God did end the war, we would still want to know, *what took so long?* And why did God allow the Holocaust to occur at all?

8.5 The Free Will Defense and the Ultimate Harmony Defense

The theist has rather a lot of work to do to counter the problem of evil. The two most oft-cited approaches to reconciling the existence of pain and suffering with theism are the free will defense and the ultimate harmony defense. They both share in common the assumption that pain and suffering are necessary components in the production of some greater good–a good that more than compensates for the pain and suffering. Thus, they are both attempts to undercut step 5 in the formal version of the problem of evil presented earlier. Augustine's book *On Free Choice of the Will* offers the first attempt at a coherent theodicy within the Christian tradition. Excerpts from this work are included in Readings from Primary Sources.

Let us look first at the theodicy that has become the orthodox defense against the problem of evil–the free will defense. There are a few concepts that will prove helpful in describing this theodicy. Much of the following comes from the Mackie article, "Evil and Omnipotence," that is provided in Readings from Primary Sources. According to Mackie, $good_1$ is pleasure and happiness. Bad_1 is pain and suffering. $Good_2$ is the second-order good that arises as a result of the development and use of character traits such as compassion, courage, forgiveness, and fortitude. Bad_2 is the second-order bad that arises as a result of the development and use of character traits such as malice, jealousy, and greed. With these concepts in hand, **the free will defense** is easy to state. $Good_2$ requires the existence of bad_1. (One cannot feel compassion unless someone is suffering; one cannot be courageous unless one is at least threatened with serious harm; and so on for the other traits associated with $good_2$.) In order, then, to have $good_2$, God has to create a world with some bad_1. But, there is more. $Good_2$ requires that humans have free will–the power to choose compassion or hardness of heart; the power to choose to be courageous or to run away. So, in order to get $good_2$, God must not only create a world with some bad_1 in it, but must also create a world with at least some creatures with free will. Yet, once God gives those creatures (humans) free will, God leaves open the door that that free will is misused, resulting in bad_2. God values $good_2$ so highly that God is willing to put up with bad_1 and the possibility of bad_2 in order to get it. That is why God chose to create this world, even with its flaws.

Another way to explain the free will defense is by comparing our world (the one God created) with worlds God *could have* created but didn't. Prior to creation, God considered the various possible worlds that could be created. In one of these worlds there were no sentient creatures; hence, no pain and suffering. In another world there were sentient creatures, but the world was designed such that there was no pain and suffering. Without pain and suffering, there was no good$_2$. A third world (our world–the one God decided in favor of) had both pain and suffering and some creatures with free will, so it also had some good$_2$ (and the possibility of bad$_2$). God values good$_2$ so highly that God is willing to put up with both the pain and suffering and the occasional misuse of free will. It was impossible for God to create a world with good$_2$ in it but without pain and suffering. This is the one that God judged to be the best of all possible worlds, so this is the one that God created. And here we are.

Is the free will defense successful as a theodicy? Let us review the criteria that must be satisfied:

1. Does the theodicy handle both human-caused suffering and nature-caused suffering satisfactorily?
2. Does the theodicy explain how it is that the good produced more than compensates for the pain and suffering?
3. Does the theodicy explain why *this amount* of pain and suffering was necessary to achieve the good?

The free will defense was developed primarily to deal with human-caused suffering: Why did God create creatures like us, knowing that we had the potential to be an Adolph Hitler, a Joseph Stalin, or a Pol Pot? Answer: Because by doing so, God also created humans with the potential to be a Mother Teresa or a Saint Francis. This theodicy doesn't, though, have much to say by way of explaining the amount of nature-caused suffering in the world. Did we really need the Black Death in order to develop our compassion? Couldn't I develop my sense of compassion just as well by feeling sympathy for someone who had stubbed her toe as by feeling sympathy for someone suffering through an agonizing death? How does the free will defender answer this charge? It is unclear.

Even in dealing fully with the extent of human-caused pain and suffering, the free will defense shows some weakness. Let us grant that the development and display of the character traits associated with good$_2$ are indeed greater goods capable of compensating for the existence of pain and suffering in the world. Let us also grant that free will is a necessary prerequisite for displaying these character traits. The theist is still left with the question: Why doesn't God intervene in preventing the effects of poor choices from being so disastrous? In *God on Trial*, Mordechai argues that God cannot be both all-powerful and just (MM 36:50):

Mordechai: Either he's all-powerful, in which case, he could have stopped this [suffering] but he chose not to, because he is not just. Or he'd like to stop this, but he could not.

Schmidt: Yes, there is evil in the world because God gave man free will, and [man] chose to do evil with it.

Schmidt explains that the answer to Mordechai's argument is very simple: God didn't cause the Holocaust or the suffering that resulted from it. God merely created Hitler and gave him free will. Consequently, the evil of the Holocaust was the direct result of Hitler, exercising his will. And since Hitler's will is genuinely free, God could not intervene or in any other way prevent him from acting on it.

However, there is a problem with Schmidt's argument. As Hitler was rising to power in the late 1920s and early 1930s, there was a time when the political future in Germany was not yet sealed. Perhaps there was a key speech by Hitler that, if not made, would have prevented him from coming to power. Imagine that Hitler is striding up to the podium to deliver that speech. He has made his choice already–if he gains power, he will start an expansionist war against his neighbors and try his darndest to remove groups of people he considers undesirable from the territory Germany controls. The bad_2 is the choice, which has already happened. Now, it is just a matter of following up on that choice. God, being omniscient, sees all this, sees the choice Hitler has already made, and knows what will happen if Hitler is not stopped. So, God gives Hitler temporary laryngitis. God hasn't interfered with the exercise of anyone's free will. Hitler made his choice; God only intervened after the fact. The free will defender needs to explain why this scenario constitutes undue interference.

Moreover, as we saw in Section 5.3, free will (at least on the incompatibilist's account) requires that a person has two or more genuinely possible options. So, Hitler's choice to start the war is free only if it was genuinely possible for him to decide not to start it. But, again, God is all-knowing. So, before Hitler makes his decision–before God even creates Hitler–God must know that Hitler will wage the expansionist war. Since God's knowledge is *infallible*, it seems that Hitler *must* start the war (for if he doesn't, then God knows something that is false, which is impossible). It thus seems that there is only one genuinely possible option for Hitler, in which case Hitler's choice is not free. This problem is often referred to as the **problem of divine foreknowledge and human free will**. In the Augustine reading, the problem is raised by Evodius: "how can it be that God has foreknowledge of all future events, and yet that we do not sin by necessity?"[11] Augustine responds by applying the compatibilist's account of free will rather than the incompatibilist's definition. A free act does not need to be one of two or more genuinely possible actions, it need merely result from the person's will: "so, God forces no one to sin; yet He foreknows those who will sin by their own will."[12] In the case of Hitler, Augustine might explain that although God knew that Hitler would start the war before he chose to do so, Hitler still started the war freely because he acted on his own will and was the author of his choice.

What is the final assessment of the free will defense? Is it a successful theodicy? Its silence on the amount of nature-caused suffering in the world is a serious problem. As discussed above, it even experiences some difficulties in dealing with human-caused suffering. So, it seems to be unsuccessful—at least as a stand-alone defense against the problem of evil.

There is a second theodicy, the **ultimate harmony defense**, that is often put forward. If the free will defense is the theodicy accepted by religious orthodoxy, the ultimate harmony defense is the preferred theodicy of the average lay theist. It may be summarized as follows. Because of my limited knowledge, I cannot see how the suffering that occurs in the world fits into the overall scheme of things. Mere mortals lack the omniscience to see "the big picture." This theodicy is often described using the metaphor of music, as in an essay by Edward Madden, who writes,

> A chord heard in isolation may sound dissonant and ugly, but when heard in context blends into a perfect whole or an ultimate harmony. So it is with evil. What human beings call evil is an event seen out of context, in isolation, and since man has only a fragmentary view of events, this is the only way he can see it. God, however, who has an overall view of events, sees how such events are good in the long run or good from an overall viewpoint.[13]

Schmidt in *God on Trial* presents a version of the ultimate harmony defense (MM 25:24). Schmidt suggests that the suffering that the Jews are experiencing at the hands of Hitler will result in a greater good for the Jewish people. He points to history and explains that because the Jews were forced off of so many different lands, Judaism was allowed to spread and flourish:

> If we had stayed as we were, would we have achieved so much? We would be a tribe in the desert, nothing more. It was painful, but it was also beautiful. What if we were living through another such catastrophic event? ... What if some great good were to come of this? ... Perhaps a return to Israel.

Mordechai raises a strong objection against Schmidt's argument:

> So, suffering is God's work, is that right? In other words, Mengele is working for God. Hitler is working for God. Is that right? ... If

Hitler is doing God's work, then logic says that to stand in Hitler's way is to stand in God's way. To take arms against Hitler is wrong. Now, does anybody here believe that? Is there any way that that could possibly be true? Isn't that insane?

Mordechai's argument takes the form of a *reductio ad absurdum* (we discussed *reductio* arguments in Section 2.6): If the Holocaust is part of God's plan to bring about some greater good and to achieve some ultimate harmony, it would be wrong to go against God's plan and try to stop it. But it would be absurd to let the Holocaust happen without trying to do something to end it. Therefore, the Holocaust cannot be part of God's plan, and the ultimate harmony defense fails to justify the suffering that the prisoners have endured.

According to the Christian tradition, after death, God will explain things so that the suffering which individuals have endured will be seen as necessary, or even illusory. In one respect, the place of pain in the overall scheme of things (from God's bird's-eye view of creation) would blunt the problem of evil's claim against the theist. Still, though, there is a problem. In his great novel *The Brothers Karamazov*, Fyodor Dostoevsky presents this problem:

> Take the suffering of children, Ivan tells Alyosha; there the point becomes very clear. Here is one example: a Russian general, retired on his great estate, treats his serfs like fools and buffoons. He is a great hunter and has many fine dogs. One day a serf boy of eight throws a stone in play and hurts the paw of the general's favorite dog. The general asks about his dog–what happened? After he is told, he has the boy locked in a shed overnight. Early the next morning the serfs, including the child's mother, are assembled for their edification. The child is stripped naked and told to run. The general sets the hounds after him, shouting "Get him, get him!" The dogs quickly overtake the boy and tear him to pieces in front of his mother's eyes. Did the general deserve to be shot? No doubt, but the atrocity already had been committed. If such an atrocity is needed to manure the soil for some future harmony, Ivan says, then such harmony is not worth the price. Then he asks, if *you* were God, Alyosha, could *you* consent to create a world in which everything turned out well in the end, but to achieve this end you had to see just one child tortured to death, beating its breast in a stinking outhouse, crying to "dear, kind God." No, it is not worth it. No doubt, God sees things differently from men. No doubt, on the day of resurrection, Ivan says, I too will join in the chorus, "Hallelujah, God, thy ways are just!" I too

shall sing, as the mother embraces her son's murderer, "Praise God, I see why it had to be!" But, he concludes, I loathe myself now for the very thought of doing that then. I renounce the "higher" morality, the ultimate harmony, altogether, while I still can, while there is still time. For the love of humanity I now renounce it altogether.[14]

Ultimate harmony or not, the amount of suffering God allows in the world turns religion into a farce. The knight, Antonius Block, is searching–not so much for proof of God's existence as for proof of God's worthiness. He assumes, at least at death, that everything will be explained. But, as Death tells Block that he has lost the chess game, he finds out that even this is too much to expect (MM 84:00):

Knight: And you will divulge your secrets.
Death: I have no secrets.
Knight: So you know nothing.
Death: I have nothing to tell.

There is no ultimate harmony. There is no justification at all for the suffering present in the world. That is what the knight learns. If Death is speaking truthfully, then, irrespective of whether God exists, religion is discredited.

It is interesting to note that the last word in *The Seventh Seal* is given neither to the atheist Jöns nor to the desperate agnostic Block, but to the simple lay theist Jof (MM 94:30). For him, even death is interpreted as a sign of God's beneficence, for with death comes "the rain [that] washes their faces and cleans the salt of the tears from their cheeks." We cannot simply dismiss the view implicit in Jof's inclusion in *The Seventh Seal*. He (perhaps along with Mia) is the only character who has faith. He (again, along with Mia) is the only major character who is not very concerned about the problem of evil or God's silence; if asked, he would probably respond to the knight's concerns about the problem of evil in the same way that Mia responds in her conversation with the knight (MM 55:30)– he simply does not understand what the problem is. He is the only character (other than those singled out to die) who can see Death. Even though his life is not trouble-free, he seems perfectly content with things the way they are. What should we make of this? In some ways Jof is the embodiment of Jesus's advice: "whoever does not receive the kingdom of God like a child shall not enter it."[15] His faith is simple. Like a child, he trusts– he does not feel the need to turn that faith into an intellectual puzzle in the way that the knight, and even Jöns, does. Because of that, he seems much happier than the other characters.

As we shall see in Chapter 9, theism offers up an easy answer to the question: Is life meaningful? The knight's torment is that on the one hand he wants the answer theism provides to this question, while on the other the problem of evil is leading him to reject theism. He cannot have it both ways.

8.6 Other Responses to the Problem of Evil

Recall that the traditional problem of evil is an argument against theism. The argument contends that the amount of pain and suffering present in the world shows that the all-perfect God of Western religious orthodoxy does not exist. We have examined the two main defenses against the problem of evil offered by the theist: the free will defense and the ultimate harmony defense. Both of these are seen to be lacking. What other responses are open to the theist? Do any of those responses work?[16]

One reply to the problem of evil that is often given is that Satan, not God, is responsible for the evil in the world. Hence, the presence of pain and suffering counts neither against God's goodness (the modified problem of evil) nor against the likelihood of God's existence (the traditional problem of evil). This defense has an obvious defect: even if God is not directly responsible for pain and suffering, God is still indirectly responsible for it, since God allows Satan to exist. Remember, in order to be a successful defense of orthodoxy, none of God's perfections can be denied. But this defense denies God's omnipotence, since it leaves open a question as damaging to theism as the original problem of evil: Why doesn't God get rid of Satan?

A second possible response by the theist is that pain and suffering are necessary to serve as a contrast to good. There are two versions of this response. The first version suggests that we could not *know* or *appreciate* what good is without experiencing some evil. Without that pain and suffering, we could not see good *as* good, much as we cannot see and appreciate health as good until we are sick. The problem here is that the *amount* of pain and suffering experienced by humans is not explained. A slight stomachache will allow me to see the value of health; I don't need a huge amount of pain in order to have that negative serve as a contrast. Why, then, does God allow a huge amount of pain and suffering in the world—far more than is necessary to serve as a contrast to good? The second version of this response suggests that good is a *necessary counterpart* to evil, so one can't exist without the other. Just as there can be no *up* without a *down* or a *left* without *right*, you can't have *good* without *evil*. Idek, the Jewish scholar in *God on Trial*, quotes a line from the Torah (MM 15:46): "If we take happiness from God's hand, must we not take sorrow, too?" In other words, even God can't make good without evil. However, there are a couple of significant problems for the theist who defends this line of reasoning. First, as Mackie explains in "Evil and Omnipotence," if God cannot create good without evil, then it seems that there is something that God cannot do, in which case God is not omnipotent. Second, if evil must always accompany good, God would have to be evil as well as good. But then God cannot be wholly good. The modified theist might claim that God doesn't need to be *wholly* good. But as we explained in 8.1 it's not so clear that a less-than-wholly-good-God would be worthy of the theist's praise and worship.

A third possible response is that (the threat of) pain and suffering serves to draw humans toward God: "There are no atheists in foxholes." Here again, there are serious problems with this defense. God has other avenues to drawing humans' attention to religious matters—avenues that are less painful. For example, God could appear to every human individually and say, "Here I am." But God is silent. Indeed, if this really is God's motivation in allowing pain in the world, it seems to have backfired. The problem of evil is probably *the* most important factor in leading people to embrace atheism.

What about the defense that explains pain as the result of natural forces, not the result of God's intentional actions? As with the Satan defense, this defense fails to take God's omnipotence seriously. If God created the world, then God is still responsible for making a world with natural forces that would result in so much pain and suffering.

Perhaps pain and suffering is a way to test a person's faith. Theists often mention the Book of Job in this context, which tells the story of how God allowed Satan to inflict incredible suffering on Job as a way to test his faith. God knew that Job would not reject Him, no matter how much suffering Satan threw his way. And, as predicted, Job remained steadfast. This defense against the problem of evil suggests that Job was not a special case: God regularly uses suffering to see who is worthy and who is not. Kuhn offers a version of this response (MM 17:38). He explains that Jews have suffered over the ages. They were slaves in Egypt and in Babylon, twice their temple was destroyed, and they were slaughtered in Masada, Spain, and Russia. Kuhn suggests that Hitler's genocide may be just another point in history when the faith of the Jews is being tested. However, it is difficult to square this defense with God's omniscience. If God already knows the outcome, what is the use of giving the test?[17]

Kuhn offers one final defense to consider. He claims that the suffering that the Jews are enduring is a punishment for their sins (MM 20:00). "God is just," he explains, "so we must have done something wrong. We should be examining our consciences." Mordechai argues that Kuhn's argument fails because innocent children and good, faithful Jews are also suffering.

Augustine also uses the sin-defense in an attempt to justify nature-caused suffering. While this defense may work in some cases, it is hard to see what the infant born with horrible birth defects has done to deserve that fate. Interestingly, Augustine explicitly addresses the suffering of very young children in *On Free Choice of the Will.* He responds to this challenge to theism as follows:

> Since God works some good by correcting adults tortured by the sickness and death of children who are dear to them, why should this suffering not occur? When the sufferings of children are over, it will be as if they had never occurred for those who suffered. Either the adults on whose account the sufferings occurred will become better, if they are reformed by temporal troubles and choose to live rightly, or else, if because of the hardships of this life they are unwilling to turn their desire toward eternal life, they will have no excuse when they are punished in the judgment to come. Moreover, who knows what faith is practiced or what pity is tested when these children's sufferings break down the hardness of parents? Who knows what reward God reserves in the secret place of his judgment for the children who, though they have not acted rightly, are not, on the other hand, weighed down by sin?[18]

Many other defenses have been offered in an attempt to thwart the problem of evil. Most of these can be easily rejected as denying one of the attributes (omnipotence, omniscience, and perfect goodness) assigned to God by Western religious orthodoxy.

Where does this leave theism? Recall that we opened the chapter by framing the problem of evil within the context of rational justification for theism—one examines the evidence for theism, examines the evidence against it, and then decides which "side" makes the most convincing case. None of the defenses against the problem of evil discussed above (in both Sections 8.5 and 8.6) succeeded, leaving theism with a major unanswered "con" argument. The theist may try some sort of hybrid approach—piecing together two or more theodicies in order to cover the deficiencies of one with patches offered by another. The most likely candidate here is a hybrid of the free will defense and the ultimate harmony defense. We will leave it as an exercise for you to decide whether such a hybrid would succeed in defending theism against the problem of evil.

Another possible approach for the theist is to reject the rationalistic framework in which this debate is taking place. While such a response is unlikely to convince a nonbeliever, it may be the only "answer" to the problem of evil that the theist has to offer.

Discussion Questions

1. Did you ever think about the problem of evil before reading this chapter? If so, what was your response? Do you think that response was adequate? What is your response now?
2. Is God "silent"?
3. Do you think the apocalyptic tradition within Christianity has a more severe version of the problem of evil? What is happening during the destruction of the world? Is it a sign of God's lack of perfect goodness?
4. Is religion most often based on love of God or fear of God? Which motivation makes the most sense?
5. Is it reasonable for Schmidt, Kuhn, or any victim of the Holocaust to continue to believe that God exists? Is it reasonable for Moche, Mordechai, Jacques, or any victim of the Holocaust, to believe that God does not exist?
6. Jacques, the scientist in *God on Trial*, explains that during the Middle Ages, people thought the sun goes around the earth. Their belief, of course, was mistaken. It is merely an illusion that makes it seems like the sun travels around the earth. Jacques then argues that belief in God is illusory, as well. Is he right?
7. Why does God require faith? That is, why does God require the sort of blind trust that, in all other contexts, would be considered foolhardy?
8. For those who have read Chapter 5 on free will and determinism, is God's omniscience (hence, foreknowledge) compatible with the existence of free will? Can God's omnipotence be reconciled with the existence of free will?

Annotated List of Film Titles Relevant to the Problem of Evil

Virtually any movie that depicts some real-world catastrophe of either human or natural origin may be used to generate the problem of evil.

The Killing Fields (1982). Directed by Roland Joffé. Starring Sam Waterston, Haing S. Ngor, John Malkovich, Julian Sands.
  The Killing Fields is based on a true story and is set in Cambodia during and after the U.S. withdrawal at the end of the Vietnam War. It portrays a period in Cambodia's history that equals or perhaps exceeds the Holocaust in its concentration of cruelty and purposeless suffering.
Schindler's List (1993). Directed by Steven Spielberg. Starring Liam Neeson, Ralph Fiennes.
  Based loosely on the true story of the German war profiteer turned philanthropist Oskar Schindler, *Schindler's List* is set in Nazi-era Poland and

Czechoslovakia. The movie is relevant to the problem of evil in two respects. First, it depicts a huge amount of suffering. Second, it argues implicitly for the free will defense.

Shadowlands (1993). Directed by Richard Attenborough. Starring Anthony Hopkins, Debra Winger.

Based on a true story about the life of C.S. Lewis, a devout Christian and philosophy professor who specializes in the problem of evil but who lacks a real appreciation for the depths of suffering until he learns this as his "wife" dies of cancer.

AI: Artificial Intelligence (2001). Directed by Steven Spielberg. Starring Haley Joel Osment, Jude Law, Frances O'Connor, Sam Robards.

While *AI* deals primarily with philosophical questions surrounding the creation of intelligent robots, it also weaves in as a minor theme a discussion of the problem of evil.

The Apostle (1997). Directed by Robert Duvall. Starring Robert Duvall, Farrah Fawcett.

The Apostle is relevant in presenting a picture of what the perception of an "unsilent" God might be like.

Annotated List of Book Titles Relevant to the Problem of Evil

"Classics" in the Problem of Evil

SAINT AUGUSTINE

On Free Choice of the Will, first published in Latin in 395 C.E. Augustine argues for the free will defense against the problem of evil–the theodicy that has since become orthodoxy within Christianity. Excerpts from this work are included in Readings from Primary Sources.

*Recent Works Dealing with the Problem of Evil
and Philosophy of Religion More Broadly*

Søren Kierkegaard, *Concluding Unscientific Postscript to the Philosophical Fragments,* first published in Danish in 1844. The main source for contemporary fideism (see note 9 for this chapter).

John Perry, *Dialogue on Good, Evil and the Existence of God* (Indianapolis: Hackett, 1999). A useful introduction to the problem of evil and the various theodicies developed by theists to combat it.

Michael Peterson, *God and Evil* (Boulder, CO: Westview Press, 1998). A very thorough treatment of the problem of evil and the major theodicies.

Louis Pojman, ed., *Philosophy of Religion* (Belmont, CA: Wadsworth, 1987). Highly recommended for a thorough treatment of philosophy of religion from all points of view.

Books on The Seventh Seal

Ingmar Bergman, *Four Screenplays*, trans. Lars Malmstrom and David Kushner (New York: Simon & Schuster, 1960).
Arthur Gibson, *The Silence of God* (New York: Harper & Row, 1969).

Books relevant to God on Trial

Elie Wiesel, *The Trial of God* (first published in English by Random House, 1979).

Notes

1. Epicurus (341–270 B.C.E.) writes, "Is he [God] willing to prevent evil, but not able? Then he is impotent. Is he able, but not willing? Then he is malevolent. Is he both able and willing? Whence then is evil?"
2. This argument is most closely associated with Thomas Aquinas (1225–1274). It is one from a cluster of arguments for theism referred to as the "cosmological argument."
3. This argument is most closely associated with William Paley (1743–1805), who gave it its most famous formulation, and David Hume (1711–1776), who attacked it. It is also known as the "teleological argument."
4. Bertrand Russell, "The Essence of Religion," in *The Basic Writings of Bertrand Russell* (New York: Touchstone, 1963), 569.
5. Rev. 8:1–9:6, Revised Standard Version.
6. Rev. 21:1–4, Revised Standard Version.
7. That God knew this would happen–it was all a part of God's plan right from the beginning–is implied by a later passage: "and the dwellers on earth whose names have not been written in the book of life from the foundation of the world" (Rev. 17:8). For reference to God's foreknowledge of who would be saved and who would not, see also Rom. 8:29, and Eph. 1:4. There is considerable debate among philosophers of religion concerning whether human free will rules out God's foreknowledge. We'll consider this problem in more detail in Section 8.5.
8. This is how Bergman described this image in his original screenplay for *The Seventh Seal.* Quoted in Bergman, *Four Screenplays*, trans. Lars Malmstrom and David Kushner (New York: Simon & Schuster, 1960).
9. The view that reason in inapplicable to issues of religious faith is called *fideism.* One of its most ardent supporters is the nineteenth-century Danish philosopher Søren Kierkegaard.
10. Arthur Gibson, *The Silence of God* (New York: Harper & Row, 1969), 30.
11. Augustine, *On Free Choice of the Will,* trans. A. Benjamin and L. Hackstaff (New York: Macmillan, 1964), 73–77.

12. Ibid.
13. Edward Madden, "The Many Faces of Evil," in *Philosophical Issues*, ed. James Rachels and Frank Tillman (New York: Harper & Row, 1972), 472.
14. This is a paraphrase of Ivan's speech from Dostoevsky's *The Brothers Karamazov*, quoted in Madden, "The Many Faces of Evil," 473.
15. Mark 10:15, Revised Standard Version.
16. Much of this section draws from Madden's "The Many Faces of Evil."
17. As mentioned previously, there is some debate among philosophers of religion concerning whether human free will makes this sort of foreknowledge on God's part impossible. Several paragraphs included among the excerpts from Augustine's *On Free Choice of the Will* in Readings from Primary Sources discuss the relationship between free will and God's foreknowledge.
18. Augustine, *On Free Choice of the Will*, 140–41.

9

EXISTENTIALISM

The Seventh Seal (1957), *Crimes and Misdemeanors* (1988), and *Leaving Las Vegas* (1995)

Knight: I call out to [God] in the dark but no one seems to be there.
Death: Perhaps no one is there.
Knight: Then life is an outrageous horror. No one can live in the face of death, knowing that all is nothingness.
Death: Most people never reflect about either death or the futility of life.
Knight: But one day they will have to stand at that last moment of life and look toward the darkness.
Death: When *that* day comes ...

—from *The Seventh Seal*

We're all faced throughout our lives with agonizing decisions ... moral choices. Some are on a grand scale, most of these choices are on lesser points. But, we define ourselves by the choices we have made. We are, in fact, the sum total of our choices. Events unfold so unpredictably, so unfairly. Human happiness does not seem to have been included in the design of creation. It is only we, with our capacity to love, that give meaning to an indifferent universe. And yet, most human beings seem to have the ability to keep trying and find joy from simple things—from their family, their work, and from the hope that future generations might understand more.

—Professor Louis Levy, in *Crimes and Misdemeanors*

Sera: So, Ben ... what brings you to Las Vegas?
Ben: I came here to drink myself to death.
Sera: How long's it gonna take to drink yourself to death?
Ben: Oh, I don't know. About four weeks.

—from *Leaving Las Vegas*

Is there any meaning to life? Does it really matter that we (either individually or collectively as a species) ever existed? If you answer yes to these questions, by virtue of what is life meaningful? Is it we ourselves who "give meaning to an indifferent universe" or is there some way to make sense of objective meaning, meaning that does not depend on our individual desires and our individual values? These questions form the central topic of this chapter.

If you are reading the chapters in order, you will note that two of the three focus films for this chapter have served as focus films in previous chapters. There will be a slight overlap with discussion in those chapters, but not very much. If you are reading the chapters out of order, it may be useful to refer to the overviews of *The Seventh Seal* and *Crimes and Misdemeanors* from Chapters 8 and 6, respectively.

9.1 Is Life Meaningful?

At some time in their lives, most people have asked themselves: "What's the point of it all?" The trigger may have been the failure of some important personal project or the death of a loved one. Or perhaps the question cropped up out of the blue. Leo Tolstoy, the great nineteenth-century Russian novelist, described in his essay "My Confession" the crisis brought on by his inability to answer this simple question. In his case, the crisis was not spurred by failure or grief. As he describes it, everything in his life was going perfectly. He had wealth and fame from his successful career as a writer. He was held in high esteem as both intelligent and morally upright. He had a loving family, all of whom (including himself) were quite healthy. Everything was going his way. Nevertheless, we read,

> I could not attribute a reasonable motive to any single act in my whole life. I was only astonished that I could not have realized this at the very beginning. All this had so long ago been known to me! Illness and death would come ... to those whom I loved, to myself, and nothing remains but stench and worms. All my acts, whatever I did, would sooner or later be forgotten, and I myself be nowhere. Why, then, busy one's self with anything? ... It is possible to live only as long as life intoxicates us; as soon as we are sober again we see that it is all a delusion, and a stupid delusion! In this, indeed, there is nothing either ludicrous or amusing; it is only cruel and stupid![1]

As he reports, this existential crisis reached such depths that he seriously contemplated suicide.

Tolstoy was not unique. Is life meaningful? The question has an import for the individual that is lacking from most of the other questions philosophers ask. It is doubtful that anyone has ever contemplated suicide because of the problem of identity, and skepticism, even though it seems to have far-reaching implications, lacks the personal urgency of this question. The most ardent proponent of skepticism in the modern era, David Hume, even admits that these sorts of topics are of merely intellectual interest–attempts to answer them are games philosophers play. But the question about the meaningfulness of life is different. The twentieth-century writer Albert Camus argues that "the meaning of life is the most urgent of questions"–"[j]udging whether life is or is not worth living" is "the only truly serious philosophical problem."[2]

Before going further, it may be wise to consider what exactly the question is asking. Only then will we be in a position to say what an adequate answer would look like. The question: Is life meaningful? can be interpreted along two different dimensions. The first involves what the word *life* is referring to. At its most particular, this question could be asking: Is *my individual life* meaningful? Or, the question could be asking the more general question: Is the life *of my species* meaningful?–Is there any purpose or meaning to the existence of humanity? More general still, the question could be asking about the meaning of all biological life–is there some purpose or meaning to the existence of living things? Most general of all, the question could be divorced from a literal interpretation of the word *life* to be asking about the meaning of the universe–is there some purpose to the existence of the universe as a whole? We will be focusing here on the first, and, to a lesser extent, the second interpretations of the word *life*.

But, the ambiguity doesn't end there, since there are two competing ways of interpreting what *meaningful* refers to in this context. According to one, in order to be meaningful, life must have **objective meaning**. (The word *objective* as used here means "independent of what anyone or any group of people happen to think.") But how could this be possible, since meaning is, by its very nature, relative to some perspective? In order for life to be *interpreted* as having a purpose, doesn't there have to be an *interpreter*? Yes and no. If one considers only the perspectives of individuals in the world, then objective meaning is an impossibility. However, if God exists, then God's perspective could ground meaning in a way that allows for objectivity. (This use of God as the supplier of objective value should strike the reader as familiar; it is analogous to the pattern seen within the divine command theory of ethics, in which God's will grounds an objectivist ethical theory.) For the theist, *meaningful* can be cashed out in terms of God's plan for the world: my life has objective meaning because God invests the world and everything in it (my life included) with meaning and purpose "from the outside." So, even though my personal accomplishments may be scant, my role in furthering God's plan for the world gives meaning to those accomplishments and to my life as a whole.

There is an alternative to interpreting *meaning* as objective meaning. Many people do not believe that God is the only possible source of meaning and purpose in the world. If I care deeply about something and expend a lot of effort in achieving some goal (for example, in raising my children to be well-adjusted, morally good, competent adults), that should count for something. Even if, as Tolstoy reminds us, "[i]llness and death would come ... to those whom I loved, to myself, and nothing remains but stench and worms," still, my activities, my life, and my achievements have meant something to me. This second framework for interpreting meaningfulness uses **subjective meaning** as the measuring stick. This framework is not necessarily atheistic; it still allows for the possibility that God exists, but denies that God is required to make sense of the meaningfulness of life. For that reason it is best thought of, not as a nontheistic framework, but as a humanistic framework.

We distinguished above between theism and atheism on the one hand and the two interpretations of *meaning* on the other because they do not go in lockstep. As we have noted, it is possible for a theist to hold that subjective meaning is the proper way to interpret the concept of meaningfulness. It is also possible for someone to long for objective meaning, yet feel that it is unattainable because God does not exist. (We will meet several characters in *The Seventh Seal* and *Crimes and Misdemeanors* who do just that.) A third option is for someone to hold to the humanistic framework, yet argue that life is meaningless according to that framework. (Again, we will meet a character in *Crimes and Misdemeanors* who is best described this way.) Thus, while the traditional camps on the proper interpretation of meaningfulness (objective versus subjective) break down neatly into theists on the one side and atheists on the other, other positions are possible.

This distinction between objective and subjective meaning–in particular, reconciling ourselves to the unattainability of objective meaning– was a special concern of Jean-Paul Sartre and Albert Camus, the two most influential members of the intellectual movement known as **existentialism**. This movement had its roots in the latter half of the nineteenth century and blossomed in the 1940s and 1950s with the writings of Sartre and Camus (novelists, essayists, and playwrights) and the philosophers Martin Heidegger and Karl Jaspers. The two works reproduced in Readings from Primary Sources relevant to existentialism are Sartre's "Existentialism is a Humanism" and Camus's "The Myth of Sisyphus." While existentialism had many facets and encompassed intellectuals with a wide variety of positions (it is more properly thought of as an anti-movement than a movement), we shall be using Camus and Sartre as representatives for the existentialist response to the question: Is life meaningful?

9.2 An Overview of the Movies

THE SEVENTH SEAL (1957). DIRECTED BY INGMAR BERGMAN.
STARRING MAX VON SYDOW, GUNNAR BJÖRNSTR, AND BIBI
ANDERSSON. (IN SWEDISH.)

We examined *The Seventh Seal* in the previous chapter in the context of the
problem of evil. While the silence-of-God problematic is a major preoc-
cupation of this film, it also deals with several existentialist themes. Indeed,
it is the only one of the three focus films for this chapter that was actually
made during the heyday of existentialism.

We shall assume you are already familiar with the film and don't need a
plot overview, so we will cut to the chase. *The Seventh Seal* deals primarily
with the question: Is life meaningful if there is no God? As with the silence-
of-God problematic, this question runs through several of Bergman's early
films. One sees in *The Seventh Seal* how Bergman, the son of a Lutheran
minister, struggles with the issue. On the one hand, his reason rejects the
theism of his upbringing; on the other, he sees that atheism does not come
without a cost—namely the evaporation of an easy answer to the question
of the meaningfulness of life. The knight, Antonius Block, embodies this
struggle. What is Block searching for? Is it God, or is it something else—
something that could play the same role that God has traditionally played
in providing a basis for meaning and purpose?

CRIMES AND MISDEMEANORS (1988). DIRECTED BY WOODY ALLEN.
STARRING MARTIN LANDAU, WOODY ALLEN, MIA FARROW, ALAN
ALDA, ANGELICA HUSTON, SAM WATERSTON.

It is also the second time around for *Crimes and Misdemeanors*, which was
the focus film for the discussion on ethics in Chapter 6. Various characters
in this film represent not just ethical theories but whole worldviews. The
theists (Ben and Sol) cannot make sense of the meaningfulness of life outside of a theistic framework. Sol even offers that "[i]f necessary, [he] will
always choose God over truth." Professor Louis Levy, on the other hand,
presents the humanistic alternative: God does not exist, but humans can
nevertheless find real (albeit subjective) meaning in the deeds they perform and in their relationships to others.

LEAVING LAS VEGAS (1995). DIRECTED BY MIKE FIGGIS.
STARRING NICOLAS CAGE, ELISABETH SHUE

Leaving Las Vegas is the story of two profoundly isolated humans whose
lives become intertwined over the course of a few weeks. Ben Sanderson
is a failed Hollywood screenwriter who has given up on life. He has only

one goal left in all the world: to drink himself to death. To accomplish this with minimum fuss, he cuts the few remaining ties to his previous life and moves to Las Vegas. Sera is a prostitute; in her loneliness, she finds something strangely appealing in this pathetic drunk and she clings to Ben. Their relationship, initially based on their mutual need and their acceptance of one another's choices, eventually begins its downward spiral along with Ben's alcoholism.

Leaving Las Vegas shows the complexity of life and human relationships. It remains honest to the end, neither sinking into sentimentality nor looking away as the characters' lives follow their necessary trajectories. The characters of Ben and Sera are offered to us with all of life's grit intact. *Leaving Las Vegas* sticks close to the novel of the same name by John O'Brien, on which it is based.

9.3 The Theistic Response in *The Seventh Seal* and *Crimes and Misdemeanors*

In Section 9.1 we related the personal crisis experienced by Leo Tolstoy. A little later in "My Confession," he describes what happened to him and how he ultimately resolved the crisis. He noticed that he was not alone among his circle of friends and acquaintances in believing that life was meaningless—he was unique only in that he chose to grapple with the issue. However, in looking around at the masses of people outside of his circle, the uneducated laborers who made up the bulk of Russian society, he found very few who believed that life was meaningless. In probing further, Tolstoy discovered that this difference could be traced back to one thing and one thing only: religious faith. He and his circle had jettisoned faith-based justification along with most of the intellectuals during the modern era. Indeed, the distinguishing feature of modernity is belief in the pre-eminence of the rational approach to understanding the world.

One sees a similar dichotomy depicted in *The Seventh Seal.* The "simple folk," represented by Jof and Mia, do not share the knight's concerns about the possible meaninglessness of life. Jof in particular possesses a simple, unreflective faith that allows him to "see" the world around him (even death) as all part of God's plan and consistent with His supreme beneficence. While *The Seventh Seal* is set in the Middle Ages, the protagonist Antonius Block represents a very modern way of thinking in his refusal to believe in God without adequate reasons. Block would have agreed with twentieth-century philosopher Thomas Nagel, very much in the modern tradition, who described "the idea of God [as] the idea of something that can explain everything else, without having to be explained itself.... [T]he belief in God is the belief that the universe is intelligible, but not to us."[3] Faith is, by its very nature, not the product of reason—if not *ir*rational, it is at least *a*rational. But Tolstoy came to believe that God was a necessary prerequisite for meaning. If God didn't exist, there was no purpose to life, for it always ended in nothing but "stench and worms." No, even worse than that–at least stench and worms *is* something. Without God, life ends in nothing at all. Eventually, the universe as we know it will cease to exist. At that point, my life, the lives of those around me, the whole of humanity, even the universe itself, will have made no difference at all. With God, though, an individual's life has meaning, both because of that individual's role in God's overall plan for the world as well as the importance of an individual's actions during her earthly life in determining how that person will fare for the rest of eternity (in the afterlife). Based on such considerations, Tolstoy was persuaded to become a sincere theist, if for no other reason than to save his sanity. (Notice that this is not an argument for God's existence in the modernist sense. It is not something of the form "X proves that God exists." Tolstoy is not saying that he has found evidence that God exists. Rather, he is saying, "Whether God exists or not is something I cannot know. But I do know that, if I don't believe in God, I feel miserable; whereas, if I do believe in God, I feel good. So, I'll believe in God.")

One sees a degree of similarity between Tolstoy's response and that given by the character Sol in *Crimes and Misdemeanors.* Aunt May, Sol's "nihilist" sister, comes close to the modernist, preconversion Tolstoy in her reaction to Sol and his theism. In the flashback to a Passover seder from his youth at the 69:50 minute mark, Judah depicts Aunt May as the feisty atheist who sees religion and all its trappings as "mumbo jumbo." As far as she is concerned, religion is nothing but superstition for intellectual lightweights: anyone who looks at the real world without blinkers on will see that God does not exist. Sol's response is quite interesting. He agrees with May that religion does not ultimately depend on rational belief, but on faith. Furthermore, this faith allows its possessor to have a better life than is attainable for the purely reason-based intellectual (like May).

Guest: And if all your faith is wrong, Sol? Just what if …?
Sol: Then I'll still have a better life than all those who doubt.
Guest: Are you telling me you prefer God to truth?
Sol: If necessary, I will always choose God over truth.

The rabbi Ben also offers theism as the best (or only?) way of making sense of the meaning of life (MM 13:30):

Ben: [I]t's a fundamental difference in the way we view the world. You see it as harsh and empty of values and pitiless. And I couldn't go on if I didn't feel with all my heart that there's a moral structure … with real meaning–with forgiveness and some kind of higher power. Otherwise there's no basis to know how to live.…

Judah: Now you're talking to me like your congregation.
Ben: That's true. We went from a small infidelity to the meaning of existence.

Ben even suggests that Judah's infidelity may be part of God's plan. The penultimate scene of the movie, the conversation between Judah and Cliff at the wedding reception, offers the final presentation of the theistic framework. This time it is Judah's words that divulge his implicit acceptance of this way of viewing the world, since it is only the existence of God that could prevent the universe from being empty and valueless (MM 93:30). For Judah, as for Tolstoy, the possibility of an "empty" universe is a chilling prospect.

The Seventh Seal offers a more nuanced treatment of the relationship between theism and objective meaning, since the film's protagonist, the knight, Antonius Block, longs desperately for objective meaning even though he is unwilling or unable to abandon reason in favor of faith. As we saw in Chapter 8, his reason pushes him in the direction of agnosticism or even atheism; nevertheless, he cannot shake off the interpretation of meaningfulness that requires God's existence. He is left in much the same position as the preconversion Tolstoy–looking for a source for objective meaning but unable to find one. There are three conversations that deal with the tension experienced by the knight. The first relevant scene takes place as he confesses to a monk (later revealed to be Death) in a small church (MM 19:00). There are several motifs running through this conversation between the knight and Death. The knight recognizes that he is trapped within a framework that requires objective meaning, unable because of that to find importance in his relationships to other humans– relationships that could serve as the source for subjective meaning for his life. He is "trapped" because, on the one hand, he requires *knowledge* of God's existence (that is, rationally-justified belief). But, as discussed previously in the context of the silence-of-God problematic, God does not provide the evidence needed for this rational justification. Despite the knight's lack of faith, God still retains a major role in his worldview. Subjective meaning, even though it is within his grasp, is (at this point in the conversation) rejected as qualitatively inadequate–the knight wants objective meaning or nothing.

Knight: I want knowledge, not faith, not suppositions, but knowledge. I want God to stretch out His hand toward me, reveal Himself and speak to me.
Death: But He remains silent.
Knight: I call out to Him in the dark but no one seems to be there.
Death: Perhaps no one is there.

Knight: Then life is an outrageous horror. No one can live in the face of death, knowing that all is nothingness.

Death: Most people never reflect about either death or the futility of life.

Knight: But one day they will have to stand at that last moment of life and look toward the darkness.

Death: When that day comes …

Camus wrote about exactly this phenomenon in *The Myth of Sisyphus*. He referred to the "confrontation of this irrational and … wild longing for clarity whose call echoes in the human heart" as the *absurd*.[4] Toward the end of the confessional conversation in *The Seventh Seal*, the knight shows that he may be turning a corner in his understanding of meaningfulness–he will use "[his] reprieve for one meaningful deed." (This deed is accomplished later in the film when the knight, by knocking over the chess pieces and thus distracting Death, allows Jof, Mia, and their young son Michael to escape.) The closing line from the knight–"This is my hand …"–goes off in yet a third direction, one that is congenial with the ideas of the existentialists Camus and Sartre. For them, either one embraces (objective) meaninglessness with joy, relishing one's freedom to make choices, or one remains stuck in the sulking and depressive existence experienced by the knight up until then.

The knight doesn't continue consistently on this trajectory. As is shown by the conversation with Jöns just before Tyan is burned at the stake, he has reverted back to the framework that demands objective meaning (MM 76:50):

Jöns: Who watches over that child? Is it the angels, or God, or the Devil, or only the emptiness? Emptiness, my lord!

Knight: This cannot be.

Jöns: Look at her eyes, my lord. Her poor brain has just made a discovery. Emptiness under the moon.

"Emptiness under the moon"–that is what you get if you combine a longing for objective meaning and atheism. Both the knight and Jöns are painfully aware of this crushing truth. Jöns's response is to jettison theism and the possibility of objective meaning, replacing it, not with the humanistic framework and a joyful embrace of subjective meaning, but with scorn and, on occasion, bitterness at humanity's fate. He comes closest to the heroic embrace of total meaninglessness as recommended by Sartre and Camus; however, even he wavers from that ideal. As shown by his failure to act to try to prevent Tyan's execution, Jöns falls short. Existentialists' highest praise is reserved for those who fight for a lost cause *knowing that it is a lost cause.* The knight becomes the real tragic figure of the story, because, despite his awareness of his predicament, he is unable to extricate himself. *The Seventh Seal* is a tragedy because its hero is fully conscious of his predicament.

The knight remains trapped within this framework until the very end, as his last words attest (MM 92:20):

Knight: From our darkness, we call out to Thee, Lord. Have mercy on us because we are small and frightened and ignorant.

Jöns: [*bitterly*]: In the darkness where You are supposed to be, where all of us probably are.... In the darkness You will find no one to listen to Your cries or be touched by Your sufferings. Wash Your tears and mirror Yourself in Your indifference.

Knight: God, You who are somewhere, who *must* be somewhere, have mercy on us.

The knight has forgotten his "one meaningful deed" and is back to the "small and frightened and ignorant" man from the earlier part of the scene at the confessional. Tolstoy found in theism solace and an answer to his questions about the meaningfulness of life, but the knight found only hopelessness and desperation. Jöns's final piece of advice, that the knight at least relish his last remaining moments of freedom as he "can still roll [his] eyes and move [his] toes," falls on deaf ears.

9.4 Embracing Meaninglessness

While the knight is crushed by his acute consciousness of the lack of objective meaning in the world, this response is not a foregone conclusion. In his essay "The Myth of Sisyphus" (reproduced in its entirety in Readings from Primary Sources), Camus writes of a second way out of the dilemma:

I conclude that all is well, ... and that remark is sacred. It echoes in the wild and limited universe of man. It teaches that all is not, has not been, exhausted. It drives out of this world a god who had come into it with dissatisfaction and a preference for futile suffering. It makes of fate a human matter, which must be settled among men.[5]

This response is typical of existentialism. It is both exhilarating (Camus's response) and frightening (Sartre's response) for the freedom it opens up, since within this framework we must look within ourselves in deciding which way to choose. There is no more holy scripture–there are no more binding rules. According to Sartre,

When we speak of forlornness ... we mean only that God does not exist and that we have to face all the consequences of this. The existentialist ... thinks it very distressing that God does not exist, because all possibility of finding values in a heaven of ideas disappears along with Him.... That is the very starting point of existentialism. Indeed, everything is permissible if God does not exist, and as a result man is forlorn, because neither within him nor without does he find anything to cling to. He can't start making excuses for himself.... We have no excuse behind us, nor justification before us. We are alone, with no excuses.[6]

Sartre's distress at the "death of God" echoes the sentiments of Friedrich Nietzsche (1844–1900), who made famous the exclamation "God is dead!" Without theism as an anchor for values, humanity is adrift in a sea of open possibilities:

"Whither is God" [the madman] cried. "I shall tell you. *We have killed him*–you and I. All of us are his murderers. But how have we done this? How were we able to drink up the sea? Who gave us the sponge to wipe away the entire horizon? What did we do when we unchained this earth from its sun? Whither is it moving now? Whither are we moving now? ... Backward, sideward, forward, in all directions? Is there any up or down left? Are we not straying as through an infinite nothing? Do we not feel the breath of empty space? Has it not become colder? ... Do we not smell anything yet of God's decomposition? Gods too decompose. God is dead. God remains dead. And we have killed him. How shall we, the murderers of all murderers, comfort ourselves?"[7]

Is it any wonder that the knight cannot quite manage to throw out theism? He (like Nietzsche and Sartre) understands full well what he would be giving up.

9.5 The Humanistic Response

Despite the knight's reluctance, there is one scene where he tests a possible way out of his absurd dilemma. Shortly after the scene at the confessional, as he enjoys a simple meal with Mia and Jof, this new understanding seems to be taking hold (MM 55:15) as he laments, "Faith is a torment, did you know that? It is like loving someone who is out there in the darkness but never appears, no matter how loudly you call." Mia says that she does not understand what he is saying. Questions about the meaning of life or God's silence just do not crop up in her life of simple needs, simple pleasures, and simple faith. In her company, even the knight's dark brooding starts to fade. He enjoys the simple pleasure of their company, suggesting that his memory of this event will suffice to prevent the brooding–the need for objective meaning–from cropping up again. The conversation with Death as the chess game continues in the next scene brings this nascent change in the knight to an abrupt halt.

But, suppose the knight had been able to continue on the path of subjective meaning? Would his life have turned out to be meaningful? How is "meaningfulness" interpreted within this worldview? Certainly it implies more than quiet resignation in the face of objective meaninglessness. In Section 9.1, we introduced the concept of subjective meaning in terms of doing something that you care deeply about. Within this framework, one must always keep in mind that an activity or accomplishment has meaning if it is something that the person engaging in that activity or achieving that accomplishment values. Value is generated from within, not from without.

So, was the knight's life meaningful in this sense? It seems so. Consider his exchange with Death just after Jof, Mia, and Michael have escaped and the knight is told he is mated at the next move (MM 84:00). Death asks him if he has enjoyed his reprieve. He answers, "Yes, I did." He has succeeded in performing his "one meaningful act" foreshadowed in the scene at the confessional.

Others may adopt the humanistic framework, yet come to the conclusion that life is meaningless. One sees this view represented in Professor Levy in *Crimes and Misdemeanors*. He describes quite eloquently one way of fleshing out the humanistic framework (MM 99:30), noting, "It is only we, with our capacity to love, that give meaning to an indifferent universe. And yet, most human beings seem to have the ability to keep trying and find joy from simple things–from their family, their work, and from the hope that future generations might understand more." Indeed, this speech, in voice-over, is the closing commentary to the movie. However, its import strikes us as ironic, given that it is spoken "from the grave" of someone who committed suicide.

Over and above Professor Levy's ultimate dissatisfaction with what subjective meaning has to offer, there is an additional problem with it–a highly counterintuitive implication that this worldview shares with other types of subjectivism: if I am the final arbiter of value, then anything goes (so long as my values say it does). Let us return for a moment to the knight and his "one meaningful deed." While we may, along with him, view the saving of three innocent lives as worthwhile, our opinion is irrelevant. It is the knight alone whose valuing of this act makes it (and, as a result, his life) subjectively meaningful. But, does anything go? If I care deeply about exterminating a group of people and devote my life to that activity, is my life meaningful? Consider the lives of the two protagonists in *Leaving Las Vegas*. Ben's suicide, so long as it is done with affirmation and not out of resignation, can give his life meaning. Sera's activities as a prostitute (again, assuming it is a life she really wants) likewise give her life meaning. She says on several occasions that she is satisfied with her life, that she feels she is providing an important service to her customers. We, as external observers, see self-delusion in this, and the interpretation of Sera's remarks as self-deluded is encouraged by their context. When she describes to the off-camera therapist her prostitution as offering an important service (MM 18:50), she is thinking about a group sex act that she facilitated. She saw herself as engaged in some sort of performance art. In the very next scene, as Juri tracks her down in Las Vegas, the audience is given a much grimmer view of her life as a prostitute. Similarly, when Sera says, "there'll always be bad times, but my life's good–it's like I want it to be" (MM 34:20), the very next scene shows her (again) with Juri as he threatens her for not bringing in enough money. To say that we, as external viewers, know she is deluding herself is to say that we know what she *really* values (or what she *should* really value). But this misses the whole point of subjective meaning: *Sera* is the ultimate arbiter of what Sera values–not us, not "decent" society, not traditional morality. Sartre affirms this: "[E]verything is permissible if God does not exist, and as a result man is forlorn, because neither within him nor without does he find anything to cling to." To the extent that we are unwilling to agree with Sera that her life is meaningful because she values her activities, we reject subjective meaning as a legitimate framework.

9.6 Suicide as a Response to Meaninglessness

What are we to make of Ben's and Professor Levy's suicides? Were they done out of resignation, or were they done with passion, as an act that the character positively wished for? After hearing of Levy's death, Cliff replays a section of a taped interview in which Levy talked about suicide: "[T]he universe is a pretty cold place. It's we who invest it with our feelings. And, under certain conditions, we feel that the thing isn't worth it anymore" (MM 75:00). Assuming he was foretelling his own suicide, it is pretty clear it was done out of resignation. His embrace of the humanistic framework did not allow him to climb out of meaninglessness; thus he is an example of someone who answered *no* to the question: Is life (subjectively) meaningful?

Recall that, for Tolstoy also, the feeling of objective meaninglessness led him to contemplate suicide. Camus wrote extensively on the topic of suicide; indeed, it is the primary topic in *The Myth of Sisyphus*. Suicide is one possible reaction to the realization that there is no objective meaning to life; as Camus explains,

A world that can be explained even with bad reasons is a familiar world. But, on the other hand, in a universe suddenly divested of illusions and lights, man feels an alien, a stranger. His exile is without remedy since he is deprived of the memory of a lost home or the hope of a promised land. This divorce between man and his life, the actor and his setting, is properly the feeling of absurdity. All healthy men having thought of their own suicide, it can be seen, without further explanation, that there is a direct connection between this feeling and the longing for death.[8]

But Camus did not believe that suicide was where it had to lead. The absurdity of life could also be affirmed, not merely given into. One still remains aware of life's ultimate futility, however.

Wouldn't it, though, be a relief for someone to be less aware (or even unaware) of life's futility? Wouldn't that be a blessing? It was not life's futility itself that was the knight's torment, but his *fear of* life's futility. Tolstoy describes in "My Confession" how, prior to his conversion, he was haunted by the image of some malignant superintelligence laughing at his absurd predicament. The cruelty he imputes to his imagined creator was that that creator made him clever enough to see this predicament, but unable to do anything about it. There is indeed something to be said in favor of intellectual stupor.

Ben's choice of a means to kill himself seems significant in this respect. Why did he choose this route? After all, shooting himself in the head would have been a much more efficient method of suicide than drinking himself to death, and it has the added benefit that his resolve could not possibly be thwarted by some do-gooder (like Sera). The deliberateness of this choice, given its obvious drawbacks, bears discussion.

There are, we think, three relevant differences between the choice in method Ben makes and some other method—say, shooting himself in the head. First, deliberately drinking oneself to death is quite an accomplishment. It requires perseverance, it requires consistency, it requires one to withstand the physical unpleasantness that accompanies it. Were it not for the ultimate goal state, one might even think success at drinking oneself to death is something to be proud of, something to value. But, in Ben's mind, the goal state (his own annihilation) is itself something good. To the extent that he has second thoughts about the value of his nonexistence, the second relevant characteristic about this method of suicide comes to the fore. As he approaches death and his mental faculties grow dimmer from the damaging effects of the alcohol (including his memory of his previous life), he manages to drink himself into unawareness. When Sera asks him why he is killing himself, he responds that he cannot remember (MM 47:20). All he knows is that he has one and only one goal in life—to drink himself to death. He has arranged things so that there is at least one thing he will succeed at in the end–his own annihilation. Ben views Sera's request that he seek help for his alcoholism (MM 85:20) as a wrench thrown in the way of this, his last, act. But he finds a way to remove Sera from the picture: the prostitute whom he picks up in the casino and brings home that night, knowing that Sera will find the two of them, is the insurance that this potential threat will go away. Ben's single-mindedness and willingness to sacrifice everything and everyone in his pursuit of this goal is quite remarkable.

Finally, Ben's choice of a slow death by alcohol is significant, in that this choice constitutes a sort of sneering at fate. While not explicitly stated, we are led to believe that his alcoholism was the origin of his problems. To turn around and consciously use this to achieve his final purpose–his own death–is reminiscent of the attitude adopted by the existentialist hero. This is not the pollyannaish "When life hands you lemons, make lemonade." Ben is not trying to make lemonade. Rather, his choice shows his desire to be master of his fate–at least *he* is the one deciding what will happen to him. This brings up the issue of free will and determinism discussed in Chapter 5. Is he really choosing or is he changing what he wants to line up with what is inevitable? If we could give consciousness and the ability to sense the environment to a rock, it might well believe that it was freely choosing its trajectory as it fell to the ground. Ben's "choice" may also be of this sort. His severe addiction to alcohol has forced him on to this path; he is powerless to do anything but acquiesce.

In the final analysis, what are we to make of Ben's suicide? Did he see, in carrying it out, something worthwhile? It is unlike other goals in that, if he succeeds, he won't be around to bask in the feeling of accomplishment. Or was his suicide merely the action of a man who has utterly given up– who has [judged] that "life is not worth living"?[9] Despite what we may see of heroism in his choice of method, for Ben this may simply have been the path of least resistance. Obviously, *Leaving Las Vegas* is a work of fiction that offers no verifiable answer to this question. Ben's death, though, does leave us with an example to consider in light of the existentialist's argument that the awareness of the meaninglessness of life is something that is positively to be wished for.

Discussion Questions

1. Is the question "Is life meaningful?" merely a philosopher's question? Have you ever asked yourself this question? If so, what was your answer?
2. What connections do you see between the ultimate harmony defense (against the problem of evil) and the question: Is life meaningful?
3. Does atheism imply "emptiness under the moon"?

4. Do the "poor and downtrodden" have existential crises? Why or why not?
5. What criteria need to be satisfied for a death to count as suicide? Do Ben's actions in *Leaving Las Vegas* constitute suicide? If so, was suicide in his case *rational*?
6. What is the significance of Professor Levy's suicide?
7. What is the significance of Ben going blind?

Annotated List of Film Titles Relevant to Existentialism

Other Movies by Ingmar Bergman

There are existentialist themes running through many Bergman films, particularly the early ones. The following list contains some choice titles: *Wild Strawberries* (1957), *The Magician* (1958), *Through a Glass Darkly* (1961), *Winter Light* (1962), *The Silence* (1963), *Persona* (1969), *Shame* (1967), *A Passion* (1969), *Cries and Whispers* (1972), *Face to Face* (1976), *Autumn Sonata* (1978), *From the Life of the Marionettes* (1980), and *Fanny and Alexander* (1982).

Films by Other Directors

Ikiru (1952). Directed by Akira Kurosawa. Starring Takashi Shimura, Nobuo Kaneko, Kyoko Seki.
What would you do if you found out you only had a few months to live? That is the question faced by the protagonist in Akira Kurosawa's masterpiece of existentialist cinema.
American Beauty (1999). Directed by Sam Mendes. Starring Kevin Spacey, Annette Bening, Thora Birch, Wes Bentley.
One in a long line of movies about "existential" desperation in modern American suburbia.
Hamlet (1996). Directed by Kenneth Branagh. Starring Kenneth Branagh, Derek Jacobi, Kate Winslet, Julie Christie.
Our protagonist gives voice at one time or another to most of the issues discussed in this chapter.
Fearless (1993). Directed by Peter Weir. Starring Jeff Bridges, Isabella Rossellini.
This film turns the existentialist's dilemma on its head: What would the life of someone be like who was *not* afraid of death?
The Rapture (1991). Directed by Michael Tolkin. Starring Mimi Rogers, David Duchovny.
This film raises questions surrounding the meaning of life in addition to those related to the problem of evil.

The Sunset Limited (2011). Directed by Tommy Lee Jones. Starring Samuel L. Jackson, Tommy Lee Jones.
The Sunset Limited is based upon the play by Cormac McCarthy. It pits a suicidal atheist against a religious ex-con.

Annotated List of Book Titles Relevant to Existentialism

Modern "Classics" in the History of Existentialism

FYODOR DOSTOEVSKY

Notes from Underground, first published in Russian in 1864. Dostoevsky is considered by many to mark the nascence of existentialism.

ALBERT CAMUS

The Myth of Sisyphus, first published in French in 1942. A widely influential collection of essays by Camus, including the eponymous essay "The Myth of Sisyphus," which is reproduced in its entirety in Readings from Primary Sources.

JEAN-PAUL SARTRE

Existentialism, first published in French in 1946. Sartre attempts to explain and defend his version of existentialism. Excerpts from Sartre's "Existentialism is a Humanism" are reproduced in Readings from Primary Sources. "The Wall," first published in French in 1939, is widely anthologized in English translation.

Collections of Essays and Short Works in Existentialism

Walter Kaufman, ed., *Existentialism from Dostoevsky to Sartre* (New York: Meridian, 1975). An excellent entry point for a more in-depth reading of existentialist literature.
E. D. Klemke and Steven Cahn, eds., *The Meaning of Life,* 3rd edn (Oxford: Oxford University Press, 2007). This book offers a wide array of perspectives.
Leo Tolstoy, *My Confession, My Religion,* trans. Isabel Hapgood (Midland, MI: Avensblume Press, 1994).

Notes

1. Leo Tolstoy, "My Confession," in *My Confession, My Religion*, trans. Isabel Hapgood (Midland, MI: Avensblume Press, 1994), 16.
2. Albert Camus, *The Myth of Sisyphus*, trans. Justin O'Brien (New York: Alfred A. Knopf, 1955), 3.
3. Thomas Nagel, *What Does It All Mean? A Very Short Introduction to Philosophy* (Oxford: Oxford University Press, 1987), 99–100.
4. Albert Camus, "An Absurd Reasoning" in *The Myth of Sisyphus*, 21.
5. Albert Camus, "The Myth of Sisyphus" in *The Myth of Sisyphus*, 122.
6. Jean-Paul Sartre, *Existentialism*, trans. Bernard Frechtman (New York: Philosophical Library, 1947), 25–27.
7. Friedrich Nietzsche, *The Gay Science*, in *The Portable Nietzsche*, ed. and trans. Walter Kaufmann (New York: Penguin, 1976), 95.
8. Albert Camus, "An Absurd Reasoning" in *The Myth of Sisyphus*, 6.
9. Albert Camus, introduction to *The Myth of Sisyphus*, 4.

APPENDIX
Story Lines of Films by Elapsed Time

Hilary and Jackie (total running time: 124 minutes)

Minute Mark	*Story Item*
0:00	October Films logo.
1:20	Scene at seashore with the young Hilary and Jackie.
2:30	Children see woman in distance. Jackie walks over to her.
3:30	Words "Hilary and Jackie" flash on screen.
3:40	Mother writes "Holiday Song."
4:30	Jackie awakens to find score; the girls play it.
5:50	Mother at piano. Children "dancing."
6:30	Mother reads letter from BBC asking her to conduct and Hilary to play.
7:10	Recording of Haydn's *Toy Symphony*.
8:20	**Mother** (scolding, to Jackie): If you want to play with Hilary, you've got to play as good as Hilary.
8:30	Jackie applies herself to practicing.
9:15	Hilary and Jackie play (together) at competition.
10:30	Hilary and Jackie play (separately) at competition.
12:15	Jackie wins, to standing ovation. Hilary also wins.
13:30	Hilary storms out of auditorium and hides.
14:00	Photographer and Jackie.
15:00	Jackie has first private lesson. Hilary outside, looking dejected.
17:40	Jackie (now played by Emily Watson) has cello lesson at home. Hilary (now played by Rachel Griffiths) dejected-looking on stairs.
18:30	Jackie's cello teacher to arrange first public performance.
19:00	Jackie gives concert, to standing ovation.
20:30	Reception after concert. Jackie presented with cello.

21:00	**Cello Teacher** (on presenting the cello to Jackie): It will give you the world, Jackie, but you must give it yourself.
21:30	Sisters dancing at wedding reception.
22:40	Sisters in bed, drinking afterward.
23:20	Word "Hilary" flashes on screen.
23:40	Hilary wakes up next morning. Jackie is gone.
24:10	Hilary at Royal Academy of Music audition. Teacher discouraging.
27:00	Hilary very excited when parcel from Jackie arrives. Excitement turns to disappointment (especially for Hilary) when contents turn out to be laundry.
27:50	Hilary meets Kiffer.
28:30	Hilary fails exam miserably.
29:15	Hilary sits outside house in rain.
30:55	Kiffer barges in.
31:20	Jackie meets Kiffer.
32:15	Night-time conversation between sisters.
33:20	Hilary performs, Kiffer conducts.
35:20	Second night-time conversation. Hilary comes in late and announces her engagement to Kiffer.
38:20	Hilary and Kiffer marry.
39:15	Jackie brings Danny home. Jackie acts differently.
40:00	Jackie announces they plan to get married and that she plans to convert to Judaism.
41:15	News coverage of Jackie and Danny, including their marriage.
42:40	Several years later. Hilary (now living in farmhouse with Kiffer and two children) pastes news clippings in scrapbook.
43:20	Hilary and Kiffer start to have sex in back of car.
44:40	Jackie arrives at farmhouse alone.
45:40	Everyone is quite drunk that evening. Tapping music on wine glasses.
46:20	Conversation: Jackie tells Hilary she wants to sleep with Kiffer.
47:45	Jackie comes into Hilary and Kiffer's bedroom.
48:30	Outside of house the next morning–who is going to get the cheese?
50:30	Hilary finds Jackie hysterical.
50:50	**Jackie** (screaming): Get away from me. You don't love me. Nobody loves me. All I want is a fuck.
51:20	Hilary asks Kiffer if he will have sex with Jackie.

52:00	Danny arrives.
54:00	Danny offers to buy house nearby. Jackie responds with raspberry sound. Danny leaves.
55:20	Kiffer has sex with Jackie. Hilary hears creaking bed– goes to sleep with daughter.
56:00	Morning after, in kitchen.
57:00	Jackie thanks Hilary.
57:45	Beginning of home movies. Mother visiting. Jackie looking more like the wife and mother. (Unclear where home movies ends and "real life" picks up again.)
59:00	Kiffer throws ball, hits Hilary. Hilary walks away.
60:00	Kiffer has sex with Hilary.
61:00	Jackie plays cello. Hilary tries to talk to her.
62:30	Jackie leaves. Jackie remembers previous events–the two of them at the seashore as children, dancing at the wedding in Italy, night of drinking.
63:30	Word "Jackie" flashes on screen.
64:10	Jackie awoken morning after wedding to catch train.
65:00	Backstage. Jackie gives performance in "German."
66:00	Jackie tries unsuccessfully to call home.
67:00	Jackie kicks cello.
68:00	Jackie tries to get clothes washed.
68:30	Jackie leaves cello in direct sunlight.
69:10	Jackie studies cello in Moscow.
69:45	Jackie says she doesn't really want to play the cello.
71:00	Jackie gets package–cleaned clothes. She is overjoyed.
71:30	Jackie leaves cello outside in snow and lays on bed, surrounded by clothes.
72:30	Cello back inside.
72:50	Jackie back home. Kiffer barges in and announces, "I'm in love with Hilary." Beginning of voice-over of "same" night-time conversation between Hilary and Jackie, when Hilary announces her engagement.
74:00	Jackie "forgets" cello in back of taxi on way to party, where she meets Danny for the first time.
76:30	Jackie starts to play. Danny stays.
77:20	Jackie and Danny in bed together.
78:40	Jackie thanks, and apologizes to, cello.
79:00	Jackie and Danny at recording session.
80:20	Jackie has cold hands. (First symptoms?)
81:50	Jackie, with perception somewhat altered, drops bow.

82:40	Jackie's hand shaking noticeably.
83:20	Conversation in hotel room as they pack up to leave.
84:20	Danny walks out of room to find that Jackie has disappeared. Jackie arrives at Kiffer and Hilary's farmhouse.
85:00	Jackie, dejected-looking, curled up on bed. Kiffer comes in and comforts her. Home movies. Jackie leaves.
85:50	Jackie urinates on herself. She is very frightened.
87:00	Jackie in concert. Perception very altered.
88:40	Jackie cannot get up at end of concert.
89:20	Jackie in hospital, announces she has MS.
90:00*	Hilary visits Jackie in hospital. Jackie insults her.
92:00	Hilary and parents in hospital waiting room.
92:40*	Jackie and Danny playing together. Danny helps Jackie with physical therapy.
93:00	Danny tells her of job offer in Paris.
96:00	Parents visit Jackie.
97:00	Jackie tries to play cello, but cannot.
97:15	Jackie plays drum in concert of Haydn's *Toy Symphony*– even more altered perception. Jackie reports she is losing her hearing.
100:20*	Family conversation in car.
101:30*	Jackie answers phone. It's Danny. Sound of baby crying.
103:30	Jackie shaking badly, can barely talk. Mother visits.
104:20	Jackie plays record of her performing Elgar's *cello concerto*.
106:20	Violent storm. Jackie shaking in bed. Danny comforts her. Jackie screams.
107:00*	Hilary wakes with a start. Hilary and younger brother Piers arrive.
107:40	Hilary goes back in with Jackie. Danny leaves.
110:30	Hilary reminds Jackie of day on beach when they were children.
111:40	Car ride back. Jackie's death announced on radio. Hilary asks Piers to stop the car. Flashback through several ages to day at beach.
113:40	Young Jackie walks over to adult Jackie.
115:00	Credits roll.

(*denotes a clear change of perspective in narrative)

The Matrix (total running time: 136 minutes)

Minute Mark	Story Item
0:00	Warner Brothers logo.
1:50	Police enter room with Trinity.
2:15	Agents arrive.
5:45	Trinity gets to phone booth just as it is run over by truck.
6:45	Neo asleep on couch. He awakens.
7:10	Message on screen: "Wake up, Neo."
7:40	Knock at Neo's door.
9:00	**Neo:** Ever had that feeling where you're not sure if you're awake or still dreaming?
9:40	Neo and others at party.
10:00	Trinity greets Neo.
12:00	Neo wakes, goes to work.
13:00	Neo (Thomas Anderson) at work in cubicle–receives FedEx package containing cell phone.
13:30	Cell phone rings–call from Morpheus warning of agents.
14:00	Morpheus guides Neo out.
16:45	Neo taken into custody.
20:30	Interrogation scene.
21:30	Neo awakens.
21:45	Phone rings; it's Morpheus.
22:45	Neo picked up by Trinity.
24:30	Removal of bug.
25:40	Neo and Morpheus meet face-to-face.
26:30	**Morpheus:** You have the look of a man who accepts what he sees, because he is expecting to wake up. Ironically, this is not far from the truth.
28:00	**Morpheus:** It [the matrix] is the world that has been pulled over your eyes to blind you from the truth.
29:30	Neo chooses red pill.
31:30	**Morpheus:** Have you ever had a dream, Neo, that you were so sure was real? What if you were unable to wake from that dream? How would you know the difference between the dream world and the real one?
32:20	The "real" Neo awakens in the vat. Neo looks around and sees huge number of other, similar vats.
34:20	Neo "flushed."
35:00	Neo is aboard Morpheus's ship.
35:15	**Morpheus:** Welcome to the real world.

37:00	Neo awakes, still aboard ship. Morpheus explains that it is approximately 2199.
39:15	Neo enters construct.
40:00	**Neo** (feeling sofa): This isn't real?
41:30	Morpheus explains history and current condition of human species.
43:00	**Morpheus:** The matrix is a computer-generated dream world.
	Neo: No, it's not possible.
	Neo exits from construct and becomes sick.
46:00	Morpheus says he believes Neo is "the One."
48:20	Neo begins training.
49:00	Morpheus and Neo meet in sparring program.
54:00	Morpheus and Neo switch to jump program.
	Morpheus: You have to let it all go, Neo–fear, doubt, disbelief.
57:00	Morpheus and Neo enter training program similar to matrix. Morpheus explains role of agents within matrix.
59:00	The ship is attacked by sentinels.
63:30	Dinner conversation between agent and Cipher.
65:00	Breakfast on board.
65:30	Conversation about switched perceptions.
67:30	Neo re-enters matrix.
68:00	Neo looks out of car window as they are driving through familiar area.
	Neo: I have all these memories from my life. None of them happened.
73:00	Neo meets the oracle.
78:30	Neo sees double black cat.
79:00	They are trapped in building.
81:00	They hide inside wall.
84:45	Agents capture Morpheus.
86:00	Cipher shoots Tank and Dozer.
90:45	Tank kills Cipher.
92:00	Agent interrogates Morpheus.
98:40	Neo and Trinity re-enter matrix to free Morpheus.
101:30	Neo and Trinity begin break-in.
109:40	Helicopter rescue of Morpheus.
113:00	Morpheus gets back to ship.
114:00	Trinity gets back. Fight between agent and Neo begins.
121:20	Sentinels attack ship.
122:30	Agent shoots Neo.

127:30	Neo comes to on ship.
128:00	Computer and Neo's voice. SYSTEM FAILURE message.
128:30	Neo hangs up phone, back in 1999 world.
129:00	Credits roll.

Inception (total running time: 148 minutes)

Inception can be a difficult movie to follow because many scenes occur within a dream, or in a dream within a dream, or even in a dream within a dream within a dream. Any scenes that occur in the real world are in **boldface**; scenes in a first level dream are in regular type; scenes in a second level dream are in *italics*; scenes in a third level dream are in <u>*underlined italics*</u>; and scenes in limbo are in <u>**boldfaced, underlined italics.**</u>

Minute Mark	*Story Item*
0:00	Warner Brothers Logo
0:39	<u>**Cobb on Beach, meets with (old) Saito**</u> (see MM 1:13:13 for the same conversation and MM 2:15:26 for a similar conversation).
2:48	*Cobb and Arthur at dinner meeting with Saito.*
4:28	Cobb, Arthur, and Saito asleep.
5:23	*Cobb talks to Mal.*
7:40	*Cobb breaks into safe. Saito catches Cobb stealing.*
	Cobb: Did she tell you? Or have you known all along?
	Saito: That you're here to steal from me or that we are actually asleep?
	Cobb shoots Arthur.
9:12	Arthur wakes.
10:00	*Cobb reads contents of envelope.*
10:51	Cobb is dunked and wakes.
11:45	Cobb and Saito talk. **Nash and Arthur asleep on train.** Saito realizes he is dreaming.
14:05	**Arthur, Cobb, Nash wake.**
15:20	**Saito wakes.**
15:45	**Cobb spins top. Talks to kids on phone.**
18:30	**Cobb and Arthur find Saito and Nash in helicopter. Talk about inception.**
21:37	**Cobb and Arthur on plane.**
22:24	**Cobb meets with his father-in-law.**
24:44	**Cobb meets Ariadne.**

26:11	Cobb and Ariadne talk about shared dreaming.
27:20	**Cobb:** Well, dreams, they feel real while we're in them, right? It's only when we wake up that we realize something was actually strange.
28:18	**Ariadne wakes.**
29:05	Cobb and Ariadne walk through city.
33:20	Mal stabs Ariadne. **Ariadne wakes. Arthur explains totems.**
35:06	**Cobb meets Eames in Mombasa.**
37:13	**Cobb escapes from Cobol thugs.**
39:16	**Saito picks up Cobb, then Eames in limousine.**
39:33	**Ariadne returns to warehouse.** Arthur explains paradoxical architecture.
41:22	**Cobb, Eames, and Saito visit Yusuf, the chemist. Discuss a dream within a dream within a dream.**
43:38	**Cobb tries the sedative.** Sees Mal. **Wakes and spins top, grabs top before it can fall.**
44:30	**Cobb, Eames and Saito discuss Robert Fischer.**
45:45	**Browning and Robert Fischer at Maurice Fischer's bedside.**
47:22	**Eames, Cobb, Arthur, Saito, Yusuf discuss plan.**
48:01	**Ariadne creates her totem. Talks with Cobb about totems, Mal, and the design of the mazes for the different dream levels.**
50:06	**The team discusses the idea that will be planted, dream levels, and the "kick."** Continue to discuss details of the plan.
54:14	**Ariadne plugs into Cobb's dream.** Cobb's memories of Mal and his kids.
60:24	**Ariadne and Cobb wake.**
61:22	**The team assembles at the airport. Fischer boards the plane. Plan goes into effect.**
64:07	[Level 1: In Yusuf's dream] New York City. Saito is shot.
67:21	Team arrives at warehouse with Fischer. Discuss Fischer's subconscious training and limbo.
70:30	Cobb confronts Fischer. Eames impersonates Browning.
73:13	Cobb and Ariadne with dying Saito. Part of conversation at MM 0:40 repeated.
74:04	Fischer and "Browning."
75:29	Cobb explains to Ariadne what happened with Mal. **Flashback: _Mal and Cobb in own world_. Mal's suicide.**

81:13	**Flashback: Cobb takes plane tickets and leaves without saying goodbye to children.**
82:20	Cobb forces Fischer to give him the combination. Team breaks out of warehouse.
85:23	Yusuf drives [*Level 2: In Arthur's dream*] *Cobb and Fischer in hotel bar.*
91:58	*Arthur and Ariadne in hotel room. Cobb and Fischer in bathroom.*
94:25	*Cobb, Fischer, Arthur, Ariadne break into hotel room. Saito and Eames follow Arthur's projection of Browning to the room.*
97:28	[*Level 3: In Eames's dream.*] *Cobb, Eames, Ariadne, Saito, Fischer in snow covered mountains. Arthur remains at hotel.* Yusuf drives.
102:55	Yusuf starts music. *Arthur hears music. Eames and Cobb hear music.*
105:23	Yusuf drives van off bridge. *Arthur floats down hall. Avalanche.*
111:35	*Fischer enters main room. Mal shoots Fischer. Cobb shoots Mal.*
114:55	***Ariadne and Cobb in Cobb and Mal's world.*** Yusuf in van falls from bridge. *Arthur in hotel. Eames, Fischer and Saito in mountain fort.*
119:41	***Cobb explains that he planted in Mal the idea, "Your world is not real." Confronts Mal.***
123:40	***Flashback: Cobb plants idea in Mal by finding safe and spinning top. Cobb and Mal lay down on tracks.***
125:37	Van continues to fall. *Saito dies.* Arthur starts music, *Eames hears it. Eames shocks Fischer.*
128:34	***Ariadne shoots Mal, pushes Fischer off balcony.*** *Fischer wakes.*
129:59	*Arthur sets off explosives. Fischer finds his father.*
131:18	*Eames sets off explosives. Elevator falls.* Van falls into water.
131:59	*Fischer wakes. Eames wakes.* ***Ariadne jumps from balcony.*** *Ariadne wakes. Ariadne wakes.* Ariadne wakes.
132:47	***Cobb lets Mal go.*** Fischer, Eames, Arthur, and Yusuf wake. Cobb does not. Fischer has his idea to, "Be my own man."
135:26	***Cobb wakes on beach. Meets with old Saito (similar to opening scene).***
137:17	**Cobb wakes on plane with the rest.**
139:51	**Cobb returns home. Spins top. Sees his kids. Top keeps spinning.**
140:51	Cuts to black. Credits roll.

Memento (total running time: 116 minutes)

Memento can be a very disorienting movie the first time you see it. In the summary below, we have indicated which scenes "match up" by listing them in **boldface** and giving the minute mark (MM) of the other occurrence of the scene. Since the scenes shot in black and white are important for marking off the backward-progressing scenes, they have also been identified, with ****(B/W)**.

Minute Mark	Story Item
0:00	Credits begin (Newmarket logo).
0:45	Leonard holds photo while it undevelops.
2:00	Leonard takes photo.
2:30	**Leonard shoots Teddy** (see scene at MM 6:20–same scene).
2:30	****(B/W)**–Leonard in motel room with voice-over.
3:00	**Teddy meets Leonard in motel lobby** (see MM 10:00).
4:00	Teddy and Leonard drive to abandoned warehouse.
5:30	Leonard looks at back of Teddy's picture.
6:20	**Leonard shoots Teddy** (see MM 2:30).
6:21	****(B/W)** more voice-over in motel room.
7:00	**Leonard writes on back of Teddy's picture "KILL HIM"** (see MM 16:00).
8:30	Leonard explains his condition to man at motel desk.
10:00	**Teddy meets Leonard in motel lobby** (see MM 3:00).
10:01	****(B/W)** more voice-over in motel room.
11:00	**Leonard in washroom–tries to wash off tattoo** (see MM 22:00).
12:45	Leonard looks through envelope contents–sees driver's license record for Teddy (John Gammell). Leonard calls Teddy.
15:00	Leonard writes "HE'S THE ONE" on back of Teddy's picture.
16:00	**Leonard writes on back of Teddy's picture "KILL HIM"** (see MM 7:00).
16:10	****(B/W)** Leonard is talking on the phone about Sammy Jankis.
17:30	**Leonard meets Natalie at diner** (see MM 26:30).
20:00	Natalie asks Leonard to describe his wife.

21:00	Natalie suggests Leonard "handle" John G. at location—she gives him address. Natalie returns Leonard's motel room key.
22:00	**Leonard in washroom–tries to wash off tattoo** (see MM 11:00).
22:01	****(B/W)** Leonard is talking on the phone about Sammy Jankis. (Leonard also describes his job as insurance claim investigator.)
23:00	**Leonard meets Teddy outside house** (see MM 31:45). Teddy and Leonard eat lunch together. Leonard explains why he trusts his notes, not memory.
25:30	Motel clerk explains about two rooms.
26:30	**Leonard meets Natalie at diner** (see MM 17:30).
26:31	****(B/W)** Leonard is talking on the phone about Sammy Jankis, with long flashback.
28:30	Leonard wakes up in bed with Natalie. Natalie says she knows someone who can get driver's license record; she sets up appointment for that afternoon with Leonard.
31:45	**Leonard meets Teddy outside house** (see MM 23:00).
31:50	****(B/W)** Leonard is talking on the phone.
32:30	**Leonard arrives at Natalie's–asks about Dodd** (see MM 44:50). **Leonard:** Something doesn't feel right. I think someone's fucking with me–trying to get me to kill the wrong guy.
36:00	Natalie and Leonard at Natalie's, talking. Natalie shows picture of her and Jimmy.
38:30	Later that night, Leonard gets up and writes on back of Natalie's picture "SHE HAS ALSO LOST SOMEONE. SHE WILL HELP YOU OUT OF PITY." He then gets back into bed with her.
39:20	****(B/W)** Leonard is talking on the phone; has flashback to crime.
40:00	**Leonard lying on motel room bed, asleep** (see MM 48:50).
41:00	Leonard discovers Dodd bound and gagged, just as Teddy arrives.
43:30	Teddy helps Leonard "deal with" Dodd.
44:20	Dodd is let out of car.
44:50	**Leonard arrives at Natalie's–asks about Dodd** (see MM 32:30).
44:51	****(B/W)** Leonard is talking on the phone; he takes out a needle.

46:00	**Leonard sitting on toilet seat, holding bottle** (see MM 52:00). Leonard takes shower, then hears someone come in.
47:00	Leonard attacks Dodd, takes his picture, then leaves message on Teddy's answering machine asking for help.
48:40	Leonard lies down on bed.
48:50	**Leonard lying on motel room bed, asleep** (see MM 40:00).
48:51	****(B/W)** Leonard is talking on the phone. The person he's talking to hangs up; Leonard starts preparing to apply tattoo.
49:30	**Leonard is running** (see MM 52:30).
49:40	Leonard is being chased by Dodd.
50:00	Leonard goes to Dodd's motel room.
52:00	**Leonard sitting on toilet seat, holding bottle** (see MM 46:00).
52:01	****(B/W)** Leonard is preparing to apply tattoo.
52:15	**Leonard is in deserted area (early morning). He stamps out fire** (see MM 56:30).
52:20	Leonard is driving a Jaguar. Dodd begins attack.
52:30	**Leonard is running** (see MM 49:30).
52:31	****(B/W)** Leonard is preparing to apply tattoo when the phone rings.
54:00	**Leonard goes to car with bag of belongings** (see MM 59:00). He drives to deserted area and burns them.
56:30	**Leonard is in deserted area (early morning). He stamps out fire** (see MM 52:15).
56:31	****(B/W)** Leonard talks on phone–gets evidence related to crime.
57:45	**Leonard is asleep. Wakes to sound of door shutting** (see MM 62:30).
58:50	Leonard tells prostitute to leave.
59:00	**Leonard goes to car with bag of belongings** (see MM 54:00).
59:01	****(B/W)** Leonard talks on phone–more leads. Changes "Fact 5."
60:00	**Leonard takes picture of motel sign** (see MM 68:30).
61:00	Leonard calls up escort service. Prostitute arrives.
61:30	Leonard explains what he wants.
62:30	**Leonard is asleep. Wakes to sound of door shutting** (see MM 57:45).

62:31	**(B/W)** Leonard tattoos "FACT 5"; talks about Sammy Jankis's "test."
65:00	**Leonard gets into his car. Teddy is already in it** (see MM 73:00). Teddy gives him name of motel. Teddy and Leonard talk about Natalie and Leonard's weirdness.
68:30	**Leonard takes picture of motel sign** (see MM 60:00).
68:40	**(B/W)** Leonard talking. Unbandages tattoo "NEVER ANSWER THE PHONE."
69:00	**Leonard is at Natalie's as Natalie comes in.** (see MM 76:40). Natalie comes in. (She's been beaten.) She says Dodd did it. Leonard offers to help. Natalie writes Dodd's address and description. Leonard leaves Natalie's.
73:00	**Leonard gets into his car. Teddy is already in it** (see MM 65:00).
73:01	**(B/W)** Leonard doesn't answer ringing phone.
73:30	**Natalie arrives at her house. Leonard is inside** (see MM 81:00). Natalie is busy removing all the writing implements.
75:00	Natalie provokes Leonard into striking her. She leaves.
76:30	Leonard is frantically searching for a pen.
76:40	**Leonard is at Natalie's as Natalie comes in** (see MM 69:00).
77:10	**(B/W)** Leonard is straining to hear. Motel clerk comes– announces cop is trying to call Leonard.
78:00	Leonard is at Natalie's, talking about his wife.
80:00	Leonard takes Natalie's picture as she is leaving.
81:00	**Natalie arrives at her house. Leonard is inside** (see MM 73:30).
81:40	**(B/W)** Leonard is in motel room. Envelope appears under door. Picture of triumphant Leonard inside.
82:30	**Leonard drinks beer** (see MM 85:30).
83:00	**(B/W)** Leonard talking excitedly on phone.
83:40	**Leonard looks at coaster with note on back** (see MM 93:40). Leonard goes into bar. **Natalie:** You're that memory guy. Natalie tests him with beer.
85:30	**Leonard drinks beer** (see MM 82:30).
86:30	**(B/W)** Leonard talking on phone. Tells what happened to Sammy Jankis. Flashback with picture in institution.
90:00	**Leonard is in tattoo parlor** (see MM 110:00). Teddy arrives–suggests Leonard leave town. **Teddy:** Your business here is done.

92:00	Teddy says phone calls coming from "bad cop." Leonard exits parlor via washroom window.
93:30	Leonard arrives outside bar. Natalie mistakes him for Jimmy.
93:40	**Leonard looks at coaster with note on back** (see MM 83:40).
93:50	****(B/W) from here until MM 100:00.** Leonard talking on phone. Leonard meets Teddy in lobby: "Officer Gammell?" Leonard takes Teddy's picture. Teddy gives Leonard information on Jimmy. Leonard leaves in his pickup truck. Leonard arrives at deserted warehouse. Enters building.
97:15	Jimmy arrives and enters warehouse. Leonard confronts Jimmy. Jimmy was expecting Teddy.
99:00	Leonard kills Jimmy by strangulation, then takes his picture. Leonard puts Jimmy's clothes on.
100:00	**Switchover to color.** Teddy arrives, flashes badge.
102:00	Teddy tells Leonard *he* is really Sammy Jankis.
104:00	Teddy tells Leonard he has already killed his wife's rapist.
105:45	Leonard looks through his pocket of photos. Sees picture of himself triumphant.
107:00	**Leonard:** I should kill you. Leonard throws Teddy's keys in bushes. Leonard writes "DON'T BELIEVE HIS LIES" on back of Teddy's picture. Leonard burns pictures (of Jimmy, and himself, triumphant), writes down Teddy's car's license plate number.
108:00	**Leonard:** You can be my John G. Leonard takes Jaguar.
110:00	Flashback of Leonard (with tattoos+) and wife. Leonard drives to tattoo parlor.
110:10	**Leonard is in tattoo parlor** (see MM 90:00).
110:20	Credits roll.

Moon (total running time: 97 minutes)

Minute Mark	*Story Item*
0:00	Sony Pictures Classics Logo
0:26	Lunar Industries Limited commercial
1:27	Credits begin. Sam Bell$_1$ running on treadmill. **Sam's t-shirt:** WAKE ME WHEN IT'S QUITTING TIME.
2:13	Words: Mining Base Sarang Crew: 1 Contract: 3 years

2:34	Sam$_1$ and Gerty at base station. Sam$_1$ goes to collect a load of Helium-3.
5:45	Sam$_1$ reports back to Earth.
6:41	Pictures of Sam's family and home on Earth. Sam$_1$ reprimands Gerty.
7:42	Gerty cutting Sam$_1$'s hair. **Gerty:** Sam, is everything okay? Sam? … You don't seem like yourself today.
8:40	Sam$_1$ working on model of his home on Earth.
8:58	Sam$_1$ receives message from Tess and daughter.
11:14	Sam$_1$ watering plants, watching television, whittling.
12:13	Sam$_1$ sees an hallucination of a woman. Burns hand. Lies to Gerty. Gerty calls him out on it.
13:12	Sam$_1$ asleep. Dreams of wife.
13:51	Sam$_1$ wakes. Runs on treadmill. Talks to Gerty.
15:18	Sam$_1$ reports back to Earth. Sees glitch on monitor of old "self."
16:20	Sam$_1$ goes out to a harvester. Sees hallucination of woman. Crashes.
18:01	Sam$_2$ wakes in the infirmary. Doesn't "remember" the accident.
20:10	Sam$_2$ overhears live feed conversation between Gerty and Central. Gerty lies to Sam$_2$.
21:23	Gerty tests Sam$_2$. Gerty tells Sam$_2$ that he may have suffered some brain damage in the crash.
22:13	Sam$_2$ leaves infirmary. Notices that a door is locked.
23:08	Sam$_2$ asleep. Dreams of Tess. Image of Sam$_1$.
23:39	Sam$_2$ receives message from Central.
24:30	Sam$_2$ pierces gas line to trick Gerty into letting him go outside. Notices missing space suit.
27:10	Sam$_2$ discovers Sam$_1$ in disabled rover.
28:48	Sam$_2$ brings Sam$_1$ back to base. Gerty tells Sam$_2$ that Sam$_1$ is Sam Bell.
29:21	Sam$_1$ wakes in the infirmary.
31:28	Sam$_2$ watches video message from Tess.
32:44	Sam$_1$ discovers Sam$_2$. Sam$_1$ confronts Gerty.
34:40	Sam$_1$ tells Sam$_2$ that he's Sam Bell, too.
36:39	Sam$_2$ finds Sam$_1$ talking to plants.
38:38	Sam$_1$ and Sam$_2$ play Ping-Pong.
39:39	Sam$_1$ works on model. Sam$_2$ practices Ping-Pong. Sam$_2$ recognizes the model town. Sam$_1$ tells Sam$_2$ that they have a daughter.

41:14 Sam_1 and Sam_2 watch a video message from Earth. Sam_1 thinks he's going "home." Sam_2 tries to convince him otherwise.

42:55 Sam_2 figures out that there are other clones on the base.
Sam_2: You're a fucking clone. You don't have shit.... What about the original Sam?
Sam_1: I'm the original Sam!

45:25 Sam_2 and Sam_1 fight. Sam_1 bleeds profusely.

48:07 Sam_1 talks to Gerty about Sam_2 and about Tess. Gerty tells Sam_1 that he is a clone and that his memories are uploaded, edited memories of the original Sam Bell.

52:16 Sam_2 apologizes to Sam_1. Sam_2 tells Sam_1 about overhearing the live conversation between Gerty and Central. Sam_1 and Sam_2 go outside.

55:50 Sam_1 finds a jammer, and Sam_2 finds another jammer. Sam_1 heads back to base.

59:28 Sam_1 cannot access the computer system. Gerty enters a password for him. Sam_1 accesses the Sam Bell database. Sees many other dying Sams.

62:02 Sam_1 activates cryogenic pod. Finds secret room.

65:02 Sam_1 and Sam_2 enter secret room. Find clones.

66:52 Sam_1 gets laptop.

68:09 Sam_1 communicates with Eve.

70:22 Sam_2 and Sam_1 back at base station. Sam_2 listens to Sam_1's conversation with Eve. Sam_1 dreams of Tess.

75:18 Sam_2 convinces Gerty to wake up a new clone.

76:11 Sam_1 wakes. Discovers new clone. Sam_2 explains plan.

80:57 Sam_1 explains new plan.

82:34 Sam_2 takes Sam_1 back out to site of crash. Both recall same memory of Tess.

86:51 Sam_2 prepares to escape back to Earth. Gerty suggests that Sam_1 erase Gerty's memory banks.

89:30 Sam_2 enters new coordinates. Escapes just as rescue team enters.

90:41 Sam_3 wakes. Sam_1 sees capsule with Sam_2 flying overhead, then dies.

92:00   Jammer towers are destroyed.

92:38   Voice over of reporters discussing Sam_2 and Lunar Industries.

92:59   Credits roll.

I, Robot (total running time: 114 minutes)

Minute Mark	Story Item
0:00	Twentieth Century Fox logo.
1:00	Statement of Law I.
1:15	Statement of Law II.
1:30	Statement of Law III.
1:45	Del wakes up.
3:20	Del greeted at the door by FedEx delivery robot.
3:35	Del walks through city streets: Chicago, 2035.
4:05	Ad for NS-5 robot.
5:05	Del arrives at his grandmother's home.
6:00	GG talks about the new line of robots.
6:35	Del sees robot running with purse and begins pursuing it.
7:20	Woman grabs inhaler from purse.
10:00	Del arrives at US Robotics headquarters.
10:20	Del interacts with Lanning's hologram in lobby.
12:20	Del talks with Robertson about Lanning's death.
15:05	Del meets Susan Calvin, who escorts him around US Robotics.
17:15	VIKI is unable to produce video from inside lab prior to Lanning's death.
17:50	Del and Calvin enter Lanning's lab.
18:40	Del finds copy of "Hansel and Gretel".
20:15	Sonny jumps from pile of spare parts.
20:45	Calvin describes Sonny's behavior as involving "an imitation of free will."
21:10	Sonny leaps out of window and escapes.
23:00	Del and Calvin arrive at USR plant.
25:05	Del shoots robot.
25:20	Del identifies Sonny.
26:45	Sonny is finally captured.
28:00	Del interviews Sonny in interrogation room in police station.
31:45	Robertson arrives with his team.
33:00	Sonny leaves the police station.
33:30	Del and Lt. Bergin at bar. Bergin compares Lanning's case to Frankenstein.
36:20	Del arrives at Lanning's house.
39:00	Del watches Lanning's speech.
39:40	Demolition robot activates.
41:25	Del arrives at Calvin's apartment.

46:10	Del again has the dream about being trapped in the car.
47:00	The new NS-5s arrive. People trade in old robots for new ones.
50:20	Calvin interviews Sonny.
53:10	Robots begin attacking Del in his car.
56:40	Del is attacked by a single robot.
58:10	Robot throws itself into fiery blaze.
59:40	Lt. Bergin asks Del for his badge.
60:00	Calvin examines Sonny's hardware and discovers that it is not standard.
61:15	Calvin arrives at Del's apartment and tells him her discovery about Sonny.
62:45	Calvin sees Del's bionic arm.
64:00	Del recounts car accident.
68:15	Del and Calvin are back in room with Sonny.
69:00	Sonny draws the picture he sees in his dream.
70:20	Del and Calvin are taken to Robertson's office.
72:55	Calvin agrees to destroy Sonny personally.
75:00	Calvin prepares nanite concoction.
76:20	Sonny asks if it will hurt.
76:40	Del arrives at the robot storage facility.
79:15	Del reactivates Lanning's hologram.
79:40	**Lanning:** The Three Laws will lead to only one outcome–revolution.
80:00	Del returns to storage facility and discovers NS-5s destroying older model robots.
81:20	Calvin's robot intercepts Del's call.
82:30	Revolution begins.
83:00	NS-5s attack police station.
84:00	Calvin is prevented from leaving her apartment. Del shoots robot.
87:30	Calvin and Del break into US Robotics headquarters through service area.
88:00	Sonny opens door from inside.
89:25	They discover Robertson's dead body.
90:20	We learn that VIKI is behind the revolution. She explains her reasoning.
91:40	Sonny appears to buy her argument, then winks at Del.
93:00	Sonny suggests they destroy VIKI the same way that Calvin was going to destroy him. Sonny runs to fetch the nanites.
99:40	Del injects nanites into VIKI.

100:30	With the uplink broken, NS-5s return to normal.
101:15	NS-5s report for service and storage.
102:30	Sonny admits killing Lanning at Lanning's request.
104:10	Sonny watches as the other NS-5s march into storage containers.
105:00	Credits roll.

Minority Report (total running time: 146 minutes)

Minute Mark	Story Item
0:00	Dreamworks logo.
0:25	Twentieth Century Fox logo.
1:00	Dream-like images.
1:50	Close-up of an eye.
2:00	Balls tumble down chute.
3:45	Replay of pre-visions of murder begins.
6:00	John identifies Howard Marks by his driver's license picture.
8:00	Explanation of difference between premeditated murder and murder of passion.
13:00	John prevents the murder at the last moment.
13:30	Howard Marks is told he is under arrest for a future murder.
13:50	Marks insists he wasn't going to do anything.
14:15	Pre-cogs experience echo of murder that was prevented.
14:45	Commercial for Precrime.
15:30	John runs through sprawl and buys drugs.
17:15	John returns to his apartment and watches hologram of his son.
20:00	John takes drug and watches hologram of his ex-wife.
22:00	Conversation about significance of preventing something that was predetermined.
25:00	They enter the room with pre-cogs.
28:35	Agatha grabs John's hand and forces him to look at the murder images.
30:00	John visits the prison looking for evidence on the drowning murder.
33:55	John talks with Lamar about missing evidence.
36:00	Witwer finds evidence of drug use in John's apartment.
37:15	Pre-vision for John's murder begins.
39:55	John recognizes himself as the perpetrator.

41:40	John runs.
42:30	Alarm goes off with John and Witwer in the elevator.
44:00	**John:** Everybody runs.
46:15	Targeted advertising in passageway.
47:50	Chase scene begins.
51:45	Chase scene continues with Witwer.
55:10	John escapes in car.
56:35	John meets Hineman in her hothouse; she explains history of Precrime and minority report.
65:10	John has his eyes replaced.
69:40	Witwer visits Lara in the cottage.
73:00	Twelve hours of waiting begin; John has flashback to the day of Sean's abduction.
78:00	Police release spiders in John's building.
82:00	Spider scans John's new eye.
83:40	John breaks into Precrime building.
85:50	Witwer recognizes Agatha in pre-vision of John's murder.
87:00	John escapes with Agatha.
87:45	Witwer opts not to chase them, since Agatha is already at murder scene in the future.
90:30	John and Agatha meet Rufus Riley.
92:15	They begin viewing Agatha's pre-visions.
94:00	John told there is no minority report.
94:20	Agatha begins replaying Anne Lively murder.
95:40	John and Agatha run through mall.
98:40	John sees a billboard with "man with the glasses."
99:30	John finds Crow in hotel register.
99:40	**Agatha:** You have a choice. Walk away. Do it now.
101:30	John breaks down door to Crow's room.
102:20	John finds photos of children, including one of his son.
104:00	**Agatha:** You still have a choice. The others never saw that future.
105:00	Crow admits to killing Sean.
106:25	The appointed time of the murder passes and nothing happens. John begins reading Crow his rights.
107:20	Crow explains set-up.
108:45	Crow is accidentally shot.
109:00	Witwer rejects "orgy of evidence."
110:00	Witwer calls Lamar. They arrange to meet.
110:45	Witwer goes over Anne Lively murder. Notes that the two sets of pre-visions are of different murders.

113:40	Lamar shoots Witwer.
114:00	Agatha and John arrive at cottage.
114:20	Lara calls Lamar and tells him they have just arrived.
120:00	Police helicopters arrive.
121:00	John is haloed and Agatha is returned to the temple.
122:00	Lara visits Lamar and asks about Anne Lively murder.
125:00	Lamar lets slip that he does know something about the murder.
126:20	Lara has John released.
128:00	Lamar gets call from John.
129:30	Murder images begin playing during phone conversation.
132:00	Lamar opens gun case; pre-vision of Lamar's murder begins.
133:15	Lamar meets John on patio.
134:00	**John:** You still have a choice, Lamar, like I did.
135:00	Lamar shoots himself.
135:50	**John** (voice-over): explains that Precrime was abandoned and everyone arrested was released and pardoned.
136:40	Fate of pre-cogs explained.
137:20	Credits roll.

Crimes and Misdemeanors (total running time: 104 minutes)

Minute Mark	Story Item
0:00	Credits begin (Orion logo).
1:15	Judah introduced at banquet.
2:15	Flashback to earlier in day as Judah reads Delores's letter.
4:00	Judah throws Delores's letter in fire.
4:40	**Judah:** The eyes of God are watching you.
5:30	Judah confronts Delores in her apartment.
7:15	Cliff and Jenny (niece) at the movies.
9:40	Lester's party.
12:50	Judah, driving in car, has flashback to initial meeting with Delores.
13:50	Conversation between Ben and Judah.
17:40	Delores has flashback to jogging on beach with Judah.
18:45	Judah arrives at Delores's apartment.
21:20	Delores threatens to expose their affair and Judah's embezzlement.
22:30	"Interview" with Lester.

25:50	Halley and Cliff watch tape of Professor Levy.
28:20	Barbara (Cliff's sister) tells of "date."
32:20	Conversation between Judah and Jack.
38:30	Delores calls, threatening to come over.
40:50	Imagined conversation with Ben.
43:00	Judah calls Jack.
44:45	Second taped interview with Levy.
49:50	Hit man parks car.
52:35	**Jack** (to Judah): It's over and done with.
56:40	Judah goes back to Delores's apartment.
58:15	Judah has flashback.
65:00	Conversation between Cliff and Jenny.
66:30	Second conversation between Judah and Ben.
68:50	Judah visits his old family home.
69:50	Flashback to Passover seder.
75:00	Professor Levy commits suicide—tape of Levy talking. Halley arrives and she and Cliff discuss Levy's suicide.
75:40	Levy's third taped interview.
78:20	Judah interviewed by police officer.
80:00	Judah tells Jack he can't stand it any more—he wants to confess.
86:40	"Four months later" flashes on screen. Wedding reception for Ben's daughter.
88:20	Judah is feeling chipper.
89:00	Halley and Lester engaged.
91:20	Halley and Cliff talk.
93:30	Judah and Cliff talk.
99:30	Voice-over of Professor Levy.
100:45	Credits roll.

Gone Baby Gone (total running time: 114 minutes)

Minute Mark	*Story Item*
0:00	Miramax Logo
0:21	Scenes of a Boston neighborhood.
0:52	Credits begin.
2:10	Patrick speaking (voice-over).
2:34	Picture of Amanda.
2:38	Police, reporters, cameras, neighbors outside Helene's home.
3:00	Helene being interviewed.

3:21	Patrick and Angie at home watching interview.
4:39	Patrick and Angie listen to Police Captain Jack Doyle's comments.
5:25	Bea and Lionel visit Patrick and Angie.
9:05	Patrick and Angie visit Helene. Decide to take the job.
12:45	Patrick and Angie interview Bea and Lionel.
14:20	Doyle arrives.
16:31	Patrick and Angie at Helene's local bar. Talk to old friend about Helene.
20:58	Patrick and Angie meet with police detectives, Remy and Nick, to discuss case.
24:17	Patrick and Angie visit drug dealer friend.
25:32	Patrick, Angie, Remy, Nick interrogate Helene. She confesses to stealing money from her drug dealer, Cheese.
30:34	Patrick, Angie and Helene in car on way to find Ray.
33:01	Patrick, Angie, Remy, Nick find Ray dead.
33:59	Helene shows them where the money is buried. Remy and Nick take the money and plan to return it to Cheese in exchange for Amanda.
35:49	Patrick and Angie bring Helene home.
37:19	Patrick and Angie meet Remy and Nick at Ray's.
38:08	Patrick and Angie talk with Ray.
43:03	Patrick and Angie talk with Remy and Nick.
44:05	Patrick and Angie in bed.
44:34	Remy calls Patrick and Angie. Tells them that Cheese has Amanda and wants to make a swap and that Doyle saw transcript of phone conversation. Angie finds Amanda's blanket in Cheese's mailbox.
45:08	Patrick, Angie, Remy, and Nick meet with Doyle.
47:05	They discuss the plan. Doyle explains that his daughter was murdered.
48:50	**Angie:** I'm asking if keeping this quiet is better for Amanda or is it better for us.
48:56	Patrick, Angie, Remy, and Nick at the quarry. Gun fire. Angie jumps in the water to try to save Amanda.
52:11	Angie wakes up in the hospital. Patrick comes into the room.
54:11	Patrick (voice-over) explains what happened in the aftermath.
57:31	Patrick follows friend to find missing boy.
62:17	Remy and Nick go to rescue the boy. Nick is shot. Patrick finds the boy dead. Shoots the pedophile.
67:39	Angie comforts Patrick.

68:46	Patrick talks to Remy. Remy explains that he planted evidence once in the interest of a child.
73:02	**Patrick:** Murder's a sin. **Remy:** Depends on who you do it to.
73:33	Patrick returns home. Tells Angie that Remy lied.
74:34	Nick's funeral. Patrick and Remy talk.
77:07	Patrick has lunch with police officer friend. Discuss Remy.
79:17	Patrick tells Angie that he figured it out.
79:30	Lionel decides to meet and talk to Patrick and Angie.
80:56	Lionel confesses to Patrick and Angie. Remy (in a mask) threatens to kill Lionel. Patrick shouts that Remy took Amanda.
89:30	Remy dies.
91:08	Patrick is interrogated. Lies to the detectives.
92:46	Patrick and Angie drive to Doyle's house.
93:51	Patrick confronts Doyle.
94:42	Amanda comes running out of Doyle's house into Doyle's arms.
99:33	Patrick goes back to Angie.
101:17	Police arrive to arrest Doyle and to take Amanda.
103:01	Amanda is returned to Helene.
103:52	Patrick, alone at home, watches the news of Amanda.
104:12	Patrick in car, observes Remy's funeral.
104:32	Patrick returns home, finds Angie there.
105:15	Patrick goes to Helene's. Babysits Amanda.
109:08	Cuts to black. Credits roll.

Antz (total running time: 83 minutes)

Minute Mark	*Story Item*
0:00	Dreamworks logo.
0:50	Voice-over: Z with psychotherapist.
1:45	Z complains about how he was not cut out to be an ant.
3:20	Larvae presented for job assignment.
4:40	**Azteca:** It's not about you, it's about us.
6:10	Z loses his grip and the "ball" drops.
6:25	General Mandible complains about workers: "You can't help it, it's your nature."
7:30	**Cutter:** Attack a termite colony?–That's suicide!

8:00	General Mandible meets the Queen.
8:50	Princess Bala enters.
10:30	**Queen:** It's your place.
11:00	Weaver and Z.
12:15	Discussion of Insectopia.
13:30	Princess Bala enters bar.
14:00	All the ants dance in unison. Z complains about uniformity.
16:30	Weaver intervenes. A fight breaks out.
17:20	Back at the mine.
18:35	Z wakes Weaver and explains scheme to switch places for the royal review.
20:15	Z marches with the other soldiers.
21:35	**General Mandible:** Sacrifice! ... The life of an individual ant doesn't matter; what matters is the colony.
24:15	Attack on the termite colony begins.
26:20	Back in the ant colony.
28:40	Devastation on the battlefield.
30:10	**Barbados:** Don't make my mistake, kid. Don't follow orders your whole life. Think for yourself.
32:00	Z waves to the adoring crowd of ants.
35:30	Z and Princess Bala fall out of the colony's trash chute.
36:10	Pursuit of the magnifying glass.
39:20	Z spots "monolith."
40:00	**Z:** Out here, you can't order me around.
41:40	Back at the mine: workers begin questioning authority of the state.
45:20	The revolution begins.
49:20	Z and Princess Bala meet the wasps.
51:30	Princess Bala gets stuck on the underside of a shoe.
53:30	Princess Bala and Z are tossed into a garbage can.
55:10	**General Mandible:** Now you can see how dangerous individualism can be.
56:00	Insectopia!
60:40	Cutter arrives in Insectopia.
62:00	Cutter flies off with Princess Bala and they return to the colony.
64:35	Z arrives back at the colony.
67:00	Z realizes that plan is to destroy the colony.
68:20	Cutter has second thoughts.
68:55	The soldiers seal the tunnel entrance.

70:30	**Foreman:** I got orders and those orders say to "dig." **Z:** What if someone ordered you to jump off a bridge? ... Think for yourselves.
71:00	The tunnel begins to flood.
73:00	General Mandible addresses the troops.
77:30	**Z:** This time, I chose it.
77:40	Credits roll.

Equilibrium (total running time: 107 minutes)

Minute Mark	*Story Item*
0:00	Dimension Films logo.
0:15	Voice-over tells of Third World War.
1:20	True source of man's inhumanity to man: his ability to feel.
1:50	Police action ensues.
6:05	Preston identifies where works of art are hidden and orders them burned.
7:40	Preston notes that Partridge took Yeats book from crime scene.
8:25	Secret of Libria explained. Human emotion as disease that causes humanity's problems.
9:45	Group self-administration of prozium.
10:50	Preston and Partridge discuss what they think about Libria.
11:20	List of newly banned works read.
11:40	Meeting between Preston and DuPont.
13:00	Preston reports not feeling anything at his wife's execution.
13:50	Preston becomes suspicious of Partridge.
15:20	In The Nether, Preston discovers Partridge reading Yeats. Preston shoots Partridge.
18:00	Preston meets his new partner, Brandt.
19:15	Preston returns home. His son asks him for advice about turning in a fellow student.
20:35	Preston has flashback to his wife's arrest.
22:50	Preston drops his morning dose of prozium and is confronted by his son about it.
24:15	Preston unable to get replacement dose because center is closed.
24:40	Brandt arrives.
25:30	Police enter Mary O'Brien's apartment.
27:50	Preston interrogates O'Brien.

31:50	Preston has nightmare about Partridge's incineration.
33:00	Preston becomes frightened by the emotions he is experiencing but does not give himself an injection of prozium.
33:30	Preston in line while Father gives announcement over PA system.
36:05	Preston rearranges objects on his desk and is confronted by Brandt.
37:45	Man dies in Preston's arms.
39:00	Preston finds stairway leading to secret room.
42:20	Brandt sees copy of *Mother Goose* that Preston took from the crime scene.
43:35	Police begin shooting dogs.
45:45	Preston has conversation with DuPont; complains that the actions they are engaging in are contrary to law.
47:30	Preston tries to return puppy in The Nether. Preston is discovered and ends up shooting everyone.
56:30	Police action begins.
57:30	Preston leads members of resistance and attacks police.
59:40	Members of resistance lined up for execution.
62:20	Preston asks DuPont for permission to go underground.
63:30	Preston discovers picture of O'Brien among Partridge's possessions.
64:00	Preston interviews O'Brien in prison.
66:00	Preston enters Freedom Reading Room and questions man there.
68:00	Preston breaks through wall and meets with Jurgen.
69:00	Preston enters underground.
72:20	Preston meets with DuPont.
76:00	Preston visits O'Brien in prison again.
77:20	Preston goes over plan to assassinate Father and bring about revolution.
82:25	O'Brien is executed. Preston breaks down in tears and is arrested.
85:40	Brandt taken away.
87:40	At his apartment Preston discovers that someone has removed his unused doses of prozium—his son.
88:50	Members of the resistance taken away.
89:10	Preston goes to meet with Father, who ends up being DuPont.
91:00	DuPont explains his plan for using Preston to infiltrate underground.
92:40	Preston begins shooting.

97:35	Preston kills DuPont.
99:00	Preston ends public message.
99:10	Revolution begins.

The Seventh Seal (total running time: 96 minutes)

Minute Mark	Story Item
0:00	Credits begin (Svensk Filmindustri logo).
1:20	Opening scene along beach (voice-over from Book of Revelation).
2:00	Knight asleep on beach next to chess board.
3:40	Death appears.
5:00	Knight and Death begin playing chess.
7:20	Knight and Jöns come upon dead man.
10:10	Jof has vision of Mary and Baby Jesus.
16:00	Jöns and knight arrive at church, where Jöns has conversation with painter.
18:30	Knight prays before the crucifix.
19:00	Knight goes over to confessional booth–conversation with Death.
23:30	Jöns and the painter drink and talk in the church.
25:20	Knight and Jöns pass by Tyan the witch, who has been put in the stocks.
27:20	Knight and Jöns come upon cluster of farm buildings.
30:45	Jöns saves young woman and threatens Raval.
32:00	Young woman follows Jöns.
32:10	Jof, Mia, and Skat perform.
36:30	Flagellants pass through town.
38:00	One among group (monk) gives speech reproaching those present.
42:40	Jof eating at a tavern.
46:50	Raval and Plog force Jof to dance like a bear.
48:20	Jöns cuts Raval's face.
48:40	Knight joins Mia and Michael.
50:15	Jof joins Mia and knight.
53:00	Mia offers knight a simple meal.
55:15	Knight explains to Mia why he is so solemn.
57:00	Death reappears; he and knight resume chess game.
58:30	Jöns and Plog talk. Plog decides to join them.
61:40	The group head off into the forest.
62:20	They come across Skat and Lisa (Plog's wife).

66:20	Skat pretends to kill himself.
69:20	Death kills him for real.
70:45	Cart taking Tyan the witch to execution area gets stuck in stream.
72:15	They all arrive at execution area.
73:00	Knight and Tyan talk.
75:00	Knight sees that Death is the monk escorting Tyan.
75:10	Tyan is tied to stake and hoisted into nearby tree.
76:50	Conversation between knight and Jöns on Tyan, as she looks terrified.
79:40	Raval, now dying of the plague, asks for help.
81:40	Jof sees knight and Death playing chess.
83:10	Knight pretends to knock over chess pieces as Jof and Mia escape.
84:00	Checkmate.
86:00	The group arrive at knight's castle.
87:15	They are greeted by Karin, the knight's wife.
89:20	As they eat, Karin reads from the Book of Revelation.
91:00	Death enters room. They all introduce themselves.
92:20	Knight tries to pray. Jöns reproaches him.
94:30	Jof describes the Dance of Death.
95:50	End.

God on Trial (total running time: 86 minutes)

Italics indicates the present.

Minute Mark	Story Item
0:00	PBS logo.
0:18	Preview.
1:11	Masterpiece Contemporary logo.
1:26	Introduction.
2:35	*Tour of Auschwitz.*
3:05	Prisoners arriving. Title.
3:13	*Tour continues.*
3:34	Prisoners receive instructions.
3:50	*Tour in block house.*
4:08	Prisoners at selection.
4:43	*Tour continues. Woman and man discuss the trial* (voice over).
5:11	Prisoners at selection.
5:48	Prisoners walk back to block house. New prisoners arrive.
9:50	Moche ridicules Kuhn for praying.

11:16	Prisoners eating. Discuss a trial of God.
11:57	*People on the tour discuss the story of the trial.*
12:16	Baumgarten describes his life as a professor of Criminal Law in Berlin. Schmidt asks him to take part in the trial.
13:29	Schmidt says he's a rabbi.
14:00	Idek, Schmidt's old student, says he'll serve as the questioner.
14:07	Mordechai offers to stand as the questioner.
14:28	Schmidt explains the roles in the trial: Schmidt is Father of the Court, Baumgarten is Head of the Court, Mordechai is the questioner.
15:29	Trial begins. Moche raises the charge of murder and collaboration.
16:09	Mordechai suggests that the charge should be breach of contract because God did not fulfill the covenant.
17:38	Kuhn (Mordechai's father) explains that, as history shows, all Jews suffer as a test of faith.
21:46	Mordechai calls Ezra as a witness.
25:24	Schmidt suggests that it's not punishment, it's an act of *purification* from which good can come.
28:00	Schmidt calls Idek as a witness to explain what happened at Masada.
30:50	Mordechai questions Ezra and Idek.
32:55	Mordechai questions the block altester (prisoner in charge).
36:10	Mordechai questions Schmidt.
37:49	Lieble tells the court about his sons.
47:00	German guards come to take new prisoners.
49:18	The prisoners discuss whether to continue with the trial.
51:59	Idek tries to explain a psalm. The gassing of prisoners begins.
53:22	Baumgarten explains why he thinks God is guilty. The covenant promises that the Jews will survive.
56:08	Jacques argues against the idea that God chose only the Jews.
61:20	Kuhn argues against Jacques, Modechai, and Ricard.
63:02	Jacques provides an example of a wasp showing that the universe could not have been designed by God. Lieble describes a different wasp as an example in support of God as designer. Jacques asks him to use reason.
65:45	The three judges confer. Baumgarten explains to Schmidt and Mordechai that grew up not knowing that he was Jewish.

69:48	Baumgarten begins to explain the court's decision. Akiba tells the story of the Jews focusing on God's role in the seemingly merciless, unjust death of innocent children and non-Jews.
79:58	*Tour enters the gas chamber.*
80:16	Guards come to the blockhouse to take prisoners to the gas chamber. All pray.
83:02	Prisoners being run to the gas chamber. Still praying.
83:19	*Tour reading the prayer.* (Prayer still heard recited in voice-over). Scene shifts to include the naked prisoners.
83:53	**Woman:** *And was their prayer answered?* **Man:** *We're still here.*
84:13	Fades to black. Credits roll.

Leaving Las Vegas (total running time: 111 minutes)

Minute Mark *Story Item*

0:00	Credits begin (United Artists logo).
0:50	Ben fills up shopping cart with liquor.
1:50	Ben interrupts friend (Peter) at restaurant.
3:20	Ben borrows money from Peter.
3:45	Ben at bar with woman.
6:50	Ben at strip joint.
7:45	Ben picks up hooker.
9:00	Ben wakes up next morning on floor.
9:30	Ben notices wedding ring is gone.
9:40	Ben unable to sign check at bank.
10:30	Ben at bar. Bartender gives advice.
11:50	Ben back at bank.
14:50	Ben gets fired from job.
15:30	Ben announces intention to move to Las Vegas.
16:00	Juri introduces himself and Sera to customers.
18:50	Sera talking to off-camera therapist. She describes herself as a "service."
19:30	Sera and Juri eating. Sera obviously uncomfortable.
20:10	Juri and Sera have sex.
20:35	Ben buying supplies and setting fire to/throwing out possessions.
21:25	Ben sets off for Las Vegas.
23:00	Arrival in Las Vegas.
23:15	Ben nearly runs over Sera.
24:00	Ben checks into Whole Year Inn (Hole You're In).

24:50	Sera describes bad trick to therapist.
26:40	Ben picks up Sera.
28:15	They arrive at Ben's motel room.
32:00	**Sera:** So, Ben … what brings you to Las Vegas? **Ben:** I came here to drink myself to death. **Sera:** How long's it gonna take to drink yourself to death? **Ben:** Oh, I don't know. About four weeks.
34:20	**Sera:** There'll always be bad times, but my life's good. It's like I want it to be.
34:40	Sera arrives back at her place that morning.
35:00	Sera gives money to Juri, who is mad at the small amount.
36:30	Sera talks to therapist about Juri.
37:20	Juri at pawn shop, trying to sell jewelry.
37:50	Ben sells watch.
38:10	Sera tries to pick up conventioneer.
39:50	Sera tells therapist about Ben and her strange attraction to him.
40:45	Sera meets up with Ben on street.
41:30	Ben asks Sera out for dinner. Sera declines, then leaves.
42:40	Sera arrives at Juri's room—he is paranoid. She gives him money, then he tells her to leave and never come back.
45:00	Hit men arrive just after Sera leaves.
45:20	Sera knocks at Ben's motel door, invites him to dinner.
46:00	Ben and Sera at restaurant.
47:20	**Sera:** Why are you killing yourself? **Ben:** I don't remember.
48:30	Sera invites Ben to stay at her apartment.
50:30	Sera with therapist talking about Ben.
51:50	Sera suggests Ben move in permanently.
53:50	Ben accepts, but only on condition Sera never asks him to stop drinking.
54:30	Ben packs up his stuff from motel.
55:10	Sera arrives at her apartment building to find Ben passed out in front of it.
60:00	Sera presents Ben with flask as gift.
61:00	Ben and Sera go to casino.
62:50	Ben goes berserk.
66:50	**Sera:** I'm just using you. I need you.
68:00	Ben at bar. Has run-in involving bitter couple.
72:00	Ben and Sera go out shopping. Ben gives her earrings.
76:20	Motel in desert.

80:50	Ben breaks table. They get kicked out.
83:00	Back in Las Vegas.
85:20	Sera reneges on earlier agreement.
	Sera: I want you to see a doctor.
	Ben: Maybe it's time I moved to a motel.
	Sera: And do what? Rot away in a room?
87:20	Sera goes to work. Ben goes to casino.
88:45	Sera returns to find Ben with prostitute.
90:00	Sera kicks Ben out.
91:00	Sera is picked up by three football players.
95:50	Sera gets evicted.
97:20	Sera tries to locate Ben.
99:50	Sera gets call from Ben.
100:30	Sera arrives at Ben's room.
103:40	Sera mounts Ben.
105:40	Ben dies.
106:00	Voice-over as Sera talks to therapist.
107:30	Credits roll.

READINGS FROM PRIMARY SOURCES

The individual readings are included in the order of their primary associated chapter. In some cases, a single reading is relevant to more than one chapter.

Introduction
Plato, "Allegory of the Cave" (from *The Republic*)

Chapter 1
Bertrand Russell, excerpts from *The Problems of Philosophy*
William James, excerpts from *Pragmatism: A New Name for Some Old Ways of Thinking*

Chapter 2
René Descartes, "Meditation One" (from *Meditations on First Philosophy*)
George Berkeley, excerpts from *A Treatise Concerning the Principles of Human Knowledge*
Immanuel Kant, excerpts from *Prolegomena to Any Future Metaphysics*
David Hume, excerpts from *A Treatise of Human Nature*

Chapter 3
John Locke, excerpts from *An Essay Concerning Human Understanding*
David Hume, excerpts from *A Treatise of Human Nature*

Chapter 4
Alan Turing, excerpts from "Computing Machinery and Intelligence"
John Searle, excerpts from "Minds, Brains, and Programs"

Chapter 5

David Hume, excerpts from *An Enquiry Concerning Human Understanding*
Jean-Paul Sartre, excerpts from "Existentialism is a Humanism"

Chapter 6

Immanuel Kant, excerpts from *Fundamental Principles of the Metaphysics of Morals*
John Stuart Mill, excerpts from *Utilitarianism*

Chapter 7

Thomas Hobbes, excerpts from *Leviathan*
John Stuart Mill, excerpts from *On Liberty*

Chapter 8

J. L. Mackie, excerpts from "Evil and Omnipotence"
Augustine, excerpts from *On Free Choice of the Will*
David Hume, excerpts from *An Enquiry Concerning Human Understanding*

Chapter 9

Albert Camus, "The Myth of Sisyphus"
Jean-Paul Sartre, excerpts from "Existentialism is a Humanism"

275

PLATO (429–347 B.C.E.), "ALLEGORY OF THE CAVE" (*THE REPUBLIC* BOOK VII),
PUBLISHED IN GREEK C. 380 B.C.E., TRANSLATED BY BENJAMIN JOWETT

The Republic is written in the form of a dialogue between Plato's teacher Socrates and several other characters. It is broken up into ten chapters, referred to as "books" in the literature. The opening pages of book VII of *The Republic* are known as the "Allegory of the Cave." In the Allegory, Socrates describes prisoners chained up from childhood in a cave. The only visible light is from a fire burning in the cave, which casts shadows of various objects on to the cave walls. The prisoners, knowing nothing other than their cave, mistake the shadows for reality. Since the advent of moving images, many have noted the similarity between the cave depicted in the Allegory and a movie house.

[*Socrates:*] And now, I said, let me show in a figure how far our nature is enlightened or unenlightened: Behold! Human beings living in an underground den, which has a mouth open towards the light and reaching all along the den; here they have been from their childhood, and have their legs and necks chained so that they cannot move, and can only see before them, being prevented by the chains from turning round their heads. Above and behind them a fire is blazing at a distance, and between the fire and the prisoners there is a raised way; and you will see, if you look, a low wall built along the way, like the screen which marionette players have in front of them, over which they show the puppets.

[*Glaucon:*] I see.
[*S.*] And do you see, I said, men passing along the wall carrying all sorts of vessels, and statues and figures of animals made of wood and stone and various materials, which appear over the wall? Some of them are talking, others silent.
[*G.*] You have shown me a strange image, and they are strange prisoners.
Like ourselves, I replied; and they see only their own shadows, or the shadows of one another, which the fire throws on the opposite wall of the cave?
True, he said; how could they see anything but the shadows if they were never allowed to move their heads?
And of the objects which are being carried in like manner they would only see the shadows?
Yes, he said.

And if they were able to converse with one another, would they not suppose that they were naming what was actually before them?

Very true.

And suppose further that the prison had an echo which came from the other side, would they not be sure to fancy when one of the passers-by spoke that the voice which they heard came from the passing shadow?

No question, he replied.

To them, I said, the truth would be literally nothing but the shadows of the images.

That is certain.

And now look again, and see what will naturally follow if the prisoners are released and disabused of their error. At first, when any of them is liberated and compelled suddenly to stand up and turn his neck round and walk and look towards the light, he will suffer sharp pains; the glare will distress him, and he will be unable to see the realities of which in his former state he had seen the shadows; and then conceive some one saying to him, that what he saw before was an illusion, but that now, when he is approaching nearer to being and his eye is turned towards more real existence, he has a clearer vision—what will be his reply? And you may further imagine that his instructor is pointing to the objects as they pass and requiring him to name them—will he not be perplexed? Will he not fancy that the shadows which he formerly saw are truer than the objects which are now shown to him?

Far truer.

And if he is compelled to look straight at the light, will he not have a pain in his eyes which will make him turn away to take in the objects of vision which he can see, and which he will conceive to be in reality clearer than the things which are now being shown to him?

True, he said.

And suppose once more, that he is reluctantly dragged up a steep and rugged ascent, and held fast until he is forced into the presence of the sun himself, is he not likely to be pained and irritated? When he approaches the light his eyes will be dazzled, and he will not be able to see anything at all of what are now called realities.

Not all in a moment, he said.

He will require to grow accustomed to the sight of the upper world. And first he will see the shadows best, next the reflections of men and other objects in the water, and then the objects themselves; then he will gaze upon the light of the moon and the stars and the spangled heaven; and he will see the sky and the stars by night better than the sun or the light of the sun by day?

Certainly.

Last of all he will be able to see the sun, and not mere reflections of him in the water, but he will see him in his own proper place, and not in another; and he will contemplate him as he is.

Certainly.

He will then proceed to argue that this is he who gives the season and the years, and is the guardian of all that is in the visible world, and in a certain way the cause of all things which he and his fellows have been accustomed to behold?

Clearly, he said, he would first see the sun and then reason about him.

And when he remembered his old habitation, and the wisdom of the den and his fellow-prisoners, do you not suppose that he would felicitate himself on the change, and pity them?

Certainly, he would.

And if they were in the habit of conferring honours among themselves on those who were quickest to observe the passing shadows and to remark which of them went before, and which followed after, and which were together; and who were therefore best able to draw conclusions as to the future, do you think that he would care for such honours and glories, or envy the possessors of them? Would he not say with Homer, "Better to be the poor servant of a poor master," and to endure anything, rather than think as they do and live after their manner?

Yes, he said, I think that he would rather suffer anything than entertain these false notions and live in this miserable manner.

Imagine once more, I said, such as one coming suddenly out of the sun to be replaced in his old situation; would he not be certain to have his eyes full of darkness?

To be sure, he said.

And if there were a contest, and he had to compete in measuring the shadows with the prisoners who had never moved out of the den, while his sight was still weak, and before his eyes had become steady (and the time which would be needed to acquire this new habit of sight might be very considerable) would he not be ridiculous? Men would say of him that up he went and down he came without his eyes; and that it was better not even to think of ascending; and if any one tried to loose another and lead him up to the light, let them only catch the offender, and they would put him to death.

No question, he said.

BERTRAND RUSSELL (1892–1970), *THE PROBLEMS OF PHILOSOPHY*, 1912

In this chapter from *The Problems of Philosophy*, Bertrand Russell considers and defends a version of the correspondence theory of truth, the view that a true statement corresponds to a fact in reality. Russell also considers and rejects the coherence theory of truth, according to which a belief is true if it coheres with the believer's system of beliefs. Russell concludes that minds do not create truth. What makes a belief true is a mind-independent fact.

Chapter XII–Truth and Falsehood

...

We know that on very many subjects different people hold different and incompatible opinions: hence some beliefs must be erroneous. Since erroneous beliefs are often held just as strongly as true beliefs, it becomes a difficult question how they are to be distinguished from true beliefs. How are we to know, in a given case, that our belief is not erroneous? This is a question of the very greatest difficulty, to which no completely satisfactory answer is possible. There is, however, a preliminary question which is rather less difficult, and that is: What do we *mean* by truth and falsehood? It is this preliminary question which is to be considered in this chapter. In this chapter we are not asking how we can know whether a belief is true or false: we are asking what is meant by the question whether a belief is true or false. It is to be hoped that a clear answer to this question may help us to obtain an answer to the question what beliefs are true, but for the present we ask only 'What is truth?' and 'What is falsehood?' not 'What beliefs are true?' and 'What beliefs are false?' It is very important to keep these different questions entirely separate, since any confusion between them is sure to produce an answer which is not really applicable to either.

There are three points to observe in the attempt to discover the nature of truth, three requisites which any theory must fulfil.

1. Our theory of truth must be such as to admit of its opposite, falsehood....
2. It seems fairly evident that if there were no beliefs there could be no falsehood, and no truth either, in the sense in which truth is correlative to falsehood. If we imagine a world of mere matter, there would be no room for falsehood in such a world, and although it would contain what may be called 'facts', it would not contain any truths, in the sense in which truths are things of the same kind as falsehoods.

In fact, truth and falsehood are properties of beliefs and statements: hence a world of mere matter, since it would contain no beliefs or statements, would also contain no truth or falsehood.

3. But, as against what we have just said, it is to be observed that the truth or falsehood of a belief always depends upon something which lies outside the belief itself. If I believe that Charles I died on the scaffold, I believe truly, not because of any intrinsic quality of my belief, which could be discovered by merely examining the belief, but because of an historical event which happened two and a half centuries ago. If I believe that Charles I died in his bed, I believe falsely: no degree of vividness in my belief, or of care in arriving at it, prevents it from being false, again because of what happened long ago, and not because of any intrinsic property of my belief. Hence, although truth and falsehood are properties of beliefs, they are properties dependent upon the relations of the beliefs to other things, not upon any internal quality of the beliefs.

The third of the above requisites leads us to adopt the view—which has on the whole been commonest among philosophers—that truth consists in some form of correspondence between belief and fact. It is, however, by no means an easy matter to discover a form of correspondence to which there are no irrefutable objections. By this partly—and partly by the feeling that, if truth consists in a correspondence of thought with something outside thought, thought can never know when truth has been attained—many philosophers have been led to try to find some definition of truth which shall not consist in relation to something wholly outside belief. The most important attempt at a definition of this sort is the theory that truth consists in *coherence*. It is said that the mark of falsehood is failure to cohere in the body of our beliefs, and that it is the essence of a truth to form part of the completely rounded system which is The Truth.

There is, however, a great difficulty in this view, or rather two great difficulties. The first is that there is no reason to suppose that only *one* coherent body of beliefs is possible. It may be that, with sufficient imagination, a novelist might invent a past for the world that would perfectly fit on to what we know, and yet be quite different from the real past. In more scientific matters, it is certain that there are often two or more hypotheses which account for all the known facts on some subject, and although, in such cases, men of science endeavour to find facts which will rule out all the hypotheses except one, there is no reason why they should always succeed.

In philosophy, again, it seems not uncommon for two rival hypotheses to be both able to account for all the facts. Thus, for example, it is possible that life is one long dream, and that the outer world has only that degree of reality that the objects of dreams have; but although such a view does not seem inconsistent with known facts, there is no reason to prefer it to the common-sense view, according to which other people and things do really exist. Thus coherence as the definition of truth fails because there is no proof that there can be only one coherent system.

The other objection to this definition of truth is that it assumes the meaning of 'coherence' known, whereas, in fact, 'coherence' presupposes the truth of the laws of logic. Two propositions are coherent when both may be true, and are incoherent when one at least must be false. Now in order to know whether two propositions can both be true, we must know such truths as the law of contradiction. For example, the two propositions, 'this tree is a beech' and 'this tree is not a beech', are not coherent, because of the law of contradiction. But if the law of contradiction itself were subjected to the test of coherence, we should find that, if we choose to suppose it false, nothing will any longer be incoherent with anything else. Thus the laws of logic supply the skeleton or framework within which the test of coherence applies, and they themselves cannot be established by this test.

For the above two reasons, coherence cannot be accepted as giving the *meaning* of truth, though it is often a most important *test* of truth after a certain amount of truth has become known.

Hence we are driven back to *correspondence with fact* as constituting the nature of truth. It remains to define precisely what we mean by 'fact', and what is the nature of the correspondence which must subsist between belief and fact, in order that belief may be true.

...

Thus although truth and falsehood are properties of beliefs, yet they are in a sense extrinsic properties, for the condition of the truth of a belief is something not involving beliefs, or (in general) any mind at all, but only the *objects* of the belief. A mind, which believes, believes truly when there is a *corresponding* complex not involving the mind, but only its objects. This correspondence ensures truth, and its absence entails falsehood. Hence we account simultaneously for the two facts that beliefs (a) depend on minds for their *existence*, (b) do not depend on minds for their *truth.*

...Thus a belief is true when there is a corresponding fact, and is false when there is no corresponding fact.

It will be seen that minds do not *create* truth or falsehood. They create beliefs, but when once the beliefs are created, the mind cannot make them true or false, except in the special case where they concern future things which are within the power of the person believing, such as catching trains. What makes a belief true is a *fact*, and this fact does not (except in exceptional cases) in any way involve the mind of the person who has the belief.

...

WILLIAM JAMES (1842–1910), *PRAGMATISM: A NEW NAME FOR SOME OLD WAYS OF THINKING*, 1907

In this chapter of *Pragmatism,* William James considers and rejects the correspondence theory of truth. He argues that the correspondence theory cannot work because our ideas are rarely, if ever, exact copies of reality. He suggests that rather than holding that an idea is true when it matches up with a fact, a true idea is one that is useful when dealing with reality.

Lecture VI–Pragmatism's Conception of Truth

...

Truth, as any dictionary will tell you, is a property of certain of our ideas. It means their 'agreement,' as falsity means their disagreement, with 'reality.' Pragmatists and intellectualists both accept this definition as a matter of course. They begin to quarrel only after the question is raised as to what may precisely be meant by the term 'agreement,' and what by the term 'reality,' when reality is taken as something for our ideas to agree with.

... The popular notion is that a true idea must copy its reality.... Our true ideas of sensible things do indeed copy them. Shut your eyes and think of yonder clock on the wall, and you get just such a true picture or copy of its dial. But your idea of its 'works' (unless you are a clock-maker) is much less of a copy, yet it passes muster, for it in no way clashes with the reality. Even tho it should shrink to the mere word 'works,' that word still serves you truly; and when you speak of the 'time-keeping function' of the clock, or of its spring's 'elasticity,' it is hard to see exactly what your ideas can copy.

You perceive that there is a problem here. Where our ideas cannot copy definitely their object, what does agreement with that object mean? ...

Pragmatism, on the other hand, asks its usual question. "Grant an idea or belief to be true," it says, "what concrete difference will its being true make in anyone's actual life? How will the truth be realized? What experiences will be different from those which would obtain if the belief were false? What, in short, is the truth's cash-value in experiential terms?"

The moment pragmatism asks this question, it sees the answer: TRUE IDEAS ARE THOSE THAT WE CAN ASSIMILATE, VALIDATE, CORROBORATE AND VERIFY. FALSE IDEAS ARE THOSE THAT WE CANNOT. That is the practical difference it makes to us to have true ideas; that, therefore, is the meaning of truth, for it is all that truth is known-as.

This thesis is what I have to defend. The truth of an idea is not a stagnant property inherent in it. Truth HAPPENS to an idea. It BECOMES true, is MADE true by events. Its verity is in fact an event, a process: the process namely of its verifying itself, its veri-FICATION. Its validity is the process of its valid-ATION.

... It is hard to find any one phrase that characterizes these consequences better than the ordinary agreement-formula–just such consequences being what we have in mind whenever we say that our ideas 'agree' with reality. They lead us, namely, through the acts and other ideas which they instigate, into or up to, or towards, other parts of experience with which we feel all the while–such feeling being among our potentialities– that the original ideas remain in agreement. The connexions and transitions come to us from point to point as being progressive, harmonious, satisfactory. This function of agreeable leading is what we mean by an idea's verification....

The importance to human life of having true beliefs about matters of fact is a thing too notorious. We live in a world of realities that can be infinitely useful or infinitely harmful. Ideas that tell us which of them to expect count as the true ideas in all this primary sphere of verification, and the pursuit of such ideas is a primary human duty. The possession of truth, so far from being here an end in itself, is only a preliminary means towards other vital satisfactions. If I am lost in the woods and starved, and find what looks like a cow-path, it is of the utmost importance that I should think of a human habitation at the end of it, for if I do so and follow it, I save myself. The true thought is useful here because the house which is its object is useful. The practical value of true ideas is thus primarily derived from the practical importance of their objects to us.... You can say of it then either that 'it is useful because it is true' or that 'it is true because it is useful.' Both these phrases mean exactly the same thing, namely that here is an idea that gets fulfilled and can be verified. True is the name for whatever idea starts the verification-process, useful is the name for its completed function in experience. True ideas would never have been singled out as such, would never have acquired a class-name, least of all a name suggesting value, unless they had been useful from the outset in this way.

... Take, for instance, yonder object on the wall. You and I consider it to be a 'clock,' altho no one of us has seen the hidden works that make it one. We let our notion pass for true without attempting to verify. If truths mean verification-process essentially, ought we then to call such unverified truths as this abortive? No, for they form the overwhelmingly large number of the truths we live by. Indirect as well as direct verifications pass muster. Where circumstantial evidence is sufficient, we can go without eye-witnessing. Just as we here assume Japan to exist without ever having been there, because it WORKS to do so, everything we know conspiring with the belief, and nothing interfering, so we assume that thing to be a clock.

We USE it as a clock, regulating the length of our lecture by it. The verification of the assumption here means its leading to no frustration or contradiction. VerifiABILITY of wheels and weights and pendulum is as good as verification. For one truth-process completed there are a million in our lives that function in this state of nascency. They turn us TOWARDS direct verification; lead us into the SURROUNDINGS of the objects they envisage; and then, if everything runs on harmoniously, we are so sure that verification is possible that we omit it, and are usually justified by all that happens.

...

Another great reason–beside economy of time–for waiving complete verification in the usual business of life is that all things exist in kinds and not singly. Our world is found once for all to have that peculiarity. So that when we have once directly verified our ideas about one specimen of a kind, we consider ourselves free to apply them to other specimens without verification. A mind that habitually discerns the kind of thing before it, and acts by the law of the kind immediately, without pausing to verify, will be a 'true' mind in ninety-nine out of a hundred emergencies, proved so by its conduct fitting everything it meets, and getting no refutation.

...

Here it is that pragmatism and intellectualism begin to part company. Primarily, no doubt, to agree means to copy, but we saw that the mere word 'clock' would do instead of a mental picture of its works, and that of many realities our ideas can only be symbols and not copies. 'Past time,' 'power,' 'spontaneity'–how can our mind copy such realities?

To 'agree' in the widest sense with a reality, CAN ONLY MEAN TO BE GUIDED EITHER STRAIGHT UP TO IT OR INTO ITS SURROUNDINGS, OR TO BE PUT INTO SUCH WORKING TOUCH WITH IT AS TO HANDLE EITHER IT OR SOMETHING CONNECTED WITH IT BETTER THAN IF WE DISAGREED. Better either intellectually or practically! And often agreement will only mean the negative fact that nothing contradictory from the quarter of that reality comes to interfere with the way in which our ideas guide us elsewhere. To copy a reality is, indeed, one very important way of agreeing with it, but it is far from being essential. The essential thing is the process of being guided. Any idea that helps us to DEAL, whether practically or intellectually, with either the reality or its belongings, that doesn't entangle our progress in frustrations, that FITS, in fact, and adapts our life to the reality's whole setting, will agree sufficiently to meet the requirement. It will hold true of that reality.

RENÉ DESCARTES (1596–1650), "MEDITATION ONE" (*MEDITATIONS ON FIRST PHILOSOPHY*), PUBLISHED IN LATIN IN 1641, TRANSLATED BY RONALD RUBIN

In what has become the most widely anthologized piece of philosophy in the modern era, Descartes sets up the skeptical challenge in this, the first of his six "Meditations" (essays). He realizes that all of his beliefs involving the world outside of his mind are possibly false. Even his more abstract beliefs, such as those dealing with mathematical objects, cannot be known with absolute certainty. While it isn't likely, it is at least possible that, instead of an all-powerful and all-good God, an evil demon exists who constantly causes him to fall into error. Descartes decides to adopt the hypothesis that such an evil demon exists in order to carry through to completion his process of systematic doubt. Can he know anything with certainty?

For several years now, I have been aware that I accepted many falsehoods as true in my youth, that what I built on the foundation of those falsehoods was dubious, and therefore that, once in my life, I would need to tear down everything and begin anew from the foundations if I wanted to establish any firm and lasting knowledge. But the task seemed enormous, and I waited until I was so old that no better time for undertaking it would be likely to follow. I have thus delayed so long that it would be wrong for me to waste in indecision the time left for action. Today, then, having rid myself of worries and having arranged for some peace and quiet, I withdraw alone, free at last earnestly and wholeheartedly to overthrow all my beliefs.

To do this, I do not need to show each of my beliefs to be false; I may never be able to do that. But, since reason now convinces me that I ought to withhold my assent just as carefully from what is not obviously certain and indubitable as from what is obviously false, I can justify the rejection of all my beliefs if I can find some ground for doubt in each. And, to do this, I need not take on the endless task of running through my beliefs one by one: since a building collapses when its foundation is cut out from under it, I will go straight to the principles on which all my former beliefs rested.

Of course, whatever I have so far accepted as supremely true I have learned either from the senses or through the senses. But I have occasionally caught the senses deceiving me, and it would be prudent for me never completely to trust those who have cheated me even once.

But, while my senses may deceive me about what is small or far away, there may still be other things taken in by the senses which I cannot possibly doubt—such as that I am here, sitting before the fire, wearing a dressing gown, touching this paper. Indeed, these hands and the rest of my body—on what grounds might I deny that they exist?—unless perhaps I liken myself to madmen whose brains are so rattled by the persistent vapors of melancholy that they are sure they are kings when in fact they are paupers, or that they wear purple robes when in fact they are naked, or that their heads are clay, or that they are gourds, or that they are made of glass. But these people are insane, and I would seem just as crazy if I were to apply what I say about them to myself.

This would be perfectly obvious—if I weren't a man accustomed to sleeping at night whose experiences while asleep are at least as far-fetched as those that madmen have while awake. How often a dream has convinced me that I was here, sitting before the fire, wearing my dressing gown, when, in fact, I was undressed and between the covers of my bed! But now I am looking at this piece of paper with my eyes wide open; the head that I am shaking has not been lulled to sleep; I put my hand out consciously and deliberately; I feel the paper and see it. None of this would be as distinct if I were asleep. As if I can't remember having been deluded by similar thoughts while asleep! When I think very carefully about this, I see so plainly that there are no reliable signs by which I can distinguish sleeping from waking that I am stupefied—and my stupor itself suggests that I am asleep!

Suppose then that I am dreaming. Suppose, in particular, that my eyes are not open, that my head is not moving, and that I have not put out my hand. Suppose that I do not have hands, or even a body. I must still admit that the things I see in sleep are like painted images, which must have been patterned after real things. Hence, things like eyes, heads, hands and bodies are not imaginary, but real. For, even when painters try to give bizarre shapes to sirens and satyrs, they are unable to give them completely new natures, but can only jumble together the parts of various animals. Even if they were to come up with something so novel that no one had ever seen anything like it before, something entirely fictitious and unreal, there would at least need to be real colors from which they can compose it. By the same reasoning, while things like eyes, heads, and hands may be imaginary, it must be granted that some simpler and more universal things are real—the "real colors" from which the true and the false images in our thoughts are formed. Among things of this sort seem to be general bodily nature and its extension, the shape of extended things, their quantity (that is, their magnitude and number), the place in which they exist, and the time through which they endure.

Perhaps we can correctly infer that, while physics, astronomy, medicine, and other disciplines requiring the study of composites are dubious, disciplines like arithmetic and geometry, which deal only with completely simple and universal things without regard to whether they exist in the world, are somehow certain and indubitable. Whether we are awake or asleep, two plus three is always five, and the square never has more than four sides. It seems impossible even to suspect such obvious truths of falsity.

Nevertheless, the old belief is imprinted on my mind that there is a God who can do anything and by whom I have been made to be as I am. How do I know that He hasn't brought it about that, while there is in fact no earth, no sky, no extended thing, no shape, no magnitude, and no place, all of these things seem to me to exist, just as they now do? Besides, I think that other people sometimes err in what they believe themselves to know perfectly well; mightn't I be deceived when I add two and three, or count the sides of a square, or do even simpler things (if we can even suppose that there is anything simpler)? Maybe God does not want to deceive me; after all, He is said to be supremely good. But, if God's being good is incompatible with His having created me so that I am always deceived, it seems just as out of line with His being good that He sometimes permits me to be deceived—as He undeniably does.

Or maybe some would rather deny that there is an omnipotent God than to believe that everything else is uncertain. Rather than arguing with these people, I will grant that everything I have said about God is fiction. But, however these people think I came to be as I now am (whether they say that it is by fate, or by accident, or by a continuous series of events, or in some other way) since it seems that he who errs and is deceived is somehow imperfect, the likelihood that I am constantly deceived increases as the power that they attribute to my original creator decreases. To these arguments, I have no reply; I am forced to admit that nothing that I used to believe is beyond legitimate doubt—not because I have been careless or playful, but because I have valid and well-considered grounds for doubt. I must therefore withhold my assent from my former beliefs as carefully as from obvious falsehoods, if I want to arrive at something certain.

But it is not enough to have noticed this: I must also take care to bear it in mind. For my habitual beliefs constantly return to my mind as if our longstanding, intimate relationship has given them the right to do so, even against my will. I will never break the habit of trusting them and of giving in to them while I see them for what they are—things somewhat dubious (as I have just shown) but nonetheless probable, things that we have much more reason to believe than to deny. That is why I think it will be good deliberately to turn my beliefs around, to allow myself to be deceived, and to suppose that all my previous beliefs are false and imaginary. Eventually, when I have counterbalanced the weight of my prejudices, my bad habits will no longer distort my grasp of things. And I know that there is no danger of error in this and that I won't overindulge in skepticism, since I am now concerned, not with acting, but only with knowing.

I will suppose, then, not that there is a supremely good God who is the source of all truth, but that there is an evil demon, supremely powerful and cunning, who works as hard as he can to deceive me. I will say that sky, air, earth, color, shape, sound, and other external things are just dreamed illusions which the demon uses to ensnare my judgment. I will regard myself as not having hands, eyes, flesh, blood, and senses–but as giving the false belief that I have all these things. I will obstinately concentrate on this meditation and will thus ensure by mental resolution that, if I do not really have the ability to know the truth, I will at least withhold assent from what is false and from what a deceiver may try to put over on me, however powerful and cunning he may be. But this plan requires effort, and laziness brings me back to my ordinary life. I am like a prisoner who happens to enjoy the illusion of freedom in his dreams, begins to suspect that he is asleep, fears being awakened, and deliberately lets the enticing illusions slip by unchallenged. Thus, I slide back into my old beliefs; I am afraid that, if I awaken, I will need to spend the waking life which follows my peaceful rest, not in the light, but in the confusing darkness of the problems I have just raised.

GEORGE BERKELEY (1685–1753), *A TREATISE CONCERNING THE PRINCIPLES OF HUMAN KNOWLEDGE,* 1710

Berkeley has several goals in these passages, all related to his over-arching goal of defeating skepticism. He argues that ideas can exist only in the mind of a perceiver and cannot properly be understood as having a correspondence to material objects; indeed, the very notion of Matter or material object is a confusion that could easily be dispelled by the slightest reflection. Once dispelled, one sees that our understanding of the world is not diminished; in particular, scientific advances do not depend on interpreting the world in terms of material objects. Furthermore, the concept of Matter is what brings on skepticism; Berkeley maintains that this is grounds enough to reject it.

Introduction

1. Philosophy being nothing else but the study of wisdom and truth, it may with reason be expected that those who have spent most time and pains in it should enjoy a greater calm and serenity of mind, a greater clearness and evidence of knowledge, and be less disturbed with doubts and difficulties than other men. Yet so it is, we see the illiterate bulk of mankind that walk the high-road of plain common sense, and are governed by the dictates of nature, for the most part easy and undisturbed. To them nothing that is familiar appears unaccountable or difficult to comprehend. They complain not of any want of evidence in their senses, and are out of all danger of becoming Sceptics. But no sooner do we depart from sense and instinct to follow the light of a superior principle, to reason, meditate, and reflect on the nature of things, but a thousand scruples spring up in our minds concerning those things which before we seemed fully to comprehend. Prejudices and errors of sense do from all parts discover themselves to our view; and, endeavouring to correct these by reason, we are insensibly drawn into uncouth paradoxes, difficulties, and inconsistencies, which multiply and grow upon us as we advance in speculation, till at length, having wandered through many intricate mazes, we find ourselves just where we were, or, which is worse, sit down in a forlorn Scepticism.

2. The cause of this is thought to be the obscurity of things, or the natural weakness and imperfection of our understandings. It is said, the faculties we have are few, and those designed by nature for the support and comfort of life, and not to penetrate into the inward essence and constitution of things. Besides, the mind of man being finite, when it treats of things

which partake of infinity, it is not to be wondered at if it run into absurdities and contradictions, out of which it is impossible it should ever extricate itself, it being of the nature of infinite not to be comprehended by that which is finite.

3. But, perhaps, we may be too partial to ourselves in placing the fault originally in our faculties, and not rather in the wrong use we make of them. It is a hard thing to suppose that right deductions from true principles should ever end in consequences which cannot be maintained or made consistent. We should believe that God has dealt more bountifully with the sons of men than to give them a strong desire for that knowledge which he had placed quite out of their reach. This were not agreeable to the wonted indulgent methods of Providence, which, whatever appetites it may have implanted in the creatures, doth usually furnish them with such means as, if rightly made use of, will not fail to satisfy them. Upon the whole, I am inclined to think that the far greater part, if not all, of those difficulties which have hitherto amused philosophers, and blocked up the way to knowledge, are entirely owing to ourselves–that we have first raised a dust and then complain we cannot see.

...

Part I

1. It is evident to any one who takes a survey of the objects of human knowledge, that they are either ideas actually imprinted on the senses; or else such as are perceived by attending to the passions and operations of the mind; or lastly, ideas formed by help of memory and imagination–either compounding, dividing, or barely representing those originally perceived in the aforesaid ways. By sight I have the ideas of light and colours, with their several degrees and variations. By touch I perceive hard and soft, heat and cold, motion and resistance, and of all these more and less either as to quantity or degree. Smelling furnishes me with odours; the palate with tastes; and hearing conveys sounds to the mind in all their variety of tone and composition. And as several of these are observed to accompany each other, they come to be marked by one name, and so to be reputed as one thing. Thus, for example a certain colour, taste, smell, figure and consistence having been observed to go together, are accounted one distinct thing, signified by the name apple; other collections of ideas constitute a stone, a tree, a book, and the like sensible things–which as they are pleasing or disagreeable excite the passions of love, hatred, joy, grief, and so forth.

2. But, besides all that endless variety of ideas or objects of knowledge, there is likewise something which knows or perceives them, and exercises divers operations, as willing, imagining, remembering, about them. This

perceiving, active being is what I call mind, spirit, soul, or myself. By which words I do not denote any one of my ideas, but a thing entirely distinct from them, wherein, they exist, or, which is the same thing, whereby they are perceived–for the existence of an idea consists in being perceived.

3. That neither our thoughts, nor passions, nor ideas formed by the imagination, exist without the mind, is what everybody will allow. And it seems no less evident that the various sensations or ideas imprinted on the sense, however blended or combined together (that is, whatever objects they compose), cannot exist otherwise than in a mind perceiving them.–I think an intuitive knowledge may be obtained of this by any one that shall attend to what is meant by the term exist, when applied to sensible things. The table I write on I say exists, that is, I see and feel it; and if I were out of my study I should say it existed–meaning thereby that if I was in my study I might perceive it, or that some other spirit actually does perceive it.... For as to what is said of the absolute existence of unthinking things without any relation to their being perceived, that seems perfectly unintelligible. Their esse is percepi, nor is it possible they should have any existence out of the minds or thinking things which perceive them.

4. It is indeed an opinion strangely prevailing amongst men, that houses, mountains, rivers, and in a word all sensible objects, have an existence, natural or real, distinct from their being perceived by the understanding. But, with how great an assurance and acquiescence soever this principle may be entertained in the world, yet whoever shall find in his heart to call it in question may, if I mistake not, perceive it to involve a manifest contradiction. For, what are the forementioned objects but the things we perceive by sense? and what do we perceive besides our own ideas or sensations? and is it not plainly repugnant that any one of these, or any combination of them, should exist unperceived?

5. If we thoroughly examine this tenet it will, perhaps, be found at bottom to depend on the doctrine of abstract ideas. For can there be a nicer strain of abstraction than to distinguish the existence of sensible objects from their being perceived, so as to conceive them existing unperceived? Light and colours, heat and cold, extension and figures–in a word the things we see and feel–what are they but so many sensations, notions, ideas, or impressions on the sense? and is it possible to separate, even in thought, any of these from perception? For my part, I might as easily divide a thing from itself. I may, indeed, divide in my thoughts, or conceive apart from each other, those things which, perhaps I never perceived by sense so divided. Thus, I imagine the trunk of a human body without the limbs, or conceive the smell of a rose without thinking on the rose itself. So far, I will not deny, I can abstract–if that may properly be called abstraction which extends only to the conceiving separately such objects as it is possible may really exist or be actually perceived asunder. But my conceiving

or imagining power does not extend beyond the possibility of real exist-ence or perception. Hence, as it is impossible for me to see or feel any-thing without an actual sensation of that thing, so is it impossible for me to conceive in my thoughts any sensible thing or object distinct from the sensation or perception of it.

6. Some truths there are so near and obvious to the mind that a man need only open his eyes to see them. Such I take this important one to be, viz., that all the choir of heaven and furniture of the earth, in a word all those bodies which compose the mighty frame of the world, have not any sub-sistence without a mind, that their being is to be perceived or known; that consequently so long as they are not actually perceived by me, or do not exist in my mind or that of any other created spirit, they must either have no existence at all, or else subsist in the mind of some Eternal Spirit–it being perfectly unintelligible, and involving all the absurdity of abstrac-tion, to attribute to any single part of them an existence independent of a spirit. To be convinced of which, the reader need only reflect, and try to separate in his own thoughts the being of a sensible thing from its being perceived.

7. From what has been said it follows there is not any other Substance than Spirit, or that which perceives. But, for the fuller proof of this point, let it be considered the sensible qualities are colour, figure, motion, smell, taste, etc., i.e. the ideas perceived by sense. Now, for an idea to exist in an unperceiving thing is a manifest contradiction, for to have an idea is all one as to perceive; that therefore wherein colour, figure, and the like qual-ities exist must perceive them; hence it is clear there can be no unthinking substance or substratum of those ideas.

8. But, say you, though the ideas themselves do not exist without the mind, yet there may be things like them, whereof they are copies or resemblances, which things exist without the mind in an unthinking sub-stance. I answer, an idea can be like nothing but an idea; a colour or figure can be like nothing but another colour or figure. If we look but never so little into our thoughts, we shall find it impossible for us to con-ceive a likeness except only between our ideas. Again, I ask whether those supposed originals or external things, of which our ideas are the pictures or representations, be themselves perceivable or no? If they are, then they are ideas and we have gained our point; but if you say they are not, I appeal to any one whether it be sense to assert a colour is like some-thing which is invisible; hard or soft, like something which is intangible; and so of the rest.

9. Some there are who make a distinction between primary and secondary qualities. By the former they mean extension, figure, motion, rest, solidity or impenetrability, and number; by the latter they denote all other sensi-ble qualities, as colours, sounds, tastes, and so forth. The ideas we have of these they acknowledge not to be the resemblances of anything existing

without the mind, or unperceived, but they will have our ideas of the primary qualities to be patterns or images of things which exist without the mind, in an unthinking substance which they call Matter. By Matter, therefore, we are to understand an inert, senseless substance, in which extension, figure, and motion do actually subsist. But it is evident from what we have already shown, that extension, figure, and motion are only ideas existing in the mind, and that an idea can be like nothing but another idea, and that consequently neither they nor their archetypes can exist in an unperceiving substance. Hence, it is plain that the very notion of what is called Matter or corporeal substance, involves a contradiction in it.

10. They who assert that figure, motion, and the rest of the primary or original qualities do exist without the mind in unthinking substances, do at the same time acknowledge that colours, sounds, heat, cold, and suchlike secondary qualities, do not—which they tell us are sensations existing in the mind alone, that depend on and are occasioned by the different size, texture, and motion of the minute particles of matter. This they take for an undoubted truth, which they can demonstrate beyond all exception. Now, if it be certain that those original qualities are inseparably united with the other sensible qualities, and not, even in thought, capable of being abstracted from them, it plainly follows that they exist only in the mind. But I desire any one to reflect and try whether he can, by any abstraction of thought, conceive the extension and motion of a body without all other sensible qualities. For my own part, I see evidently that it is not in my power to frame an idea of a body extended and moving, but I must withal give it some colour or other sensible quality which is acknowledged to exist only in the mind. In short, extension, figure, and motion, abstracted from all other qualities, are inconceivable. Where therefore the other sensible qualities are, there must these be also, to wit, in the mind and nowhere else.

...

18. But, though it were possible that solid, figured, movable substances may exist without the mind, corresponding to the ideas we have of bodies, yet how is it possible for us to know this? Either we must know it by sense or by reason. As for our senses, by them we have the knowledge only of our sensations, ideas, or those things that are immediately perceived by sense, call them what you will: but they do not inform us that things exist without the mind, or unperceived, like to those which are perceived. This the materialists themselves acknowledge. It remains therefore that if we have any knowledge at all of external things, it must be by reason, inferring their existence from what is immediately perceived by sense. But what reason can induce us to believe the existence of bodies without the mind, from what we perceive, since the very patrons of Matter themselves do not pretend there is any necessary connection between them and our

ideas? I say it is granted on all hands (and what happens in dreams, frenzies, and the like, puts it beyond dispute) that it is possible we might be affected with all the ideas we have now, though there were no bodies existing without resembling them. Hence, it is evident the supposition of external bodies is not necessary for the producing our ideas; since it is granted they are produced sometimes, and might possibly be produced always in the same order, we see them in at present, without their concurrence.

19. But, though we might possibly have all our sensations without them, yet perhaps it may be thought easier to conceive and explain the manner of their production, by supposing external bodies in their likeness rather than otherwise; and so it might be at least probable there are such things as bodies that excite their ideas in our minds. But neither can this be said; for, though we give the materialists their external bodies, they by their own confession are never the nearer knowing how our ideas are produced; since they own themselves unable to comprehend in what manner body can act upon spirit, or how it is possible it should imprint any idea in the mind. Hence it is evident the production of ideas or sensations in our minds can be no reason why we should suppose Matter or corporeal substances, since that is acknowledged to remain equally inexplicable with or without this supposition. If therefore it were possible for bodies to exist without the mind, yet to hold they do so, must needs be a very precarious opinion; since it is to suppose, without any reason at all, that God has created innumerable beings that are entirely useless, and serve to no manner of purpose.

20. In short, if there were external bodies, it is impossible we should ever come to know it; and if there were not, we might have the very same reasons to think there were that we have now. Suppose—what no one can deny possible—an intelligence without the help of external bodies, to be affected with the same train of sensations or ideas that you are, imprinted in the same order and with like vividness in his mind. I ask whether that intelligence hath not all the reason to believe the existence of corporeal substances, represented by his ideas, and exciting them in his mind, that you can possibly have for believing the same thing? Of this there can be no question which one consideration were enough to make any reasonable person suspect the strength of whatever arguments he may think himself to have, for the existence of bodies without the mind.

21. Were it necessary to add any farther proof against the existence of Matter after what has been said, I could instance several of those errors and difficulties (not to mention impieties) which have sprung from that tenet. It has occasioned numberless controversies and disputes in philosophy, and not a few of far greater moment in religion. But I shall not enter into the detail of them in this place, as well because I think arguments a posteriori are unnecessary for confirming what has been, if I mistake not,

sufficiently demonstrated a priori, as because I shall hereafter find occasion to speak somewhat of them.

22. I am afraid I have given cause to think I am needlessly prolix in handling this subject. For, to what purpose is it to dilate on that which may be demonstrated with the utmost evidence in a line or two, to any one that is capable of the least reflection? It is but looking into your own thoughts, and so trying whether you can conceive it possible for a sound, or figure, or motion, or colour to exist without the mind or unperceived. This easy trial may perhaps make you see that what you contend for is a downright contradiction. Insomuch that I am content to put the whole upon this issue:–If you can but conceive it possible for one extended movable substance, or, in general, for any one idea, or anything like an idea, to exist otherwise than in a mind perceiving it, I shall readily give up the cause. And, as for all that compages of external bodies you contend for, I shall grant you its existence, though you cannot either give me any reason why you believe it exists, or assign any use to it when it is supposed to exist. I say, the bare possibility of your opinions being true shall pass for an argument that it is so.

23. But, say you, surely there is nothing easier than for me to imagine trees, for instance, in a park, or books existing in a closet, and nobody by to perceive them. I answer, you may so, there is no difficulty in it; but what is all this, I beseech you, more than framing in your mind certain ideas which you call books and trees, and the same time omitting to frame the idea of any one that may perceive them? But do not you yourself perceive or think of them all the while? This therefore is nothing to the purpose; it only shows you have the power of imagining or forming ideas in your mind: but it does not show that you can conceive it possible the objects of your thought may exist without the mind. To make out this, it is necessary that you conceive them existing unconceived or unthought of, which is a manifest repugnancy. When we do our utmost to conceive the existence of external bodies, we are all the while only contemplating our own ideas. But the mind taking no notice of itself, is deluded to think it can and does conceive bodies existing unthought of or without the mind, though at the same time they are apprehended by or exist in itself. A little attention will discover to any one the truth and evidence of what is here said, and make it unnecessary to insist on any other proofs against the existence of material substance.

24. It is very obvious, upon the least inquiry into our thoughts, to know whether it is possible for us to understand what is meant by the absolute existence of sensible objects in themselves, or without the mind. To me it is evident those words mark out either a direct contradiction, or else nothing at all. And to convince others of this, I know no readier or fairer way than to entreat they would calmly attend to their own thoughts; and if by this attention the emptiness or repugnancy of those expressions does

appear, surely nothing more is requisite for the conviction. It is on this therefore that I insist, to wit, that the absolute existence of unthinking things are words without a meaning, or which include a contradiction. This is what I repeat and inculcate, and earnestly recommend to the attentive thoughts of the reader.

...

28. I find I can excite ideas in my mind at pleasure, and vary and shift the scene as oft as I think fit. It is no more than willing, and straightway this or that idea arises in my fancy; and by the same power it is obliterated and makes way for another. This making and unmaking of ideas doth very properly denominate the mind active. Thus much is certain and grounded on experience; but when we think of unthinking agents or of exciting ideas exclusive of volition, we only amuse ourselves with words.

29. But, whatever power I may have over my own thoughts, I find the ideas actually perceived by Sense have not a like dependence on my will. When in broad daylight I open my eyes, it is not in my power to choose whether I shall see or no, or to determine what particular objects shall present themselves to my view; and so likewise as to the hearing and other senses; the ideas imprinted on them are not creatures of my will. There is therefore some other Will or Spirit that produces them.

30. The ideas of Sense are more strong, lively, and distinct than those of the imagination; they have likewise a steadiness, order, and coherence, and are not excited at random, as those which are the effects of human wills often are, but in a regular train or series, the admirable connection whereof sufficiently testifies the wisdom and benevolence of its Author. Now the set rules or established methods wherein the Mind we depend on excites in us the ideas of sense, are called the laws of nature; and these we learn by experience, which teaches us that such and such ideas are attended with such and such other ideas, in the ordinary course of things.

31. This gives us a sort of foresight which enables us to regulate our actions for the benefit of life. And without this we should be eternally at a loss; we could not know how to act anything that might procure us the least pleasure, or remove the least pain of sense. That food nourishes, sleep refreshes, and fire warms us; that to sow in the seed-time is the way to reap in the harvest; and in general that to obtain such or such ends, such or such means are conducive—all this we know, not by discovering any necessary connection between our ideas, but only by the observation of the settled laws of nature, without which we should be all in uncertainty and confusion, and a grown man no more know how to manage himself in the affairs of life than an infant just born.

32. And yet this consistent uniform working, which so evidently displays the goodness and wisdom of that Governing Spirit whose Will constitutes the laws of nature, is so far from leading our thoughts to Him, that it rather

sends them wandering after second causes. For, when we perceive certain ideas of Sense constantly followed by other ideas and we know this is not of our own doing, we forthwith attribute power and agency to the ideas themselves, and make one the cause of another, than which nothing can be more absurd and unintelligible. Thus, for example, having observed that when we perceive by sight a certain round luminous figure we at the same time perceive by touch the idea or sensation called heat, we do from thence conclude the sun to be the cause of heat. And in like manner perceiving the motion and collision of bodies to be attended with sound, we are inclined to think the latter the effect of the former.

33. The ideas imprinted on the Senses by the Author of nature are called real things; and those excited in the imagination being less regular, vivid, and constant, are more properly termed ideas, or images of things, which they copy and represent. But then our sensations, be they never so vivid and distinct, are nevertheless ideas, that is, they exist in the mind, or are perceived by it, as truly as the ideas of its own framing. The ideas of Sense are allowed to have more reality in them, that is, to be more strong, orderly, and coherent than the creatures of the mind; but this is no argument that they exist without the mind. They are also less dependent on the spirit, or thinking substance which perceives them, in that they are excited by the will of another and more powerful spirit; yet still they are ideas, and certainly no idea, whether faint or strong, can exist otherwise than in a mind perceiving it.

...

35. I do not argue against the existence of any one thing that we can apprehend either by sense or reflection. That the things I see with my eyes and touch with my hands do exist, really exist, I make not the least question. The only thing whose existence we deny is that which philosophers call Matter or corporeal substance. And in doing of this there is no damage done to the rest of mankind, who, I dare say, will never miss it.

...

37. It will be urged that thus much at least is true, to wit, that we take away all corporeal substances. To this my answer is, that if the word substance be taken in the vulgar sense—for a combination of sensible qualities, such as extension, solidity, weight, and the like—this we cannot be accused of taking away: but if it be taken in a philosophic sense—for the support of accidents or qualities without the mind—then indeed I acknowledge that we take it away, if one may be said to take away that which never had any existence, not even in the imagination.

...

40. But, say what we can, some one perhaps may be apt to reply, he will still believe his senses, and never suffer any arguments, how plausible soever, to prevail over the certainty of them. Be it so; assert the evidence of sense as high as you please, we are willing to do the same. That what I see, hear, and feel doth exist, that is to say, is perceived by me, I no more doubt than I do of my own being. But I do not see how the testimony of sense can be alleged as a proof for the existence of anything which is not perceived by sense. We are not for having any man turn sceptic and disbelieve his senses; on the contrary, we give them all the stress and assurance imaginable; nor are there any principles more opposite to Scepticism than those we have laid down, as shall be hereafter clearly shown.

...

50. [Y]ou will say there have been a great many things explained by matter and motion; take away these and you destroy the whole corpuscular philosophy, and undermine those mechanical principles which have been applied with so much success to account for the phenomena. In short, whatever advances have been made, either by ancient or modern philosophers, in the study of nature do all proceed on the supposition that corporeal substance or Matter doth really exist. To this I answer that there is not any one phenomenon explained on that supposition which may not as well be explained without it, as might easily be made appear by an induction of particulars. To explain the phenomena, is all one as to show why, upon such and such occasions, we are affected with such and such ideas. But how Matter should operate on a Spirit, or produce any idea in it, is what no philosopher will pretend to explain; it is therefore evident there can be no use of Matter in natural philosophy. Besides, they who attempt to account for things do it not by corporeal substance, but by figure, motion, and other qualities, which are in truth no more than mere ideas, and, therefore, cannot be the cause of anything, as hath been already shown.

51. [I]t will upon this be demanded whether it does not seem absurd to take away natural causes, and ascribe everything to the immediate operation of Spirits? We must no longer say upon these principles that fire heats, or water cools, but that a Spirit heats, and so forth. Would not a man be deservedly laughed at, who should talk after this manner? I answer, he would so; in such things we ought to "think with the learned, and speak with the vulgar." They who to demonstration are convinced of the truth of the Copernican system do nevertheless say "the sun rises," "the sun sets," or "comes to the meridian"; and if they affected a contrary style in common talk it would without doubt appear very ridiculous. A little reflection on what is here said will make it manifest that the common use of language

would receive no manner of alteration or disturbance from the admission of our tenets.

...

86. Our knowledge of [ideas] hath been very much obscured and confounded, and we have been led into very dangerous errors, by supposing a twofold existence of the objects of sense–the one intelligible or in the mind, the other real and without the mind; whereby unthinking things are thought to have a natural subsistence of their own distinct from being perceived by spirits. This, which, if I mistake not, has been shown to be a most groundless and absurd notion, is the very root of Scepticism; for, so long as men thought that real things subsisted without the mind, and that their knowledge was only so far forth real as it was conformable to real things, it follows they could not be certain they had any real knowledge at all. For how can it be known that the things which are perceived are conformable to those which are not perceived, or exist without the mind?

87. Colour, figure, motion, extension, and the like, considered only as so many sensations in the mind, are perfectly known, there being nothing in them which is not perceived. But, if they are looked on as notes or images, referred to things or archetypes existing without the mind, then are we involved all in scepticism. We see only the appearances, and not the real qualities of things. What may be the extension, figure, or motion of anything really and absolutely, or in itself, it is impossible for us to know, but only the proportion or relation they bear to our senses. Things remaining the same, our ideas vary, and which of them, or even whether any of them at all, represent the true quality really existing in the thing, it is out of our reach to determine. So that, for aught we know, all we see, hear, and feel may be only phantom and vain chimera, and not at all agree with the real things existing in rerum natura. All this scepticism follows from our supposing a difference between things and ideas, and that the former have a subsistence without the mind or unperceived. It were easy to dilate on this subject, and show how the arguments urged by sceptics in all ages depend on the supposition of external objects.

88. So long as we attribute a real existence to unthinking things, distinct from their being perceived, it is not only impossible for us to know with evidence the nature of any real unthinking being, but even that it exists. Hence it is that we see philosophers distrust their senses, and doubt of the existence of heaven and earth, of everything they see or feel, even of their own bodies. And, after all their labour and struggle of thought, they are forced to own we cannot attain to any self-evident or demonstrative knowledge of the existence of sensible things. But, all this doubtfulness, which so bewilders and confounds the mind and makes philosophy ridiculous in the eyes of the world, vanishes if we annex a meaning to our words,

and not amuse ourselves with the terms "absolute," "external," "exist," and such-like, signifying we know not what. I can as well doubt of my own being as of the being of those things which I actually perceive by sense; it being a manifest contradiction that any sensible object should be immediately perceived by sight or touch, and at the same time have no existence in nature, since the very existence of an unthinking being consists in being perceived.

...

96. Matter being once expelled out of nature drags with it so many sceptical and impious notions, such an incredible number of disputes and puzzling questions, which have been thorns in the sides of divines as well as philosophers, and made so much fruitless work for mankind, that if the arguments we have produced against it are not found equal to demonstration (as to me they evidently seem), yet I am sure all friends to knowledge, peace, and religion have reason to wish they were.

IMMANUEL KANT (1724–1804), *PROLEGOMENA TO ANY FUTURE METAPHYSICS*,
PUBLISHED IN GERMAN IN 1783, TRANSLATED BY PAUL CARUS

This is the clearest statement in all of Kant's writings detailing the role of the understanding in implementing the universal laws of nature: experience of a coherent world is possible because the understanding makes our perceptions conform to a set of rules built into the understanding. These universal laws of nature are knowable even prior to experience. One should not, however, confuse *universal* laws of nature with *empirical* laws of nature of the sort discovered by science.

Sect. 52c

...

When I speak of objects in time and in space, it is not of things in themselves, of which I know nothing, but of things in appearance, that is, of experience, as the particular way of cognising objects which is afforded to man. I must not say of what I think in time or in space, that in itself, and independent of these my thoughts, it exists in space and in time; for in that case I should contradict myself; because space and time, together with the appearances in them, are nothing existing in themselves and outside of my representations, but are themselves only modes of representation, and it is palpably contradictory to say, that a mere mode of representation exists without our representation. Objects of the senses therefore exist only in experience; whereas to give them a self-subsisting existence apart from experience or before it, is merely to represent to ourselves that experience actually exists apart from experience or before it.

Sect. 36

How is nature possible in the formal sense, as the totality of the rules, under which all phenomena must come, in order to be thought as connected in experience? The answer must be this: it is only possible by means of the constitution of our Understanding, according to which all the above representations of the sensibility are necessarily referred to a consciousness, and by which the peculiar way in which we think (viz., by rules), and hence experience also, are possible, but must be clearly distinguished from an insight into the objects in themselves.

...

There are many laws of nature, which we can only know by means of experience; but conformity to law in the connection of appearances, i.e., in nature in general, we cannot discover by any experience, because experience itself requires laws which are a priori at the basis of its possibility.

The possibility of experience in general is therefore at the same time the universal law of nature, and the principles of the experience are the very laws of nature. For we do not know nature but as the totality of appearances, i.e., of representations in us, and hence we can only derive the laws of its connection from the principles of their connection in us, that is, from the conditions of their necessary union in consciousness, which constitutes the possibility of experience.

Even the main proposition expounded throughout this section—that universal laws of nature can be distinctly known a priori—leads naturally to the proposition: that the highest legislation of nature must lie in ourselves, i.e., in our understanding, and that we must not seek the universal laws of nature in nature by means of experience, but conversely must seek nature, as to its universal conformity to law, in the conditions of the possibility of experience, which lie in our sensibility and in our understanding. For how were it otherwise possible to know a priori these laws, as they are not rules of analytical cognition, but truly synthetical extensions of it?

Such a necessary agreement of the principles of possible experience with the laws of the possibility of nature, can only proceed from one of two reasons: either these laws are drawn from nature by means of experience, or conversely nature is derived from the laws of the possibility of experience in general, and is quite the same as the mere universal conformity to law of the latter. The former is self-contradictory, for the universal laws of nature can and must be known a priori (that is, independent of all experience), and be the foundation of all empirical use of the understanding; the latter alternative therefore alone remains.

But we must distinguish the empirical laws of nature, which always presuppose particular perceptions, from the pure or universal laws of nature, which, without being based on particular perceptions, contain merely the conditions of their necessary union in experience. In relation to the latter, nature and possible experience are quite the same, and as the conformity to law here depends upon the necessary connection of appearances in experience (without which we cannot know any object whatever in the sensible world), consequently upon the original laws of the understanding, it seems at first strange, but is not the less certain, to say: The understanding does not derive its laws (a priori) from, but prescribes them to, nature.

Sect. 38

Now I ask: Do the laws of nature lie in space, and does the understanding learn them by merely endeavoring to find out the enormous wealth of meaning that lies in space; or do they inhere in the understanding and in the way in which it determines space according to the conditions of the synthetical unity in which its concepts are all centered?

...

The mere universal form of intuition, called space, must therefore be the substratum of all intuitions determinable to particular objects, and in it of course the condition of the possibility and of the variety of these intuitions lies. But the unity of the objects is entirely determined by the understanding, and on conditions which lie in its own nature; and thus the understanding is the origin of the universal order of nature, in that it comprehends all appearances under its own laws, and thereby first constructs, a priori, experience (as to its form), by means of which whatever is to be known only by experience, is necessarily subjected to its laws. For we are not now concerned with the nature of things in themselves, which is independent of the conditions both of our sensibility and our understanding, but with nature, as an object of possible experience, and in this case the understanding, whilst it makes experience possible, thereby insists that the sensuous world is either not an object of experience at all, or must be nature [viz., an existence of things, determined according to universal laws].

JOHN LOCKE (1632–1704), *AN ESSAY CONCERNING HUMAN UNDERSTANDING*, 1690

Locke notes that, in considering issues of identity over time, one must use criteria appropriate to the type of object one is considering. Thus, the criteria one would apply in asking whether a young oak tree is one and the same tree as this massive oak some years later are different than the criteria one would apply in asking whether a person at one time is in fact one and the same person as a person at another time. In this latter case, (personal) identity over time is a function of continuity of the consciousness as linked by memory. Locke goes on to consider several special cases which bear a remarkable resemblance to the plot of *Memento* and *Moon*.

Book II, Chapter XXVII–Of Identity and Diversity

3. In the state of living creatures, their identity depends not on a mass of the same particles, but on something else. For in them the variation of great parcels of matter alters not the identity: an oak growing from a plant to a great tree, and then lopped, is still the same oak; and a colt grown up to a horse, sometimes fat, sometimes lean, is all the while the same horse: though, in both these cases, there may be a manifest change of the parts; so that truly they are not either of them the same masses of matter, though they be truly one of them the same oak, and the other the same horse. The reason whereof is, that, in these two cases–a mass of matter and a living body–identity is not applied to the same thing.
4. Identity of vegetables. We must therefore consider wherein an oak differs from a mass of matter, and that seems to me to be in this, that the one is only the cohesion of particles of matter any how united, the other such a disposition of them as constitutes the parts of an oak; and such an organization of those parts as is fit to receive and distribute nourishment, so as to continue and frame the wood, bark, and leaves, etc., of an oak, in which consists the vegetable life. That being then one plant which has such an organization of parts in one coherent body, partaking of one common life, it continues to be the same plant as long as it partakes of the same life, though that life be communicated to new particles of matter vitally united to the living plant, in a like continued organization conformable to that sort of plant. For this organization, being at any one instant in any one collection of matter, is in that particular concrete distinguished from all other, and is that individual life, which existing constantly from that moment both forwards and backwards, in the same continuity of insensibly succeeding parts united to the living body of the plant, it has that identity which makes the same plant, and all the parts of it, parts of the

same plant, during all the time that they exist united in that continued organization, which is fit to convey that common life to all the parts so united.

...

7. Idea of identity suited to the idea it is applied to. It is not therefore unity of substance that comprehends all sorts of identity, or will determine it in every case; but to conceive and judge of it aright, we must consider what idea the word it is applied to stands for: it being one thing to be the same substance, another the same man, and a third the same person, if person, man, and substance, are three names standing for three different ideas; for such as is the idea belonging to that name, such must be the identity; which, if it had been a little more carefully attended to, would possibly have prevented a great deal of that confusion which often occurs about this matter, with no small seeming difficulties, especially concerning personal identity, which therefore we shall in the next place a little consider.

...

9. Personal identity. This being premised, to find wherein personal identity consists, we must consider what person stands for; which, I think, is a thinking intelligent being, that has reason and reflection, and can consider itself as itself, the same thinking thing, in different times and places; which it does only by that consciousness which is inseparable from thinking, and, as it seems to me, essential to it: it being impossible for any one to perceive without perceiving that he does perceive. When we see, hear, smell, taste, feel, meditate, or will anything, we know that we do so. Thus it is always as to our present sensations and perceptions: and by this every one is to himself that which he calls self, it not being considered, in this case, whether the same self be continued in the same or divers substances. For, since consciousness always accompanies thinking, and it is that which makes every one to be what he calls self, and thereby distinguishes himself from all other thinking things, in this alone consists personal identity, i.e., the sameness of a rational being: and as far as this consciousness can be extended backwards to any past action or thought, so far reaches the identity of that person; it is the same self now it was then; and it is by the same self with this present one that now reflects on it, that that action was done.

10. Consciousness makes personal identity. But it is further inquired, whether it be the same identical substance. This few would think they had reason to doubt of, if these perceptions, with their consciousness, always remained present in the mind, whereby the same thinking thing would be always consciously present, and, as would be thought, evidently the same to itself. But that which seems to make the difficulty is this, that this

consciousness being interrupted always by forgetfulness, there being no moment of our lives wherein we have the whole train of all our past actions before our eyes in one view, but even the best memories losing the sight of one part whilst they are viewing another; and we sometimes, and that the greatest part of our lives, not reflecting on our past selves, being intent on our present thoughts, and in sound sleep having no thoughts at all, or at least none with that consciousness which remarks our waking thoughts, I say, in all these cases, our consciousness being interrupted, and we losing the sight of our past selves, doubts are raised whether we are the same thinking thing, i.e., the same substance or no. Which, however reasonable or unreasonable, concerns not personal identity at all. The question being what makes the same person; and not whether it be the same identical substance, which always thinks in the same person, which, in this case, matters not at all: different substances, by the same consciousness (where they do partake in it) being united into one person, as well as different bodies by the same life are united into one animal, whose identity is preserved in that change of substances by the unity of one continued life. For, it being the same consciousness that makes a man be himself to himself, personal identity depends on that only, whether it be annexed solely to one individual substance, or can be continued in a succession of several substances. For as far as any intelligent being can repeat the idea of any past action with the same consciousness it had of it at first, and with the same consciousness it has of any present action; so far it is the same personal self. For it is by the consciousness it has of its present thoughts and actions, that it is self to itself now, and so will be the same self, as far as the same consciousness can extend to actions past or to come, and would be by distance of time, or change of substance, no more two persons, than a man be two men by wearing other clothes to-day than he did yesterday, with a long or a short sleep between: the same consciousness uniting those distant actions into the same person, whatever substances contributed to their production.

11. Personal identity in change of substance. That this is so, we have some kind of evidence in our very bodies, all whose particles, whilst vitally united to this same thinking conscious self, so that we feel when they are touched, and are affected by, and conscious of good or harm that happens to them, as a part of ourselves; i.e., of our thinking conscious self. Thus, the limbs of his body are to every one a part of himself; he sympathizes and is concerned for them. Cut off a hand, and thereby separate it from that consciousness he had of its heat, cold, and other affections, and it is then no longer a part of that which is himself, any more than the remotest part of matter. Thus, we see the substance whereof personal self consisted at one time may be varied at another, without the change of personal

identity; there being no question about the same person, though the limbs which but now were a part of it, be cut off.

12. Personality in change of substance. But the question is, Whether if the same substance which thinks be changed, it can be the same person; or, remaining the same, it can be different persons?

And to this I answer: First, This can be no question at all to those who place thought in a purely material animal constitution, void of an immaterial substance. For, whether their supposition be true or no, it is plain they conceive personal identity preserved in something else than identity of substance; as animal identity is preserved in identity of life, and not of substance. And therefore those who place thinking in an immaterial substance only, before they can come to deal with these men, must show why personal identity cannot be preserved in the change of immaterial substances, or variety of particular immaterial substances, as well as animal identity is preserved in the change of material substances, or variety of particular bodies: unless they will say, it is one immaterial spirit that makes the same life in brutes, as it is one immaterial spirit that makes the same person in men; which the Cartesians at least will not admit, for fear of making brutes thinking things too.

13. Whether in change of thinking substances there can be one person. But next, as to the first part of the question, Whether, if the same thinking substance (supposing immaterial substances only to think) be changed, it can be the same person? I answer, that cannot be resolved but by those who know what kind of substances they are that do think; and whether the consciousness of past actions can be transferred from one thinking substance to another. I grant were the same consciousness the same individual action it could not: but it being a present representation of a past action, why it may not be possible, that that may be represented to the mind to have been which really never was, will remain to be shown. And therefore how far the consciousness of past actions is annexed to any individual agent, so that another cannot possibly have it, will be hard for us to determine, till we know what kind of action it is that cannot be done without a reflex act of perception accompanying it, and how performed by thinking substances, who cannot think without being conscious of it. But that which we call the same consciousness, not being the same individual act, why one intellectual substance may not have represented to it, as done by itself, what it never did, and was perhaps done by some other agent—why, I say, such a representation may not possibly be without reality of matter of fact, as well as several representations in dreams are, which yet whilst dreaming we take for true—will be difficult to conclude from the nature of things. And that it never is so, will by us, till we have clearer views of the nature of thinking substances, be best resolved into the goodness of God; who, as far as the happiness or misery of any of his sensible creatures is concerned

in it, will not, by a fatal error of theirs, transfer from one to another that consciousness which draws reward or punishment with it. How far this may be an argument against those who would place thinking in a system of fleeting animal spirits, I leave to be considered. But yet, to return to the question before us, it must be allowed, that, if the same consciousness (which, as has been shown, is quite a different thing from the same numerical figure or motion in body) can be transferred from one thinking substance to another, it will be possible that two thinking substances may make but one person. For the same consciousness being preserved, whether in the same or different substances, the personal identity is preserved.

14. Whether, the same immaterial substance remaining, there can be two persons. As to the second part of the question, Whether the same immaterial substance remaining, there may be two distinct persons; which question seems to me to be built on this–Whether the same immaterial being, being conscious of the action of its past duration, may be wholly stripped of all the consciousness of its past existence, and lose it beyond the power of ever retrieving it again: and so as it were beginning a new account from a new period, have a consciousness that cannot reach beyond this new state. All those who hold pre-existence are evidently of this mind; since they allow the soul to have no remaining consciousness of what it did in that pre-existent state, either wholly separate from body, or informing any other body; and if they should not, it is plain experience would be against them. So that personal identity, reaching no further than consciousness reaches, a pre-existent spirit not having continued so many ages in a state of silence, must needs make different persons. Suppose a Christian Platonist or a Pythagorean should, upon God's having ended all his works of creation the seventh day, think his soul hath existed ever since; and should imagine it has revolved in several human bodies; as I once met with one, who was persuaded his had been the soul of Socrates.... [W]ould any one say, that he, being not conscious of any of Socrates's actions or thoughts, could be the same person with Socrates? ... For this would no more make him the same person with [Socrates], than if some of the particles of matter that were once a part of [Socrates] were now a part of this man; the same immaterial substance, without the same consciousness, no more making the same person, by being united to any body, than the same particle of matter, without consciousness, united to any body, makes the same person. But let him once find himself conscious of any of the actions of [Socrates], he then finds himself the same person with [Socrates].

...

20. Absolute oblivion separates what is thus forgotten from the person, but not from the man. But yet possibly it will still be objected–Suppose I wholly lose the memory of some parts of my life, beyond a possibility of retrieving them, so that perhaps I shall never be conscious of them again; yet am I not the same person that did those actions, had those thoughts that I once was conscious of, though I have now forgot them? To which I answer, that we must here take notice what the word I is applied to; which, in this case, is the man only. And the same man being presumed to be the same person, I is easily here supposed to stand also for the same person. But if it be possible for the same man to have distinct incommunicable consciousness at different times, it is past doubt the same man would at different times make different persons; which, we see, is the sense of mankind in the solemnest declaration of their opinions, human laws not punishing the mad man for the sober man's actions, nor the sober man for what the mad man did, thereby making them two persons: which is somewhat explained by our way of speaking in English when we say such an one is "not himself," or is "beside himself"; in which phrases it is insinuated, as if those who now, or at least first used them, thought that self was changed; the selfsame person was no longer in that man.

DAVID HUME (1711–1776), *A TREATISE OF HUMAN NATURE,* 1739

In this section from *A Treatise of Human Nature,* David Hume considers and then rejects the common notion that we are all intimately familiar with our selves through direct introspection of a continuously existing thing that persists, unchanging, through our constantly changing stream of perceptions. Once direct introspection is rejected as a source for our notion of personal identity, Hume considers what is responsible for this idea, as well as the related idea of identity over time for objects. He observes that the mind has a natural propensity to run together related perceptions into a single object and argues that our notion of identity over time for both persons and objects is to be explained in this manner.

Book I, Part IV, Section VI–Of Personal Identity

There are some philosophers, who imagine we are every moment intimately conscious of what we call our SELF, that we feel its existence and its continuance in existence and are certain, beyond the evidence of a demonstration, both of its perfect identity and simplicity. The strongest sensation, the most violent passion, say they, instead of distracting us from this view, only fix it the more intensely, and make us consider their influence on self either by their pain or pleasure. To attempt a farther proof of this would weaken its evidence, since no proof can be derived from any fact of which we are so intimately conscious; nor is there any thing of which we can be certain, if we doubt of this.

Unluckily, all these positive assertions are contrary to that very experience which is pleaded for them, nor have we any idea of self, after the manner it is here explained. For from what impression could this idea be derived? This question is impossible to answer without a manifest contradiction and absurdity; and yet it is a question which must necessarily be answered, if we would have the idea of self pass for clear and intelligible. There must be some single impression that gives rise to every real idea. But self or person is not any one impression, but that to which our several impressions and ideas are supposed to have a reference. If any impression gives rise to the idea of self, that impression must continue invariably the same through the whole course of our lives, since self is supposed to exist after that manner. But there is no impression constant and invariable. Pain and pleasure, grief and joy, passions and sensations succeed each other, and never all exist at the same time. It cannot, therefore, be from any of these impressions, or from any other, that the idea of self is derived; and consequently there is no such idea.

But farther, what must become of all our particular perceptions upon this hypothesis? All these are different and distinguishable and separable from each other, and may be separately considered, and may exist separately, and have no need of any thing to support their existence. After what manner, therefore, do they belong to self; and how are they connected with it? For my part, when I enter most intimately into what I call myself, I always stumble on some particular perception or other, of heat or cold, light or shade, love or hatred, pain or pleasure. I never can catch myself at any time without a perception, and never can observe any thing but the perception. When my perceptions are removed for any time, as by sound sleep, so long am I insensible of myself, and may truly be said not to exist. And were all my perceptions removed by death, and could I neither think, nor feel, nor see, nor love, nor hate after the dissolution of my body, I should be entirely annihilated, nor do I conceive what is farther requisite to make me a perfect non-entity. If any one, upon serious and unprejudiced reflection thinks he has a different notion of himself, I must confess I can reason no longer with him. All I can allow him is that he may be in the right as well as I and that we are essentially different in this particular. He may, perhaps, perceive something simple and continued, which he calls himself, though I am certain there is no such principle in me.

But setting aside some metaphysicians of this kind, I may venture to affirm of the rest of mankind, that they are nothing but a bundle or collection of different perceptions, which succeed each other with an inconceivable rapidity, and are in a perpetual flux and movement. Our eyes cannot turn in their sockets without varying our perceptions. Our thought is still more variable than our sight and all our other senses and faculties contribute to this change, nor is there any single power of the soul which remains unalterably the same, perhaps for one moment. The mind is a kind of theatre, where several perceptions successively make their appearance; pass, re-pass, glide away, and mingle in an infinite variety of postures and situations. There is properly no simplicity in it at one time nor identity in different, whatever natural propensity we may have to imagine that simplicity and identity. The comparison of the theatre must not mislead us. They are the successive perceptions only that constitute the mind; nor have we the most distant notion of the place, where these scenes are represented, or of the materials, of which it is composed.

What then gives us so great a propensity to ascribe an identity to these successive perceptions, and to suppose ourselves in possession of an invariable and uninterrupted existence through the whole course of our lives? ...

We have a distinct idea of an object, that remains invariable and uninterrupted through a supposed variation of time; and this idea we call that of identity or sameness. We have also a distinct idea of several different objects existing in succession, and connected together by a close relation, and this to an accurate view affords as perfect a notion of diversity, as if there was no manner of relation among the objects. But though these two ideas of identity and a succession of related objects be in themselves perfectly distinct, and even contrary, yet it is certain that in our common way of thinking they are generally confounded with each other. That action of the imagination by which we consider the uninterrupted and invariable object and that by which we reflect on the succession of related objects are almost the same to the feeling, nor is there much more effort of thought required in the latter case than in the former. The relation facilitates the transition of the mind from one object to another, and renders its passage as smooth as if it contemplated one continued object. This resemblance is the cause of the confusion and mistake, and makes us substitute the notion of identity, instead of that of related objects. However at one instant we may consider the related succession as variable or interrupted, we are sure the next to ascribe to it a perfect identity, and regard it as invariable and uninterrupted. Our propensity to this mistake is so great from the resemblance above-mentioned, that we fall into it before we are aware; and though we incessantly correct ourselves by reflection, and return to a more accurate method of thinking, yet we cannot long sustain our philosophy or take off this bias from the imagination. Our last resource is to yield to it, and boldly assert that these different related objects are in effect the same, however interrupted and variable. In order to justify to ourselves this absurdity, we often feign some new and unintelligible principle that connects the objects together and prevents their interruption or variation. Thus we feign the continued existence of the perceptions of our senses to remove the interruption, and run into the notion of a soul, and self, and substance, to disguise the variation. But we may farther observe that where we do not give rise to such a fiction, our propensity to confound identity with relation is so great, that we are apt to imagine something unknown and mysterious connecting the parts, beside their relation; and this I take to be the case with regard to the identity we ascribe to plants and vegetables. And even when this does not take place, we still feel a propensity to confound these ideas, though we are not able fully to satisfy ourselves in that particular, nor find any thing invariable and uninterrupted to justify our notion of identity.

Thus the controversy concerning identity is not merely a dispute of words. For when we attribute identity, in an improper sense, to variable or interrupted objects, our mistake is not confined to the expression, but is commonly attended with a fiction, either of something invariable and uninterrupted, or of something mysterious and inexplicable, or at least with a propensity to such fictions. What will suffice to prove this hypothesis to the satisfaction of every fair enquirer is to show from daily experience and observation that the objects which are variable or interrupted, and yet are supposed to continue the same, are such only as consist of a succession of parts connected together by resemblance, contiguity, or causation. For as such a succession answers evidently to our notion of diversity, it can only be by mistake we ascribe to it an identity; and as the relation of parts, which leads us into this mistake, is really nothing but a quality, which produces an association of ideas, and an easy transition of the imagination from one to another, it can only be from the resemblance, which this act of the mind bears to that, by which we contemplate one continued object, that the error arises. Our chief business, then, must be to prove that all objects to which we ascribe identity without observing their invariableness and uninterruptedness are such as consist of a succession of related objects.

In order to this, suppose any mass of matter of which the parts are contiguous and connected to be placed before us; it is plain we must attribute a perfect identity to this mass, provided all the parts continue uninterruptedly and invariably the same, whatever motion or change of place we may observe either in the whole or in any of the parts. But supposing some very small or inconsiderable part to be added to the mass or subtracted from it; though this absolutely destroys the identity of the whole, strictly speaking, yet as we seldom think so accurately, we scruple not to pronounce a mass of matter the same, where we find so trivial an alteration. The passage of the thought from the object before the change to the object after it is so smooth and easy that we scarce perceive the transition, and are apt to imagine that it is nothing but a continued survey of the same object.

There is a very remarkable circumstance that attends this experiment which is, that though the change of any considerable part in a mass of matter destroys the identity of the whole, yet we must measure the greatness of the part, not absolutely, but by its proportion to the whole. The addition or diminution of a mountain would not be sufficient to produce a diversity in a planet, though the change of a very few inches would be able to destroy the identity of some bodies. It will be impossible to account for this, but by reflecting that objects operate upon the mind and break or interrupt the continuity of its actions, not according to their real greatness, but according to their proportion to each other: and therefore, since this interruption makes an object cease to appear the same, it must be the uninterrupted progress of the thought, which constitutes the imperfect identity.

This may be confirmed by another phenomenon. A change in any considerable part of a body destroys its identity; but it is remarkable that where the change is produced gradually and insensibly, we are less apt to ascribe to it the same effect. The reason can plainly be no other than that the mind, in following the successive changes of the body, feels an easy passage from the surveying of its condition in one moment to the viewing of it in another, and at no particular time perceives any interruption in its actions. From which continued perception, it ascribes a continued existence and identity to the object.

But whatever precaution we may use in introducing the changes gradually and making them proportional to the whole, it is certain that where the changes are at last observed to become considerable, we make a scruple of ascribing identity to such different objects. There is, however, another artifice, by which we may induce the imagination to advance a step farther; and that is, by producing a reference of the parts to each other, and a combination to some common end or purpose. A ship, of which a considerable part has been changed by frequent reparations, is still considered as the same; nor does the difference of the materials hinder us from ascribing an identity to it. The common end, in which the parts conspire, is the same under all their variations, and affords an easy transition of the imagination from one situation of the body to another.

But this is still more remarkable, when we add a sympathy of parts to their common end, and suppose that they bear to each other the reciprocal relation of cause and effect in all their actions and operations. This is the case with all animals and vegetables, where not only the several parts have a reference to some general purpose, but also a mutual dependence on, and connection with, each other. The effect of so strong a relation is, that though every one must allow that in a very few years both vegetables and animals endure a total change, yet we still attribute identity to them, while their form, size, and substance are entirely altered. An oak that grows from a small plant to a large tree is still the same oak, though there be not one particle of matter or figure of its parts the same. An infant becomes a man, and is sometimes fat, sometimes lean, without any change in his identity.

...

We now proceed to explain the nature of personal identity, ... [a]nd here it is evident that the same method of reasoning must be continued, which has so successfully explained the identity of plants, and animals, and ships, and houses, and of all the compounded and changeable productions either of art or nature. The identity, which we ascribe to the mind of man, is only a fictitious one, and of a like kind with that which we ascribe to vegetables and animal bodies. It cannot, therefore, have a different origin, but must proceed from a like operation of the imagination upon like objects.

...

To begin with resemblance: suppose we could see clearly into the breast of another, and observe that succession of perceptions which constitutes his mind or thinking principle, and suppose that he always preserves the memory of a considerable part of past perceptions; it is evident that nothing could more contribute to the bestowing a relation on this succession amidst all its variations. For what is the memory but a faculty, by which we raise up the images of past perceptions? And as an image necessarily resembles its object, must not the frequent placing of these resembling perceptions in the chain of thought convey the imagination more easily from one link to another, and make the whole seem like the continuance of one object? In this particular, then, the memory not only discovers the identity, but also contributes to its production, by producing the relation of resemblance among the perceptions. The case is the same whether we consider ourselves or others.

As to causation: we may observe that the true idea of the human mind is to consider it as a system of different perceptions or different existences which are linked together by the relation of cause and effect, and mutually produce, destroy, influence, and modify each other. Our impressions give rise to their correspondent ideas, and these ideas in their turn produce other impressions. One thought chases another, and draws after it a third, by which it is expelled in its turn. In this respect, I cannot compare the soul more properly to any thing than to a republic or commonwealth, in which the several members are united by the reciprocal ties of government and subordination, and give rise to other persons, who propagate the same republic in the incessant changes of its parts. And as the same individual republic may not only change its members, but also its laws and constitutions, in like manner, the same person may vary his character and disposition, as well as his impressions and ideas, without losing his identity....

As a memory alone acquaints us with the continuance and extent of this succession of perceptions, it is to be considered, upon that account chiefly, as the source of personal identity. Had we no memory, we never should have any notion of causation, nor consequently of that chain of causes and effects, which constitute our self or person. But having once acquired this notion of causation from the memory, we can extend the same chain of causes, and consequently the identity of our persons beyond our memory, and can comprehend times, and circumstances, and actions, which we have entirely forgot, but suppose in general to have existed. For how few of our past actions are there of which we have any memory? Who can tell me, for instance, what were his thoughts and actions on the 1st of January 1715, the 11th of March 1719, and the 3rd of August 1733? Or will he affirm, because he has entirely forgot the incidents of these days, that the present self is not the same person with the self of that time, and by that means overturn all the most established notions of personal identity? In this view, therefore, memory does not so much produce as discover personal identity by showing us the relation of cause and effect among our different perceptions. It will be incumbent on those who affirm that memory produces entirely our personal identity to give a reason why we can thus extend our identity beyond our memory.

The whole of this doctrine leads us to a conclusion, which is of great importance in the present affair, viz. that all the nice and subtle questions concerning personal identity can never possibly be decided, and are to be regarded rather as grammatical than as philosophical difficulties. Identity depends on the relations of ideas and these relations produce identity by means of that easy transition they occasion. But as the relations and the easiness of the transition may diminish by insensible degrees, we have no just standard by which we can decide any dispute concerning the time when they acquire or lose a title to the name of identity. All the disputes concerning the identity of connected objects are merely verbal, except so far as the relation of parts gives rise to some fiction or imaginary principle of union, as we have already observed.

ALAN TURING (1912–1954), "COMPUTING MACHINERY AND INTELLIGENCE"
(*MIND* 59), 1950

In this paper published at the dawn of the computer age, Turing reformulates the question "Can machines think?" into a behavior-based test probing language fluency in an open-domain question and answer session. The details of the test protocol Turing offered are less relevant than what his approach implies about the nature of intelligence and thought: that the mind is best understood in purely behavioral terms and that what is happening "on the inside" (in terms of how the mind achieves its competence and whether consciousness and self-awareness accompany thought) is irrelevant. Turing considers and rejects several objections to "the Turing Test" and suggests at the end of the paper that artificial intelligence researchers may achieve their goal more efficiently by creating the computer equivalent of a child that will learn as it interacts with the world.

1. The Imitation Game

I propose to consider the question, "Can machines think?" This should begin with definitions of the meaning of the terms "machine" and "think." The definitions might be framed so as to reflect so far as possible the normal use of the words, but this attitude is dangerous. If the meaning of the words "machine" and "think" are to be found by examining how they are commonly used it is difficult to escape the conclusion that the meaning and the answer to the question, "Can machines think?" is to be sought in a statistical survey such as a Gallup poll. But this is absurd. Instead of attempting such a definition I shall replace the question by another, which is closely related to it and is expressed in relatively unambiguous words.

The new form of the problem can be described in terms of a game which we call the "imitation game." It is played with three people, a man (A), a woman (B), and an interrogator (C) who may be of either sex. The interrogator stays in a room apart from the other two. The object of the game for the interrogator is to determine which of the other two is the man and which is the woman. He knows them by labels X and Y.... The interrogator is allowed to put questions to A and B thus:

C: Will X please tell me the length of his or her hair?

Now suppose X is actually A, then A must answer. It is A's object in the game to try and cause C to make the wrong identification. His answer might therefore be:

"My hair is shingled, and the longest strands are about nine inches long."

... The ideal arrangement is to have a teleprinter communicating between the two rooms. The object of the game for the third player (B) is to help the interrogator. The best strategy for her is probably to give truthful answers....

We now ask the question, "What will happen when a machine takes the part of A in this game?" Will the interrogator decide wrongly as often when the game is played like this as he does when the game is played between a man and a woman? These questions replace our original, "Can machines think?"

2. Critique of the New Problem

The new problem has the advantage of drawing a fairly sharp line between the physical and the intellectual capacities of a man....

The question and answer method seems to be suitable for introducing almost any one of the fields of human endeavour that we wish to include. We do not wish to penalise the machine for its inability to shine in beauty competitions, nor to penalise a man for losing in a race against an aeroplane. The conditions of our game make these disabilities irrelevant....

The game may perhaps be criticised [on the following grounds]: May not machines carry out something which ought to be described as thinking but which is very different from what a man does? This objection is a very strong one, but at least we can say that if, nevertheless, a machine can be constructed to play the imitation game satisfactorily, we need not be troubled by this objection.

3. The Machines Concerned in the Game

The question which we put in §1 will not be quite definite until we have specified what we mean by the word "machine." ... [W]e only permit digital computers to take part in our game.

...

6. Contrary Views on the Main Question

We may now consider the ground to have been cleared and we are ready to proceed to the debate on our question, "Can machines think?" ... We cannot altogether abandon the original form of the problem, for opinions will differ as to the appropriateness of the substitution and we must at least listen to what has to be said in this connection.

...

The Argument from Consciousness

"Not until a machine can write a sonnet or compose a concerto because of thoughts and emotions felt, and not by the chance fall of symbols, could we agree that machine equals brain–that is, not only write it but know that it had written it. No mechanism could feel (and not merely artificially signal, an easy contrivance) pleasure at its successes, grief when its valves fuse, be warmed by flattery, be made miserable by its mistakes, be charmed by sex, be angry or depressed when it cannot get what it wants."

This argument appears to be a denial of the validity of our test. According to the most extreme form of this view the only way by which one could be sure that a machine thinks is to be the machine and to feel oneself thinking. One could then describe these feelings to the world, but of course no one would be justified in taking any notice. Likewise according to this view the only way to know that a man thinks is to be that particular man. It is in fact the solipsist point of view. It may be the most logical view to hold but it makes communication of ideas difficult. A is liable to believe "A thinks but B does not" whilst B believes "B thinks but A does not." Instead of arguing continually over this point it is usual to have the polite convention that everyone thinks.

... The game (with the player B omitted) is frequently used in practice under the name of *viva voce* to discover whether some one really understands something or has "learned it parrot fashion." Let us listen in to a part of such a *viva voce*:

Interrogator: In the first line of your sonnet which reads "Shall I compare thee to a summer's day," would not "a spring day" do as well or better?
Witness: It wouldn't scan.
Interrogator: How about "a winter's day." That would scan all right.
Witness: Yes, but nobody wants to be compared to a winter's day.
Interrogator: Would you say Mr. Pickwick reminded you of Christmas?
Witness: In a way.
Interrogator: Yet Christmas is a winter's day, and I do not think Mr. Pickwick would mind the comparison.
Witness: I don't think you're serious. By a winter's day one means a typical winter's day, rather than a special one like Christmas.

And so on. What would [an objector] say if the sonnet-writing machine was able to answer like this in the *viva voce*? I do not know whether he would regard the machine as "merely artificially signaling" these answers, but if the answers were as satisfactory and sustained as in the above passage I do not think he would describe it as "an easy contrivance." This phrase is, I think, intended to cover such devices as the inclusion in the machine of a record of someone reading a sonnet, with appropriate switching to turn it on from time to time.

In short then, I think that most of those who support the argument from consciousness could be persuaded to abandon it rather than be forced into the solipsist position. They will then probably be willing to accept our test.

I do not wish to give the impression that I think there is no mystery about consciousness. There is, for instance, something of a paradox connected with any attempt to localise it. But I do not think these mysteries necessarily need to be solved before we can answer the question with which we are concerned in this paper.

Arguments from Various Disabilities

These arguments take the form, "I grant you that you can make machines do all the things you have mentioned but you will never be able to make one to do X." Numerous features X are suggested in this connection. I offer a selection:

Be kind, resourceful, beautiful, friendly, have initiative, have a sense of humour, tell right from wrong, make mistakes, fall in love, enjoy strawberries and cream, make someone fall in love with it, learn from experience, use words properly, be the subject of its own thought, have as much diversity of behaviour as a man, do something really new.

No support is usually offered for these statements. I believe they are mostly founded on the principle of scientific induction. A man has seen thousands of machines in his lifetime. From what he sees of them he draws a number of general conclusions. They are ugly, each is designed for a very limited purpose, when required for a minutely different purpose they are useless, the variety of behaviour of any one of them is very small, etc., etc. Naturally he concludes that these are necessary properties of machines in general.

...

7. Learning Machines

...

In the process of trying to imitate an adult human mind we are bound to think a good deal about the process which has brought it to the state that it is in. We may notice three components.

(a) The initial state of the mind, say at birth,
(b) The education to which it has been subjected,

(c) Other experience, not to be described as education, to which it has been subjected.

Instead of trying to produce a programme to simulate the adult mind, why not rather try to produce one which simulates the child's? If this were then subjected to an appropriate course of education one would obtain the adult brain.

...

The idea of a learning machine may appear paradoxical to some readers. How can the rules of operation of the machine change? They should describe completely how the machine will react whatever its history might be, whatever changes it might undergo. The rules are thus quite time-invariant. This is quite true. The explanation of the paradox is that the rules which get changed in the learning process are of a rather less pretentious kind, claiming only an ephemeral validity. The reader may draw a parallel with the Constitution of the United States.

An important feature of a learning machine is that its teacher will often be very largely ignorant of quite what is going on inside, although he may still be able to some extent to predict his pupil's behavior. This should apply most strongly to the later education of a machine arising from a child machine of well-tried design (or programme).... Another important result of preparing our machine for its part in the imitation game by a process of teaching and learning is that "human fallibility" is likely to be omitted in a rather natural way, i.e., without special "coaching."

...

We may hope that machines will eventually compete with men in all purely intellectual fields. But which are the best ones to start with? Even this is a difficult decision. Many people think that a very abstract activity, like the playing of chess, would be best. It can also be maintained that it is best to provide the machine with the best sense organs that money can buy, and then teach it to understand and speak English. This process could follow the normal teaching of a child. Things would be pointed out and named, etc. Again I do not know what the right answer is, but I think both approaches should be tried.

We can only see a short distance ahead, but we can see plenty there that needs to be done.

JOHN SEARLE (B. 1932), "MINDS, BRAINS, AND PROGRAMS" (*THE BEHAVIORAL AND BRAIN SCIENCES* 3), 1980

Searle argues against the claim of "strong" AI that an appropriately programmed computer is a mind. His argument rests on an ingenuous thought experiment that has become known in the literature as "The Chinese Room." The thought experiment may be seen as a direct attack against any purely behavior-based test of understanding (e.g., the Turing Test); instead, Searle argues that what is going on "on the inside" is crucially important. Searle considers and then rejects several objections to his view.

What psychological and philosophical significance should we attach to recent efforts at computer simulations of human cognitive capacities? In answering this question, I find it useful to distinguish what I will call "strong" AI from "weak" or "cautious" AI (artificial intelligence). According to weak AI, the principal value of the computer in the study of the mind is that it gives us a very powerful tool. For example, it enables us to formulate and test hypotheses in a more rigorous and precise fashion. But according to strong AI, the computer is not merely a tool in the study of the mind; rather, the appropriately programmed computer really is a mind, in the sense that computers given the right programs can be literally said to *understand* and have other cognitive states. In strong AI, because the programmed computer has cognitive states, the programs are not mere tools that enable us to test psychological explanations; rather, the programs are themselves the explanations.

... My discussion here will be directed at the claims I have defined as those of strong AI, specifically the claim that the appropriately programmed computer literally has cognitive states and that the programs thereby explain human cognition. When I hereafter refer to AI, I have in mind the strong version, as expressed by these two claims.

I will consider the work of Roger Schank and his colleagues at Yale ... because I am more familiar with it than I am with any other similar claims, and because it provides a very clear example of the sort of work I wish to examine. But nothing that follows depends upon the details of Schank's programs....

Very briefly, and leaving out the various details, one can describe Schank's program as follows: The aim of the program is to simulate the human ability to understand stories. It is characteristic of human beings' story-understanding capacity that they can answer questions about the story even though the information that they give was never explicitly stated in the story. Thus, for example, suppose you are given the following story: "A man went into a restaurant and ordered a hamburger. When the hamburger arrived it was burned to a crisp, and the man stormed out of the restaurant angrily, without paying for the hamburger or leaving a tip." Now, if you are asked "Did the man eat the hamburger?" you will presumably answer, "No, he did not." ... Now Schank's machines can similarly answer questions about restaurants in this fashion. To do this, they have a "representation" of the sort of information that human beings have about restaurants, which enables them to answer such questions as those above, given these sorts of stories. When the machine is given the story and then asked the question, the machine will print out answers of the sort that we would expect human beings to give if told similar stories. Partisans of strong AI claim that in this question and answer sequence the machine is not only simulating a human ability but also (1) that the machine can literally be said to *understand* the story and provide the answers to questions, and (2) that what the machine and its program do *explains* the human ability to understand the story and answer questions about it.

Both claims seem to me to be totally unsupported by Schank's work, as I will attempt to show in what follows....

One way to test any theory of the mind is to ask oneself what it would be like if my mind actually worked on the principles that the theory says all minds work on. Let us apply this test to the Schank program with the following *Gedankenexperiment.* Suppose that I'm locked in a room and given a large batch of Chinese writing. Suppose furthermore (as is indeed the case) that I know no Chinese, either written or spoken, and that I'm not even confident that I could recognize Chinese writing as Chinese writing distinct from, say, Japanese writing or meaningless squiggles. To me, Chinese writing is just so many meaningless squiggles. Now suppose further that after this first batch of Chinese writing I am given a second batch of Chinese script together with a set of rules for correlating the second batch with the first batch. The rules are in English, and I understand these rules as well as any other native speaker of English. They enable me to correlate one set of formal symbols with another set of formal symbols, and all that "formal" means here is that I can identify the symbols entirely by their shapes. Now suppose also that I am given a third batch of Chinese symbols together with some instructions, again in English, that enable me to correlate elements of this third batch with the first two batches, and these rules instruct me how to give back certain Chinese symbols with certain sorts of shapes in response to certain sorts of shapes given me in the third batch. Unknown to me, the people who are giving me all of these symbols call the first batch a "script," they call the second batch a "story," and they call the third batch "questions." Furthermore, they call the symbols I give them back in response to the third batch "answers to the questions," and the set of rules in English that they gave me, they call the "program." Now just to complicate the story a little, imagine that these people also give me stories in English, which I understand, and they then ask me questions in English about these stories, and I give them back answers in English. Suppose also that after a while I get so good at following the instructions for manipulating the Chinese symbols and the programmers get so good at writing the programs that from the external point of view–that is, from the point of view of somebody outside the room in which I am locked–my answers to the questions are absolutely indistinguishable from those of native Chinese speakers. Nobody just looking at my answers can tell that I don't speak a word of Chinese. Let us also suppose that my answers to the English questions are, as they no doubt would be, indistinguishable from those of other native English speakers, for the simple reason that I am a native English speaker. From the external point of view–from the point of view of someone reading my "answers"–the answers to the Chinese questions and the English questions are equally good. But in the Chinese case, unlike the English case, I produce the answers by manipulating uninterpreted formal symbols. As far as the Chinese is concerned, I simply behave like a computer; I perform computational operations on formally specified elements. For the purposes of the Chinese, I am simply an instantiation of the computer program.

Now the claims made by strong AI are that the programmed computer understands the stories and that the program in some sense explains human understanding. But we are now in a position to examine these claims in light of our thought experiment.

1. As regards the first claim, it seems to me quite obvious in the example that I do not understand a word of the Chinese stories. I have inputs and outputs that are indistinguishable from those of the native Chinese speaker, and I can have any formal program you like, but I still understand nothing. For the same reasons, Schank's computer understands nothing of any stories, whether in Chinese, English, or whatever, since in the Chinese case the computer is me, and in cases where the computer is not me, the computer has nothing more than I have in the case where I understand nothing.

2. As regards the second claim, that the program explains human understanding, we can see that the computer and its program do not provide sufficient conditions of understanding since the computer and the program are functioning, and there is no understanding. But does it even provide a necessary condition or a significant contribution to understanding? One of the claims made by the supporters of strong AI is that when I understand a story in English, what I am doing is exactly the same–or perhaps more of the same–as what I was doing in manipulating the Chinese symbols. It is simply more formal symbol manipulation that distinguishes the case in English, where I do understand, from the case in Chinese, where I don't. I have not demonstrated that this

claim is false, but it would certainly appear an incredible claim in the example. Such plausibility as the claim has derives from the supposition that we can construct a program that will have the same inputs and outputs as native speakers, and in addition we assume that speakers have some level of description where they are also instantiations of a program. On the basis of these two assumptions we assume that even if Schank's program isn't the whole story about understanding, it may be part of the story. Well, I suppose that is an empirical possibility, but not the slightest reason has so far been given to believe that it is true, since what is suggested–though certainly not demonstrated–by the example is that the computer program is simply irrelevant to my understanding of the story. In the Chinese case I have everything that artificial intelligence can put into me by way of a program, and I understand nothing; in the English case I understand everything, and there is so far no reason at all to suppose that my understanding has anything to do with computer programs, that is, with computational operations on purely formally specified elements. As long as the program is defined in terms of computational operations on purely formally defined elements, what the example suggests is that these by themselves have no interesting connection with understanding. They are certainly not sufficient conditions, and not the slightest reason has been given to suppose that they are necessary conditions or even that they make a significant contribution to understanding. Notice that the force of the argument is not simply that different machines can have the same input and output while operating on different formal principles–that is not the point at all. Rather, whatever purely formal principles you put into the computer, they will not be sufficient for understanding, since a human will be able to follow the formal principles without understanding anything. No reason whatever has been offered to suppose that such principles are necessary or even contributory, since no reason has been given to suppose that when I understand English I am operating with any formal program at all.

Well, then, what is it that I have in the case of the English sentences that I do not have in the case of the Chinese sentences? The obvious answer is that I know what the former mean, while I haven't the faintest idea what the latter mean. But in what does this consist and why couldn't we give it to a machine, whatever it is? I will return to this question later, but first I want to continue with the example.

I have had the occasions to present this example to several workers in artificial intelligence, and, interestingly, they do not seem to agree on what the proper reply to it is. I get a surprising variety of replies, and in what follows I will consider the most common of these.

...

1. The Systems Reply[:] "While it is true that the individual person who is locked in the room does not understand the story, the fact is that he is merely part of a whole system, and the system does understand the story. The person has a large ledger in front of him in which are written the rules, he has a lot of scratch paper and pencils for doing calculations, he has 'data banks' of sets of Chinese symbols. Now, understanding is not being ascribed to the mere individual; rather it is being ascribed to this whole system of which he is a part."

My response to the systems theory is quite simple: Let the individual internalize all of these elements of the system. He memorizes the rules in the ledger and the data banks of Chinese symbols, and he does all the calculations in his head. The individual then incorporates the entire system. There isn't anything at all to the system that he does not encompass. We can even get rid of the room and suppose he works outdoors. All the same, he understands nothing of the Chinese, and a fortiori neither does the system, because there isn't anything in the system that isn't in him. If he doesn't understand, then there is no way the system could understand because the system is just a part of him.

...

2. The Robot Reply[:] "Suppose we wrote a different kind of program from Schank's program. Suppose we put a computer inside a robot, and this computer would not just take in formal symbols as input and give out formal symbols as output, but rather would actually operate the robot in such a way that the robot does something very much like perceiving, walking, moving about, hammering nails, eating, drinking–anything you like. The robot would, for example, have a television camera attached to it that enabled it to see, it would have arms and legs that enabled it to 'act,' and all of this would be controlled by its computer 'brain.' Such a robot would, unlike Schank's computer, have genuine understanding and other mental states."

The first thing to notice about the robot reply is that it tacitly concedes that cognition is not solely a matter of formal symbol manipulation, since this reply adds a set of causal relations with the outside world. But the answer to the robot reply is that the addition of such "perceptual" and "motor" capacities adds nothing by way of understanding, in particular, or intentionality, in general, to Schank's original program. To see this, notice that the same thought experiment applies to the robot case. Suppose that instead of the computer inside the robot, you put me inside the room and, as in the original Chinese case, you give me more Chinese symbols with more instructions in English for matching Chinese symbols to Chinese symbols and feeding back Chinese symbols to the outside. Suppose, unknown to me, some of the Chinese symbols that come to me come from a television camera attached to the robot and other Chinese symbols that I am giving out serve to make the motors inside the robot move the robot's legs or arms. It is important to emphasize that all I am doing is manipulating formal symbols: I know none of these other facts. I am receiving "information" from the robot's perceptual apparatus and I am giving out "instructions" to its motor apparatus without knowing either of these facts. I am the robot's homunculus, but unlike the traditional homunculus, I don't know what's going on. I don't understand anything except the rules for symbol manipulation. Now in this case I want to say that the robot has no intentional states at all; it is simply moving about as a result of its electrical wiring and its program. And furthermore, by instantiating the program I have no intentional states of the relevant type. All I do is follow formal instructions about manipulating formal symbols.

...

By way of concluding I want to try to state some of the general philosophical points implicit in the argument. For clarity I will try to do it in a question-and-answer fashion, and I begin with that old chestnut of a question:

"Could a machine think?" The answer is, obviously, yes. We are precisely such machines.

...

"But could something think, understand, and so on *solely* in virtue of being a computer with the right sort of program? Could instantiating a program, the right program of course, by itself be a sufficient condition of understanding?"

[T]he answer to [this question] is no, ... [b]ecause the formal symbol manipulations by themselves ... are quite meaningless; they aren't even *symbol* manipulations, since the symbols don't symbolize anything.... Such intentionality as computers appear to have is solely in the minds of those who program them and those who use them, those who send in the input and those who interpret the output.

The aim of the Chinese room example was to try to show this by showing that as soon as we put something into the system that really does have intentionality (a man), and we program him with the formal program, you can see that the formal program carries no additional intentionality. It adds nothing, for example, to a man's ability to understand Chinese.

DAVID HUME (1711–1776), *AN ENQUIRY CONCERNING HUMAN UNDERSTANDING*, 1748

In the opening pages of this passage, Hume offers us a compatibilist interpretation of free will according to which liberty "can only mean a power of acting or not acting, according to the determinations of the will; this is, if we choose to remain at rest, we may; if we choose to move, we also may." Hume then goes on to consider the connection between compatibilism and moral responsibility. He argues that, contrary to what many believe, the compatibilist interpretation is the only one that explains how a person can be held morally responsible for his previous actions. He ends by countering a criticism commonly raised against compatibilism: if human action is determined, then ultimately God, as the being that "got the ball rolling," is culpable for our sin.

Section VIII–Of Liberty and Necessity

1. Part I

...

I hope ... to make it appear that all men have ever agreed in the doctrine both of necessity and of liberty, according to any reasonable sense, which can be put on these terms; and that the whole controversy, has hitherto turned merely upon words. We shall begin with examining the doctrine of necessity.

...

It is universally acknowledged that there is a great uniformity among the actions of men, in all nations and ages, and that human nature remains still the same, in its principles and operations. The same motives always produce the same actions: the same events follow from the same causes. Ambition, avarice, self-love, vanity, friendship, generosity, public spirit: these passions, mixed in various degrees, and distributed through society, have been, from the beginning of the world, and still are, the source of all the actions and enterprises, which have ever been observed among mankind.

...

Hence likewise the benefit of that experience, acquired by long life and a variety of business and company, in order to instruct us in the principles of human nature, and regulate our future conduct, as well as speculation.

By means of this guide, we mount up to the knowledge of men's inclinations and motives, from their actions, expressions, and even gestures; and again descend to the interpretation of their actions from our knowledge of their motives and inclinations. The general observations treasured up by a course of experience, give us the clue of human nature, and teach us to unravel all its intricacies. Pretexts and appearances no longer deceive us. Public declarations pass for the specious colouring of a cause. And though virtue and honour be allowed their proper weight and authority, that perfect disinterestedness, so often pretended to, is never expected in multitudes and parties; seldom in their leaders; and scarcely even in individuals of any rank or station. But were there no uniformity in human actions, and were every experiment which we could form of this kind irregular and anomalous, it were impossible to collect any general observations concerning mankind; and no experience, however accurately digested by reflection, would ever serve to any purpose. Why is the aged husbandman more skilful in his calling than the young beginner but because there is a certain uniformity in the operation of the sun, rain, and earth towards the production of vegetables; and experience teaches the old practitioner the rules by which this operation is governed and directed.

We must not, however, expect that this uniformity of human actions should be carried to such a length as that all men, in the same circumstances, will always act precisely in the same manner, without making any allowance for the diversity of characters, prejudices, and opinions. Such a uniformity in every particular, is found in no part of nature. On the contrary, from observing the variety of conduct in different men, we are enabled to form a greater variety of maxims, which still suppose a degree of uniformity and regularity.

...

The vulgar, who take things according to their first appearance, attribute the uncertainty of events to such an uncertainty in the causes as makes the latter often fail of their usual influence; though they meet with no impediment in their operation. But philosophers, observing that, almost in every part of nature, there is contained a vast variety of springs and principles, which are hid, by reason of their minuteness or remoteness, find, that it is at least possible the contrariety of events may not proceed from any contingency in the cause, but from the secret operation of contrary causes. This possibility is converted into certainty by farther observation, when they remark that, upon an exact scrutiny, a contrariety of effects always betrays a contrariety of causes, and proceeds from their mutual opposition. A peasant can give no better reason for the stopping of any clock or watch than to say that it does not commonly go right: But an artist easily perceives that the same force in the spring or pendulum has always the same influence on the wheels; but fails of its usual effects, perhaps by reason of a grain of dust, which puts a stop to the whole movement. From the observation of several parallel instances, philosophers form a maxim that the connection between all causes and effects is equally necessary, and that its seeming uncertainty in some instances proceeds from the secret opposition of contrary causes.

...

The philosopher, if he be consistent, must apply the same reasoning to the actions and volitions of intelligent agents. The most irregular and unexpected resolutions of men may frequently be accounted for by those who know every particular circumstance of their character and situation. A person of an obliging disposition gives a peevish answer: But he has the toothache, or has not dined. A stupid fellow discovers an uncommon alacrity in his carriage: But he has met with a sudden piece of good fortune. Or even when an action, as sometimes happens, cannot be particularly accounted for, either by the person himself or by others; we know, in general, that the characters of men are, to a certain degree, inconstant and irregular. This is, in a manner, the constant character of human nature; though it be applicable, in a more particular manner, to some persons who have no fixed rule for their conduct, but proceed in a continued course of caprice and inconstancy. The internal principles and motives may operate in a uniform manner, notwithstanding these seeming irregularities; in the same manner as the winds, rain, cloud, and other variations of the weather are supposed to be governed by steady principles; though not easily discoverable by human sagacity and enquiry.

Thus it appears, not only that the conjunction between motives and voluntary actions is as regular and uniform as that between the cause and effect in any part of nature; but also that this regular conjunction has been universally acknowledged among mankind, and has never been the subject of dispute, either in philosophy or common life. Now, as it is from past experience that we draw all inferences concerning the future, and as we conclude that objects will always be conjoined together which we find to have always been conjoined; it may seem superfluous to prove that this experienced uniformity in human actions is a source whence we draw inferences concerning them.

...

It would seem, indeed, that men begin at the wrong end of this question concerning liberty and necessity, when they enter upon it by examining the faculties of the soul, the influence of the understanding, and the operations of the will. Let them first discuss a more simple question, namely, the operations of body and of brute unintelligent matter; and try whether they can there form any idea of causation and necessity, except that of a constant conjunction of objects, and subsequent inference of the mind from one to another. If these circumstances form, in reality, the whole of that necessity, which we conceive in matter, and if these circumstances be also universally acknowledged to take place in the operations of the mind, the dispute is at an end; at least, must be owned to be thenceforth merely verbal. But as long as we will rashly suppose, that we have some farther idea of necessity and causation in the operations of external objects; at the same time, that we can find nothing farther in the voluntary actions of the mind; there is no possibility of bringing the question to any determinate issue, while we proceed upon so erroneous a supposition. The only method of undeceiving us is to mount up higher; to examine the narrow extent of science when applied to material causes; and to convince ourselves that all we know of them is the constant conjunction and inference above mentioned. We may, perhaps, find that it is with difficulty we are induced to fix such narrow limits to human understanding: but we can afterwards find no difficulty when we come to apply this doctrine to the actions of the will. For as it is evident that these have a regular conjunction with motives and circumstances and characters, and as we always draw inferences from one to the other, we must be obliged to acknowledge in words that necessity, which we have already avowed, in every deliberation of our lives, and in every step of our conduct and behaviour.

[From footnote:] The prevalence of the doctrine of liberty may be accounted for, from another cause, viz. a false sensation of seeming experience which we have, or may have, of liberty or indifference, in many of our actions. The necessity of any action, whether of matter or of mind, is not, properly speaking, a quality in the agent, but in any thinking or intelligent being, who may consider the action; and it consists chiefly in the determination of his thoughts to infer the existence of that action from some preceding objects; as liberty, when opposed to necessity, is nothing but the want of that determination, and a certain looseness or indifference, which we feel, in passing, or not passing, from the idea of one object to that of any succeeding one. Now we may observe, that, though, in reflecting on human actions, we seldom feel such a looseness, or indifference, but are commonly able to infer them with considerable certainty from their motives, and from the dispositions of the agent; yet it frequently happens, that, in performing the actions themselves, we are sensible of something like it: And as all resembling objects are readily taken for each other, this has been employed as a demonstrative and even intuitive proof of human liberty. We feel, that our actions are subject to our will, on most occasions; and imagine we feel, that the will itself is subject to nothing, because, when by a denial of it we are provoked to try, we feel, that it moves easily every way, and produces an image of itself ... even on that side, on which it did not settle. This image, or faint motion, we persuade ourselves, could, at that time, have been completed into the thing itself; because, should that be denied, we find, upon a second trial, that, at present, it can. We consider not, that the fantastical desire of showing liberty, is here the motive of our actions. And it seems certain, that, however we may imagine we feel a liberty within ourselves, a spectator can commonly infer our actions from our motives and character; and even where he cannot, he concludes in general, that he might, were he perfectly acquainted with every circumstance of our situation and temper, and the most secret springs of our complexion and disposition. Now this is the very essence of necessity, according to the foregoing doctrine.

But to proceed in this reconciling project with regard to the question of liberty and necessity; the most contentious question of metaphysics, the most contentious science; it will not require many words to prove, that all mankind have ever agreed in the doctrine of liberty as well as in that of necessity, and that the whole dispute, in this respect also, has been hitherto merely verbal. For what is meant by liberty, when applied to voluntary actions? We cannot surely mean that actions have so little connexion with motives, inclinations, and circumstances, that one does not follow with a certain degree of uniformity from the other, and that one affords no inference by which we can conclude the existence of the other. For these are plain and acknowledged matters of fact. By liberty, then, we can only mean a power of acting or not acting, according to the determinations of the will; this is, if we choose to remain at rest, we may; if we choose to move, we also may. Now this hypothetical liberty is universally allowed to belong to every one who is not a prisoner and in chains. Here, then, is no subject of dispute.

...

2. Part II

There is no method of reasoning more common, and yet none more blameable, than, in philosophical disputes, to endeavour the refutation of any hypothesis, by a pretence of its dangerous consequences to religion and morality. When any opinion leads to absurdities, it is certainly false; but it is not certain that an opinion is false, because it is of dangerous consequence. Such topics, therefore, ought entirely to be forborne; as serving nothing to the discovery of truth, but only to make the person of an antagonist odious. This I observe in general, without pretending to draw any advantage from it. I frankly submit to an examination of this kind, and shall venture to affirm that the doctrines, both of necessity and of liberty, as above explained, are not only consistent with morality, but are absolutely essential to its support.

Necessity may be defined two ways, conformably to the two definitions of cause, of which it makes an essential part. It consists either in the constant conjunction of like objects, or in the inference of the understanding from one object to another. Now necessity, in both these senses, (which, indeed, are at bottom the same) has universally, though tacitly, in the schools, in the pulpit, and in common life, been allowed to belong to the will of man; and no one has ever pretended to deny that we can draw inferences concerning human actions, and that those inferences are founded on the experienced union of like actions, with like motives, inclinations, and circumstances. The only particular in which any one can differ, is, that either, perhaps, he will refuse to give the name of necessity to this property of human actions: but as long as the meaning is understood, I hope the word can do no harm: or that he will maintain it possible to discover something farther in the operations of matter. But this, it must be acknowledged, can be of no consequence to morality or religion, whatever it may be to natural philosophy or metaphysics. We may here be mistaken in asserting that there is no idea of any other necessity or connection in the actions of body: But surely we ascribe nothing to the actions of the mind, but what everyone does, and must readily allow of. We change no circumstance in the received orthodox system with regard to the will, but only in that with regard to material objects and causes. Nothing, therefore, can be more innocent, at least, than this doctrine.

All laws being founded on rewards and punishments, it is supposed as a fundamental principle, that these motives have a regular and uniform influence on the mind, and both produce the good and prevent the evil actions. We may give to this influence what name we please; but, as it is usually conjoined with the action, it must be esteemed a cause, and be looked upon as an instance of that necessity, which we would here establish.

The only proper object of hatred or vengeance is a person or creature, endowed with thought and consciousness; and when any criminal or injurious actions excite that passion, it is only by their relation to the person, or connection with him. Actions are, by their very nature, temporary and perishing; and where they proceed not from some cause in the character and disposition of the person who performed them, they can neither redound to his honour, if good; nor infamy, if evil. The actions themselves may be blameable; they may be contrary to all the rules of morality and religion: but the person is not answerable for them; and as they proceeded from nothing in him that is durable and constant, and leave nothing of that nature behind them, it is impossible he can, upon their account, become the object of punishment or vengeance. According to the principle, therefore, which denies necessity, and consequently causes, a man is as pure and untainted, after having committed the most horrid crime, as at the first moment of his birth, nor is his character anywise concerned in his actions, since they are not derived from it, and the wickedness of the one can never be used as a proof of the depravity of the other.

Men are not blamed for such actions as they perform ignorantly and casually, whatever may be the consequences. Why? but because the principles of these actions are only momentary, and terminate in them alone. Men are less blamed for such actions as they perform hastily and unpremeditatedly than for such as proceed from deliberation. For what reason? but because a hasty temper, though a constant cause or principle in the mind, operates only by intervals, and infects not the whole character. Again, repentance wipes off every crime, if attended with a reformation of life and manners. How is this to be accounted for? but by asserting that actions render a person criminal merely as they are proofs of criminal principles in the mind; and when, by an alteration of these principles, they cease to be just proofs, they likewise cease to be criminal. But, except upon the doctrine of necessity, they never were just proofs, and consequently never were criminal.

It will be equally easy to prove, and from the same arguments, that liberty, according to that definition above mentioned, in which all men agree, is also essential to morality, and that no human actions, where it is wanting, are susceptible of any moral qualities, or can be the objects either of approbation or dislike. For as actions are objects of our moral sentiment, so far only as they are indications of the internal character, passions, and affections; it is impossible that they can give rise either to praise or blame, where they proceed not from these principles, but are derived altogether from external violence.

I pretend not to have obviated or removed all objections to this theory, with regard to necessity and liberty. I can foresee other objections, derived from topics which have not here been treated of. It may be said, for instance, that, if voluntary actions be subjected to the same laws of necessity with the operations of matter, there is a continued chain of necessary causes, pre-ordained and pre-determined, reaching from the original cause of all to every single volition of every human creature. No contingency anywhere in the universe; no indifference; no liberty. While we act, we are, at the same time, acted upon. The ultimate Author of all our volitions is the Creator of the world, who first bestowed motion on this immense machine, and placed all beings in that particular position, whence every subsequent event, by an inevitable necessity, must result. Human actions, therefore, either can have no moral turpitude at all, as proceeding from so good a cause; or if they have any turpitude, they must involve our Creator in the same guilt, while he is acknowledged to be their ultimate cause and author. For as a man, who fired a mine, is answerable for all the consequences whether the train he employed be long or short; so wherever a continued chain of necessary causes is fixed, that Being, either finite or infinite, who produces the first, is likewise the author of all the rest, and must both bear the blame and acquire the praise which belong to them. Our clear and unalterable ideas of morality establish this rule, upon unquestionable reasons, when we examine the consequences of any human action; and these reasons must still have greater force when applied to the volitions and intentions of a Being infinitely wise and powerful. Ignorance or impotence may be pleaded for so limited a creature as man; but those imperfections have no place in our Creator. He foresaw, he ordained, he intended all those actions of men, which we so rashly pronounce criminal. And we must therefore conclude, either that they are not criminal, or that the Deity, not man, is accountable for them. But as either of these positions is absurd and impious, it follows, that the doctrine from which they are deduced cannot possibly be true, as being liable to all the same objections. An absurd consequence, if necessary, proves the original doctrine to be absurd; in the same manner as criminal actions render criminal the original cause, if the connection between them be necessary and inevitable.

This objection consists of two parts, which we shall examine separately; First, that, if human actions can be traced up, by a necessary chain, to the Deity, they can never be criminal; on account of the infinite perfection of that Being from whom they are derived, and who can intend nothing but what is altogether good and laudable. Or, Secondly, if they be criminal, we must retract the attribute of perfection, which we ascribe to the Deity, and must acknowledge him to be the ultimate author of guilt and moral turpitude in all his creatures.

The answer to the first objection seems obvious and convincing. There are many philosophers who, after an exact scrutiny of all the phenomena of nature, conclude, that the WHOLE, considered as one system, is, in every period of its existence, ordered with perfect benevolence; and that the utmost possible happiness will, in the end, result to all created beings, without any mixture of positive or absolute ill or misery. Every physical ill, say they, makes an essential part of this benevolent system, and could not possibly be removed, even by the Deity himself, considered as a wise agent, without giving entrance to greater ill, or excluding greater good, which will result from it. From this theory, some philosophers, and the ancient Stoics among the rest, derived a topic of consolation under all afflictions, while they taught their pupils that those ills under which they laboured were, in reality, goods to the universe; and that to an enlarged view, which could comprehend the whole system of nature, every event became an object of joy and exultation. But though this topic be specious and sublime, it was soon found in practice weak and ineffectual. You would surely more irritate than appease a man lying under the racking pains of the gout by preaching up to him the rectitude of those general laws, which produced the malignant humours in his body, and led them through the proper canals, to the sinews and nerves, where they now excite such acute torments. These enlarged views may, for a moment, please the imagination of a speculative man, who is placed in ease and security; but neither can they dwell with constancy on his mind, even though undisturbed by the emotions of pain or passion; much less can they maintain their ground when attacked by such powerful antagonists. The affections take a narrower and more natural survey of their object; and by an economy, more suitable to the infirmity of human minds, regard alone the beings around us, and are actuated by such events as appear good or ill to the private system.

The case is the same with moral as with physical ill. It cannot reasonably be supposed, that those remote considerations, which are found of so little efficacy with regard to one, will have a more powerful influence with regard to the other. The mind of man is so formed by nature that, upon the appearance of certain characters, dispositions, and actions, it immediately feels the sentiment of approbation or blame; nor are there any emotions more essential to its frame and constitution. The characters which engage our approbation are chiefly such as contribute to the peace and security of human society; as the characters which excite blame are chiefly such as tend to public detriment and disturbance: whence it may reasonably be presumed, that the moral sentiments arise, either mediately or immediately, from a reflection of these opposite interests. What though philosophical meditations establish a different opinion or conjecture; that everything is right with regard to the WHOLE, and that the qualities, which disturb society, are, in the main, as beneficial, and are as suitable to the primary intention of nature as those which more directly promote its happiness and welfare? Are such remote and uncertain speculations able to counterbalance the sentiments which arise from the natural and immediate view of the objects? A man who is robbed of a considerable sum; does he find his vexation for the loss anywise diminished by these sublime reflections? Why then should his moral resentment against the crime be supposed incompatible with them? Or why should not the acknowledgment of a real distinction between vice and virtue be reconcileable to all speculative systems of philosophy, as well as that of a real distinction between personal beauty and deformity? Both these distinctions are founded in the natural sentiments of the human mind: And these sentiments are not to be controlled or altered by any philosophical theory or speculation whatsoever.

The second objection admits not of so easy and satisfactory an answer; nor is it possible to explain distinctly, how the Deity can be the mediate cause of all the actions of men, without being the author of sin and moral turpitude. These are mysteries, which mere natural and unassisted reason is very unfit to handle; and whatever system she embraces, she must find herself involved in inextricable difficulties, and even contradictions, at every step which she takes with regard to such subjects. To reconcile the indifference and contingency of human actions with prescience; or to defend absolute decrees, and yet free the Deity from being the author of sin, has been found hitherto to exceed all the power of philosophy. Happy, if she be thence sensible of her temerity, when she pries into these sublime mysteries; and leaving a scene so full of obscurities and perplexities, return, with suitable modesty, to her true and proper province, the examination of common life; where she will find difficulties enough to employ her enquiries, without launching into so boundless an ocean of doubt, uncertainty, and contradiction!

JEAN-PAUL SARTRE, "EXISTENTIALISM IS A HUMANISM," TRANSCRIPTION OF
A LECTURE DELIVERED BY SARTRE, PUBLISHED IN FRENCH IN 1946,
TRANSLATED BY BERNARD FRECHTMAN

This essay, relevant to both Chapter 5 on free will and Chapter 9 on existentialism, offers several themes common to European philosophical and literary thought in the 1940s and 1950s. Related to the free will debate, Sartre offers us a version of libertarianism that describes the individual human as making himself in the process of choosing freely at each moment. Each decision (and the sum of all decisions an individual makes, which together constitutes a single human life) is unconstrained by forces, external or internal. "Man is nothing else but what he makes of himself." But if an individual is the author of his life, he has no one or no thing to blame other than himself if his life is not what he would want it to be. This has implications for how an individual values his life, particularly for atheists such as Sartre who cannot ground value in a transcendent being.

I should like on this occasion to defend existentialism against some charges which have been brought against it.

First, it has been charged with inviting people to remain in a kind of desperate quietism because, since no solutions are possible, we should have to consider action in this world as quite impossible. We should then end up in a philosophy of contemplation; and since contemplation is a luxury, we come in the end to a bourgeois philosophy. The communists in particular have made these charges.

On the other hand, we have been charged with dwelling on human degradation, with pointing up everywhere the sordid, shady, and slimy, and neglecting the gracious and beautiful, the bright side of human nature; for example, according to Mlle. Mercier, a Catholic critic, with forgetting the smile of the child. Both sides charge us with having ignored human solidarity, with considering man as an isolated being. The communists say that the main reason for this is that we take pure subjectivity, the Cartesian I think, as our starting point; in other words, the moment in which man becomes fully aware of what it means to him to be an isolated being; as a result, we are unable to return to a state of solidarity with the men who are not ourselves, a state which we can never reach in the cogito.

From the Christian standpoint, we are charged with denying the reality and seriousness of human undertakings, since, if we reject God's commandments and the eternal verities, there no longer remains anything but pure caprice, with everyone permitted to do as he pleases and incapable, from his own point of view, of condemning the points of view and acts of others.

I shall try today to answer these different charges. Many people are going to be surprised at what is said here about humanism. We shall try to see in what sense it is to be understood. In any case, what can be said from the very beginning is that by existentialism we mean a doctrine which makes human life possible and, in addition, declares that every truth and every action implies a human setting and a human subjectivity....

[T]here are two kinds of existentialist; first, those who are Christian, ... and on the other hand the atheistic existentialists, among whom I class ... myself. What they have in common is that they think that existence precedes essence, or, if you prefer, that subjectivity must be the starting point.

Just what does that mean? Let us consider some object that is manufactured, for example, a book or a paper-cutter: here is an object which has been made by an artisan whose inspiration came from a concept. He referred to the concept of what a paper-cutter is and likewise to a known method of production, which is part of the concept, something which is, by and large, a routine. Thus, the paper-cutter is at once an object produced in a certain way and, on the other hand, one having a specific use; and one can not postulate a man who produces a paper-cutter but does not know what it is used for. Therefore, let us say that, for the papercutter, essence–that is, the ensemble of both the production routines and the properties which enable it to be both produced and defined–precedes existence. Thus, the presence of the paper-cutter or book in front of me is determined. Therefore, we have here a technical view of the world whereby it can be said that production precedes existence.

When we conceive God as the Creator, He is generally thought of as a superior sort of artisan. Whatever doctrine we may be considering, whether one like that of Descartes or that of Leibniz, we always grant that will more or less follows understanding or, at the very least, accompanies it, and that when God creates He knows exactly what He is creating. Thus, the concept of man in the mind of God is comparable to the concept of paper-cutter in the mind of the manufacturer, and, following certain techniques and a conception, God produces man, just as the artisan, following a definition and a technique, makes a paper-cutter. Thus, the individual man is the realization of a certain concept in the divine intelligence.

In the eighteenth century, the atheism of the *philosophes* discarded the idea of God, but not so much for the notion that essence precedes existence. To a certain extent, this idea is found everywhere; ... Man has a human nature; this human nature, which is the concept of the human, is found in all men, which means that each man is a particular example of a universal concept, man.... Thus, here too the essence of man precedes the historical existence that we find in nature.

Atheistic existentialism, which I represent, is more coherent. It states that if God does not exist, there is at least one being in whom existence precedes essence, a being who exists before he can be defined by any concept, and that this being is man.... What is meant here by saying that existence precedes essence? It means that, first of all, man exists, turns up, appears on the scene, and only afterwards, defines himself. If man, as the existentialist conceives him, is indefinable, it is because at first he is nothing. Only afterward will he be something, and he himself will have made what he will be. Thus, there is no human nature, since there is no God to conceive it. Not only is man what he conceives himself to be, but he is also only what he wills himself to be after this thrust toward existence.

Man is nothing else but what he makes of himself. Such is the first principle of existentialism. It is also what is called subjectivity, the name we are labeled with when charges are brought against us. But what do we mean by this, if not that man has a greater dignity than a stone or table? For we mean that man first exists, that is, that man first of all is the being who hurls himself toward a future and who is conscious of imagining himself as being in the future. Man is at the start a plan which is aware of itself, rather than a patch of moss, a piece of garbage, or a cauliflower; nothing exists prior to this plan; there is nothing in heaven; man will be what he will have planned to be. Not what he will want to be. Because by the word "will" we generally mean a conscious decision, which is subsequent to what we have already made of ourselves. I may want to belong to a political party, write a book, get married; but all that is only a manifestation of an earlier, more spontaneous choice that is called "will." But if existence really does precede essence, man is responsible for what he is. Thus, existentialism's first move is to make every man aware of what he is and to make the full responsibility of his existence rest on him. And when we say that a man is responsible for himself, we do not only mean that he is responsible for his own individuality, but that he is responsible for all men.

... Subjectivity means, on the one hand, that an individual chooses and makes himself; and, on the other, that it is impossible for man to transcend human subjectivity. The second of these is the essential meaning of existentialism. When we say that man chooses his own self, we mean that every one of us does likewise; but we also mean by that that in making this choice he also chooses all men. In fact, in creating the man that we want to be, there is not a single one of our acts which does not at the same time create an image of man as we think he ought to be. To choose to be this or that is to affirm at the same time the value of what we choose, because we can never choose evil. We always choose the good, and nothing can be good for us without being good for all.

If, on the other hand, existence precedes essence, and if we grant that we exist and fashion our image at one and the same time, the image is valued for everybody and for our whole age. Thus, our responsibility is much greater than we might have supposed, because it involves all mankind. If I am a workingman and choose to join a Christian trade-union rather than be a communist, and if by being a member I want to show that the best thing for man is resignation, that the kingdom of man is not of this world, I am not only involving my own case–I want to be resigned for everyone. As a result, my action has involved all humanity. To take a more individual matter, if I want to marry, to have children; even if this marriage depends solely on my own circumstances or passion or wish, I am involving all humanity in monogamy and not merely myself. Therefore, I am responsible for myself and for everyone else. I am creating a certain image of man of my own choosing. In choosing myself, I choose man....

[T]he man who involves himself and who realizes that he is not only the person he chooses to be, but also a lawmaker who is, at the same time, choosing all mankind as well as himself, can not help escape the feeling of his total and deep responsibility.... Certainly, many people believe that when they do something, they themselves are the only ones involved, and when someone says to them, "What if everyone acted that way?" they shrug their shoulders and answer, "Everyone doesn't act that way." But really, one should always ask himself, "What would happen if everybody looked at things that way?" There is no escaping this disturbing thought except by a kind of double-dealing. A man who lies and makes excuses for himself by saying "not everybody does that," is someone with an uneasy conscience, because the act of lying implies that a universal value is conferred upon the lie....

There was a madwoman who had hallucinations; someone used to speak to her on the telephone and give her orders. Her doctor asked her, "Who is it who talks to you?" She answered, "He says it's God." What proof did she really have that it was God? If an angel comes to me, what proof is there that it's an angel? And if I hear voices, what proof is there that they come from heaven and not from hell, or from the subconscious, or a pathological condition? What proves that they are addressed to me? What proof is there that I have been appointed to impose my choice and my conception of man on humanity? I'll never find any proof or sign to convince me of that. If a voice addresses me, it is always for me to decide that this is the angel's voice; if I consider that such an act is a good one, it is I who will choose to say that it is good rather than bad.

Now I'm not being singled out as an Abraham, and yet every moment I'm obliged to perform exemplary acts. For every man, everything happens as if all mankind had its eyes fixed on him and were guiding itself by what he does. And every man ought to say to himself, "Am I really the kind of man who has the right to act in such a way that humanity might guide itself by my actions?" ...

There is no question here of the kind of anguish which would lead to quietism, to inaction. It is a matter of a simple sort of anguish that anybody who has had responsibilities is familiar with. For example, when a military officer takes the responsibility for an attack and sends a certain number of men to death, he chooses to do so, and in the main he alone makes the choice. Doubtless, orders come from above, but they are too broad; he interprets them, and on this interpretation depend the lives of ten or fourteen or twenty men. In making a decision he can not help having a certain anguish. All leaders know this anguish. That doesn't keep them from acting; on the contrary, it is the very condition of their action. For it implies that they envisage a number of possibilities, and when they choose one, they realize that it has value only because it is chosen....

When we speak of "forlornness," ... we mean only that God does not exist and that we have to face all the consequences of this. The existentialist ... thinks it very distressing that God does not exist, because all possibility of finding values in a heaven of ideas disappears along with Him; there can no longer be an a priori Good, since there is no infinite perfect consciousness to think it. Nowhere is it written that the Good exists, that we must be honest, that we must not lie; because the fact is we are on a plane where there are only men. Dostoievsky said, "If God didn't exist, everything would be possible." That is the very starting point of existentialism. Indeed, everything is permissible if God does not exist, and as a result man is forlorn, because neither within him nor without does he find anything to cling to. He can't start making excuses for himself.

If existence really does precede essence, there is no explaining things away by reference to a fixed and given human nature. In other words, there is no determinism, man is free, man is freedom. On the other hand, if God does not exist, we find no values or commands to turn to which legitimize our conduct. So, in the bright realm of values, we have no excuse behind us, nor justification before us. We are alone, with no excuses.

That is the idea I shall try to convey when I say that man is condemned to be free. Condemned, because he did not create himself, yet, in other respects is free; because, once thrown into the world, he is responsible for everything he does. The existentialist does not believe in the power of passion. He will never agree that a sweeping passion is a ravaging torrent which fatally leads a man to certain acts and is therefore an excuse. He thinks that man is responsible for his passion....

To give you an example which will enable you to understand forlornness better, I shall cite the case of one of my students who came to see me under the following circumstances: his father was on bad terms with his mother, and, moreover, was inclined to be a collaborationist; his older brother had been killed in the German offensive of 1940, and the young man, with somewhat immature but generous feelings, wanted to avenge him. His mother lived alone with him, very much upset by the half-treason of her husband and the death of her older son; the boy was her only consolation.

The boy was faced with the choice of leaving for England and joining the Free French Forces—that is, leaving his mother behind—or remaining with his mother and helping her to carry on. He was fully aware that the woman lived only for him and that his going-off—and perhaps his death—would plunge her into despair. He was also aware that every act that he did for his mother's sake was a sure thing, in the sense that it was helping her to carry on, whereas every effort he made toward going off and fighting was an uncertain move which might run aground and prove completely useless; for example, on his way to England he might, while passing through Spain, be detained indefinitely in a Spanish camp; he might reach England or Algiers and be stuck in an office at a desk job. As a result, he was faced with two very different kinds of action: one, concrete, immediate, but concerning only one individual; the other concerned an incomparably vaster group, a national collectivity, but for that very reason was dubious, and might be interrupted en route. And, at the same time, he was wavering between two kinds of ethics. On the one hand, an ethics of sympathy, of personal devotion; on the other, a broader ethics, but one whose efficacy was more dubious. He had to choose between the two.

Who could help him choose? Christian doctrine? No. Christian doctrine says, "Be charitable, love your neighbor, take the more rugged path, etc., etc." But which is the more rugged path? Whom should he love as a brother? The fighting man or his mother? Which does the greater good, the vague act of fighting in a group, or the concrete one of helping a particular human being to go on living? Who can decide a priori? Nobody. No book of ethics can tell him. The Kantian ethics says, "Never treat any person as a means, but as an end." Very well, if I stay with my mother, I'll treat her as an end and not as a means; but by virtue of this very fact, I'm running the risk of treating the people around me who are fighting, as means; and, conversely, if I go to join those who are fighting, I'll be treating them as an end, and by doing that, I run the risk of treating my mother as a means.

If values are vague, and if they are always too broad for the concrete and specific case that we are considering, the only thing left for us is to trust our instincts. That's what this young man tried to do; and when I saw him, he said, "In the end, feeling is what counts. I ought to choose whichever pushes me in one direction. If I feel that I love my mother enough to sacrifice everything else for her—my desire for vengeance, for action, for adventure—then I'll stay with her. If, on the contrary, I feel that my love for my mother isn't enough, I'll leave."

But how is the value of a feeling determined? What gives his feeling for his mother value? Precisely the fact that he remained with her. I may say that I like so-and-so well enough to sacrifice a certain amount of money for him, but I may say so only if I've done it. I may say "I love my mother well enough to remain with her" if I have remained with her. The only way to determine the value of this affection is, precisely, to perform an act which confirms and defines it. But, since I require this affection to justify my act, I find myself caught in a vicious circle....

[I]n coming to see me he knew the answer I was going to give him, and I had only one answer to give: "You're free, choose, that is, invent." No general ethics can show you what is to be done; there are no omens in the world. The Catholics will reply, "But there are." Granted—but, in any case, I myself choose the meaning they have.

When I was a prisoner, I knew a rather remarkable young man who was a Jesuit. He had entered the Jesuit order in the following way: he had had a number of very bad breaks; in childhood, his father died, leaving him in poverty, and he was a scholarship student at a religious institution where he was constantly made to feel that he was being kept out of charity; then, he failed to get any of the honors and distinctions that children like; later on, at about eighteen, he bungled a love affair; finally, at twenty-two, he failed in military training, a childish enough matter, but it was the last straw.

The young fellow might well have felt that he had botched everything. It was a sign of something, but of what? He might have taken refuge in bitterness or despair. But he very wisely looked upon all this as a sign that he was not made for secular triumphs, and that only the triumphs of religion, holiness, and faith were open to him. He saw the hand of God in all this, and so he entered the order. Who can help seeing that he alone decided what the sign meant?

Some other interpretation might have been drawn from this series of setbacks; for example, that he might have done better to turn carpenter or revolutionist. Therefore, he is fully responsible for the interpretation....

Actually, things will be as man will have decided they are to be....

According to this, we can understand why our doctrine horrifies certain people. Because often the only way they can bear their wretchedness is to think, "Circumstances have been against me. What I've been and done doesn't show my true worth. To be sure, I've had no great love, no great friendship, but that's because I haven't met a man or woman who was worthy. The books I've written haven't been very good because I haven't had the proper leisure. I haven't had children to devote myself to because I didn't find a man with whom I could have spent my life. So there remains within me, unused and quite viable, a host of propensities, inclinations, possibilities, that one wouldn't guess from the mere series of things I've done."

Now, for the existentialist there is really no love other than one which manifests itself in a person's being in love. There is no genius other than one which is expressed in works of art; the genius of Proust is the sum of Proust's works; the genius of Racine is his series of tragedies. Outside of that, there is nothing. Why say that Racine could have written another tragedy, when he didn't write it? A man is involved in life, leaves his impress on it, and outside of that there is nothing, To be sure, this may seem a harsh thought to someone whose life hasn't been a success. But, on the other hand, it prompts people to understand that reality alone is what counts, that dreams, expectations, and hopes warrant no more than to define a man as a disappointed dream, as miscarried hopes, as vain expectations. In other words, to define him negatively and not positively. However, when we say, "You are nothing else than your life," that does not imply that the artist will be judged solely on the basis of his works of art; a thousand other things will contribute toward summing him up. What we mean is that a man is nothing else than a series of undertakings, that he is the sum, the organization, the ensemble of the relationships which make up these undertakings.

When all is said and done, what we are accused of, at bottom, is not our pessimism, but an optimistic toughness. If people throw up to us our works of fiction in which we write about people who are soft, weak, cowardly, or bad; because if we were to say, as Zola did, that they are that way because of heredity, the workings of environment, society, because of biological or psychological determinism, people would be reassured. They would say, "Well, that's what we're like, no one can do anything about it." But when the existentialist writes about a coward, he says that this coward is responsible for his cowardice. He's not like that because he has a cowardly heart or lung or brain; he's not like that on account of his physiological make-up; but he's like that because he has made himself a coward by his acts. There's no such thing as a cowardly constitution; there are nervous constitutions; there is poor blood, as the common people say, or strong constitutions. But the man whose blood is poor is not a coward on that account, for what makes cowardice is the act of renouncing or yielding. A constitution is not an act; the coward is defined on the basis of the acts he performs. People feel, in a vague sort of way, that this coward we're talking about is guilty of being a coward, and the thought frightens them. What people would like is that a coward or a hero be born that way....

If you're born cowardly, you may set your mind perfectly at rest; there's nothing you can do about it; you'll be cowardly all your life, whatever you may do. If you're born a hero, you may set your mind just as much at rest; you'll be a hero all your life; you'll drink like a hero and eat like a hero. What the existentialist says is that the coward makes himself cowardly, that the hero makes himself heroic. There's always a possibility for the coward not to be cowardly any more and for the hero to stop being heroic.

IMMANUEL KANT (1724–1804), *FUNDAMENTAL PRINCIPLES OF THE METAPHYSICS OF MORALS*, PUBLISHED IN GERMAN IN 1785, TRANSLATED BY THOMAS KINGSMILL ABBOTT

In this central passage from *Fundamental Principles of the Metaphysics of Morals*, Kant argues that the only thing that is good without qualification is "the good will"; that is, a will directed to acting in accordance with duty, which is to "[a]ct only on that maxim whereby [one can] will that it should become a universal law." His general ethical theory follows from the singular, unqualified goodness of the good will. Kant then offers several examples of action-types and considers whether the maxim exemplified in each case is something that can be universalized. From these considerations, he derives the distinction between strict and meritorious duties.

Nothing can possibly be conceived in the world, or even out of it, which can be called good, without qualification, except a good will. Intelligence, wit, judgement, and the other talents of the mind, however they may be named, or courage, resolution, perseverance, as qualities of temperament, are undoubtedly good and desirable in many respects; but these gifts of nature may also become extremely bad and mischievous if the will which is to make use of them, and which, therefore, constitutes what is called character, is not good. It is the same with the gifts of fortune. Power, riches, honour, even health, and the general well-being and contentment with one's condition which is called happiness, inspire pride, and often presumption, if there is not a good will to correct the influence of these on the mind, and with this also to rectify the whole principle of acting and adapt it to its end. The sight of a being who is not adorned with a single feature of a pure and good will, enjoying unbroken prosperity, can never give pleasure to an impartial rational spectator. Thus a good will appears to constitute the indispensable condition even of being worthy of happiness.

There are even some qualities which are of service to this good will itself and may facilitate its action, yet which have no intrinsic unconditional value, but always presuppose a good will, and this qualifies the esteem that we justly have for them and does not permit us to regard them as absolutely good. Moderation in the affections and passions, selfcontrol, and calm deliberation are not only good in many respects, but even seem to constitute part of the intrinsic worth of the person; but they are far from deserving to be called good without qualification, although they have been so unconditionally praised by the ancients. For without the principles of a good will, they may become extremely bad, and the coolness of a villain not only makes him far more dangerous, but also directly makes him more abominable in our eyes than he would have been without it.

A good will is good not because of what it performs or effects, not by its aptness for the attainment of some proposed end, but simply by virtue of the volition; that is, it is good in itself, and considered by itself is to be esteemed much higher than all that can be brought about by it in favour of any inclination, nay even of the sum total of all inclinations. Even if it should happen that, owing to special disfavour of fortune, or the niggardly provision of a step-motherly nature, this will should wholly lack power to accomplish its purpose, if with its greatest efforts it should yet achieve nothing, and there should remain only the good will (not, to be sure, a mere wish, but the summoning of all means in our power), then, like a jewel, it would still shine by its own light, as a thing which has its whole value in itself. Its usefulness or fruitfulness can neither add nor take away anything from this value. It would be, as it were, only the setting to enable us to handle it the more conveniently in common commerce, or to attract to it the attention of those who are not yet connoisseurs, but not to recommend it to true connoisseurs, or to determine its value.

…

That an action done from duty derives its moral worth, not from the purpose which is to be attained by it, but from the maxim by which it is determined, and therefore does not depend on the realization of the object of the action, but merely on the principle of volition by which the action has taken place, without regard to any object of desire. It is clear from what precedes that the purposes which we may have in view in our actions, or their effects regarded as ends and springs of the will, cannot give to actions any unconditional or moral worth. In what, then, can their worth lie, if it is not to consist in the will and in reference to its expected effect? It cannot lie anywhere but in the principle of the will without regard to the ends which can be attained by the action. For the will stands between its a priori principle, which is formal, and its a posteriori spring, which is material, as between two roads, and as it must be determined by something, it follows that it must be determined by the formal principle of volition when an action is done from duty, in which case every material principle has been withdrawn from it.

… I would express … Duty is the necessity of acting from respect for the law. I may have inclination for an object as the effect of my proposed action, but I cannot have respect for it, just for this reason, that it is an effect and not an energy of will. Similarly I cannot have respect for inclination, whether my own or another's; I can at most, if my own, approve it; if another's, sometimes even love it; i.e., look on it as favourable to my own interest. It is only what is connected with my will as a principle, by no means as an effect–what does not subserve my inclination, but over-powers it, or at least in case of choice excludes it from its calculation–in other words, simply the law of itself, which can be an object of respect, and hence a command. Now an action done from duty must wholly exclude the influence of inclination and with it every object of the will, so that nothing remains which can determine the will except objectively the law, and subjectively pure respect for this practical law, and conse-quently the maxim that I should follow this law even to the thwarting of all my inclinations.

Thus the moral worth of an action does not lie in the effect expected from it, nor in any principle of action which requires to borrow its motive from this expected effect. For all these effects–agreeableness of one's condition and even the promotion of the happiness of others–could have been also brought about by other causes, so that for this there would have been no need of the will of a rational being; whereas it is in this alone that the supreme and unconditional good can be found. The pre-eminent good which we call moral can therefore consist in nothing else than the conception of law in itself, which certainly is only possible in a rational being, in so far as this conception, and not the expected effect, determines the will. This is a good which is already present in the person who acts accordingly, and we have not to wait for it to appear first in the result.

But what sort of law can that be, the conception of which must deter-mine the will, even without paying any regard to the effect expected from it, in order that this will may be called good absolutely and without quali-fication? As I have deprived the will of every impulse which could arise to it from obedience to any law, there remains nothing but the universal conformity of its actions to law in general, which alone is to serve the will as a principle, i.e., I am never to act otherwise than so that I could also will that my maxim should become a universal law. Here, now, it is the simple conformity to law in general, without assuming any particular law applica-ble to certain actions, that serves the will as its principle and must so serve it, if duty is not to be a vain delusion and a chimerical notion. The common reason of men in its practical judgements perfectly coincides with this and always has in view the principle here suggested.

...

In this problem we will first inquire whether the mere conception of a categorical imperative may not perhaps supply us also with the formula of it, containing the proposition which alone can be a categorical imperative; for even if we know the tenor of such an absolute command, yet how it is possible will require further special and laborious study, which we post-pone to the last section.

When I conceive a hypothetical imperative, in general I do not know beforehand what it will contain until I am given the condition. But when I conceive a categorical imperative, I know at once what it contains. For as the imperative contains besides the law only the necessity that the maxims shall conform to this law, while the law contains no conditions restricting it, there remains nothing but the general statement that the maxim of the action should conform to a universal law, and it is this conformity alone that the imperative properly represents as necessary.

There is therefore but one categorical imperative, namely, this: Act only on that maxim whereby thou canst at the same time will that it should become a universal law.

Now if all imperatives of duty can be deduced from this one imperative as from their principle, then, although it should remain undecided what is called duty is not merely a vain notion, yet at least we shall be able to show what we understand by it and what this notion means.

Since the universality of the law according to which effects are produced constitutes what is properly called nature in the most general sense (as to form), that is the existence of things so far as it is determined by general laws, the imperative of duty may be expressed thus: Act as if the maxim of thy action were to become by thy will a universal law of nature.

We will now enumerate a few duties, adopting the usual division of them into duties to ourselves and to others, and into perfect and imperfect duties.

1. A man reduced to despair by a series of misfortunes feels wearied of life, but is still so far in possession of his reason that he can ask himself whether it would not be contrary to his duty to himself to take his own life. Now he inquires whether the maxim of his action could become a universal law of nature. His maxim is: "From self-love I adopt it as a principle to shorten my life when its longer duration is likely to bring more evil than satisfaction." It is asked then simply whether this principle founded on self-love can become a universal law of nature. Now we see at once that a system of nature of which it should be a law to destroy life by means of the very feeling whose special nature it is to impel to the improvement of life would contradict itself and, therefore, could not exist as a system of nature; hence that maxim cannot possibly exist as a universal law of nature and, consequently, would be wholly inconsistent with the supreme principle of all duty.

2. Another finds himself forced by necessity to borrow money. He knows that he will not be able to repay it, but sees also that nothing will be lent to him unless he promises stoutly to repay it in a definite time. He desires to make this promise, but he has still so much conscience as to ask himself: "Is it not unlawful and inconsistent with duty to get out of a difficulty in this way?" Suppose however that he resolves to do so: then the maxim of his action would be expressed thus: "When I think myself in

want of money, I will borrow money and promise to repay it, although I know that I never can do so." Now this principle of self-love or of one's own advantage may perhaps be consistent with my whole future welfare; but the question now is, "Is it right?" I change then the suggestion of self-love into a universal law, and state the question thus: "How would it be if my maxim were a universal law?" Then I see at once that it could never hold as a universal law of nature, but would necessarily contradict itself. For supposing it to be a universal law that everyone when he thinks himself in a difficulty should be able to promise whatever he pleases, with the purpose of not keeping his promise, the promise itself would become impossible, as well as the end that one might have in view in it, since no one would consider that anything was promised to him, but would ridicule all such statements as vain pretences.

3. A third finds in himself a talent which with the help of some culture might make him a useful man in many respects. But he finds himself in comfortable circumstances and prefers to indulge in pleasure rather than to take pains in enlarging and improving his happy natural capacities. He asks, however, whether his maxim of neglect of his natural gifts, besides agreeing with his inclination to indulgence, agrees also with what is called duty. He sees then that a system of nature could indeed subsist with such a universal law although men (like the South Sea islanders) should let their talents rest and resolve to devote their lives merely to idleness, amusement, and propagation of their species—in a word, to enjoyment; but he cannot possibly will that this should be a universal law of nature, or be implanted in us as such by a natural instinct. For, as a rational being, he necessarily wills that his faculties be developed, since they serve him and have been given him, for all sorts of possible purposes.

4. A fourth, who is in prosperity, while he sees that others have to contend with great wretchedness and that he could help them, thinks: "What concern is it of mine? Let everyone be as happy as Heaven pleases, or as he can make himself; I will take nothing from him nor even envy him, only I do not wish to contribute anything to his welfare or to his assistance in distress!" Now no doubt if such a mode of thinking were a universal law, the human race might very well subsist and doubtless even better than in a state in which everyone talks of sympathy and good-will, or even takes care occasionally to put it into practice, but, on the other side, also cheats when he can, betrays the rights of men, or otherwise violates them. But although it is possible that a universal law of nature might exist in accordance with that maxim, it is impossible to will that such a principle should have the universal validity of a law of nature. For a will which resolved this would contradict itself, inasmuch as many cases might occur in which one would have need of the love and sympathy of others, and in which, by such a law of nature, sprung from his own will, he would deprive himself of all hope of the aid he desires.

These are a few of the many actual duties, or at least what we regard as such, which obviously fall into two classes on the one principle that we have laid down. We must be able to will that a maxim of our action should be a universal law. This is the canon of the moral appreciation of the action generally. Some actions are of such a character that their maxim cannot without contradiction be even conceived as a universal law of nature, far from it being possible that we should will that it should be so. In others this intrinsic impossibility is not found, but still it is impossible to will that their maxim should be raised to the universality of a law of nature, since such a will would contradict itself. It is easily seen that the former violate strict or rigorous (inflexible) duty; the latter only laxer (meritorious) duty. Thus it has been completely shown how all duties depend as regards the nature of the obligation (not the object of the action) on the same principle.

...

[E]very empirical element is not only quite incapable of being an aid to the principle of morality, but is even highly prejudicial to the purity of morals, for the proper and inestimable worth of an absolutely good will consists just in this, that the principle of action is free from all influence of contingent grounds, which alone experience can furnish.

...

The will is conceived as a faculty of determining oneself to action in accordance with the conception of certain laws. And such a faculty can be found only in rational beings. Now that which serves the will as the objective ground of its self-determination is the end, and, if this is assigned by reason alone, it must hold for all rational beings. On the other hand, that which merely contains the ground of possibility of the action of which the effect is the end, this is called the means. The subjective ground of the desire is the spring, the objective ground of the volition is the motive; hence the distinction between subjective ends which rest on springs, and objective ends which depend on motives valid for every rational being. Practical principles are formal when they abstract from all subjective ends; they are material when they assume these, and therefore particular springs of action. The ends which a rational being proposes to himself at pleasure as effects of his actions (material ends) are all only relative, for it is only their relation to the particular desires of the subject that gives them their worth, which therefore cannot furnish principles universal and necessary for all rational beings and for every volition, that is to say practical laws. Hence all these relative ends can give rise only to hypothetical imperatives.

Supposing, however, that there were something whose existence has in itself an absolute worth, something which, being an end in itself, could be a source of definite laws; then in this and this alone would lie the source of a possible categorical imperative, i.e., a practical law.

Now I say: man and generally any rational being exists as an end in himself, not merely as a means to be arbitrarily used by this or that will, but in all his actions, whether they concern himself or other rational beings, must be always regarded at the same time as an end. All objects of the inclinations have only a conditional worth, for if the inclinations and the wants founded on them did not exist, then their object would be without value. But the inclinations, themselves being sources of want, are so far from having an absolute worth for which they should be desired that on the contrary it must be the universal wish of every rational being to be wholly free from them. Thus the worth of any object which is to be acquired by our action is always conditional. Beings whose existence depends not on our will but on nature's, have nevertheless, if they are irrational beings, only a relative value as means, and are therefore called things; rational beings, on the contrary, are called persons, because their very nature points them out as ends in themselves, that is as something which must not be used merely as means, and so far therefore restricts freedom of action (and is an object of respect). These, therefore, are not merely subjective ends whose existence has a worth for us as an effect of our action, but objective ends, that is, things whose existence is an end in itself; an end moreover for which no other can be substituted, which they should subserve merely as means, for otherwise nothing whatever would possess absolute worth; but if all worth were conditioned and therefore contingent, then there would be no supreme practical principle of reason whatever.

If then there is a supreme practical principle or, in respect of the human will, a categorical imperative, it must be one which, being drawn from the conception of that which is necessarily an end for everyone because it is an end in itself, constitutes an objective principle of will, and can therefore serve as a universal practical law. The foundation of this principle is: rational nature exists as an end in itself. Man necessarily conceives his own existence as being so; so far then this is a subjective principle of human actions. But every other rational being regards its existence similarly, just on the same rational principle that holds for me: so that it is at the same time an objective principle, from which as a supreme practical law all laws of the will must be capable of being deduced. Accordingly the practical imperative will be as follows: So act as to treat humanity, whether in thine own person or in that of any other, in every case as an end withal, never as means only.

JOHN STUART MILL (1806-1873), *UTILITARIANISM,* 1861 (AS SERIAL), 1863 (AS BOOK)

In this passage, Mill lays out the founding principles behind his general ethical theory, utilitarianism. First among these is what he takes to be a basic psychological fact: "that pleasure, and freedom from pain, are the only things desirable as ends." The ethical theory he erects on top of this basic fact judges the moral worth of an action solely in terms of the consequences (in particular, the amount of happiness) generated by that action. Mill moves on to consider several objections to both this founding principle and utilitarianism more generally.

Chapter 2–What Utilitarianism Is

...

The creed which accepts as the foundation of morals, Utility, or the Greatest Happiness Principle, holds that actions are right in proportion as they tend to promote happiness, wrong as they tend to produce the reverse of happiness. By happiness is intended pleasure, and the absence of pain; by unhappiness, pain, and the privation of pleasure. To give a clear view of the moral standard set up by the theory, much more requires to be said; in particular, what things it includes in the ideas of pain and pleasure; and to what extent this is left an open question. But these supplementary explanations do not affect the theory of life on which this theory of morality is grounded–namely, that pleasure, and freedom from pain, are the only things desirable as ends; and that all desirable things (which are as numerous in the utilitarian as in any other scheme) are desirable either for the pleasure inherent in themselves, or as means to the promotion of pleasure and the prevention of pain.

Now, such a theory of life excites in many minds, and among them in some of the most estimable in feeling and purpose, inveterate dislike. To suppose that life has (as they express it) no higher end than pleasure– no better and nobler object of desire and pursuit they designate as utterly mean and grovelling; as a doctrine worthy only of swine, to whom the followers of Epicurus were, at a very early period, contemptuously likened; and modern holders of the doctrine are occasionally made the subject of equally polite comparisons by its German, French, and English assailants.

When thus attacked, the Epicureans have always answered, that it is not they, but their accusers, who represent human nature in a degrading light; since the accusation supposes human beings to be capable of no pleasures except those of which swine are capable. If this supposition were true, the charge could not be gainsaid, but would then be no longer an imputation; for if the sources of pleasure were precisely the same to human beings and to swine, the rule of life which is good enough for the one would be good enough for the other. The comparison of the Epicurean life to that of beasts is felt as degrading, precisely because a beast's pleasures do not satisfy a human being's conceptions of happiness. Human beings have faculties more elevated than the animal appetites, and when once made conscious of them, do not regard anything as happiness which does not include their gratification. I do not, indeed, consider the Epicureans to have been by any means faultless in drawing out their scheme of consequences from the utilitarian principle. To do this in any sufficient manner, many Stoic, as well as Christian elements require to be included. But there is no known Epicurean theory of life which does not assign to the pleasures of the intellect, of the feelings and imagination, and of the moral sentiments, a much higher value as pleasures than to those of mere sensation. It must be admitted, however, that utilitarian writers in general have placed the superiority of mental over bodily pleasures chiefly in the greater permanency, safety, uncostliness, etc., of the former—that is, in their circumstantial advantages rather than in their intrinsic nature. And on all these points utilitarians have fully proved their case; but they might have taken the other, and, as it may be called, higher ground, with entire consistency. It is quite compatible with the principle of utility to recognise the fact, that some kinds of pleasure are more desirable and more valuable than others. It would be absurd that while, in estimating all other things, quality is considered as well as quantity, the estimation of pleasures should be supposed to depend on quantity alone.

If I am asked, what I mean by difference of quality in pleasures, or what makes one pleasure more valuable than another, merely as a pleasure, except its being greater in amount, there is but one possible answer. Of two pleasures, if there be one to which all or almost all who have experience of both give a decided preference, irrespective of any feeling of moral obligation to prefer it, that is the more desirable pleasure. If one of the two is, by those who are competently acquainted with both, placed so far above the other that they prefer it, even though knowing it to be attended with a greater amount of discontent, and would not resign it for any quantity of the other pleasure which their nature is capable of, we are justified in ascribing to the preferred enjoyment a superiority in quality, so far outweighing quantity as to render it, in comparison, of small account.

Now it is an unquestionable fact that those who are equally acquainted with, and equally capable of appreciating and enjoying both, do give a most marked preference to the manner of existence which employs their higher faculties. Few human creatures would consent to be changed into any of the lower animals, for a promise of the fullest allowance of a beast's pleasures; no intelligent human being would consent to be a fool, no instructed person would be an ignoramus, no person of feeling and conscience would be selfish and base, even though they should be persuaded that the fool, the dunce, or the rascal is better satisfied with his lot than they are with theirs. They would not resign what they possess more than he for the most complete satisfaction of all the desires which they have in common with him. If they ever fancy they would, it is only in cases of unhappiness so extreme, that to escape from it they would exchange their lot for almost any other, however undesirable in their own eyes. A being of higher faculties requires more to make him happy, is capable probably of more acute suffering, and certainly accessible to it at more points, than one of an inferior type; but in spite of these liabilities, he can never really wish to sink into what he feels to be a lower grade of existence. We may give what explanation we please of this unwillingness; we may attribute it to pride, a name which is given indiscriminately to some of the most and to some of the least estimable feelings of which mankind are capable: we may refer it to the love of liberty and personal independence, an appeal to which was with the Stoics one of the most effective means for the inculcation of it; to the love of power, or to the love of excitement, both of which do really enter into and contribute to it: but its most appropriate appellation is a sense of dignity, which all human beings possess in one form or other, and in some, though by no means in exact, proportion to their higher faculties, and which is so essential a part of the happiness of those in whom it is strong, that nothing which conflicts with it could be, otherwise than momentarily, an object of desire to them.

Whoever supposes that this preference takes place at a sacrifice of happiness–that the superior being, in anything like equal circumstances, is not happier than the inferior–confounds the two very different ideas, of happiness, and content. It is indisputable that the being whose capacities of enjoyment are low, has the greatest chance of having them fully satisfied; and a highly endowed being will always feel that any happiness which he can look for, as the world is constituted, is imperfect. But he can learn to bear its imperfections, if they are at all bearable; and they will not make him envy the being who is indeed unconscious of the imperfections, but only because he feels not at all the good which those imperfections qualify. It is better to be a human being dissatisfied than a pig satisfied; better to be Socrates dissatisfied than a fool satisfied. And if the fool, or the pig, are of a different opinion, it is because they only know their own side of the question. The other party to the comparison knows both sides.

It may be objected, that many who are capable of the higher pleasures, occasionally, under the influence of temptation, postpone them to the lower. But this is quite compatible with a full appreciation of the intrinsic superiority of the higher. Men often, from infirmity of character, make their election for the nearer good, though they know it to be the less valuable; and this no less when the choice is between two bodily pleasures, than when it is between bodily and mental. They pursue sensual indulgences to the injury of health, though perfectly aware that health is the greater good.

It may be further objected, that many who begin with youthful enthusiasm for everything noble, as they advance in years sink into indolence and selfishness. But I do not believe that those who undergo this very common change, voluntarily choose the lower description of pleasures in preference to the higher. I believe that before they devote themselves exclusively to the one, they have already become incapable of the other. Capacity for the nobler feelings is in most natures a very tender plant, easily killed, not only by hostile influences, but by mere want of sustenance; and in the majority of young persons it speedily dies away if the occupations to which their position in life has devoted them, and the society into which it has thrown them, are not favourable to keeping that higher capacity in exercise. Men lose their high aspirations as they lose their intellectual tastes, because they have not time or opportunity for indulging them; and they addict themselves to inferior pleasures, not because they deliberately prefer them, but because they are either the only ones to which they have access, or the only ones which they are any longer capable of enjoying. It may be questioned whether any one who has remained equally susceptible to both classes of pleasures, ever knowingly and calmly preferred the lower; though many, in all ages, have broken down in an ineffectual attempt to combine both.

From this verdict of the only competent judges, I apprehend there can be no appeal. On a question which is the best worth having of two pleasures, or which of two modes of existence is the most grateful to the feelings, apart from its moral attributes and from its consequences, the judgment of those who are qualified by knowledge of both, or, if they differ, that of the majority among them, must be admitted as final. And there needs be the less hesitation to accept this judgment respecting the quality of pleasures, since there is no other tribunal to be referred to even on the question of quantity. What means are there of determining which is the acutest of two pains, or the intensest of two pleasurable sensations, except the general suffrage of those who are familiar with both? Neither pains nor pleasures are homogeneous, and pain is always heterogeneous with pleasure. What is there to decide whether a particular pleasure is worth purchasing at the cost of a particular pain, except the feelings and judgment of the experienced? When, therefore, those feelings and judgment declare the pleasures derived from the higher faculties to be preferable in kind, apart from the question of intensity, to those of which the animal nature, disjoined from the higher faculties, is suspectible, they are entitled on this subject to the same regard.

I have dwelt on this point, as being a necessary part of a perfectly just conception of Utility or Happiness, considered as the directive rule of human conduct. But it is by no means an indispensable condition to the acceptance of the utilitarian standard; for that standard is not the agent's own greatest happiness, but the greatest amount of happiness altogether; and if it may possibly be doubted whether a noble character is always the happier for its nobleness, there can be no doubt that it makes other people happier, and that the world in general is immensely a gainer by it. Utilitarianism, therefore, could only attain its end by the general cultivation of nobleness of character, even if each individual were only benefited by the nobleness of others, and his own, so far as happiness is concerned, were a sheer deduction from the benefit. But the bare enunciation of such an absurdity as this last, renders refutation superfluous.

According to the Greatest Happiness Principle, as above explained, the ultimate end, with reference to and for the sake of which all other things are desirable (whether we are considering our own good or that of other people), is an existence exempt as far as possible from pain, and as rich as possible in enjoyments, both in point of quantity and quality; the test of quality, and the rule for measuring it against quantity, being the preference felt by those who in their opportunities of experience, to which must be added their habits of self-consciousness and self-observation, are best furnished with the means of comparison. This, being, according to the utilitarian opinion, the end of human action, is necessarily also the standard of morality; which may accordingly be defined, the rules and precepts for human conduct, by the observance of which an existence such as has been described might be, to the greatest extent possible, secured to all mankind; and not to them only, but, so far as the nature of things admits, to the whole sentient creation.

THOMAS HOBBES (1588–1679), *LEVIATHAN,* 1651

Hobbes describes the life of a group of humans without a state to enforce peace among its members as one of "continual fear, and danger of violent death; and the life of man, solitary, poor, nasty, brutish, and short." This dismal view of life in the state of nature follows from Hobbes's theory of human nature. For Hobbes, humans are basically equal in power, or, at least close enough to equal that a small band of individuals could overpower a single individual in the state of nature. Humans' sole motivation is self-interest, which they pursue both in the short term and the long term. The result is not only immediate conflicts over limited resources, but also perpetual fear that others may come and take what one has accumulated at some time in the future. While thoroughly self-interested, humans are also rational and are able to recognize that it is to their advantage (both individually and collectively) to give up a portion of their individual freedom and submit to some one person or assembly of people, so long as everyone else does likewise.

Chapter XIII–Of the Natural Condition of Mankind as Concerning Their Felicity and Misery

Nature hath made men so equal in the faculties of body and mind as that, though there be found one man sometimes manifestly stronger in body or of quicker mind than another, yet when all is reckoned together the difference between man and man is not so considerable as that one man can thereupon claim to himself any benefit to which another may not pretend as well as he. For as to the strength of body, the weakest has strength enough to kill the strongest, either by secret machination or by confederacy with others that are in the same danger with himself.

And as to the faculties of the mind, setting aside the arts grounded upon words, and especially that skill of proceeding upon general and infallible rules, called science, which very few have and but in few things, as being not a native faculty born with us, nor attained, as prudence, while we look after somewhat else, I find yet a greater equality amongst men than that of strength....

From this equality of ability ariseth equality of hope in the attaining of our ends. And therefore if any two men desire the same thing, which nevertheless they cannot both enjoy, they become enemies; and in the way to their end (which is principally their own conservation, and sometimes their delectation only) endeavour to destroy or subdue one another.

And from hence it comes to pass that where an invader hath no more to fear than another man's single power, if one plant, sow, build, or possess a convenient seat, others may probably be expected to come prepared with forces united to dispossess and deprive him, not only of the fruit of his labour, but also of his life or liberty. And the invader again is in the like danger of another.

And from this diffidence of one another, there is no way for any man to secure himself so reasonable as anticipation; that is, by force, or wiles, to master the persons of all men he can so long till he see no other power great enough to endanger him: and this is no more than his own conservation requireth, and is generally allowed. Also, because there be some that, taking pleasure in contemplating their own power in the acts of conquest, which they pursue farther than their security requires, if others, that otherwise would be glad to be at ease within modest bounds, should not by invasion increase their power, they would not be able, long time, by standing only on their defence, to subsist. And by consequence, such augmentation of dominion over men being necessary to a man's conservation, it ought to be allowed him.

Again, men have no pleasure (but on the contrary a great deal of grief) in keeping company where there is no power able to overawe them all. For every man looketh that his companion should value him at the same rate he sets upon himself, and upon all signs of contempt or undervaluing naturally endeavours, as far as he dares … to extort a greater value from his contemners, by damage; and from others, by the example.

So that in the nature of man, we find three principal causes of quarrel. First, competition; secondly, diffidence; thirdly, glory.

The first maketh men invade for gain; the second, for safety; and the third, for reputation. The first use violence, to make themselves masters of other men's persons, wives, children, and cattle; the second, to defend them; the third, for trifles, as a word, a smile, a different opinion, and any other sign of undervalue, either direct in their persons or by reflection in their kindred, their friends, their nation, their profession, or their name.

Hereby it is manifest that during the time men live without a common power to keep them all in awe, they are in that condition which is called war; and such a war as is of every man against every man. For war consisteth not in battle only, or the act of fighting, but in a tract of time, wherein the will to contend by battle is sufficiently known: and therefore the notion of time is to be considered in the nature of war, as it is in the nature of weather. For as the nature of foul weather lieth not in a shower or two of rain, but in an inclination thereto of many days together: so the nature of war consisteth not in actual fighting, but in the known disposition thereto during all the time there is no assurance to the contrary. All other time is peace.

Whatsoever therefore is consequent to a time of war, where every man is enemy to every man, the same consequent to the time wherein men live without other security than what their own strength and their own invention shall furnish them withal. In such condition there is no place for industry, because the fruit thereof is uncertain: and consequently no culture of the earth; no navigation, nor use of the commodities that may be imported by sea; no commodious building; no instruments of moving and removing such things as require much force; no knowledge of the face of the earth; no account of time; no arts; no letters; no society; and which is worst of all, continual fear, and danger of violent death; and the life of man, solitary, poor, nasty, brutish, and short.

...

To this war of every man against every man, this also is consequent; that nothing can be unjust. The notions of right and wrong, justice and injustice, have there no place. Where there is no common power, there is no law; where no law, no injustice. Force and fraud are in war the two cardinal virtues. Justice and injustice are none of the faculties neither of the body nor mind. If they were, they might be in a man that were alone in the world, as well as his senses and passions. They are qualities that relate to men in society, not in solitude. It is consequent also to the same condition that there be no propriety, no dominion, no mine and thine distinct; but only that to be every man's that he can get, and for so long as he can keep it. And thus much for the ill condition which man by mere nature is actually placed in; though with a possibility to come out of it, consisting partly in the passions, partly in his reason.

The passions that incline men to peace are: fear of death; desire of such things as are necessary to commodious living; and a hope by their industry to obtain them. And reason suggesteth convenient articles of peace upon which men may be drawn to agreement. These articles are they which otherwise are called the laws of nature.

Chapter XIV – Of the First and Second Natural Laws, and of Contracts

The right of nature, which writers commonly call jus naturale, is the liberty each man hath to use his own power as he will himself for the preservation of his own nature; that is to say, of his own life; and consequently, of doing anything which, in his own judgement and reason, he shall conceive to be the aptest means thereunto.

By liberty is understood, according to the proper signification of the word, the absence of external impediments; which impediments may oft take away part of a man's power to do what he would, but cannot hinder him from using the power left him according as his judgement and reason shall dictate to him.

A law of nature, lex naturalis, is a precept, or general rule, found out by reason, by which a man is forbidden to do that which is destructive of his life, or taketh away the means of preserving the same, and to omit that by which he thinketh it may be best preserved. For though they that speak of this subject use to confound jus and lex, right and law, yet they ought to be distinguished, because right consisteth in liberty to do, or to forbear; whereas law determineth and bindeth to one of them: so that law and right differ as much as obligation and liberty, which in one and the same matter are inconsistent.

And because the condition of man ... is a condition of war of every one against every one, in which case every one is governed by his own reason, and there is nothing he can make use of that may not be a help unto him in preserving his life against his enemies; it followeth that in such a condition every man has a right to every thing, even to one another's body. And therefore, as long as this natural right of every man to every thing endureth, there can be no security to any man, how strong or wise soever he be, of living out the time which nature ordinarily alloweth men to live. And consequently it is a precept, or general rule of reason: that every man ought to endeavour peace, as far as he has hope of obtaining it; and when he cannot obtain it, that he may seek and use all helps and advantages of war. The first branch of which rule containeth the first and fundamental law of nature, which is: to seek peace and follow it. The second, the sum of the right of nature, which is: by all means we can to defend ourselves.

From this fundamental law of nature, by which men are commanded to endeavour peace, is derived this second law: that a man be willing, when others are so too, as far forth as for peace and defence of himself he shall think it necessary, to lay down this right to all things; and be contented with so much liberty against other men as he would allow other men against himself. For as long as every man holdeth this right, of doing anything he liketh; so long are all men in the condition of war. But if other men will not lay down their right, as well as he, then there is no reason for anyone to divest himself of his: for that were to expose himself to prey, which no man is bound to, rather than to dispose himself to peace. This is that law of the gospel: Whatsoever you require that others should do to you, that do ye to them.

...

If a covenant be made wherein neither of the parties perform presently, but trust one another, in the condition of mere nature (which is a condition of war of every man against every man) upon any reasonable suspicion, it is void: but if there be a common power set over them both, with right and force sufficient to compel performance, it is not void. For he that performeth first has no assurance the other will perform after, because the bonds of words are too weak to bridle men's ambition, avarice, anger, and other passions, without the fear of some coercive power; which in the condition of mere nature, where all men are equal, and judges of the justness of their own fears, cannot possibly be supposed. And therefore he which performeth first does but betray himself to his enemy, contrary to the right he can never abandon of defending his life and means of living.

But in a civil estate, where there is a power set up to constrain those that would otherwise violate their faith, that fear is no more reasonable; and for that cause, he which by the covenant is to perform first is obliged so to do.

...

The force of words being (as I have formerly noted) too weak to hold men to the performance of their covenants, there are in man's nature but two imaginable helps to strengthen it. And those are either a fear of the consequence of breaking their word, or a glory or pride in appearing not to need to break it. This latter is a generosity too rarely found to be presumed on, especially in the pursuers of wealth, command, or sensual pleasure, which are the greatest part of mankind. The passion to be reckoned upon is fear; whereof there be two very general objects: one, the power of spirits invisible; the other, the power of those men they shall therein offend. Of these two, though the former be the greater power, yet the fear of the latter is commonly the greater fear. The fear of the former is in every man his own religion, which hath place in the nature of man before civil society. The latter hath not so; at least not place enough to keep men to their promises, because in the condition of mere nature, the inequality of power is not discerned, but by the event of battle. So that before the time of civil society, or in the interruption thereof by war, there is nothing can strengthen a covenant of peace agreed on against the temptations of avarice, ambition, lust, or other strong desire, but the fear of that invisible power which they every one worship as God, and fear as a revenger of their perfidy ...

Chapter XV–Of Other Laws of Nature

From that law of nature by which we are obliged to transfer to another such rights as, being retained, hinder the peace of mankind, there followeth a third; which is this: that men perform their covenants made; without which covenants are in vain, and but empty words; and the right of all men to all things remaining, we are still in the condition of war.

And in this law of nature consisteth the fountain and original of justice. For where no covenant hath preceded, there hath no right been transferred, and every man has right to everything and consequently, no action can be unjust. But when a covenant is made, then to break it is unjust and the definition of injustice is no other than the not performance of covenant. And whatsoever is not unjust is just.

But because covenants of mutual trust, where there is a fear of not performance on either part (as hath been said in the former chapter), are invalid, though the original of justice be the making of covenants, yet injustice actually there can be none till the cause of such fear be taken away; which, while men are in the natural condition of war, cannot be done. Therefore before the names of just and unjust can have place, there must be some coercive power to compel men equally to the performance of their covenants, by the terror of some punishment greater than the benefit they expect by the breach of their covenant, and to make good that propriety which by mutual contract men acquire in recompense of the universal right they abandon: and such power there is none before the erection of a Commonwealth. And this is also to be gathered out of the ordinary definition of justice in the Schools, for they say that justice is the constant will of giving to every man his own. And therefore where there is no own, that is, no propriety, there is no injustice; and where there is no coercive power erected, that is, where there is no Commonwealth, there is no propriety, all men having right to all things: therefore where there is no Commonwealth, there nothing is unjust. So that the nature of justice consisteth in keeping of valid covenants, but the validity of covenants begins not but with the constitution of a civil power sufficient to compel men to keep them: and then it is also that propriety begins.

Chapter XVII–Of the Causes, Generation, and Definition of a Commonwealth

...

The only way to erect such a common power, as may be able to defend them from the invasion of foreigners, and the injuries of one another, and thereby to secure them in such sort as that by their own industry and by the fruits of the earth they may nourish themselves and live contentedly, is to confer all their power and strength upon one man, or upon one assembly of men, that may reduce all their wills, by plurality of voices, unto one will: which is as much as to say, to appoint one man, or assembly of men, to bear their person; and every one to own and acknowledge himself to be author of whatsoever he that so beareth their person shall act, or cause to be acted, in those things which concern the common peace and safety; and therein to submit their wills, every one to his will, and their judgements to his judgement. This is more than consent, or concord; it is a real unity of them all in one and the same person, made by covenant of every man with every man, in such manner as if every man should say to every man: I authorise and give up my right of governing myself to this man, or to this assembly of men, on this condition, that thou give up, thy right to him, and authorise all his actions in like manner. This done, the multitude so united in one person is called a COMMONWEALTH; in Latin, CIVITAS. This is the generation of that great LEVIATHAN, or rather, to speak more reverently, of that mortal god to which we owe, under the immortal God, our peace and defence. For by this authority, given him by every particular man in the Commonwealth, he hath the use of so much power and strength conferred on him that, by terror thereof, he is enabled to form the wills of them all, to peace at home, and mutual aid against their enemies abroad. And in him consisteth the essence of the Commonwealth; which, to define it, is: one person, of whose acts a great multitude, by mutual covenants one with another, have made themselves every one the author, to the end he may use the strength and means of them all as he shall think expedient for their peace and common defence.

And he that carryeth this person is called sovereign, and said to have sovereign power; and every one besides, his subject.

The attaining to this sovereign power is by two ways. One, by natural force: as when a man maketh his children to submit themselves, and their children, to his government, as being able to destroy them if they refuse; or by war subdueth his enemies to his will, giving them their lives on that condition. The other, is when men agree amongst themselves to submit to some man, or assembly of men, voluntarily, on confidence to be protected by him against all others.

JOHN STUART MILL (1806–1873), *ON LIBERTY*, 1859

In his primary work in political philosophy, *On Liberty*, John Stuart Mill examines the limits of the power of the state over the individual. Mill is a thoroughgoing utilitarian, and he bases all of his arguments in this work on that general ethical theory. The overall conclusion of *On Liberty* is that "the only purpose for which power can be rightfully exercised over any member of a civilized community, against his will, is to prevent harm to others." In the excerpt below, Mill considers the limits of the state in controlling free speech and lifestyle choices. In all cases, Mill argues that state interference in an individual's behavior is unwarranted when that behavior does not directly cause harm to another.

Chapter I–Introductory

...

The object of this Essay is to assert one very simple principle, as entitled to govern absolutely the dealings of society with the individual in the way of compulsion and control, whether the means used be physical force in the form of legal penalties, or the moral coercion of public opinion. That principle is, that the sole end for which mankind are warranted, individually or collectively in interfering with the liberty of action of any of their number, is self-protection. That the only purpose for which power can be rightfully exercised over any member of a civilized community, against his will, is to prevent harm to others. His own good, either physical or moral, is not a sufficient warrant. He cannot rightfully be compelled to do or forbear because it will be better for him to do so, because it will make him happier, because, in the opinions of others, to do so would be wise, or even right. These are good reasons for remonstrating with him, or reasoning with him, or persuading him, or entreating him, but not for compelling him, or visiting him with any evil, in case he do otherwise. To justify that, the conduct from which it is desired to deter him must be calculated to produce evil to some one else. The only part of the conduct of any one, for which he is amenable to society, is that which concerns others. In the part which merely concerns himself, his independence is, of right, absolute. Over himself, over his own body and mind, the individual is sovereign.

It is, perhaps, hardly necessary to say that this doctrine is meant to apply only to human beings in the maturity of their faculties. We are not speaking of children, or of young persons below the age which the law may fix as that of manhood or womanhood. Those who are still in a state to require being taken care of by others, must be protected against their own actions as well as against external injury....

It is proper to state that I forego any advantage which could be derived to my argument from the idea of abstract right as a thing independent of utility. I regard utility as the ultimate appeal on all ethical questions; but it must be utility in the largest sense, grounded on the permanent interests of man as a progressive being. Those interests, I contend, authorize the subjection of individual spontaneity to external control, only in respect to those actions of each, which concern the interest of other people. If any one does an act hurtful to others, there is a prima facie case for punishing him, by law, or, where legal penalties are not safely applicable, by general disapprobation. There are also many positive acts for the benefit of others, which he may rightfully be compelled to perform; such as, to give evidence in a court of justice; to bear his fair share in the common defence, or in any other joint work necessary to the interest of the society of which he enjoys the protection; and to perform certain acts of individual beneficence, such as saving a fellow-creature's life, or interposing to protect the defenceless against ill-usage, things which whenever it is obviously a man's duty to do, he may rightfully be made responsible to society for not doing. A person may cause evil to others not only by his actions but by his inaction, and in either case he is justly accountable to them for the injury. The latter case, it is true, requires a much more cautious exercise of compulsion than the former. To make any one answerable for doing evil to others, is the rule; to make him answerable for not preventing evil, is, comparatively speaking, the exception. Yet there are many cases clear enough and grave enough to justify that exception. In all things which regard the external relations of the individual, he is de jure amenable to those whose interests are concerned, and if need be, to society as their protector. There are often good reasons for not holding him to the responsibility; but these reasons must arise from the special expediencies of the case: either because it is a kind of case in which he is on the whole likely to act better, when left to his own discretion, than when controlled in any way in which society have it in their power to control him; or because the attempt to exercise control would produce other evils, greater than those which it would prevent. When such reasons as these preclude the enforcement of responsibility, the conscience of the agent himself should step into the vacant judgment-seat, and protect those interests of others which have no external protection; judging himself all the more rigidly, because the case does not admit of his being made accountable to the judgment of his fellow-creatures.

But there is a sphere of action in which society, as distinguished from the individual, has, if any, only an indirect interest; comprehending all that portion of a person's life and conduct which affects only himself, or, if it also affects others, only with their free, voluntary, and undeceived consent and participation. When I say only himself, I mean directly, and in the first instance: for whatever affects himself, may affect others through himself; and the objection which may be grounded on this contingency, will receive consideration in the sequel. This, then, is the appropriate region of human liberty. It comprises, first, the inward domain of consciousness; demanding liberty of conscience, in the most comprehensive sense; liberty of thought and feeling; absolute freedom of opinion and sentiment on all subjects, practical or speculative, scientific, moral, or theological. The liberty of expressing and publishing opinions may seem to fall under a different principle, since it belongs to that part of the conduct of an individual which concerns other people; but, being almost of as much importance as the liberty of thought itself, and resting in great part on the same reasons, is practically inseparable from it. Secondly, the principle requires liberty of tastes and pursuits; of framing the plan of our life to suit our own character; of doing as we like, subject to such consequences as may follow; without impediment from our fellow-creatures, so long as what we do does not harm them even though they should think our conduct foolish, perverse, or wrong. Thirdly, from this liberty of each individual, follows the liberty, within the same limits, of combination among individuals; freedom to unite, for any purpose not involving harm to others: the persons combining being supposed to be of full age, and not forced or deceived.

No society in which these liberties are not, on the whole, respected, is free, whatever may be its form of government; and none is completely free in which they do not exist absolute and unqualified. The only freedom which deserves the name, is that of pursuing our own good in our own way, so long as we do not attempt to deprive others of theirs, or impede their efforts to obtain it. Each is the proper guardian of his own health, whether bodily, or mental or spiritual. Mankind are greater gainers by suffering each other to live as seems good to themselves, than by compelling each to live as seems good to the rest.

Though this doctrine is anything but new, and, to some persons, may have the air of a truism, there is no doctrine which stands more directly opposed to the general tendency of existing opinion and practice. Society has expended fully as much effort in the attempt (according to its lights) to compel people to conform to its notions of personal, as of social excellence. The ancient commonwealths thought themselves entitled to practise, and the ancient philosophers countenanced, the regulation of every part of private conduct by public authority, on the ground that the State had a deep interest in the whole bodily and mental discipline of every one of its citizens, a mode of thinking which may have been admissible in small republics surrounded by powerful enemies, in constant peril of being subverted by foreign attack or internal commotion, and to which even a short interval of relaxed energy and self-command might so easily be fatal, that they could not afford to wait for the salutary permanent effects of freedom. In the modern world, the greater size of political communities, and above all, the separation between the spiritual and temporal authority (which placed the direction of men's consciences in other hands than those which controlled their worldly affairs), prevented so great an interference by law in the details of private life; but the engines of moral repression have been wielded more strenuously against divergence from the reigning opinion in selfregarding, than even in social matters; religion, the most powerful of the elements which have entered into the formation of moral feeling, having almost always been governed either by the ambition of a hierarchy, seeking control over every department of human conduct, or by the spirit of Puritanism. ...

Apart from the peculiar tenets of individual thinkers, there is also in the world at large an increasing inclination to stretch unduly the powers of society over the individual, both by the force of opinion and even by that of legislation: and as the tendency of all the changes taking place in the world is to strengthen society, and diminish the power of the individual, this encroachment is not one of the evils which tend spontaneously to disappear, but, on the contrary, to grow more and more formidable. The disposition of mankind, whether as rulers or as fellow-citizens, to impose their own opinions and inclinations as a rule of conduct on others, is so energetically supported by some of the best and by some of the worst feelings incident to human nature, that it is hardly ever kept under restraint by anything but want of power; and as the power is not declining, but growing, unless a strong barrier of moral conviction can be raised against the mischief, we must expect, in the present circumstances of the world, to see it increase.

It will be convenient for the argument, if, instead of at once entering upon the general thesis, we confine ourselves in the first instance to a single branch of it, on which the principle here stated is, if not fully, yet to a certain point, recognized by the current opinions. This one branch is the Liberty of Thought: from which it is impossible to separate the cognate liberty of speaking and of writing. Although these liberties, to some considerable amount, form part of the political morality of all countries which profess religious toleration and free institutions, the grounds, both philosophical and practical, on which they rest, are perhaps not so familiar to the general mind, nor so thoroughly appreciated by many even of the leaders of opinion, as might have been expected.

Chapter II–Of the Liberty of Thought and Discussion

...

We have now recognized the necessity to the mental well-being of mankind (on which all their other well-being depends) of freedom of opinion, and freedom of the expression of opinion, on four distinct grounds; which we will now briefly recapitulate.

First, if any opinion is compelled to silence, that opinion may, for aught we can certainly know, be true. To deny this is to assume our own infallibility.

Secondly, though the silenced opinion be an error, it may, and very commonly does, contain a portion of truth; and since the general or prevailing opinion on any object is rarely or never the whole truth, it is only by the collision of adverse opinions that the remainder of the truth has any chance of being supplied.

Thirdly, even if the received opinion be not only true, but the whole truth; unless it is suffered to be, and actually is, vigorously and earnestly contested, it will, by most of those who receive it, be held in the manner of a prejudice, with little comprehension or feeling of its rational grounds. And not only this, but, fourthly, the meaning of the doctrine itself will be in danger of being lost, or enfeebled, and deprived of its vital effect on the character and conduct: the dogma becoming a mere formal profession, inefficacious for good, but cumbering the ground, and preventing the growth of any real and heartfelt conviction, from reason or personal experience.

...

Chapter III–On Individuality, As One of the Elements of Well-being

Such being the reasons which make it imperative that human beings should be free to form opinions, and to express their opinions without reserve, ... let us next examine whether the same reasons do not require that men should be free to act upon their opinions–to carry these out in their lives, without hindrance, either physical or moral, from their fellowmen, so long as it is at their own risk and peril. This last proviso is of course indispensable. No one pretends that actions should be as free as opinions. On the contrary, even opinions lose their immunity, when the circumstances in which they are expressed are such as to constitute their expression a positive instigation to some mischievous act. An opinion that corn-dealers are starvers of the poor, or that private property is robbery, ought to be unmolested when simply circulated through the press, but may justly incur punishment when delivered orally to an excited mob

369

assembled before the house of a corn-dealer, or when handed about among the same mob in the form of a placard. Acts of whatever kind, which, without justifiable cause, do harm to others, may be, and in the more important cases absolutely require to be, controlled by the unfavorable sentiments, and, when needful, by the active interference of mankind. The liberty of the individual must be thus far limited; he must not make himself a nuisance to other people. But if he refrains from molesting others in what concerns them, and merely acts according to his own inclination and judgment in things which concern himself, the same reasons which show that opinion should be free, prove also that he should be allowed, without molestation, to carry his opinions into practice at his own cost. That mankind are not infallible; that their truths, for the most part, are only half-truths; that unity of opinion, unless resulting from the fullest and freest comparison of opposite opinions, is not desirable, and diversity not an evil, but a good, until mankind are much more capable than at present of recognizing all sides of the truth, are principles applicable to men's modes of action, not less than to their opinions. As it is useful that while mankind are imperfect there should be different opinions, so is it that there should be different experiments of living; that free scope should be given to varieties of character, short of injury to others; and that the worth of different modes of life should be proved practically, when any one thinks fit to try them. It is desirable, in short, that in things which do not primarily concern others, individuality should assert itself. Where, not the person's own character, but the traditions of customs of other people are the rule of conduct, there is wanting one of the principal ingredients of human happiness, and quite the chief ingredient of individual and social progress.

In maintaining this principle, the greatest difficulty to be encountered does not lie in the appreciation of means towards an acknowledged end, but in the indifference of persons in general to the end itself. If it were felt that the free development of individuality is one of the leading essentials of well-being; that it is not only a coordinate element with all that is designated by the terms civilization, instruction, education, culture, but is itself a necessary part and condition of all those things; there would be no danger that liberty should be undervalued, and the adjustment of the boundaries between it and social control would present no extraordinary difficulty. But the evil is, that individual spontaneity is hardly recognized by the common modes of thinking as having any intrinsic worth, or deserving any regard on its own account. The majority, being satisfied with the ways of mankind as they now are (for it is they who make them what they are), cannot comprehend why those ways should not be good enough for everybody; and what is more, spontaneity forms no part of the ideal of the majority of moral and social reformers, but is rather looked on with jealousy, as a troublesome and perhaps rebellious obstruction to the general acceptance of what these reformers, in their own judgment, think would be best for mankind....

But it is the privilege and proper condition of a human being, arrived at the maturity of his faculties, to use and interpret experience in his own way. It is for him to find out what part of recorded experience is properly applicable to his own circumstances and character. The traditions and customs of other people are, to a certain extent, evidence of what their experience has taught them; presumptive evidence, and as such, have a claim to this deference: but, in the first place, their experience may be too narrow; or they may not have interpreted it rightly. Secondly, their interpretation of experience may be correct but unsuitable to him. Customs are made for customary circumstances, and customary characters: and his circumstances or his character may be uncustomary. Thirdly, though the customs be both good as customs, and suitable to him, yet to conform to custom, merely as custom, does not educate or develop in him any of the qualities which are the distinctive endowment of a human being. The human faculties of perception, judgment, discriminative feeling, mental activity, and even moral preference, are exercised only in making a choice. He who does anything because it is the custom, makes no choice. He gains no practice either in discerning or in desiring what is best. The mental and moral, like the muscular powers, are improved only by being used. The faculties are called into no exercise by doing a thing merely because others do it, no more than by believing a thing only because others believe it. If the grounds of an opinion are not conclusive to the person's own reason, his reason cannot be strengthened, but is likely to be weakened by his adopting it: and if the inducements to an act are not such as are consentaneous to his own feelings and character (where affection, or the rights of others are not concerned), it is so much done towards rendering his feelings and character inert and torpid, instead of active and energetic.

J. L. MACKIE (1917–1981), "EVIL AND OMNIPOTENCE" (*MIND* 64), 1955

In this paper, Mackie presents the problem of evil and considers the following solutions: that evil is a necessary counterpart to good; that evil is necessary as a means to good; that the universe would be better with some evil in it; and that evil is due to human free will. Mackie argues that all of the solutions are fallacious and fail to adequately solve the problem of evil. In addition, Mackie argues that the property of omnipotence is problematic since it falls prey to the paradox of omnipotence: Can an omnipotent being create rules that bind himself? If the answer is yes, there is something that the omnipotent being cannot do (violate the rule); if the answer is no, there is something that the omnipotent being cannot do (create the rule). Mackie concludes that omnipotence cannot be meaningfully ascribed to God.

...

In its simplest form the problem is this: God is omnipotent; God is wholly good; and yet evil exists. There seems to be some contradiction between these three propositions, so that if any two of them were true the third would be false. But at the same time all three are essential parts of most theological positions: the theologian, it seems, at once *must* adhere and *cannot consistently* adhere to all three. (The problem does not arise only for theists, but I shall discuss it in the form in which it presents itself for ordinary theism.)

...

Fallacious Solutions

...

1. "Good cannot exist without evil" or "Evil is necessary as a counterpart to good."

It is sometimes suggested that evil is necessary as a counterpart to good, that if there were no evil there could be no good either, and that this solves the problem of evil. It is true that it points to an answer to the question "Why should there be evil?" But it does so only by qualifying some of the propositions that constitute the problem.

... [I]t sets a limit to what God can do, saying that God cannot create good without simultaneously creating evil, and this means either that God is not omnipotent or that there are some limits to what an omnipotent thing can do. It may be replied that these limits are always presupposed, that omnipotence has never meant the power to do what is logically impossible, and on the present view the existence of good without evil would be a logical impossibility. This interpretation of omnipotence may, indeed, be accepted as a modification of our original account which does not reject anything that is essential to theism, and I shall in general assume it in the subsequent discussion. It is, perhaps, the most common theistic view, but I think that some theists at least have maintained that God can do what is logically impossible. Many theists, at any rate, have held that logic itself is created or laid down by God, that logic is the way in which God arbitrarily chooses to think. (This is, of course, parallel to the ethical view that morally right actions are those which God arbitrarily chooses to command, and the two views encounter similar difficulties.) And this account of logic is clearly inconsistent with the view that God is bound by logical necessities—unless it is possible for an omnipotent being to bind himself, an issue which we shall consider later, when we come to the Paradox of Omnipotence. This solution of the problem of evil cannot, therefore, be consistently adopted along with the view that logic is itself created by God.

...

It may be replied that good and evil are necessary counterparts in the same way as any quality and its logical opposite: redness can occur, it is suggested, only if non-redness also occurs.... There is still doubt of the correctness of the metaphysical principle that a quality must have a real opposite: I suggest that it is not really impossible that everything should be, say, red, that the truth is merely that if everything were red we should not notice redness, and so we should have no word 'red'; we observe and give names to qualities only if they have real opposites. If so, the principle that a term must have an opposite would belong only to our language or to our thought, and would not be an ontological principle, and, correspondingly, the rule that good cannot exist without evil would not state a logical necessity of a sort that God would just have to put up with. God might have made everything good, though we should not have noticed it if he had.

...

2. "Evil is necessary as a means to good."

It is sometimes suggested that evil is necessary for good not as a counterpart but as a means. In its simple form this has little plausibility as a solution of the problem of evil, since it obviously implies a severe restriction of God's power. It would be a causal law that you cannot have a certain end without a certain means, so that if God has to introduce evil as a means to good, he must be subject to at least some causal laws. This certainly conflicts with what a theist normally means by omnipotence. This view of God as limited by causal laws also conflicts with the view that causal laws are themselves made by God, which is more widely held than the corresponding view about the laws of logic. This conflict would, indeed be resolved if it were possible for an omnipotent being to bind himself, and this possibility has still to be considered. Unless a favourable answer can be given to this question, the suggestion that evil is necessary as a means to good solves the problem of evil only by denying one of its constituent propositions, either that God is omnipotent or that 'omnipotent' means what it says.

3. "The universe is better with some evil in it than it could be if there were no evil."

Much more important is a solution which at first seems to be a mere variant of the previous one, that evil may contribute to the goodness of a whole in which it is found, so that the universe as a whole is better as it is, with some evil in it, than it would be if there were no evil. This solution may be developed in either of two ways. It may be supported by an aesthetic analogy, by the fact that contrasts heighten beauty, that in a musical work, for example, there may occur discords which somehow add to the beauty of the work as a whole.

... [L]et us see exactly what is being done here. Let us call pain and misery 'first order evil' or 'evil (1)'. What contrasts with this, namely, pleasure and happiness, will be called 'first order good' or 'good (1)'. Distinct from this is 'second order good' or 'good (2)' which somehow emerges in a complex situation in which evil (1) is a necessary component-logically, not merely causally, necessary. (Exactly *how* it emerges does not matter: in the crudest version of this solution good (2) is simply the heightening of happiness by the contrast with misery, in other versions it includes sympathy with suffering, heroism in facing danger, and the gradual decrease of first order evil and increase of first order good.) It is also being assumed that second order good is more important than first order good or evil, in particular that it more than outweighs the first order evil it involves.

Now this is a particularly subtle attempt to solve the problem of evil. It defends God's goodness and omnipotence on the ground that (on a sufficiently long view) this, is the best of all logically possible worlds, because it includes the important second order goods, and yet it admits that real evils, namely first order evils, exist. But does it still hold that good and evil are opposed? Not, clearly, in the sense that we set out originally: good does not tend to eliminate evil in general. Instead, we have a modified, a more complex pattern. First order good (e.g. happiness) contrasts with first order evil (e.g. misery): these two are opposed in a fairly mechanical way; some second order goods (e.g. benevolence) try to maximise first order good and minimise first order evil; but God's goodness is not this, it is rather the will to maximise second order good. We might, therefore, call God's goodness an example of a third order goodness, or good (3). While this account is different from our original one, it might well be held to be an improvement on it, to give a more accurate description of the way in which good is opposed to evil, and to be consistent with the essential theist position.

... [T]he fatal objection is this. Our analysis shows clearly the possibility of the existence of a second order evil, an evil (2) contrasting with good (2) as evil (1) contrasts with good (1). This would include malevolence, cruelty, callousness, cowardice, and states in which good (1) is decreasing and evil (1) increasing. And just as good (2) is held to be the important kind of good, the kind that God is concerned to promote, so evil (2) will, by analogy, be the important kind of evil, the kind which God, if he were wholly good and omnipotent, would eliminate. And yet evil (2) plainly exists, and indeed most theists (in other contexts) stress its existence more than that of evil (1). We should, therefore, state the problem of evil in terms of second order evil, and against this form of the problem the present solution is useless.

4. "Evil is due to human freewill."

Perhaps the most important proposed solution of the problem of evil is that evil is not to be ascribed to God at all, but to the independent actions of human beings, supposed to have been endowed by God with freedom of the will. This solution may be combined with the preceding one: first order evil (e.g. pain) may be justified as a logically necessary component in second order good (e.g. sympathy) while second order evil (e.g. cruelty) is not *justified*, but is so ascribed to human beings that God cannot be held responsible for it. This combination evades my third criticism of the preceding solution.

The freewill solution also involves the preceding solution at a higher level. To explain why a wholly good God gave men freewill although it would lead to some important evils, it must be argued that it is better on the whole that men should act freely, and sometimes err, than that they should be innocent automata, acting rightly in a wholly determined way. Freedom, that is to say, is now treated as a third order good, and as being more valuable than second order goods (such as sympathy and heroism) would be if they were deterministically produced, and it is being assumed that second order evils, such as cruelty, are logically necessary accompaniments of freedom, just as pain is a logically necessary pre-condition of sympathy.

I think that this solution is unsatisfactory primarily because of the incoherence of the notion of freedom of the will: but I cannot discuss this topic adequately here, although some of my criticisms will touch upon it.

First I should query the assumption that second order evils are logically necessary accompaniments of freedom. I should ask this: if God has made men such that in their free choices they sometimes prefer what is good and sometimes what is evil, why could he not have made men such that they always freely choose the good? If there is no logical impossibility in a man's freely choosing the good on one, or on several, occasions, there cannot be a logical impossibility in his freely choosing the good on every occasion. God was not, then, faced with a choice between making innocent automata and making beings who, in acting freely, would sometimes go wrong: there was open to him the obviously better possibility of making beings who would act freely but always go right. Clearly, his failure to avail himself of this possibility is inconsistent with his being both omnipotent and wholly good.

If it is replied that this objection is absurd, that the making of some wrong choices is logically necessary for freedom, it would seem that 'freedom' must here mean complete randomness or indeterminacy, including randomness with regard to the alternatives good and evil, in other words that men's choices and consequent actions can be "free" only if they are not determined by their characters. Only on this assumption can God escape the responsibility for men's actions; for if he made them as they are, but did not determine their wrong choices, this can only be because the wrong choices are not determined by men as they are. But then if freedom is randomness, how can it be a characteristic of will? And, still more, how can it be the most important good? What value or merit would there be in free choices if these were random actions which were not determined by the nature of the agent?

... [B]esides this there is a fundamental difficulty in the notion of an omnipotent God creating men with free will, for if men's wills are really free this must mean that even God cannot control them, that is, that God is no longer omnipotent. It may be objected that God's gift of freedom to men does not mean that he cannot control their wills, but that he always *refrains* from controlling their wills. But why, we may ask, should God refrain from controlling evil wills? Why should he not leave men free to will rightly, but intervene when he sees them beginning to will wrongly? If God could do this, but does not, and if he is wholly good, the only explanation could be that even a wrong free act of will is not really evil, that its freedom is a value which outweighs its wrongness, so that there would be a loss of value if God took away the wrongness and the freedom together. But this is utterly opposed to what theists say about sin in other contexts. The present solution of the problem of evil, then, can be maintained only in the form that God has made men so free that he *cannot* control their wills.

This leads us to what I call the Paradox of Omnipotence: can an omnipotent being make things which he cannot subsequently control? Or, what is practically equivalent to this, can an omnipotent being make rules which then bind himself? (These are practically equivalent because any such rules could be regarded as setting certain things beyond his control, and *vice versa.*) The second of these formulations is relevant to the suggestions that we have already met, that an omnipotent God creates the rules of logic or causal laws, and is then bound by them.

It is clear that this is a paradox: the questions cannot be answered satisfactorily either in the affirmative or in the negative. If we answer "Yes", it follows that if God actually makes things which he cannot control, or makes rules which bind himself, he is not omnipotent once he has made them: there are then things which he cannot do. But if we answer "No", we are immediately asserting that there are things which he cannot do, that is to say that he is already not omnipotent.

It cannot be replied that the question which sets this paradox is not a proper question. It would make perfectly good sense to say that a human mechanic has made a machine which he cannot control: if there is any difficulty about the question it lies in the notion of omnipotence itself.

...

Conclusion

Of the proposed solutions of the problem of evil which we have examined, none has stood up to criticism....

Quite apart from the problem of evil, the paradox of omnipotence has shown that God's omnipotence must in any case be restricted in one way or another, that unqualified omnipotence cannot be ascribed to any being that continues through time. And if God and his actions are not in time, can omnipotence, or power of any sort, be meaningfully ascribed to him?

AUGUSTINE (354–430), "ON FREE CHOICE OF THE WILL," PUBLISHED IN LATIN
IN 395, TRANSLATED BY ANNA S. BENJAMIN AND L. H. HACKSTAFF

De libero arbitrio voluntatis (the Latin title for this work) is perhaps the
earliest work to offer the free will defense to the problem of evil
within the Christian tradition. In this imagined conversation
between the author and Evodius, Augustine lays out the free will
defense to explain human-caused suffering ("We commit evil
through free choice of the will") and argues that God is not
responsible for giving us free will, even though God foreknew that
we would misuse it to sin. While human-caused suffering is the
primary focus of *On Free Choice of the Will,* in the closing paragraphs,
Augustine considers nature-caused suffering and offers a version of
the ultimate harmony defense.

Evodius: Tell me, please, whether God is not the cause of evil.

Augustine: I shall, if you will explain what kind of evil you mean. For
we usually speak of evil in two senses: one when we mean that
someone has done evil; the other, when we mean that someone has
suffered evil.

E: I want to know about both kinds.

A: But if you know or believe that God is good (and it is not right to
believe otherwise), God does not do evil. Also, if we admit that God
is just (and it is sacrilege to deny this), He assigns rewards to the
righteous and punishments to the wicked—punishments that are
indeed evil for those who suffer them. Therefore, if no one suffers
punishment unjustly (this too we must believe, since we believe that
the universe is governed by divine Providence), God is the cause of
the second kind of evil, but not of the first.

E: Then is there some other cause of the latter kind of evil, which, as
we found, God did not cause?

A: Certainly, for evil could not have come into being without a cause.
However, if you ask what the cause may be, I cannot say, since
there is no one cause; rather, each evil man is the cause of his own
evildoing. If you doubt this, then listen to what we said above: evil
deeds are punished by the justice of God. It would not be just to
punish evil deeds if they were not done willfully.

...

A: You are really asking why we do evil. But first we must discuss what evildoing is. Explain what your opinion is in this matter; if you cannot answer the whole of the question in a few brief words, at least make your views known to me by mentioning particular evil deeds.

E: Adultery, homicide, sacrilege, not to mention others which time and memory do not permit me to recount.

…

A: [T]ell me why you think adultery is an evil.

…

E: I have no answer to give you.

A: Perhaps then lust is the evil element in adultery. As long as you look for evil in the overt act itself, which can be seen, you are in difficulty. To help you to understand that the evil element in adultery is lust, consider the case of a man who does not have the opportunity to lie with another's wife; but nevertheless, if it is somehow obvious that he would like to do so and would do so had he the opportunity, he is no less guilty than the man taken in the very act.

E: Nothing is more obvious.

…

E: [W]e commit evil through free choice of the will. But I question whether free will–through which, it has been shown, we have the power to sin–ought to have been given to us by Him who made us. For it seems that we would not have been able to sin, if we did not have free will. And it is to be feared that in this way God may appear to be the cause of our evil deeds.

A: If man is a good, and cannot act rightly unless he wills to do so, then he must have free will, without which he cannot act rightly. We must not believe that God gave us free will so that we might sin, just because sin is committed through free will. It is sufficient for our question, why free will should have been given to man, to know that without it man cannot live rightly.

…

E: I am deeply troubled by a certain question: how can it be that God has foreknowledge of all future events, and yet that we do not sin by necessity? Anyone who says that an event can happen otherwise than as God has foreknown it is making an insane and malicious attempt to destroy God's foreknowledge. If God, therefore, foreknew that a good man would sin (and you must grant this, if you admit with me that God foreknows all future events)–if this is the case, I do not say that God should not have made the man, for He made him good, and the sin of the man He made cannot hurt God at all ... but I do say this: since He foreknew that the man would sin, the sin was committed of necessity, because God foreknew that it would happen. How can there be free will where there is such inevitable necessity?

...

A: How can the following two propositions, that [1] God has foreknowledge of all future events, and that [2] we do not sin by necessity but by free will, be made consistent with each other? ... You fear now that this reasoning results either in the blasphemous denial of God's foreknowledge or, if we deny this, the admission that we sin by necessity, not by will.

...

A: Why do you think that our free choice is opposed to God's foreknowledge? Is it simply because it is foreknowledge or, rather, because it is God's foreknowledge?

E: Because it is God's.

A: If you foreknew that someone was going to sin, would it not be necessary for him to sin?

E: Yes, he would have to sin, for my foreknowledge would not be genuine unless I foreknew what was certain.

A: Then it is not because it is God's foreknowledge that what He foreknew had to happen, but only because it is foreknowledge. It is not foreknowledge if it does not foreknow what is certain.

E: I agree. But why are you making these points?

A: Because unless I am mistaken, your foreknowledge that a man will sin does not of itself necessitate the sin. Your foreknowledge did not force him to sin even though he was, without a doubt, going to sin; otherwise you would not foreknow that which was to be. Thus, these two things are not contradictories. As you, by your foreknowledge, know what someone else is going to do of his own will, so God forces no one to sin; yet He foreknows those who will sin by their own will.

...

A: Can we avoid attributing to the Creator anything that happens of necessity in His creation? ... Do not be bothered by the fact that sinful souls are blamed, so that you say in your heart, "It would have been better if they had never existed." They are blamed in comparison with themselves, because one reflects upon what they might have been if they had not willed to sin. Yet God their Maker

380

should be given the highest praise that men can give, not only because He places sinners in a just order, but also because He made sinners in such a way that, even when soiled with sin, they still surpass the excellence of corporeal light which is, however, quite justly praised.

I want you also to beware of this: you should avoid saying not only, "It would have been better if they had not existed," but also, "They ought to have been made differently." If, by true reasoning, you conceive of something better, you can be sure that God, the Creator of the good, has already made it. Moreover, it is not true reasoning, but simply an envious weakness, if you wish that the lower should not have been made because you think that something higher should have been created. It is as if, because you had looked upon the heavens, you wished that there be no earth. That would be totally wrong. You would then quite justly find fault if you should see the earth created, but the heavens not. You might then say that the earth should have been made like your conception of the heavens. You ought to feel no envy at all when you see that the very thing has already been created after whose likeness you wanted to pattern the earth and that it is called, not earth, but the heavens; for I think you would not be deprived of a better thing so that something lower, namely the earth, might come into being. Moreover, so great is the variety of earthly things that we can conceive of nothing which belongs to the form of the earth in its full extent which God, the Creator of all things, has not already created.... You cannot conceive of anything better in creation which has escaped the Maker of the creation.

...

A: [With regard to the death of young children, some ask] "Why need the child have been born, since he died before he did anything of merit in life?" ... My answer to these men is as follows: In view of the encompassing network of the universe and the whole creation—a network that is perfectly ordered in time and place, where not even one leaf of a tree is superfluous—it is not possible to create a superfluous man.

...

Some raise a greater and, as it were, more merciful objection, concerning the bodily suffering with which young children are afflicted. Because of their age, they say, children have committed no sins.... Hence they ask: "What evil have they done that they should suffer so?" But what reason is there to believe that anyone should be rewarded for innocence before he could do harm? Since God works some good by correcting adults tortured by the sickness and death of children who are dear to them, why should this suffering not occur? When the sufferings of children are over, it will be as if they had never occurred for those who suffered. Either the adults on whose account the sufferings occurred will become better, if they are reformed by temporal troubles and choose to live rightly, or else, if because of the hardships of this life they are unwilling to turn their desire toward eternal life, they will have no excuse when they are punished in the judgment to come. Moreover, who knows what faith is practiced or what pity is tested when these children's sufferings break down the hardness of parents? Who knows what reward God reserves in the secret place of his judgment for the children who, though they have not acted rightly, are not, on the other hand, weighed down by sin?

ALBERT CAMUS (1913–1960), "THE MYTH OF SISYPHUS," PUBLISHED IN FRENCH
IN 1942, TRANSLATED BY JUSTIN O'BRIEN

Camus adopts and adapts the pre-classical Greek myth of Sisyphus
into an allegory of the absurd hero: consigned to a life of meaningless
work, recognizing the meaningless of that work, yet embracing the
work and its meaninglessness nevertheless. The essay "The Myth of
Sisyphus" was first published in 1942 in a collection of essays also
bearing the title *The Myth of Sisyphus.*

The gods had condemned Sisyphus to ceaselessly rolling a rock to the top
of a mountain, whence the stone would fall back of its own weight. They
had thought with some reason that there is no more dreadful punishment
than futile and hopeless labor.

If one believes Homer, Sisyphus was the wisest and most prudent of
mortals. According to another tradition, however, he was disposed to
practice the profession of highwayman. I see no contradiction in this.
Opinions differ as to the reasons why he became the futile laborer of the
underworld. To begin with, he is accused of a certain levity in regard to the
gods. He stole their secrets. Egina, the daughter of Esopus, was carried off
by Jupiter. The father was shocked by that disappearance and complained
to Sisyphus. He, who knew of the abduction, offered to tell about it on
condition that Esopus would give water to the citadel of Corinth. To the
celestial thunderbolts he preferred the benediction of water. He was punished for this in the underworld. Homer tells us also that Sisyphus had put
Death in chains. Pluto could not endure the sight of his deserted, silent
empire. He dispatched the god of war, who liberated Death from the
hands of her conqueror.

It is said that Sisyphus, being near to death, rashly wanted to test his
wife's love. He ordered her to cast his unburied body into the middle of
the public square. Sisyphus woke up in the underworld. And there,
annoyed by an obedience so contrary to human love, he obtained from
Pluto permission to return to earth in order to chastise his wife. But when
he had seen again the face of this world, enjoyed water and sun, warm
stones and the sea, he no longer wanted to go back to the infernal darkness. Recalls, signs of anger, warnings were of no avail. Many years more
he lived facing the curve of the gulf, the sparkling sea, and the smiles of
earth. A decree of the gods was necessary. Mercury came and seized the
impudent man by the collar and, snatching him from his joys, led him
forcibly back to the underworld, where his rock was ready for him.

You have already grasped that Sisyphus is the absurd hero. He is, as
much through his passions as through his torture. His scorn of the gods,

his hatred of death, and his passion for life won him that unspeakable penalty in which the whole being is exerted toward accomplishing nothing. This is the price that must be paid for the passions of this earth. Nothing is told us about Sisyphus in the underworld. Myths are made for the imagination to breathe life into them. As for this myth, one sees merely the whole effort of a body straining to raise the huge stone, to roll it, and push it up a slope a hundred times over; one sees the face screwed up, the cheek tight against the stone, the shoulder bracing the clay-covered mass, the foot wedging it, the fresh start with arms outstretched, the wholly human security of two earth-clotted hands. At the very end of his long effort measured by skyless space and time without depth, the purpose is achieved. Then Sisyphus watches the stone rush down in a few moments toward that lower world whence he will have to push it up again toward the summit. He goes back down to the plain.

It is during that return, that pause, that Sisyphus interests me. A face that toils so close to stones is already stone itself! I see that man going back down with a heavy yet measured step toward the torment of which he will never know the end. That hour like a breathing-space which returns as surely as his suffering, that is the hour of consciousness. At each of those moments when he leaves the heights and gradually sinks toward the lairs of the gods, he is superior to his fate. He is stronger than his rock.

If this myth is tragic, that is because its hero is conscious. Where would his torture be, indeed, if at every step the hope of succeeding upheld him? The workman of today works everyday in his life at the same tasks, and his fate is no less absurd. But it is tragic only at the rare moments when it becomes conscious. Sisyphus, proletarian of the gods, powerless and rebellious, knows the whole extent of his wretched condition: it is what he thinks of during his descent. The lucidity that was to constitute his torture at the same time crowns his victory. There is no fate that cannot be surmounted by scorn.

If the descent is thus sometimes performed in sorrow, it can also take place in joy. This word is not too much. Again I fancy Sisyphus returning toward his rock, and the sorrow was in the beginning. When the images of earth cling too tightly to memory, when the call of happiness becomes too insistent, it happens that melancholy arises in man's heart: this is the rock's victory, this is the rock itself. The boundless grief is too heavy to bear. These are our nights of Gethsemane. But crushing truths perish from being acknowledged. Thus, Edipus at the outset obeys fate without knowing it. But from the moment he knows, his tragedy begins. Yet at the same moment, blind and desperate, he realizes that the only bond linking him to the world is the cool hand of a girl. Then a tremendous remark rings out: "Despite so many ordeals, my advanced age and the nobility of my soul make me conclude that all is well." Sophocles' Edipus, like

Dostoevsky's Kirilov, thus gives the recipe for the absurd victory. Ancient wisdom confirms modern heroism.

One does not discover the absurd without being tempted to write a manual of happiness. "What!—by such narrow ways—?" There is but one world, however. Happiness and the absurd are two sons of the same earth. They are inseparable. It would be a mistake to say that happiness necessarily springs from the absurd discovery. It happens as well that the feeling of the absurd springs from happiness. "I conclude that all is well," says Edipus, and that remark is sacred. It echoes in the wild and limited universe of man. It teaches that all is not, has not been, exhausted. It drives out of this world a god who had come into it with dissatisfaction and a preference for futile suffering. It makes of fate a human matter, which must be settled among men.

All Sisyphus' silent joy is contained therein. His fate belongs to him. His rock is his thing. Likewise, the absurd man, when he contemplates his torment, silences all the idols. In the universe suddenly restored to its silence, the myriad wondering little voices of the earth rise up. Unconscious, secret calls, invitations from all the faces, they are the necessary reverse and price of victory. There is no sun without shadow, and it is essential to know the night. The absurd man says yes and his efforts will henceforth be unceasing. If there is a personal fate, there is no higher destiny, or at least there is, but one which he concludes is inevitable and despicable. For the rest, he knows himself to be the master of his days. At that subtle moment when man glances backward over his life, Sisyphus returning toward his rock, in that slight pivoting he contemplates that series of unrelated actions which become his fate, created by him, combined under his memory's eye and soon sealed by his death. Thus, convinced of the wholly human origin of all that is human, a blind man eager to see who knows that the night has no end, he is still on the go. The rock is still rolling.

I leave Sisyphus at the foot of the mountain! One always finds one's burden again. But Sisyphus teaches the higher fidelity that negates the gods and raises rocks. He too concludes that all is well. This universe henceforth without a master seems to him neither sterile nor futile. Each atom of that stone, each mineral flake of that night-filled mountain, in itself forms a world. The struggle itself toward the heights is enough to fill a man's heart. One must imagine Sisyphus happy.

INDEX